ZAHRA'S PARADISE

When we are dead, seek not our tomb
in the earth, but in the hearts of men.

—Rumi

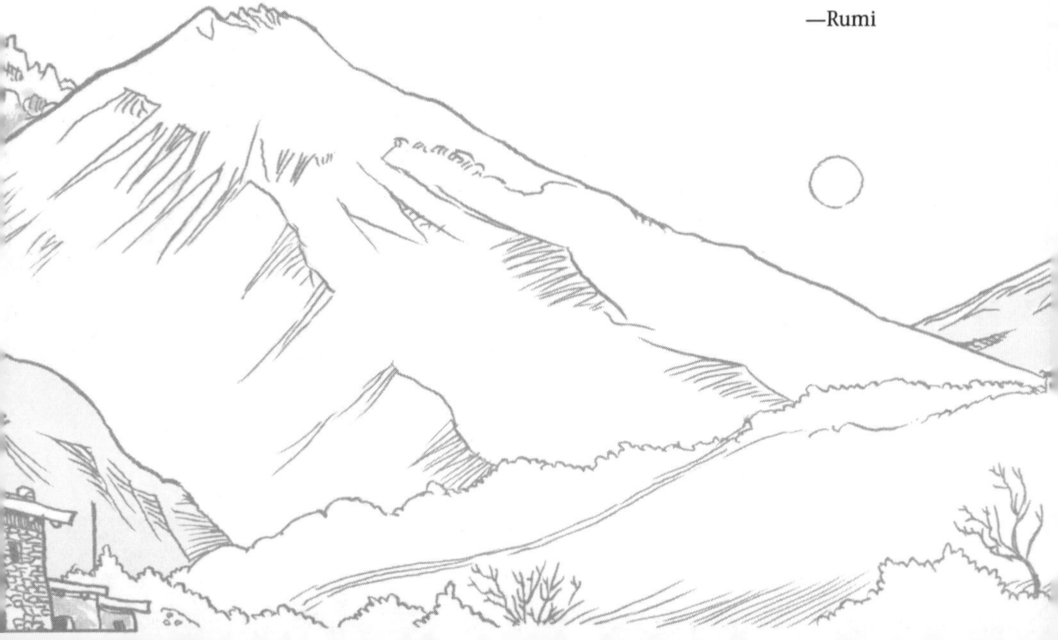

ZAHRA'S PARADISE

Story by Amir & Khalil

Written by Amir

Artwork by Khalil

First Second

NEW YORK & LONDON

To the missing, the absent and the fallen.

—A. & K.

Published by First Second
First Second is an imprint of Roaring Brook Press,
a division of Holtzbrinck Publishing Holdings Limited Partnership
175 Fifth Avenue, New York, New York 10010

Distributed in the United Kingdom by Macmillan Children's Books,
a division of Pan Macmillan.

Library of Congress Cataloging-in-Publication Data

Khalil, Amir.
Zahra's paradise/Amir Khalil. —1st ed.
p. cm.
ISBN 978-1-59643-642-8 (alk. paper)
1. Iran—Comic books, strips, etc. 2. Bloggers —Comic books, strips, etc.
3. Missing persons —Comic books, strips, etc. I. Title.
PR679.I64Z34 2011
741.5'955—dc23

2011017564

First Second books are available for special promotions and premiums.
For details, contact: Director of Special Markets, Holtzbrinck Publishers.

First edition 2011
Book design by Marion Vitus
Printed in the United States of America

3 5 7 9 10 8 6 4 2

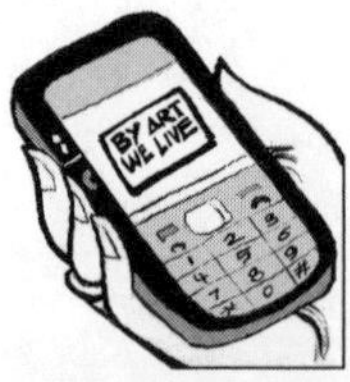
BY ART WE LIVE

PREMONITION

PROLOGUE

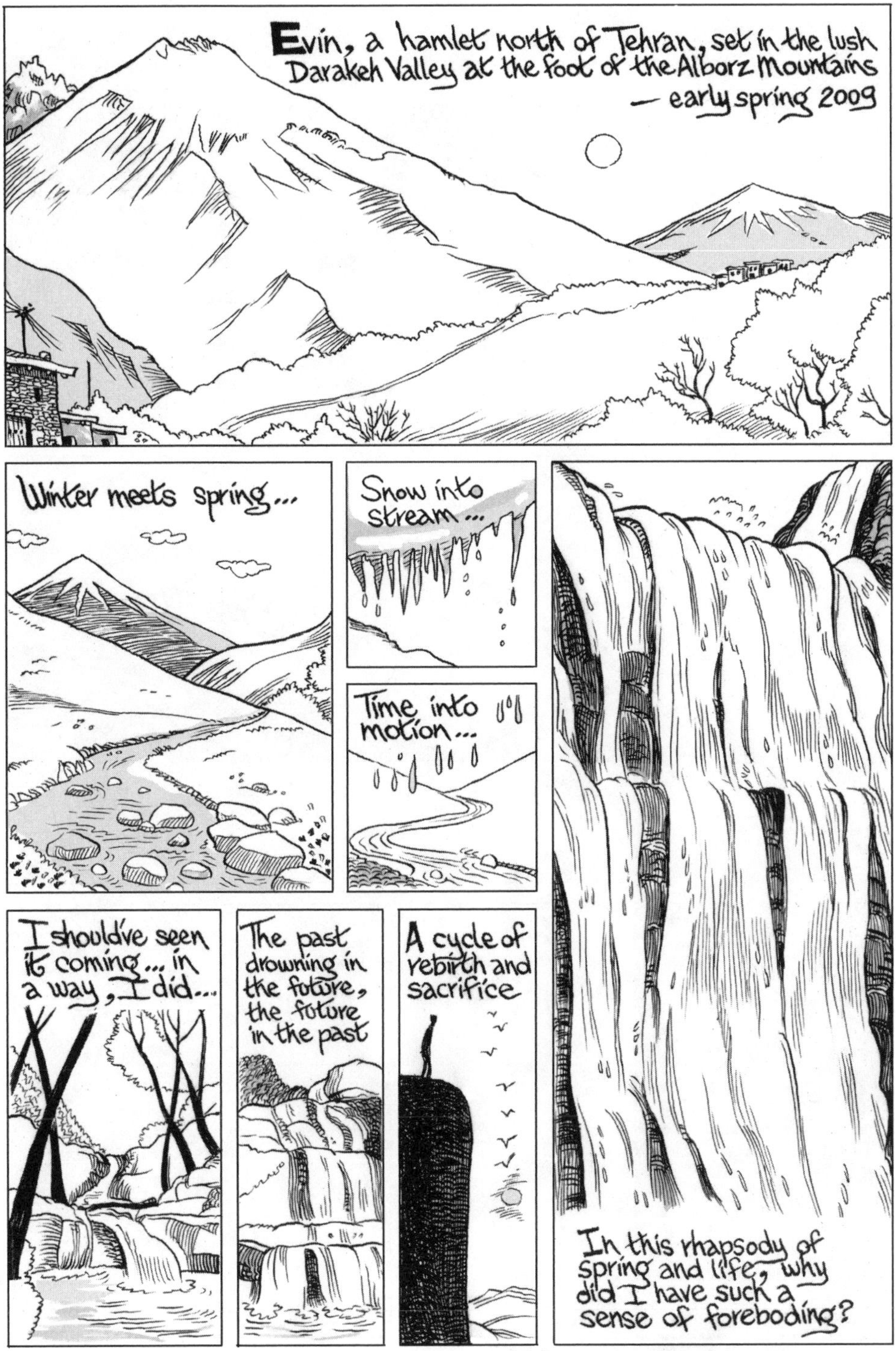
Evin, a hamlet north of Tehran, set in the lush Darakeh Valley at the foot of the Alborz Mountains
— early spring 2009
Winter meets spring...
Snow into stream...
Time into motion...
In this rhapsody of spring and life, why did I have such a sense of foreboding?
I should've seen it coming... in a way, I did...
The past drowning in the future, the future in the past
A cycle of rebirth and sacrifice

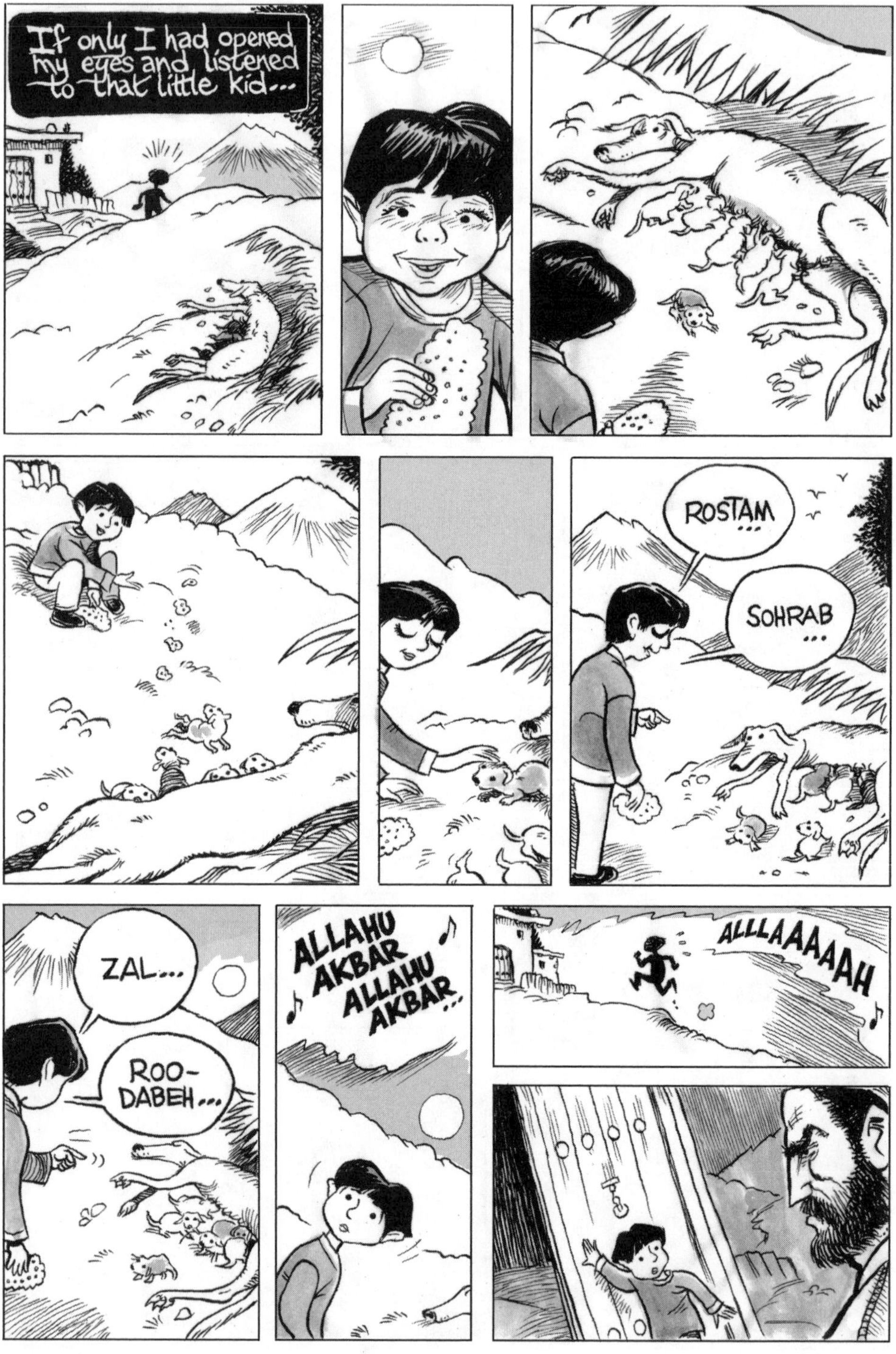
If only I had opened my eyes and listened to that little kid...
ROSTAM...
SOHRAB...
ZAL...
ROO-DABEH...
ALLAHU AKBAR ALLAHU AKBAR...
ALLLAAAAAH

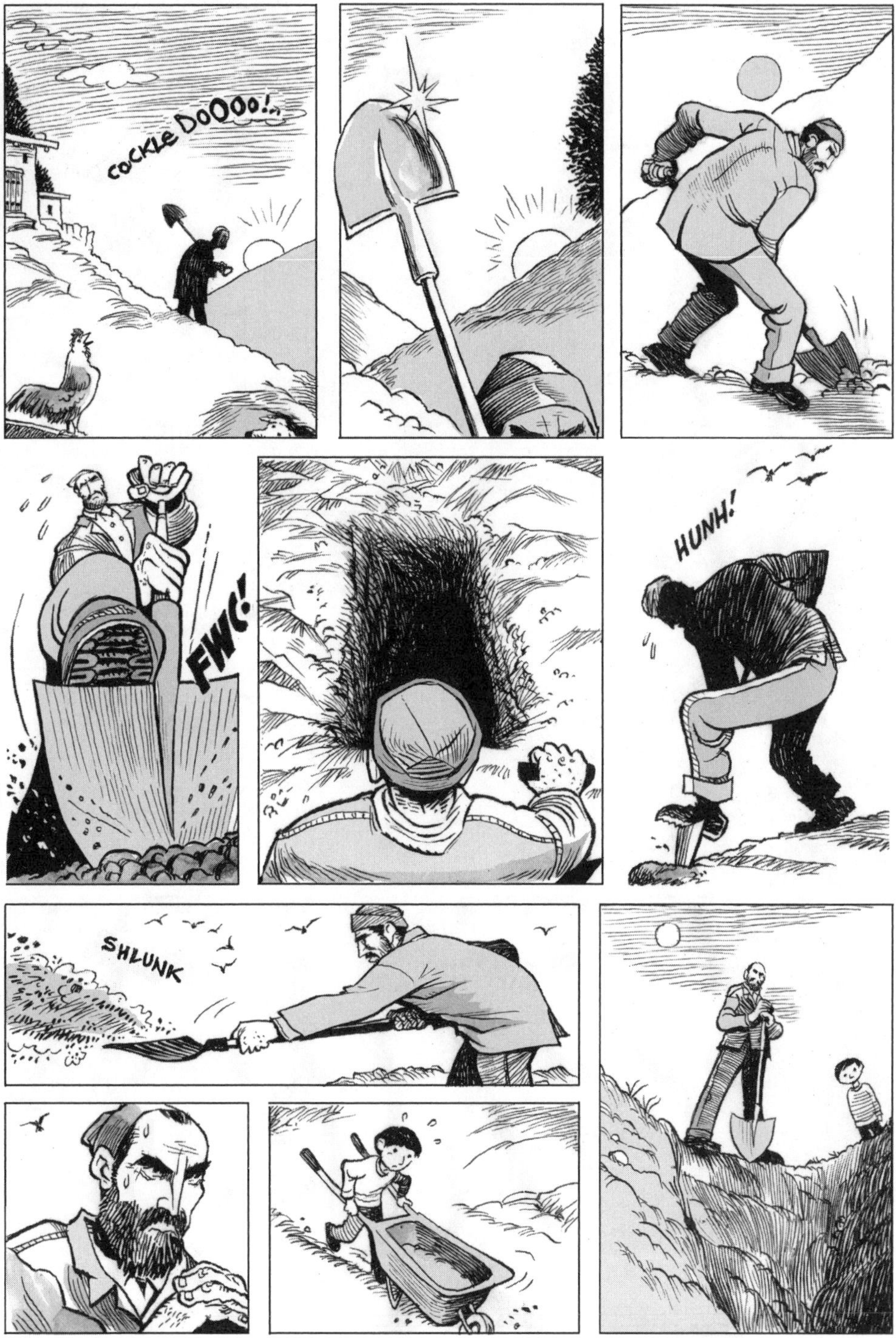
COCKLE DOOOO!
FWC!
HUNH!
SHLUNK

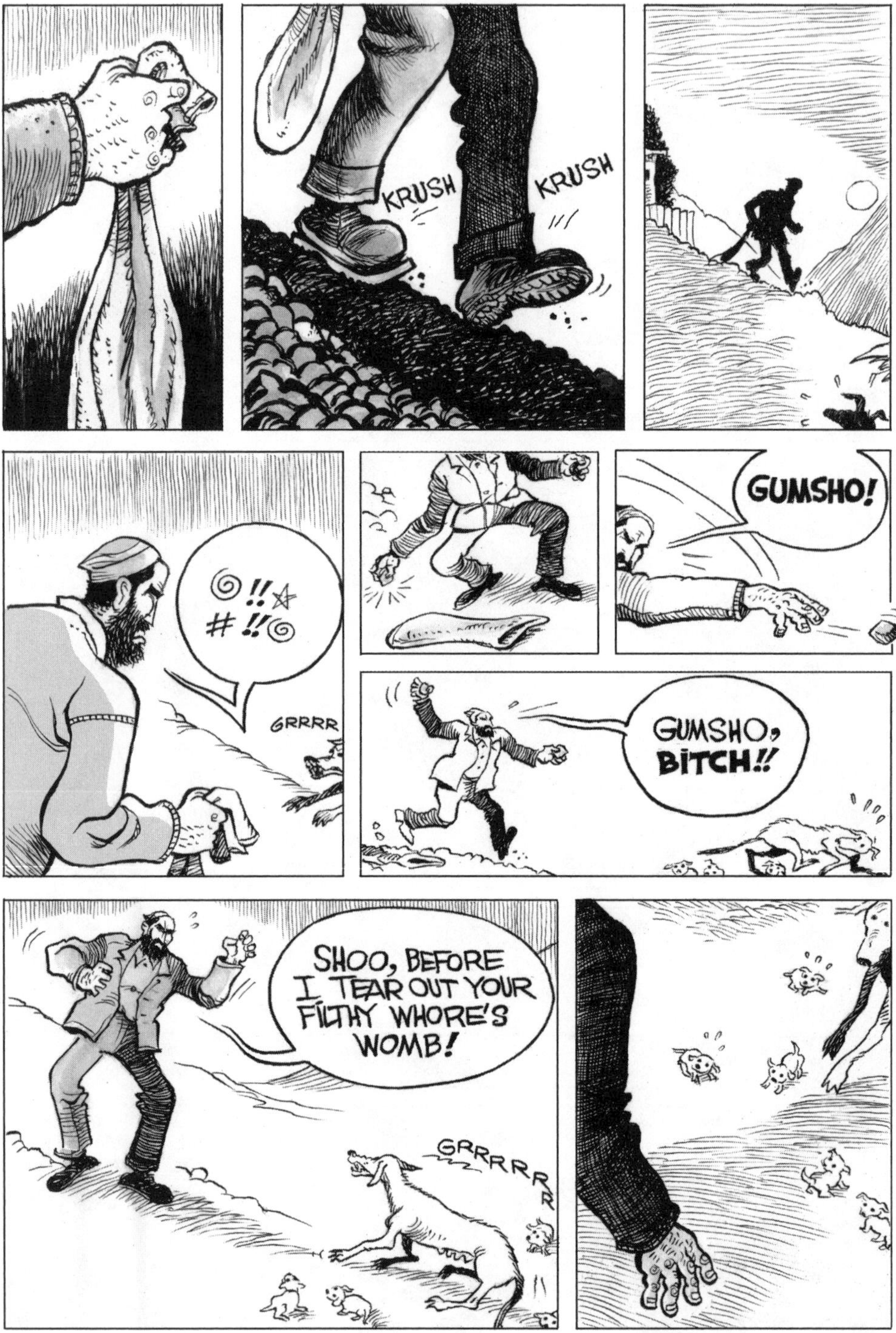
KRUSH
KRUSH
GUMSHO!
GRRRR
GUMSHO, BITCH!!
SHOO, BEFORE I TEAR OUT YOUR FILTHY WHORE'S WOMB!
GRRRRRRR

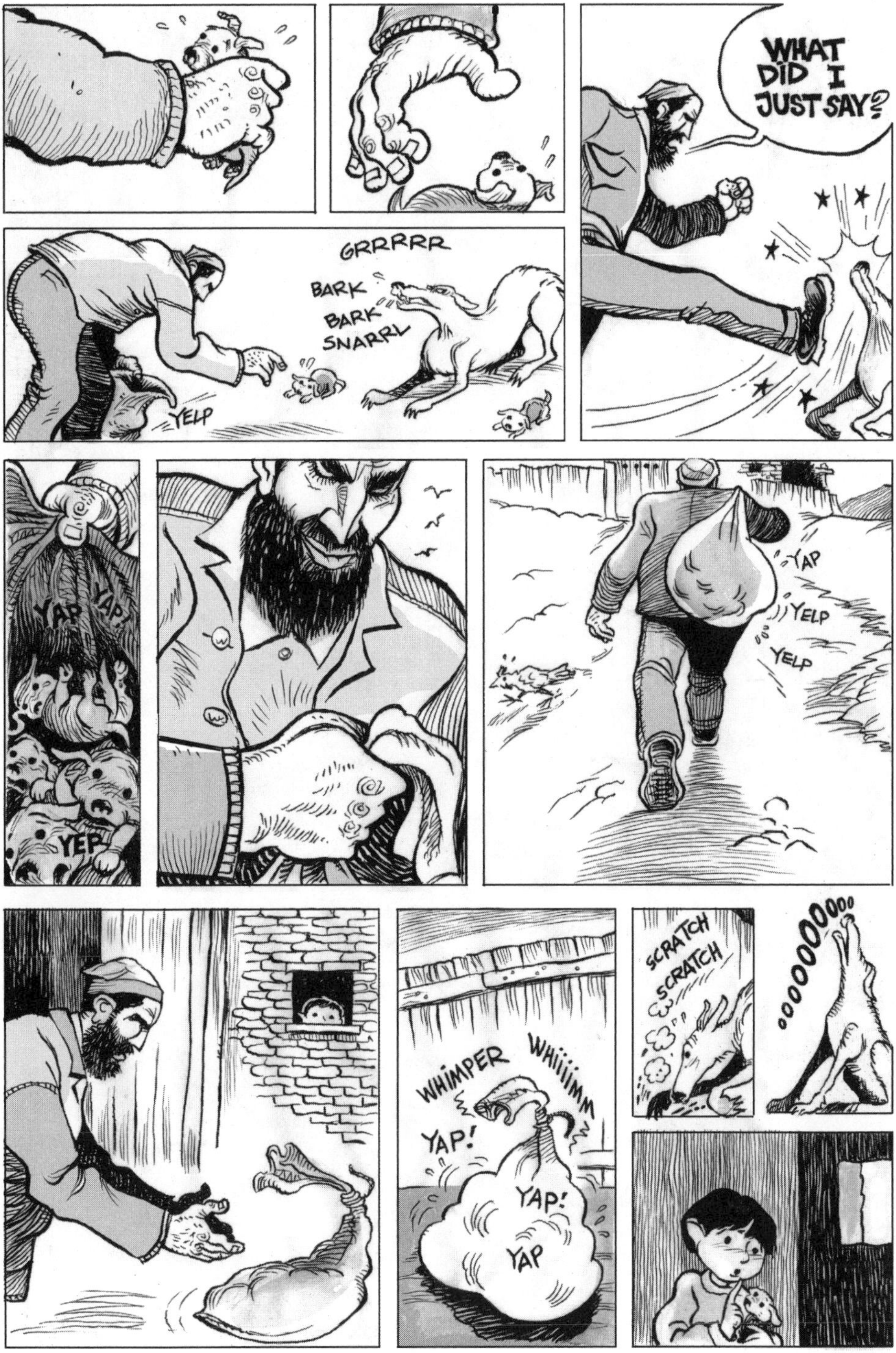
WHAT DID I JUST SAY?
GRRRRR
BARK
BARK
SNARRL
YELP
YAP
YAP
YEP
YAP
YELP
YELP
WHIMPER
WHIIIIIMM
YAP!
YAP!
YAP
SCRATCH
SCRATCH
oooOOOOOooo

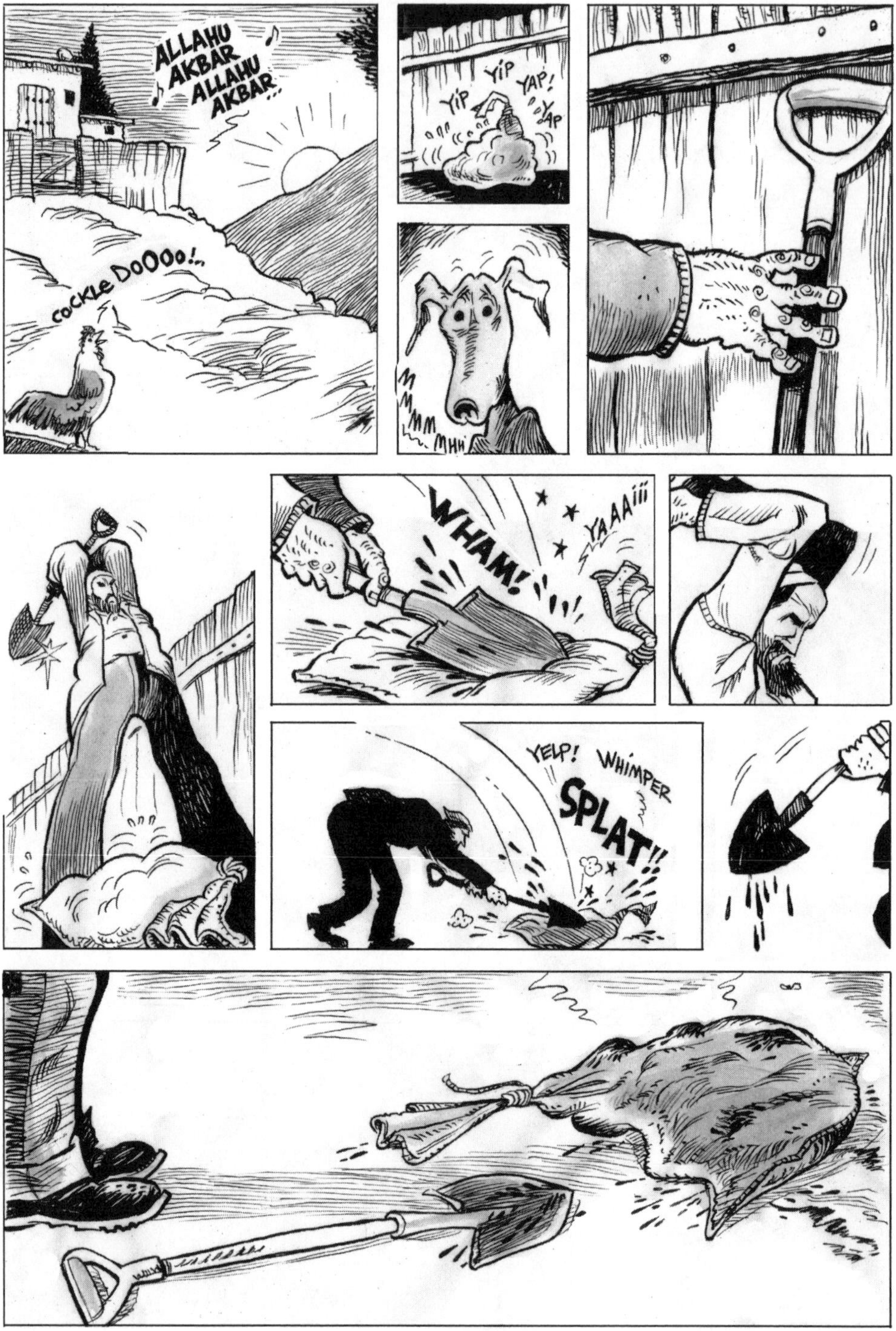
ALLAHU AKBAR ALLAHU AKBAR
COCKLE DOOOO!..
YIP YIP YAP! YAP
MMMMM MHH
WHAM!
YAAAiii
YELP! WHIMPER
SPLAT!!

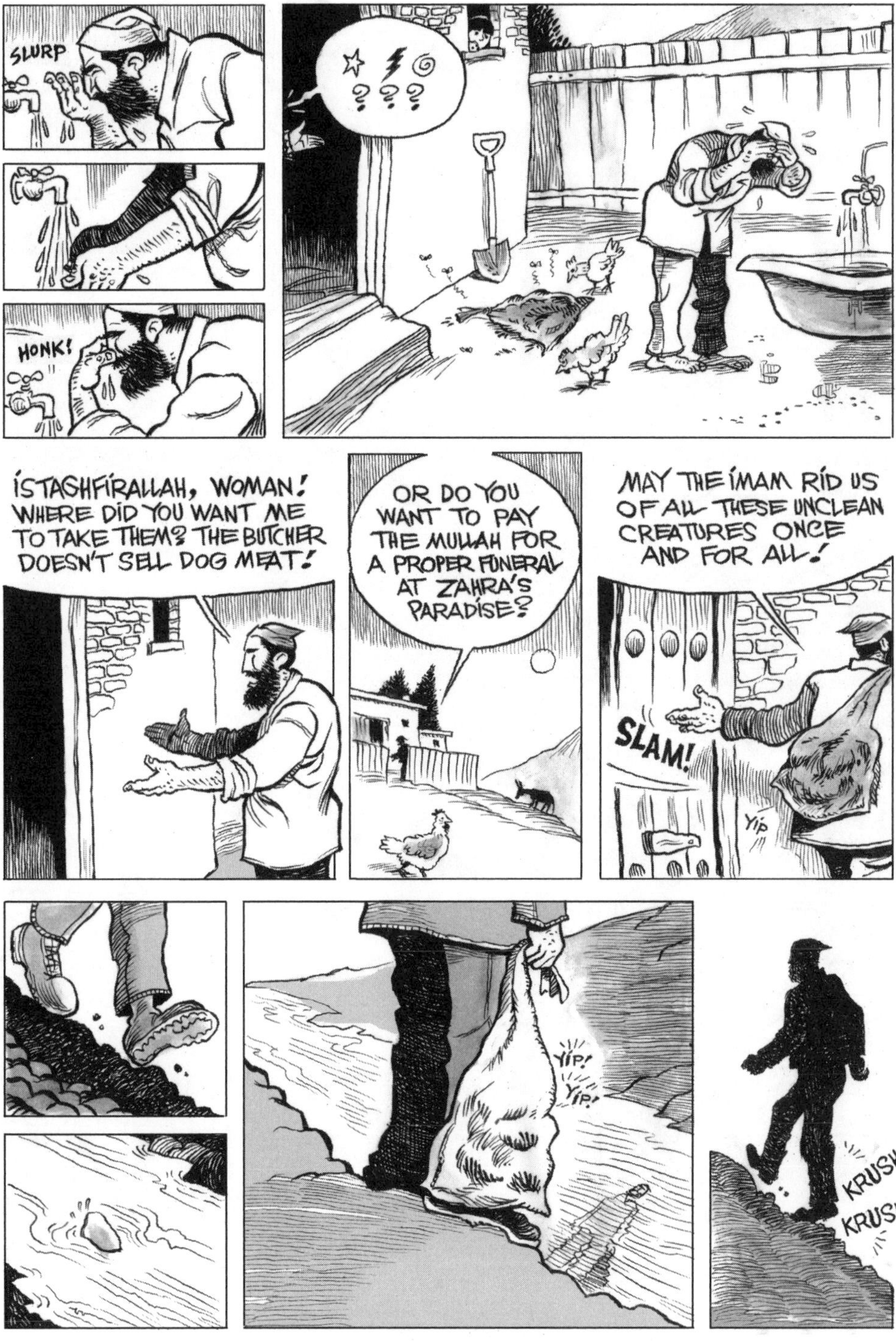
SLURP
HONK!
ISTAGHFIRALLAH, WOMAN! WHERE DID YOU WANT ME TO TAKE THEM? THE BUTCHER DOESN'T SELL DOG MEAT!
OR DO YOU WANT TO PAY THE MULLAH FOR A PROPER FUNERAL AT ZAHRA'S PARADISE?
MAY THE IMAM RID US OF ALL THESE UNCLEAN CREATURES ONCE AND FOR ALL!
SLAM!
YIP
YIP!
YIP!
KRUSH
KRUSH

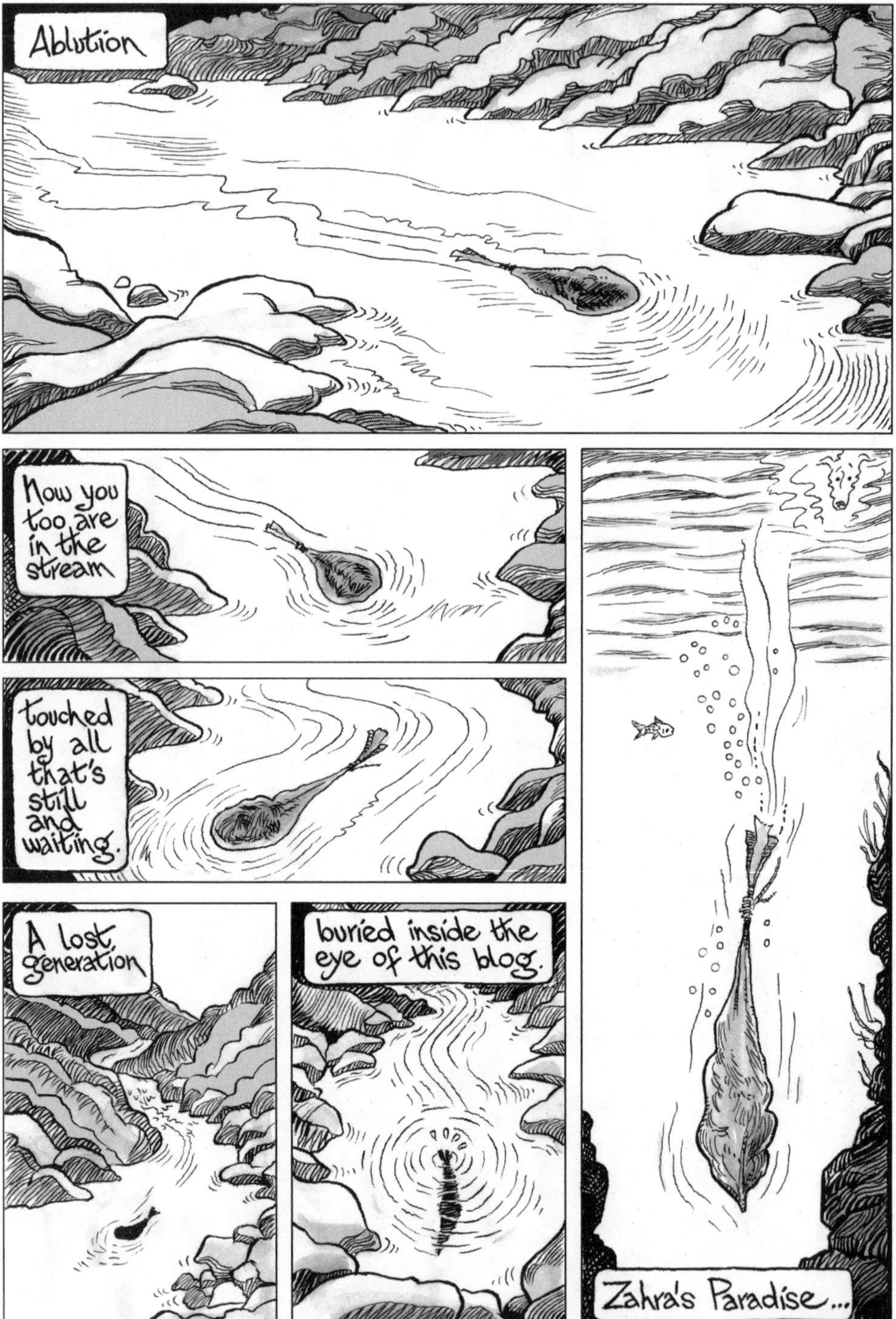
Ablution
Now you too are in the stream
touched by all that's still and waiting.
A lost generation
buried inside the eye of this blog.
Zahra's Paradise...

AFTERMATH

CHAPTER ONE

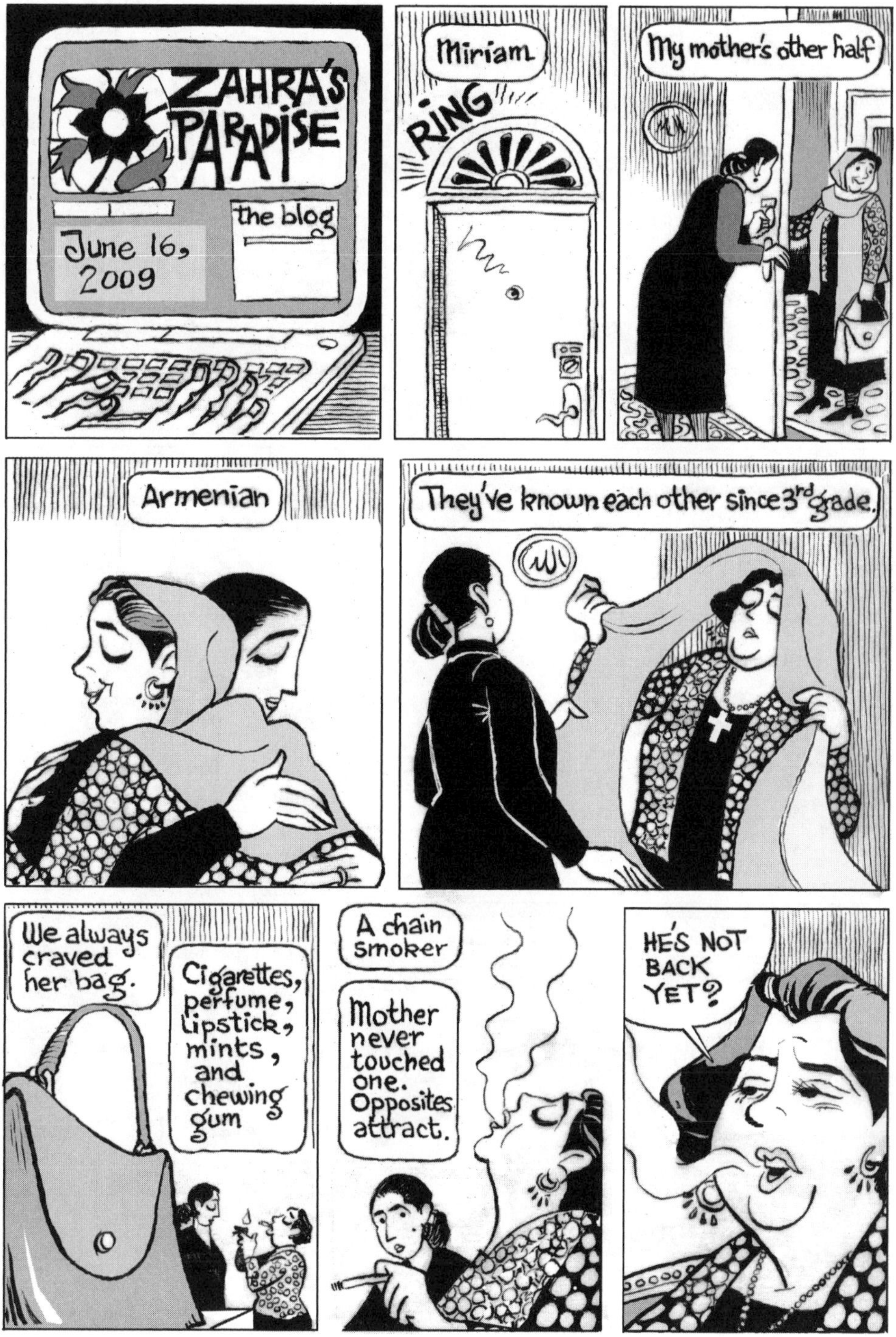
ZAHRA'S PARADISE
the blog
June 16, 2009
Miriam
RING
My mother's other half
Armenian
They've known each other since 3rd grade.
We always craved her bag.
Cigarettes, perfume, lipstick, mints, and chewing gum
A chain smoker
Mother never touched one. Opposites attract.
HE'S NOT BACK YET?

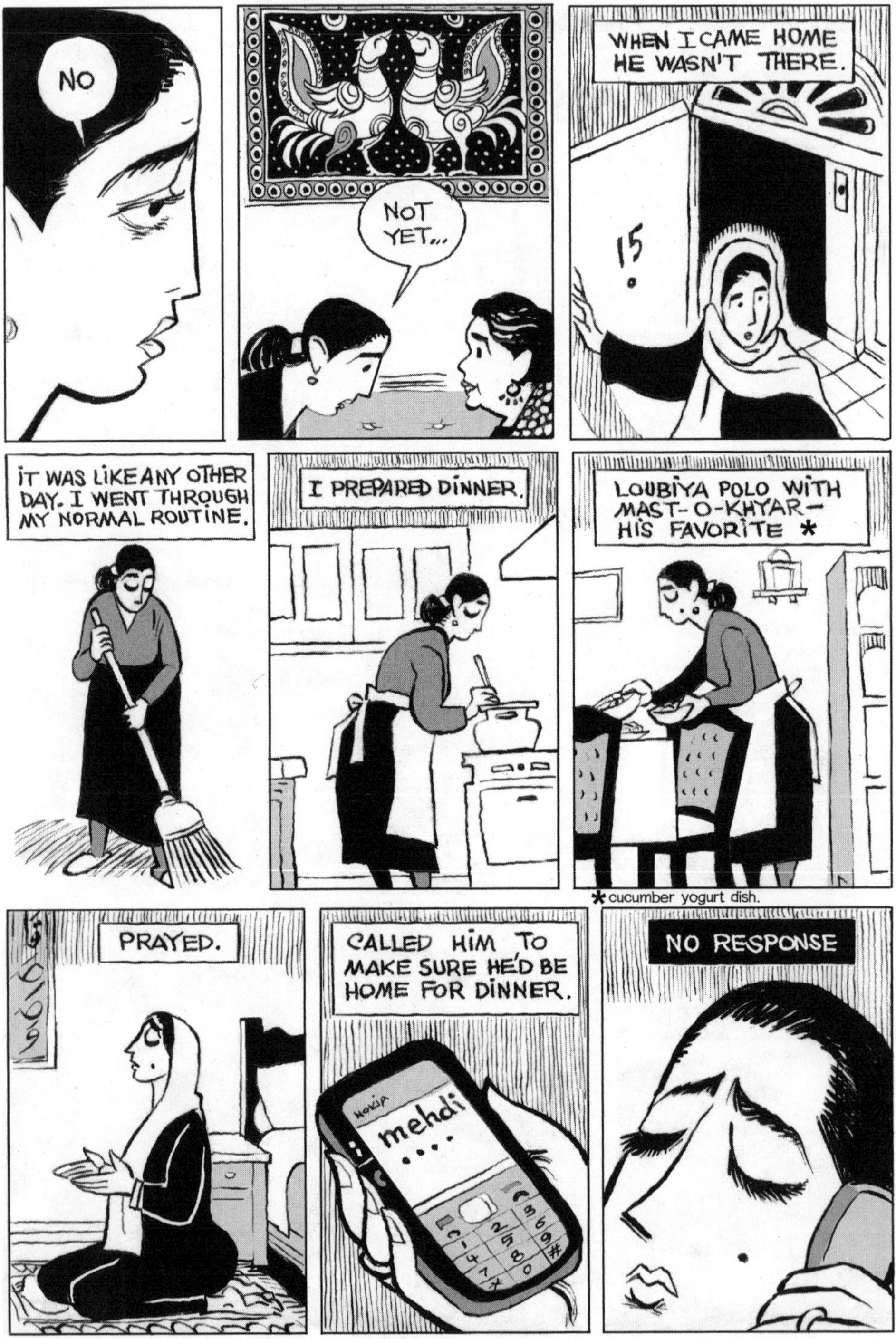
NO
NOT YET...
WHEN I CAME HOME HE WASN'T THERE.
15
IT WAS LIKE ANY OTHER DAY. I WENT THROUGH MY NORMAL ROUTINE.
I PREPARED DINNER.
LOUBIYA POLO WITH MAST-O-KHYAR—HIS FAVORITE *
PRAYED.
CALLED HIM TO MAKE SURE HE'D BE HOME FOR DINNER.
NOKIA
mehdi
....
NO RESPONSE

*cucumber yogurt dish.

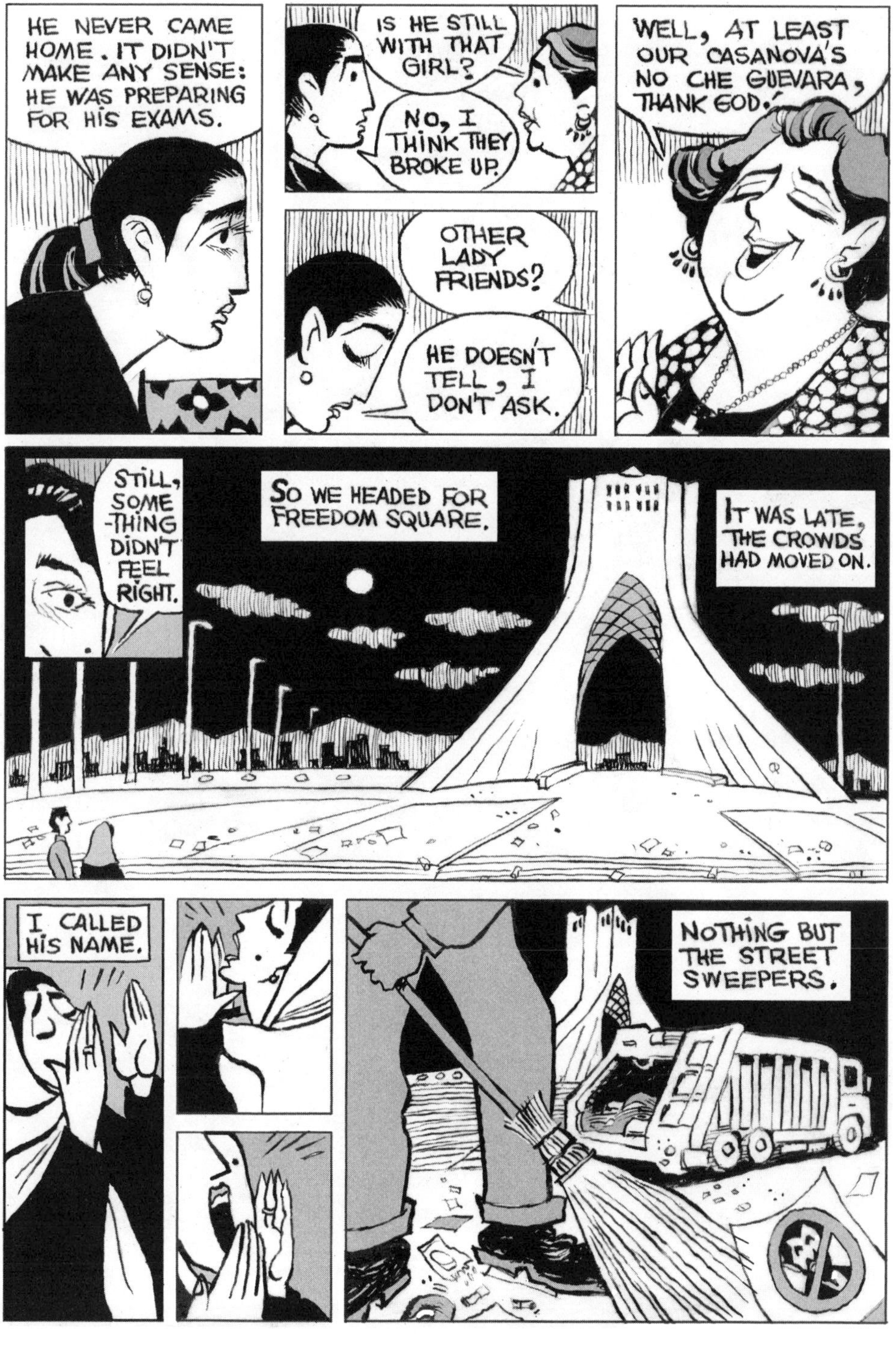
HE NEVER CAME HOME. IT DIDN'T MAKE ANY SENSE: HE WAS PREPARING FOR HIS EXAMS.
IS HE STILL WITH THAT GIRL?
NO, I THINK THEY BROKE UP.
OTHER LADY FRIENDS?
HE DOESN'T TELL, I DON'T ASK.
WELL, AT LEAST OUR CASANOVA'S NO CHE GUEVARA, THANK GOD.
STILL, SOME-THING DIDN'T FEEL RIGHT.
SO WE HEADED FOR FREEDOM SQUARE.
IT WAS LATE, THE CROWDS HAD MOVED ON.
I CALLED HIS NAME.
NOTHING BUT THE STREET SWEEPERS.

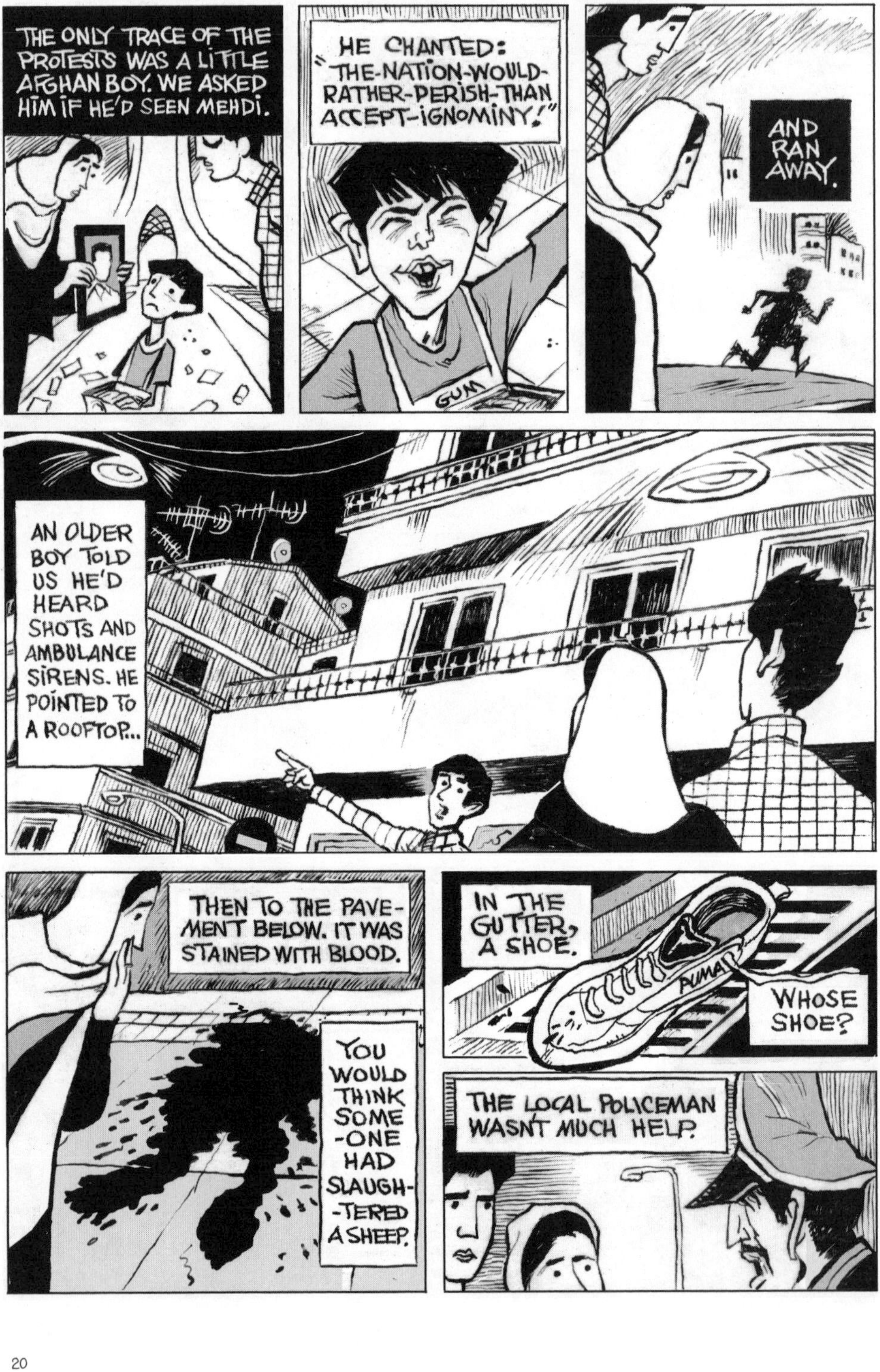
THE ONLY TRACE OF THE PROTESTS WAS A LITTLE AFGHAN BOY. WE ASKED HIM IF HE'D SEEN MEHDI.
HE CHANTED: "THE-NATION-WOULD-RATHER-PERISH-THAN ACCEPT-IGNOMINY!"
GUM
AND RAN AWAY.
AN OLDER BOY TOLD US HE'D HEARD SHOTS AND AMBULANCE SIRENS. HE POINTED TO A ROOFTOP...
THEN TO THE PAVE-MENT BELOW. IT WAS STAINED WITH BLOOD.
YOU WOULD THINK SOME-ONE HAD SLAUGH-TERED A SHEEP.
IN THE GUTTER, A SHOE.
PUMA
WHOSE SHOE?
THE LOCAL POLICEMAN WASN'T MUCH HELP.

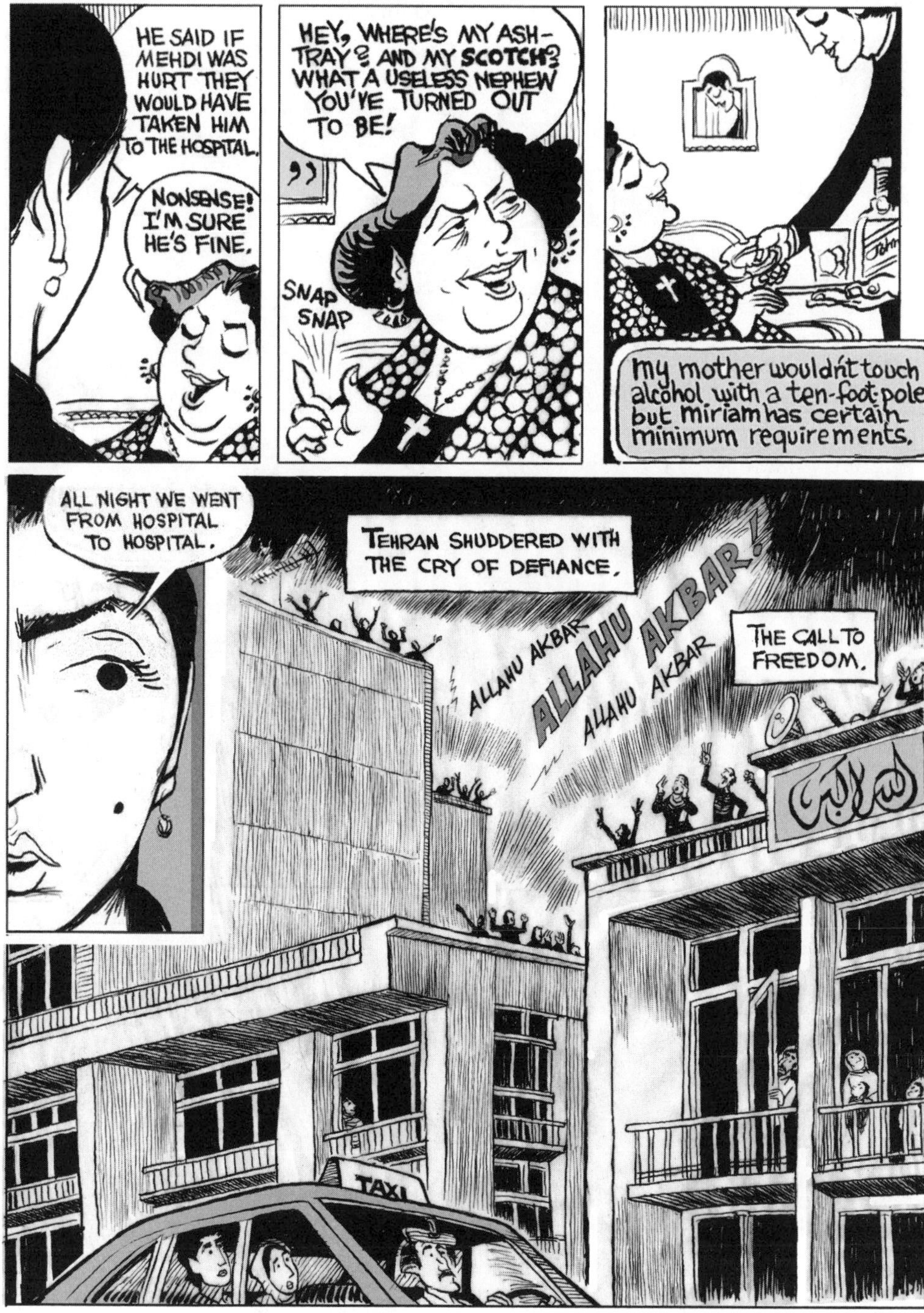
HE SAID IF MEHDI WAS HURT THEY WOULD HAVE TAKEN HIM TO THE HOSPITAL.
NONSENSE! I'M SURE HE'S FINE.
HEY, WHERE'S MY ASH-TRAY?? AND MY SCOTCH?? WHAT A USELESS NEPHEW YOU'VE TURNED OUT TO BE!
SNAP SNAP
My mother wouldn't touch alcohol with a ten-foot-pole but Miriam has certain minimum requirements.
ALL NIGHT WE WENT FROM HOSPITAL TO HOSPITAL.
TEHRAN SHUDDERED WITH THE CRY OF DEFIANCE.
ALLAHU AKBAR
ALLAHU AKBAR!
ALLAHU AKBAR
THE CALL TO FREEDOM.
TAXI

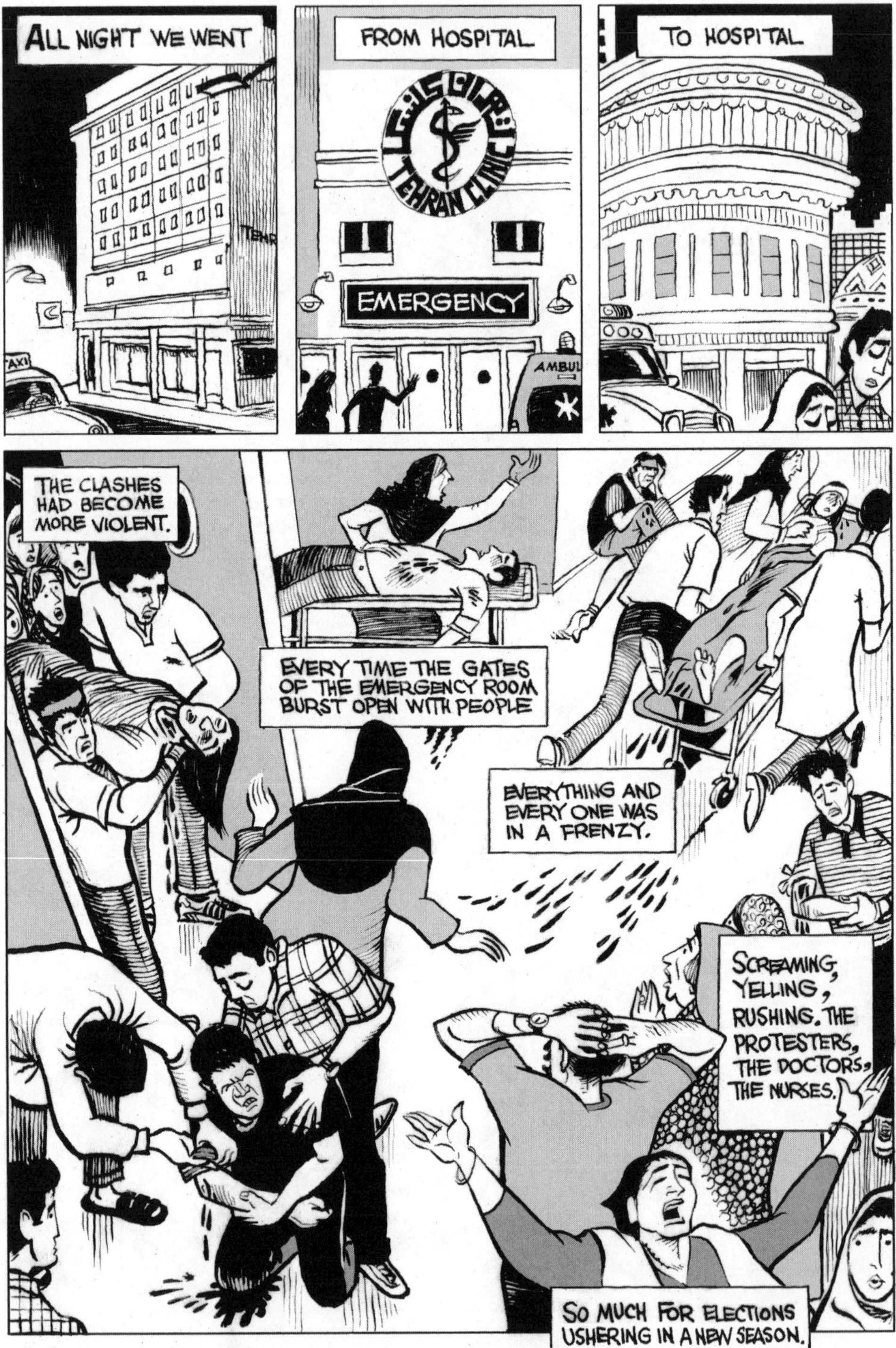
ALL NIGHT WE WENT
FROM HOSPITAL
TEHRAN CLINIC
EMERGENCY
TO HOSPITAL
THE CLASHES HAD BECOME MORE VIOLENT.
EVERY TIME THE GATES OF THE EMERGENCY ROOM BURST OPEN WITH PEOPLE
EVERYTHING AND EVERY ONE WAS IN A FRENZY.
SCREAMING, YELLING, RUSHING. THE PROTESTERS, THE DOCTORS, THE NURSES.
SO MUCH FOR ELECTIONS USHERING IN A NEW SEASON.

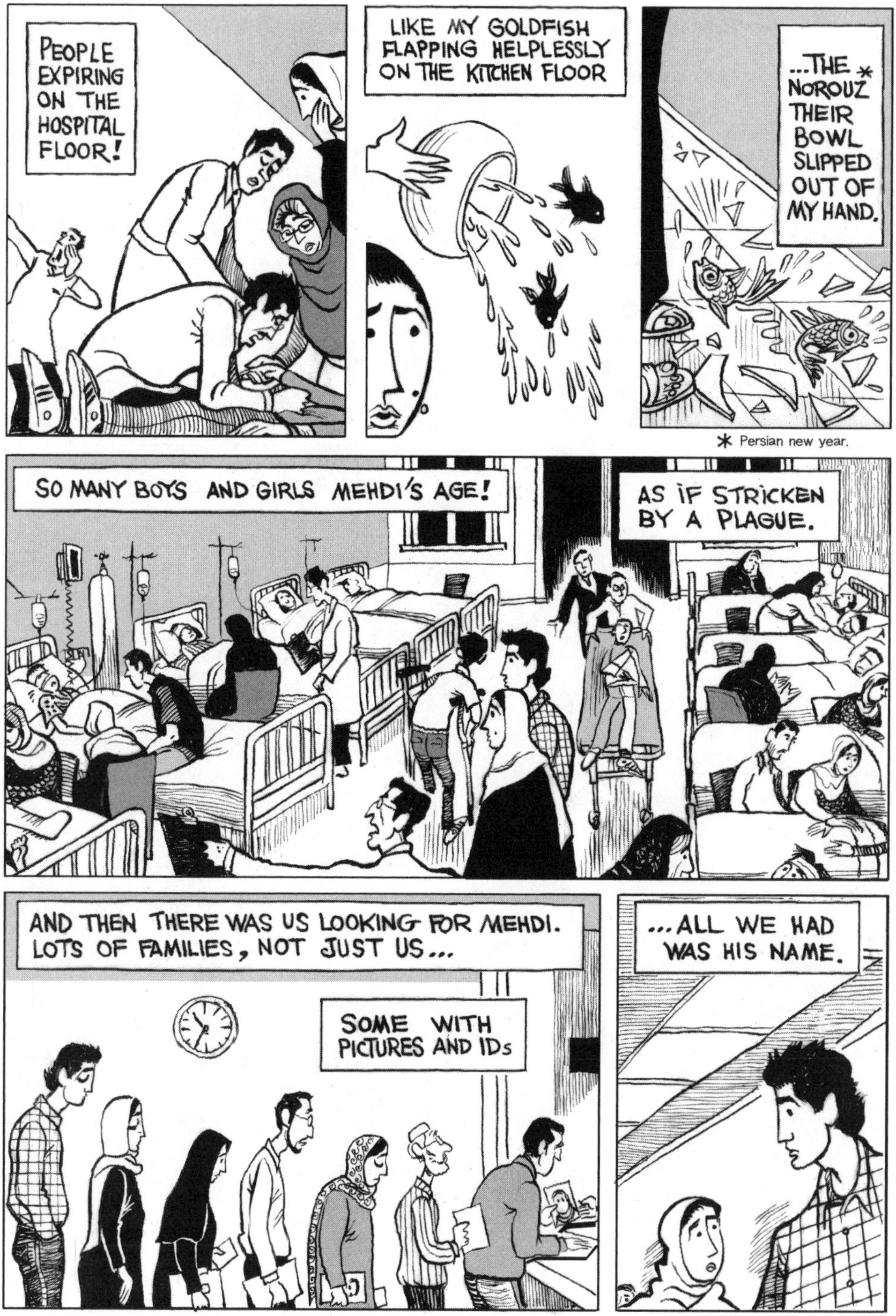
PEOPLE EXPIRING ON THE HOSPITAL FLOOR!
LIKE MY GOLDFISH FLAPPING HELPLESSLY ON THE KITCHEN FLOOR
...THE NOROUZ* THEIR BOWL SLIPPED OUT OF MY HAND.
SO MANY BOYS AND GIRLS MEHDI'S AGE!
AS IF STRICKEN BY A PLAGUE.
AND THEN THERE WAS US LOOKING FOR MEHDI. LOTS OF FAMILIES, NOT JUST US...
SOME WITH PICTURES AND IDs
...ALL WE HAD WAS HIS NAME.

* Persian new year.

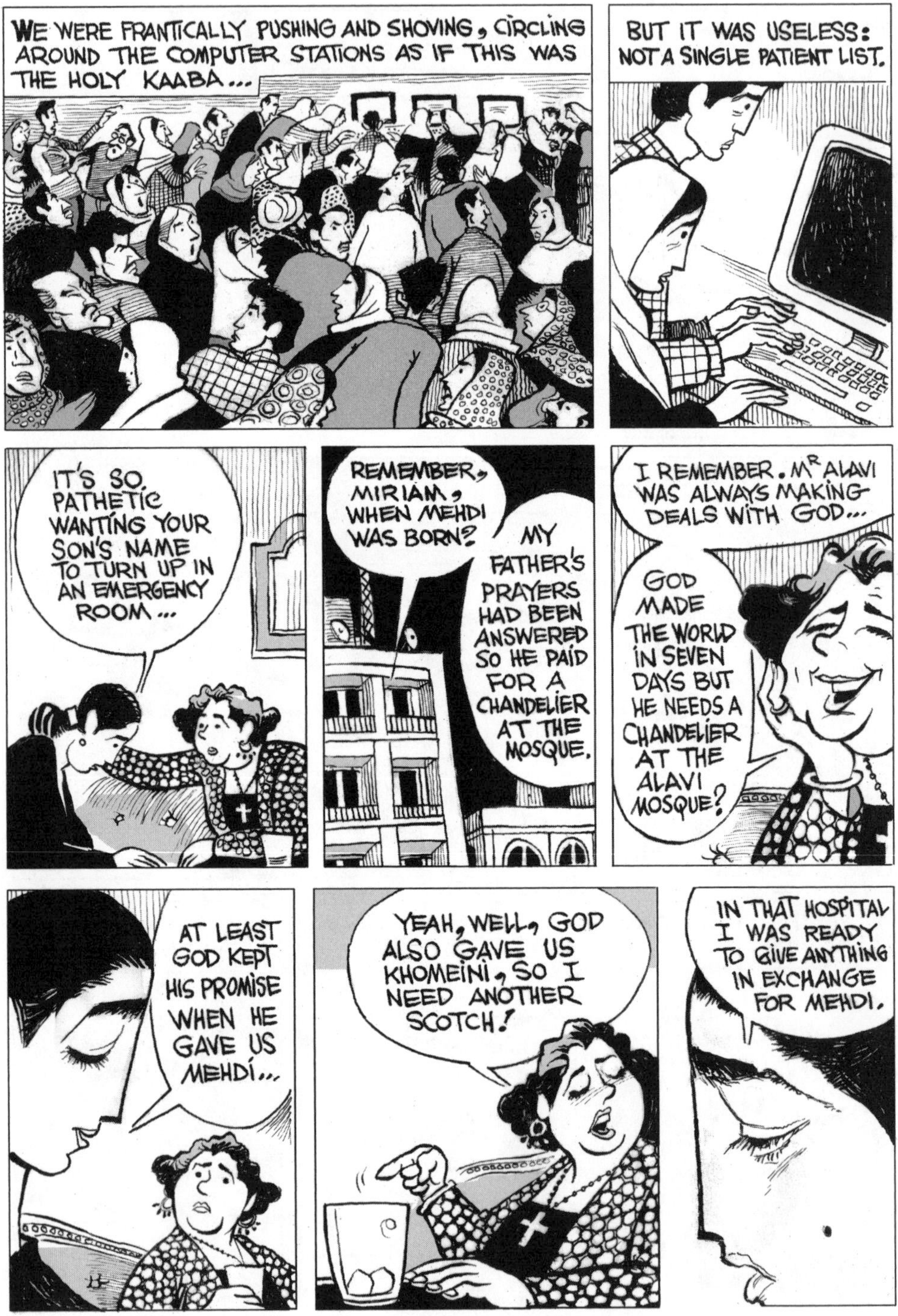

WE WERE FRANTICALLY PUSHING AND SHOVING, CIRCLING AROUND THE COMPUTER STATIONS AS IF THIS WAS THE HOLY KAABA...
BUT IT WAS USELESS: NOT A SINGLE PATIENT LIST.
IT'S SO PATHETIC WANTING YOUR SON'S NAME TO TURN UP IN AN EMERGENCY ROOM...
REMEMBER, MIRIAM, WHEN MEHDI WAS BORN?
MY FATHER'S PRAYERS HAD BEEN ANSWERED SO HE PAID FOR A CHANDELIER AT THE MOSQUE.
I REMEMBER. MR ALAVI WAS ALWAYS MAKING DEALS WITH GOD...
GOD MADE THE WORLD IN SEVEN DAYS BUT HE NEEDS A CHANDELIER AT THE ALAVI MOSQUE?
AT LEAST GOD KEPT HIS PROMISE WHEN HE GAVE US MEHDI...
YEAH, WELL, GOD ALSO GAVE US KHOMEINI, SO I NEED ANOTHER SCOTCH!
IN THAT HOSPITAL I WAS READY TO GIVE ANYTHING IN EXCHANGE FOR MEHDI.

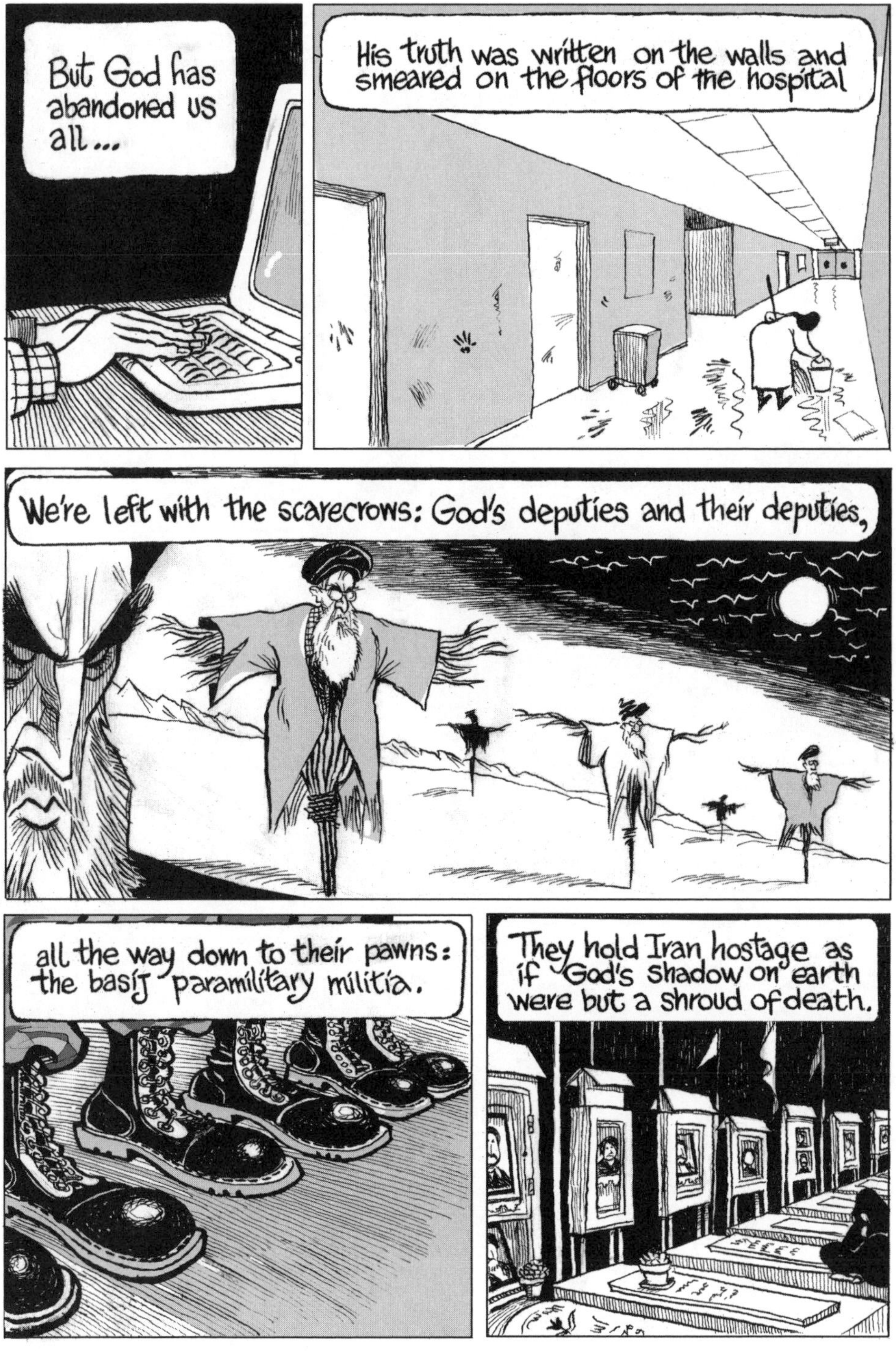

But God has abandoned us all...
His truth was written on the walls and smeared on the floors of the hospital
We're left with the scarecrows: God's deputies and their deputies,
all the way down to their pawns: the basij paramilitary militia.
They hold Iran hostage as if God's shadow on earth were but a shroud of death.

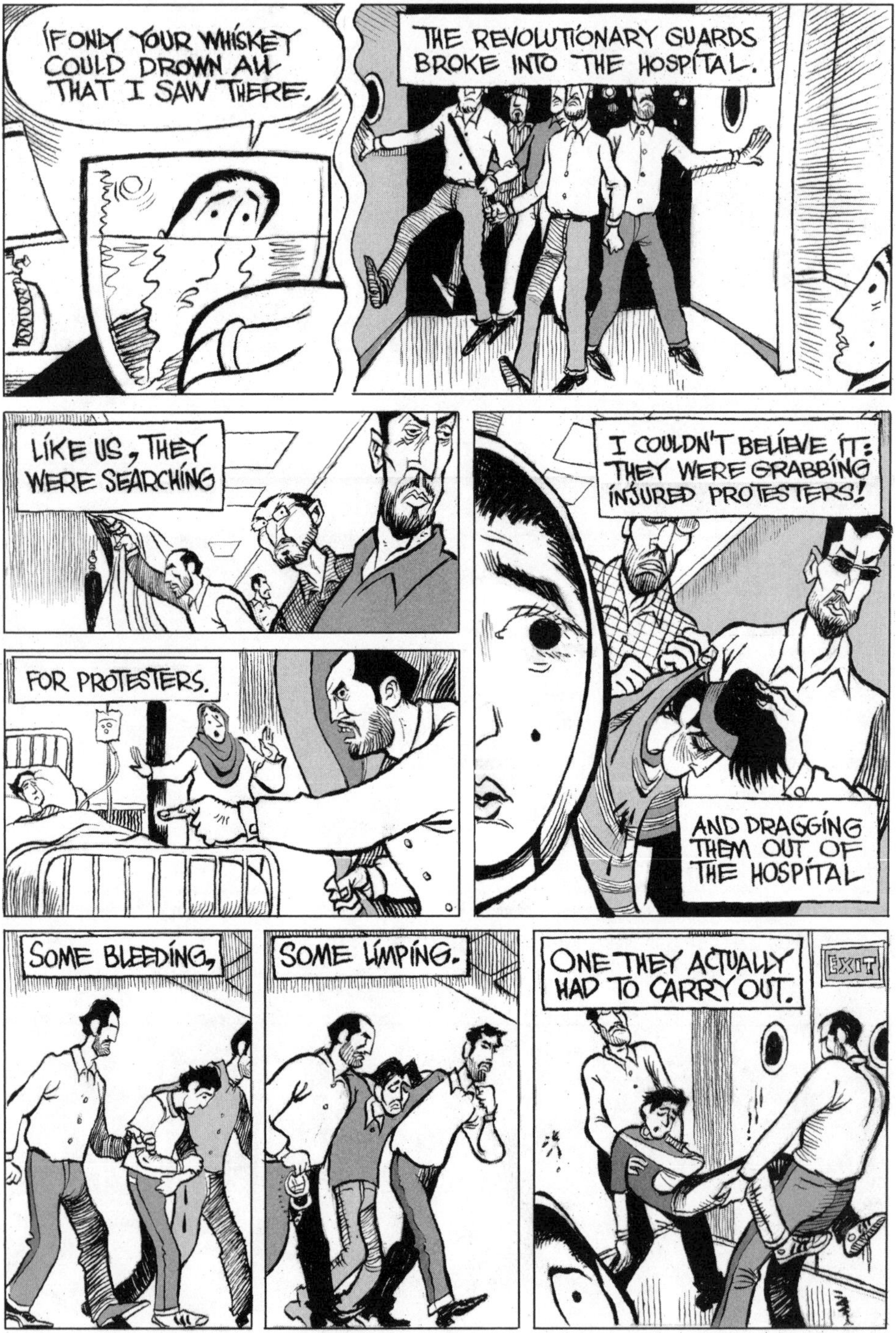
IF ONLY YOUR WHISKEY COULD DROWN ALL THAT I SAW THERE.
THE REVOLUTIONARY GUARDS BROKE INTO THE HOSPITAL.
LIKE US, THEY WERE SEARCHING
FOR PROTESTERS.
I COULDN'T BELIEVE IT: THEY WERE GRABBING INJURED PROTESTERS!
AND DRAGGING THEM OUT OF THE HOSPITAL
SOME BLEEDING,
SOME LIMPING.
ONE THEY ACTUALLY HAD TO CARRY OUT.
EXIT

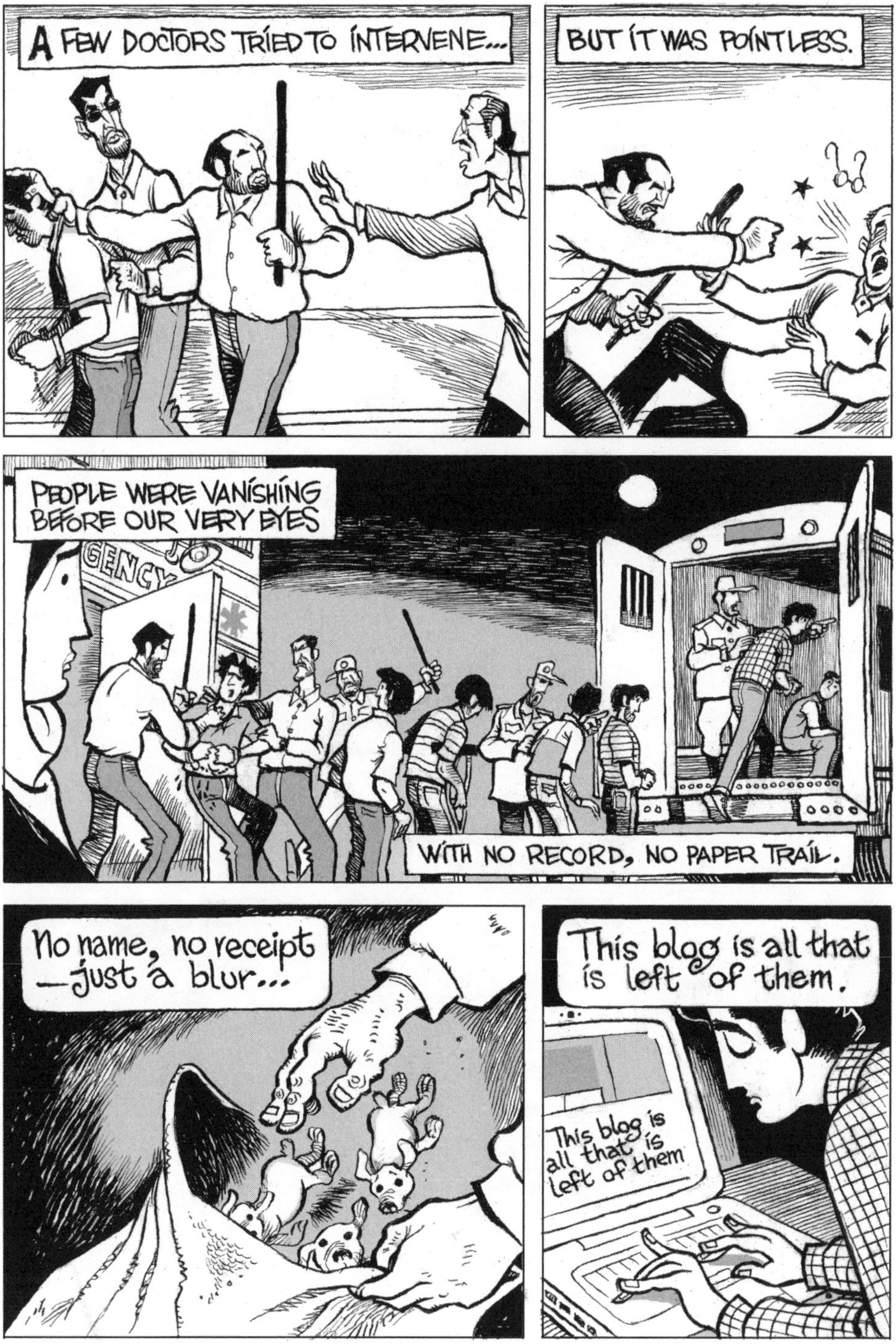
A FEW DOCTORS TRIED TO INTERVENE...
BUT IT WAS POINTLESS.
PEOPLE WERE VANISHING BEFORE OUR VERY EYES
WITH NO RECORD, NO PAPER TRAIL.
No name, no receipt —just a blur...
This blog is all that is left of them.
This blog is all that is left of them

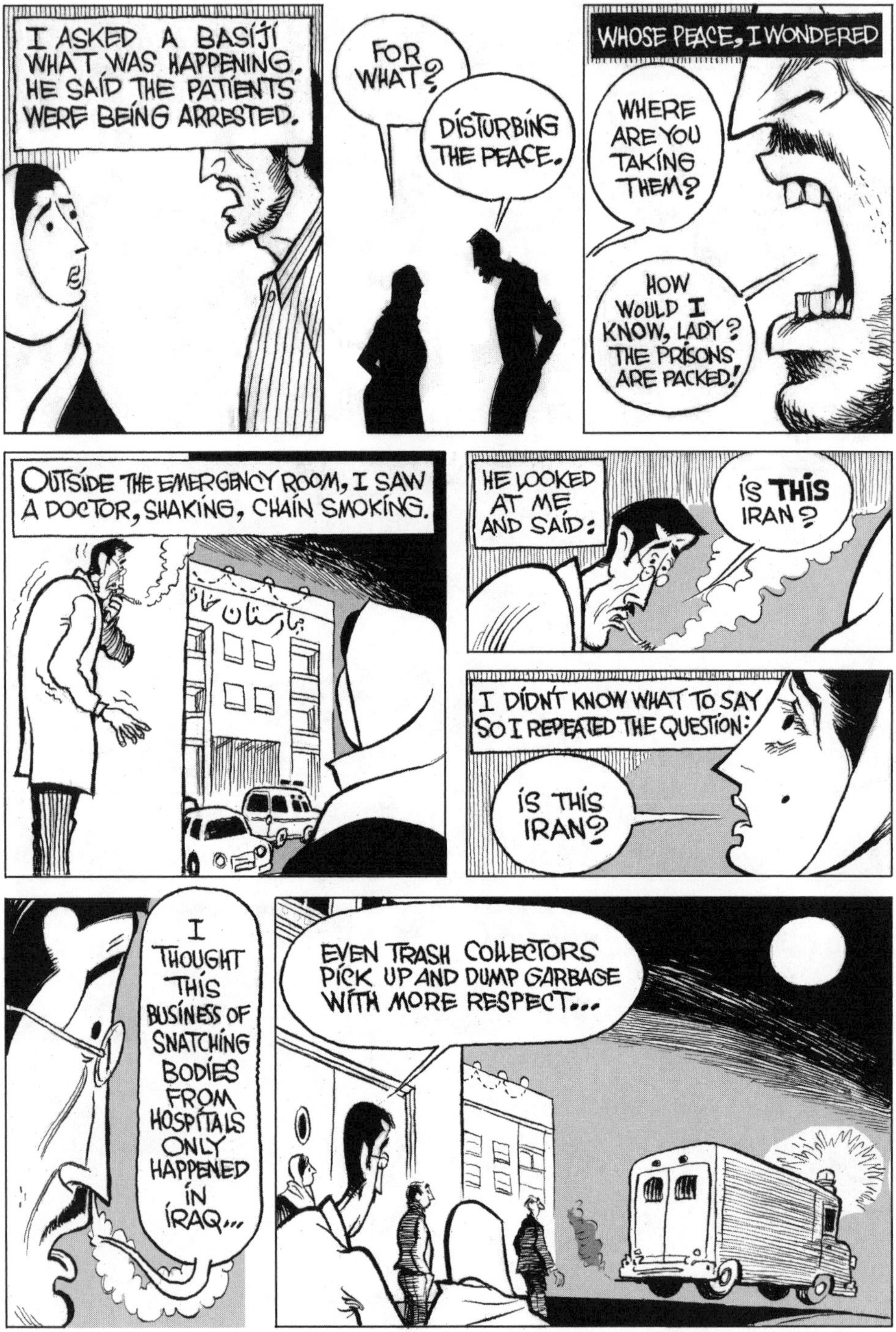
I ASKED A BASÍJÍ WHAT WAS HAPPENING. HE SAID THE PATIENTS WERE BEING ARRESTED.
FOR WHAT?
DISTURBING THE PEACE.
WHOSE PEACE, I WONDERED
WHERE ARE YOU TAKING THEM?
HOW WOULD I KNOW, LADY? THE PRISONS ARE PACKED!
OUTSIDE THE EMERGENCY ROOM, I SAW A DOCTOR, SHAKING, CHAIN SMOKING.
بیمارستان
HE LOOKED AT ME AND SAID:
IS THIS IRAN?
I DIDN'T KNOW WHAT TO SAY SO I REPEATED THE QUESTION:
IS THIS IRAN?
I THOUGHT THIS BUSINESS OF SNATCHING BODIES FROM HOSPITALS ONLY HAPPENED IN IRAQ...
EVEN TRASH COLLECTORS PICK UP AND DUMP GARBAGE WITH MORE RESPECT...

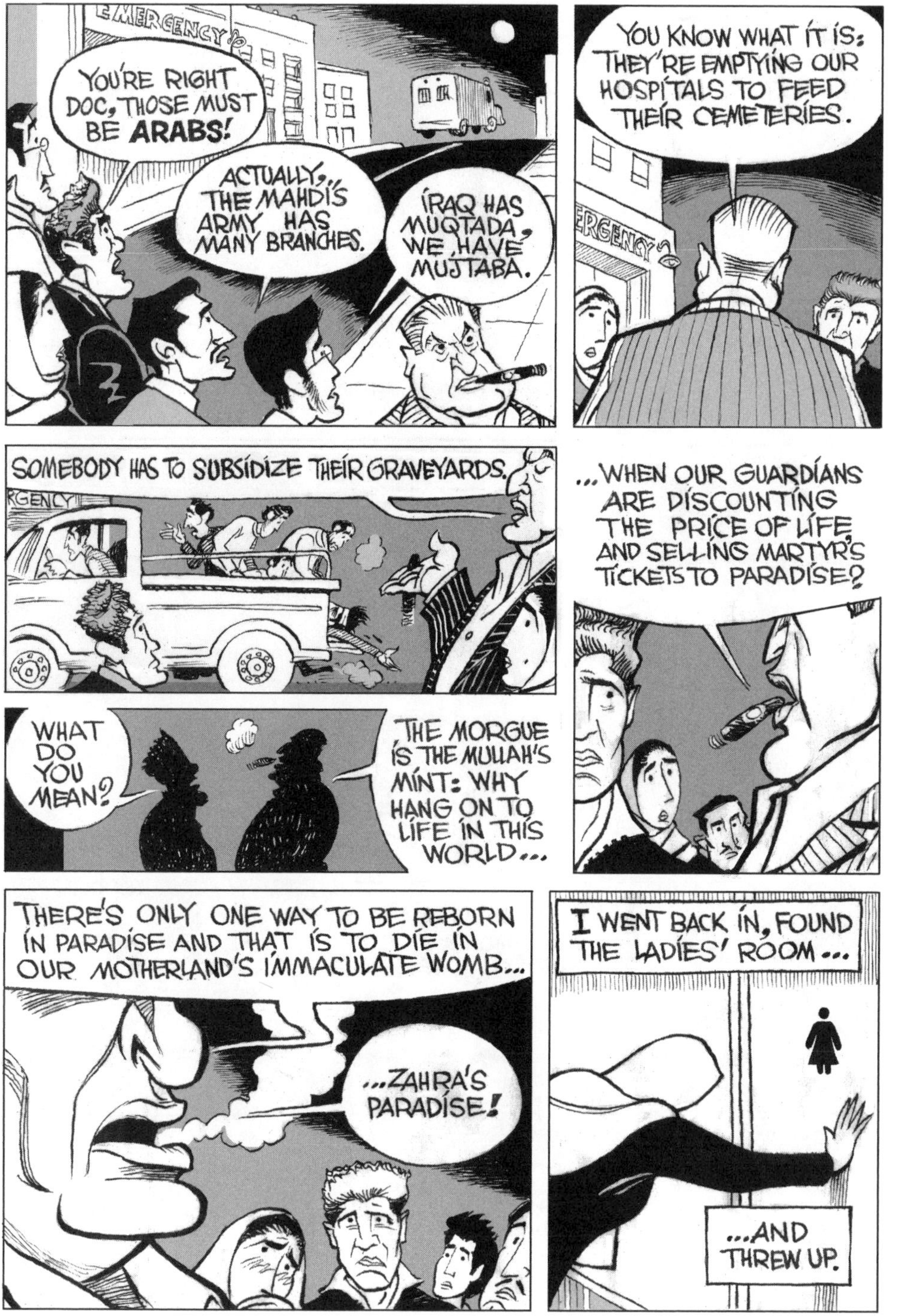
EMERGENCY
YOU'RE RIGHT DOC, THOSE MUST BE ARABS!
ACTUALLY... THE MAHDI'S ARMY HAS MANY BRANCHES.
IRAQ HAS MUQTADA, WE HAVE MUJTABA.
YOU KNOW WHAT IT IS: THEY'RE EMPTYING OUR HOSPITALS TO FEED THEIR CEMETERIES.
ERGENCY
SOMEBODY HAS TO SUBSIDIZE THEIR GRAVEYARDS.
RGENCY
...WHEN OUR GUARDIANS ARE DISCOUNTING THE PRICE OF LIFE AND SELLING MARTYR'S TICKETS TO PARADISE?
WHAT DO YOU MEAN?
THE MORGUE IS THE MULLAH'S MINT: WHY HANG ON TO LIFE IN THIS WORLD...
THERE'S ONLY ONE WAY TO BE REBORN IN PARADISE AND THAT IS TO DIE IN OUR MOTHERLAND'S IMMACULATE WOMB...
...ZAHRA'S PARADISE!
I WENT BACK IN, FOUND THE LADIES' ROOM...
...AND THREW UP.

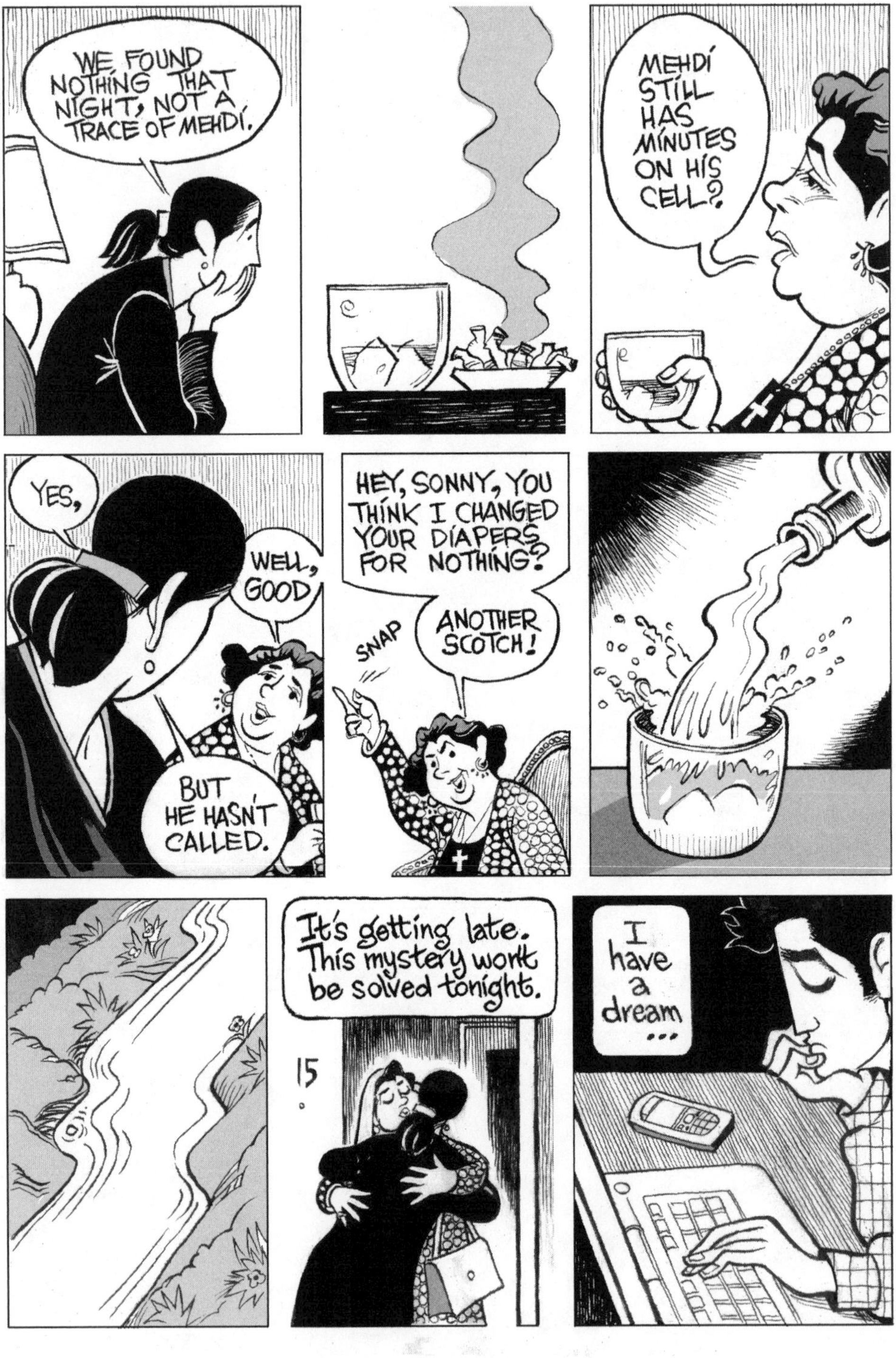
WE FOUND NOTHING THAT NIGHT, NOT A TRACE OF MEHDI.
MEHDI STILL HAS MINUTES ON HIS CELL?
YES,
WELL, GOOD
BUT HE HASN'T CALLED.
HEY, SONNY, YOU THINK I CHANGED YOUR DIAPERS FOR NOTHING?
SNAP
ANOTHER SCOTCH!
It's getting late. This mystery won't be solved tonight.
15
I have a dream ...

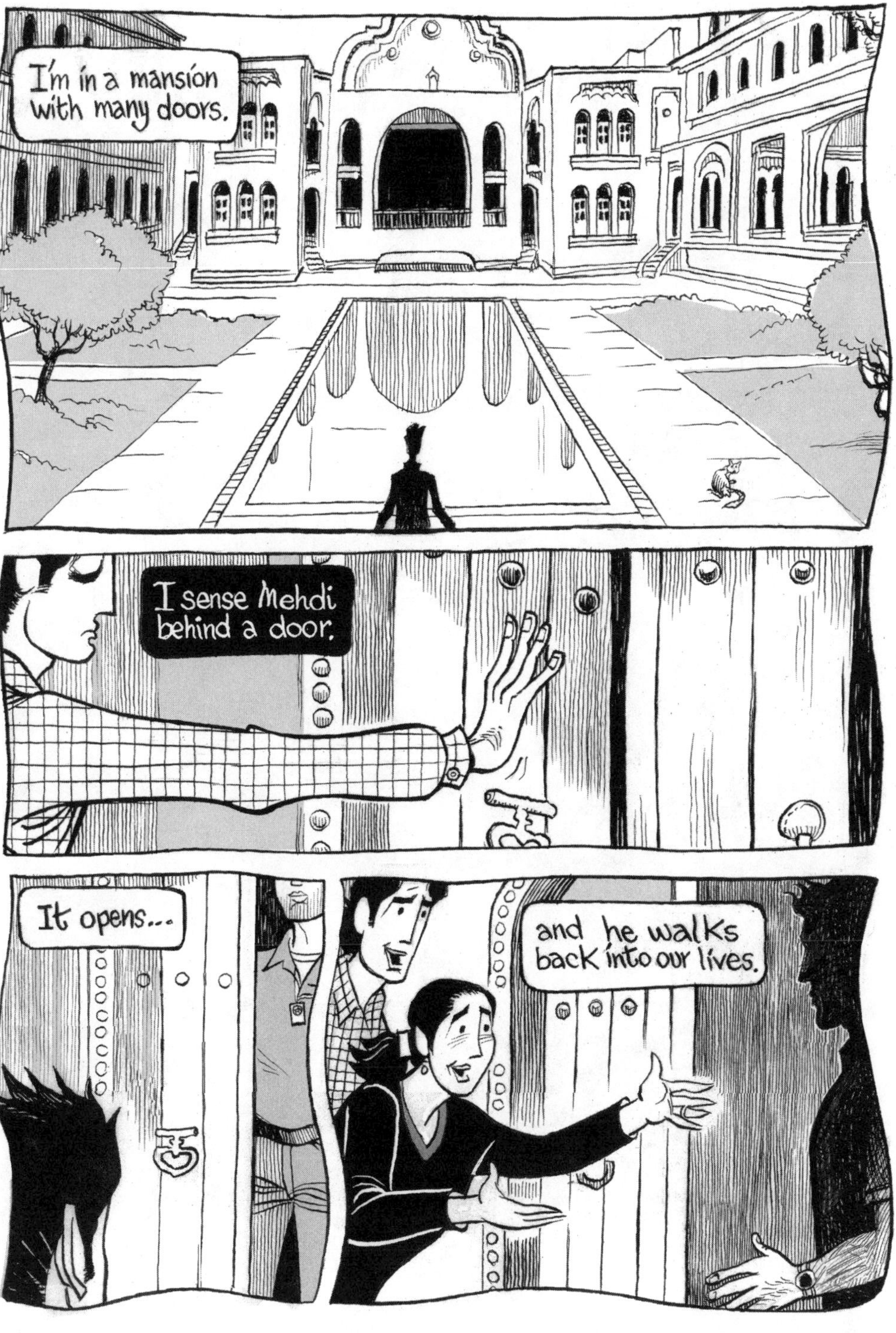
I'm in a mansion with many doors.
I sense Mehdi behind a door.
It opens...
and he walks back into our lives.

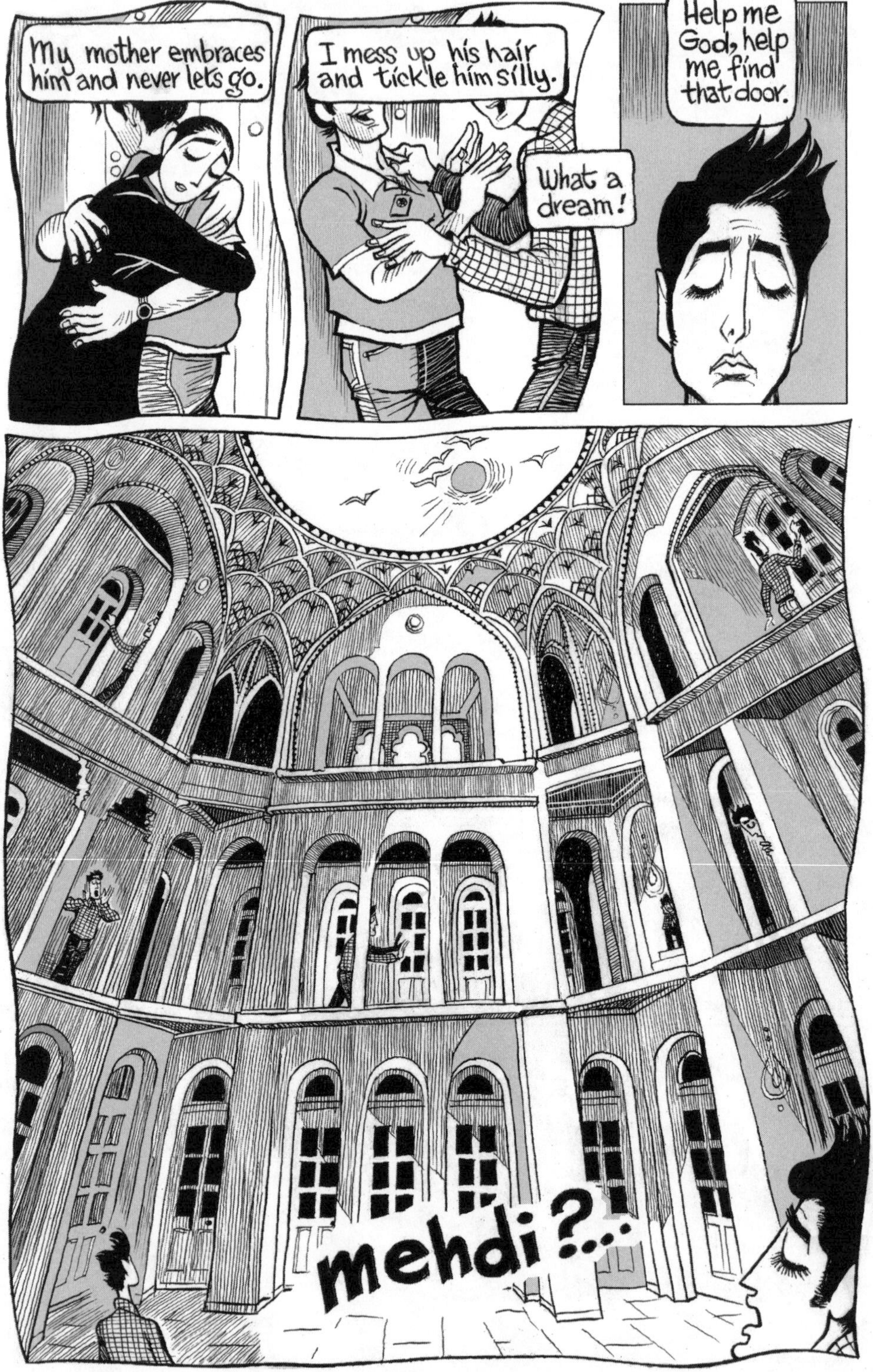
My mother embraces him and never lets go.
I mess up his hair and tickle him silly.
What a dream!
Help me God, help me find that door.
mehdi?...

EVIN

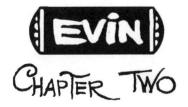

CHAPTER TWO

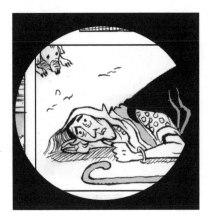

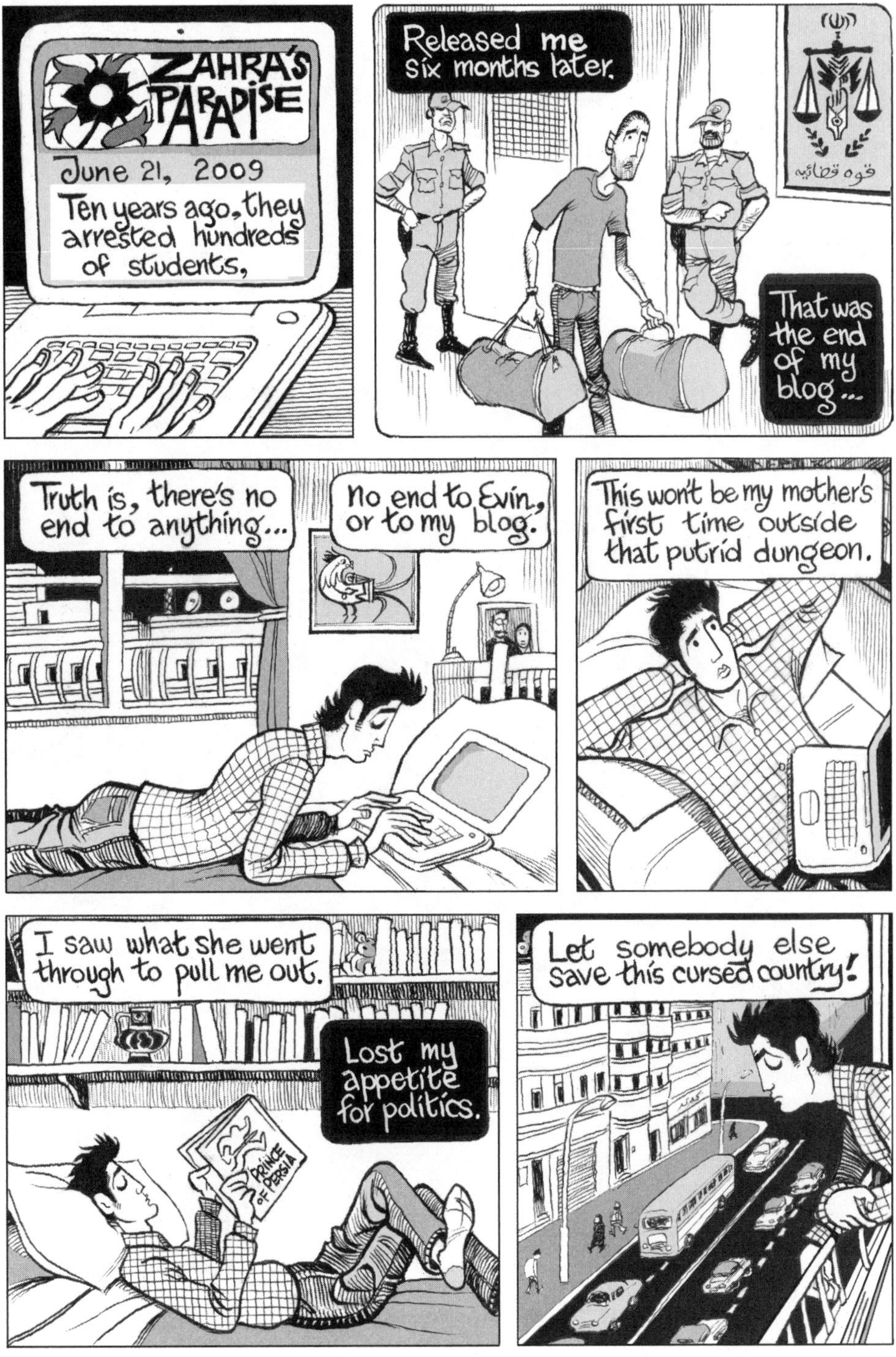
ZAHRA'S PARADISE
June 21, 2009
Ten years ago, they arrested hundreds of students,
Released me six months later.
That was the end of my blog...
Truth is, there's no end to anything...
No end to Evin, or to my blog.
This won't be my mother's first time outside that putrid dungeon.
I saw what she went through to pull me out.
Lost my appetite for politics.
PRINCE OF PERSIA
Let somebody else save this cursed country!

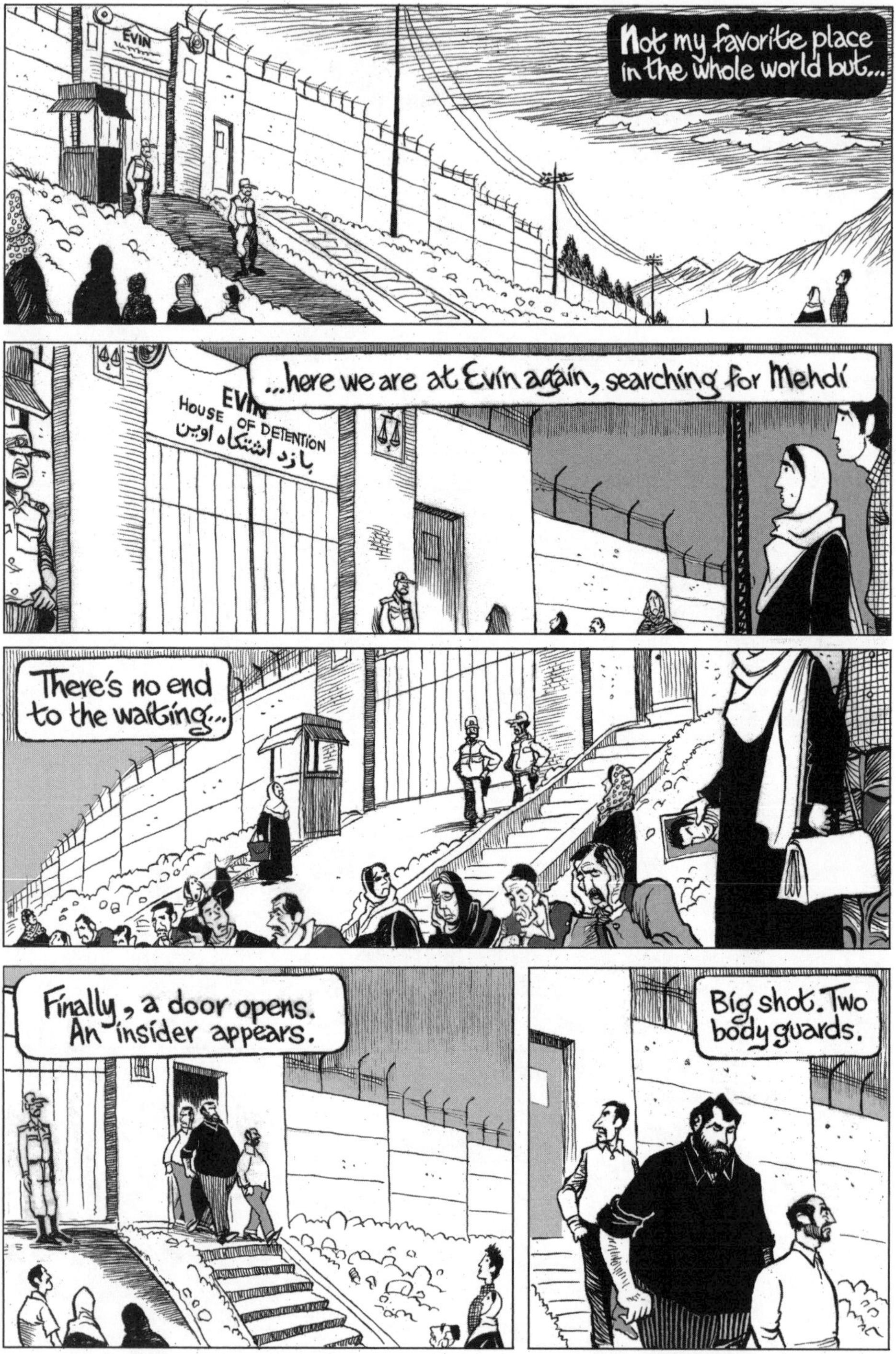
Not my favorite place in the whole world but...
EVIN
...here we are at Evín again, searching for Mehdí
EVIN HOUSE OF DETENTION
بازد اشتگاه اوین
There's no end to the waiting...
Finally, a door opens. An insider appears.
Big shot. Two body guards.

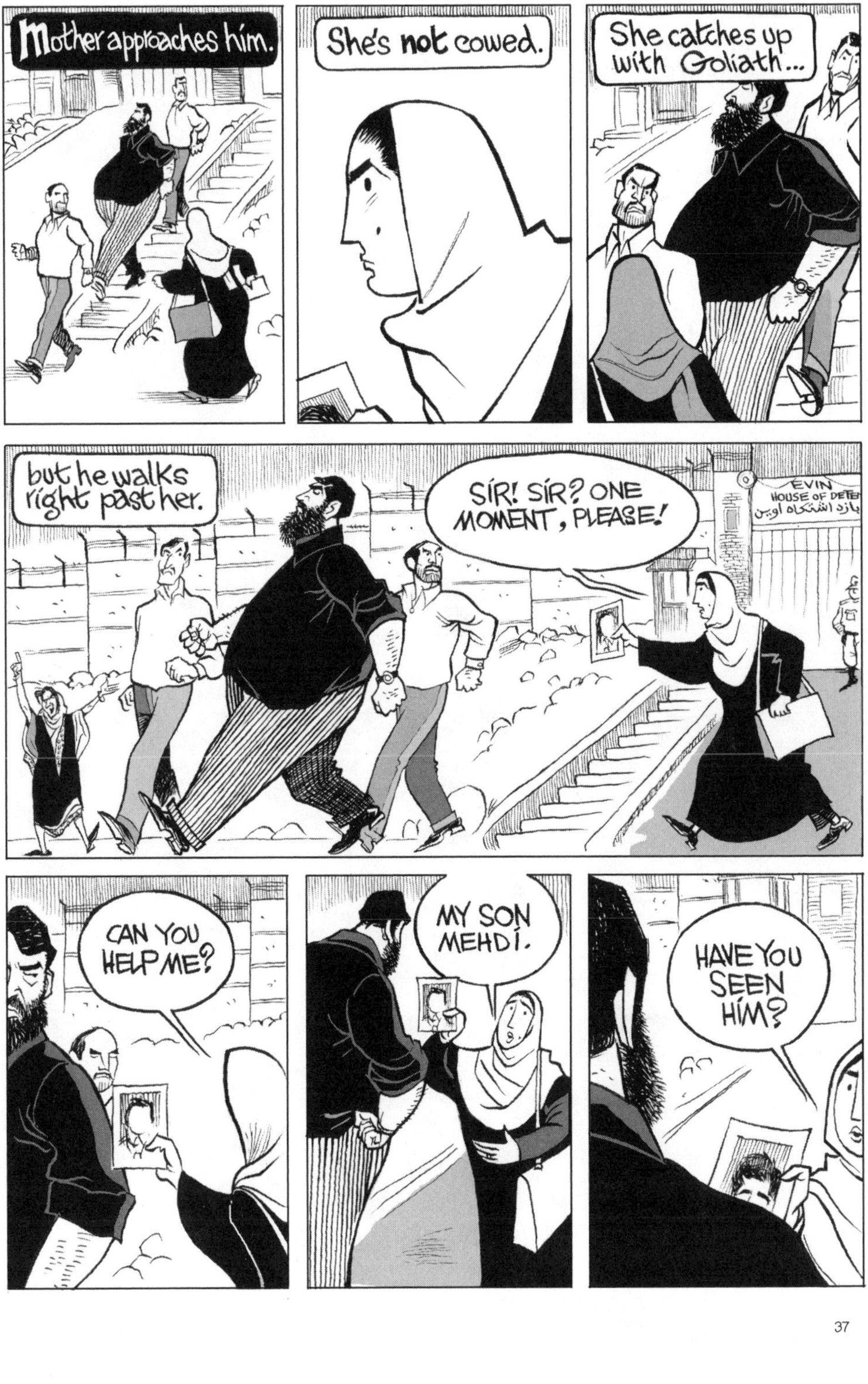
Mother approaches him.
She's not cowed.
She catches up with Goliath...
but he walks right past her.
SIR! SIR? ONE MOMENT, PLEASE!
EVIN
HOUSE OF DETE
CAN YOU HELP ME?
MY SON MEHDI.
HAVE YOU SEEN HIM?

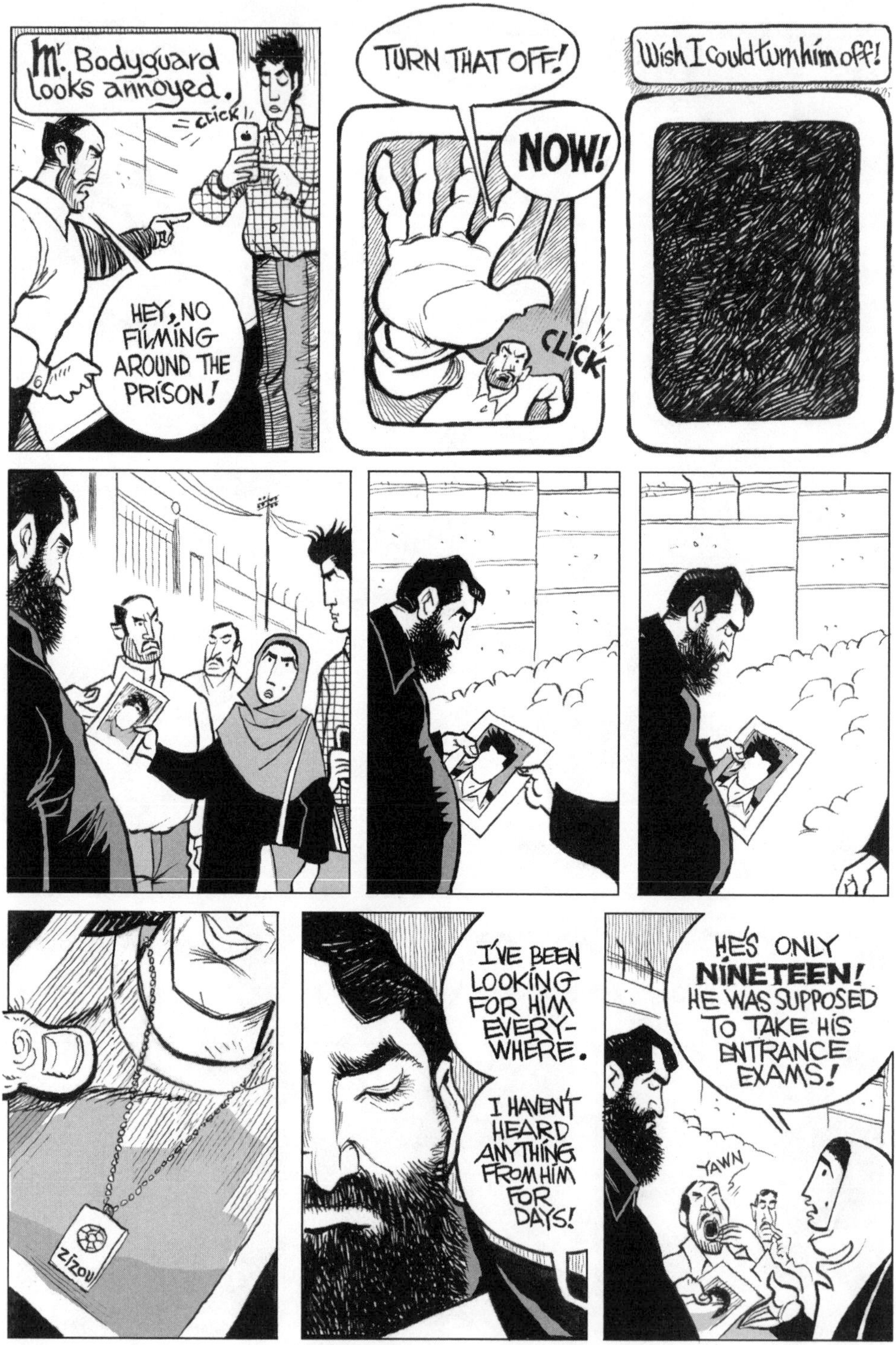
Mr. Bodyguard looks annoyed.
CLICK
HEY, NO FILMING AROUND THE PRISON!
TURN THAT OFF!
NOW!
CLICK
Wish I could turn him off!
I'VE BEEN LOOKING FOR HIM EVERY-WHERE.
I HAVEN'T HEARD ANYTHING FROM HIM FOR DAYS!
ZIZOU
HE'S ONLY **NINETEEN!** HE WAS SUPPOSED TO TAKE HIS ENTRANCE EXAMS!
YAWN

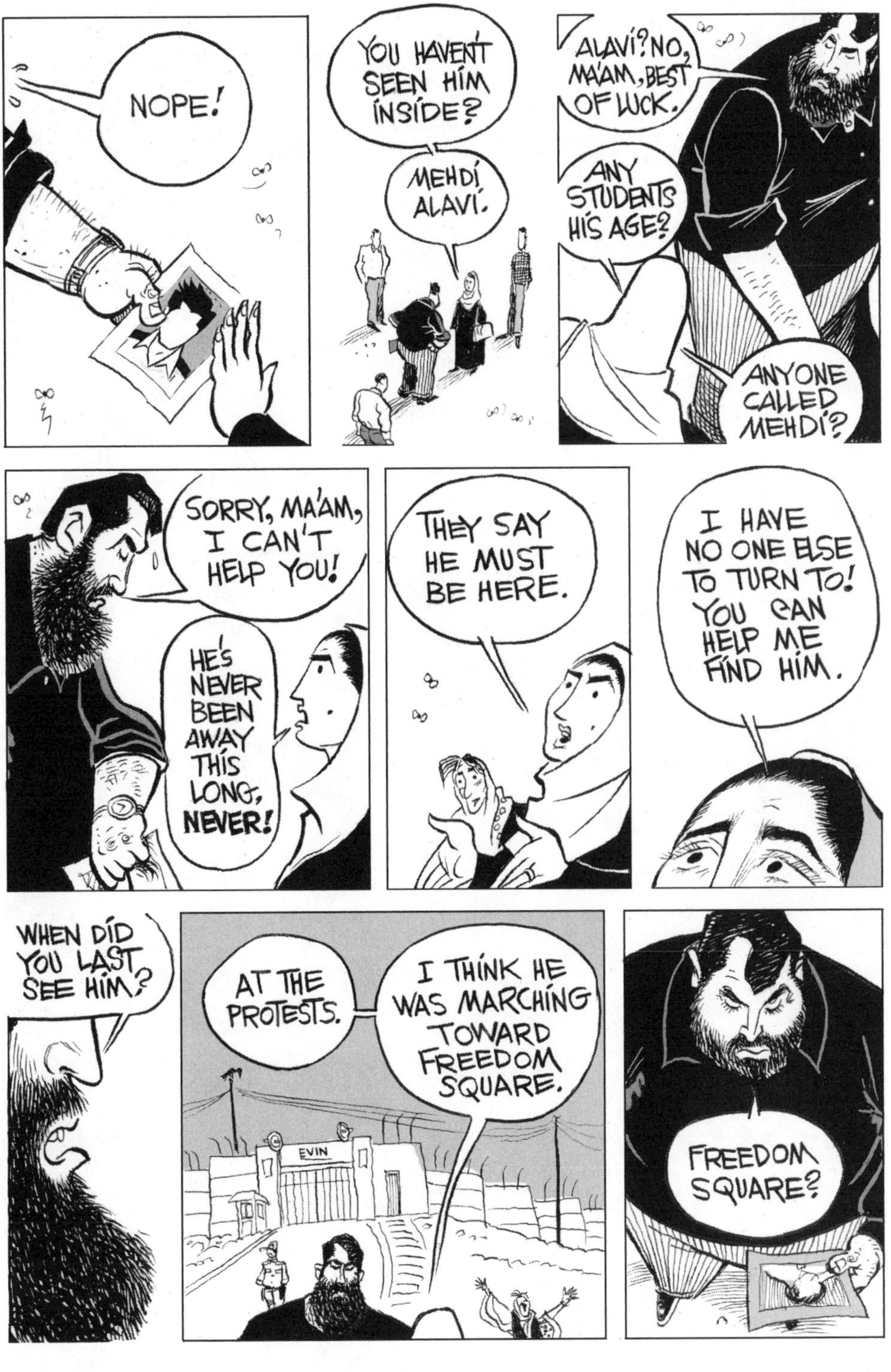
NOPE!
YOU HAVEN'T SEEN HIM INSIDE?
MEHDI ALAVI.
ALAVI? NO, MA'AM, BEST OF LUCK.
ANY STUDENTS HIS AGE?
ANYONE CALLED MEHDI?
SORRY, MA'AM, I CAN'T HELP YOU!
HE'S NEVER BEEN AWAY THIS LONG, NEVER!
THEY SAY HE MUST BE HERE.
I HAVE NO ONE ELSE TO TURN TO! YOU CAN HELP ME FIND HIM.
WHEN DID YOU LAST SEE HIM?
AT THE PROTESTS.
I THINK HE WAS MARCHING TOWARD FREEDOM SQUARE.
EVIN
FREEDOM SQUARE?

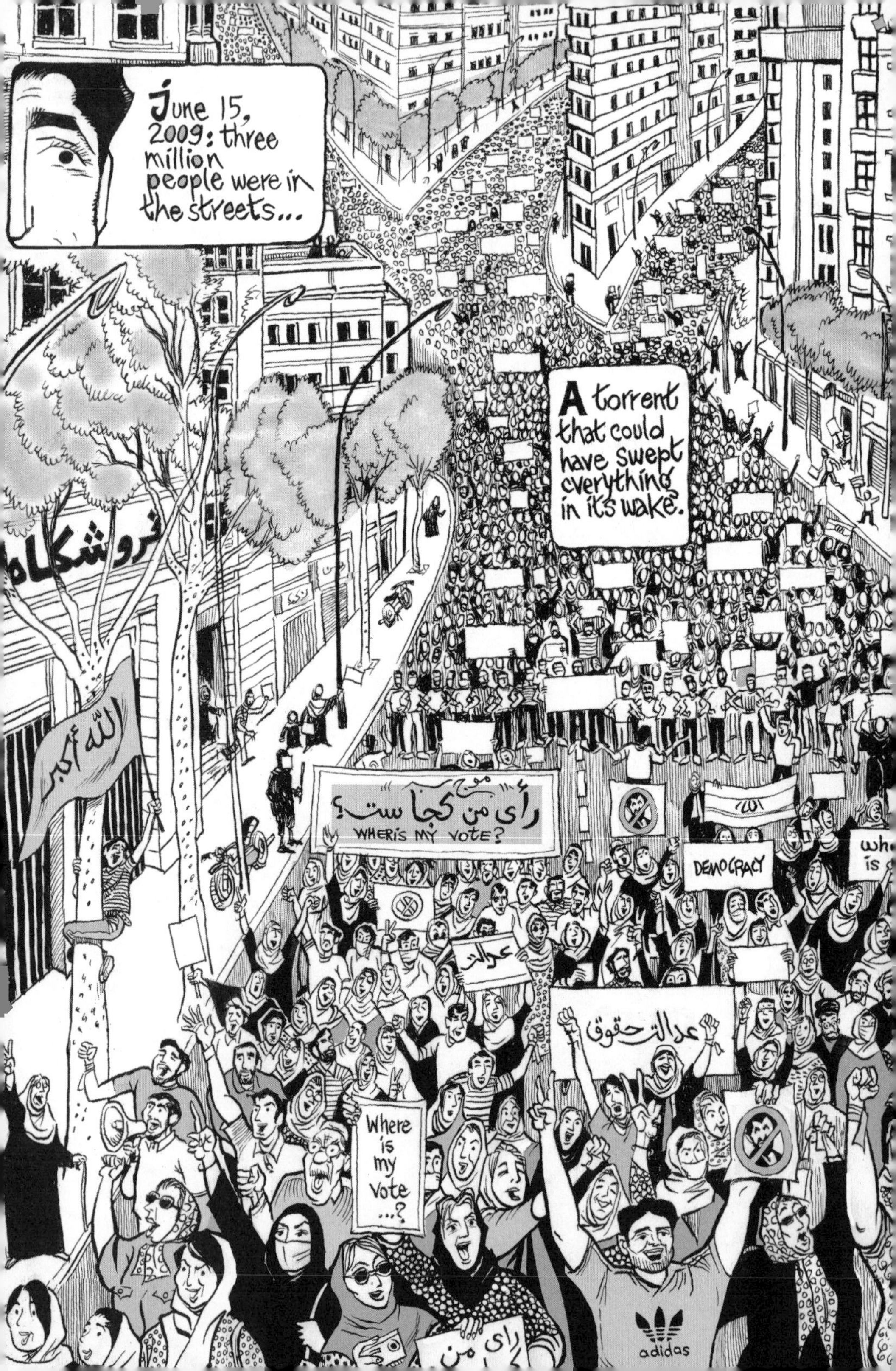
June 15, 2009: three million people were in the streets...
A torrent that could have swept everything in it's wake.
رای من کجاست؟
WHERE'S MY VOTE?
DEMOCRACY
Where is my vote ...?
adidas

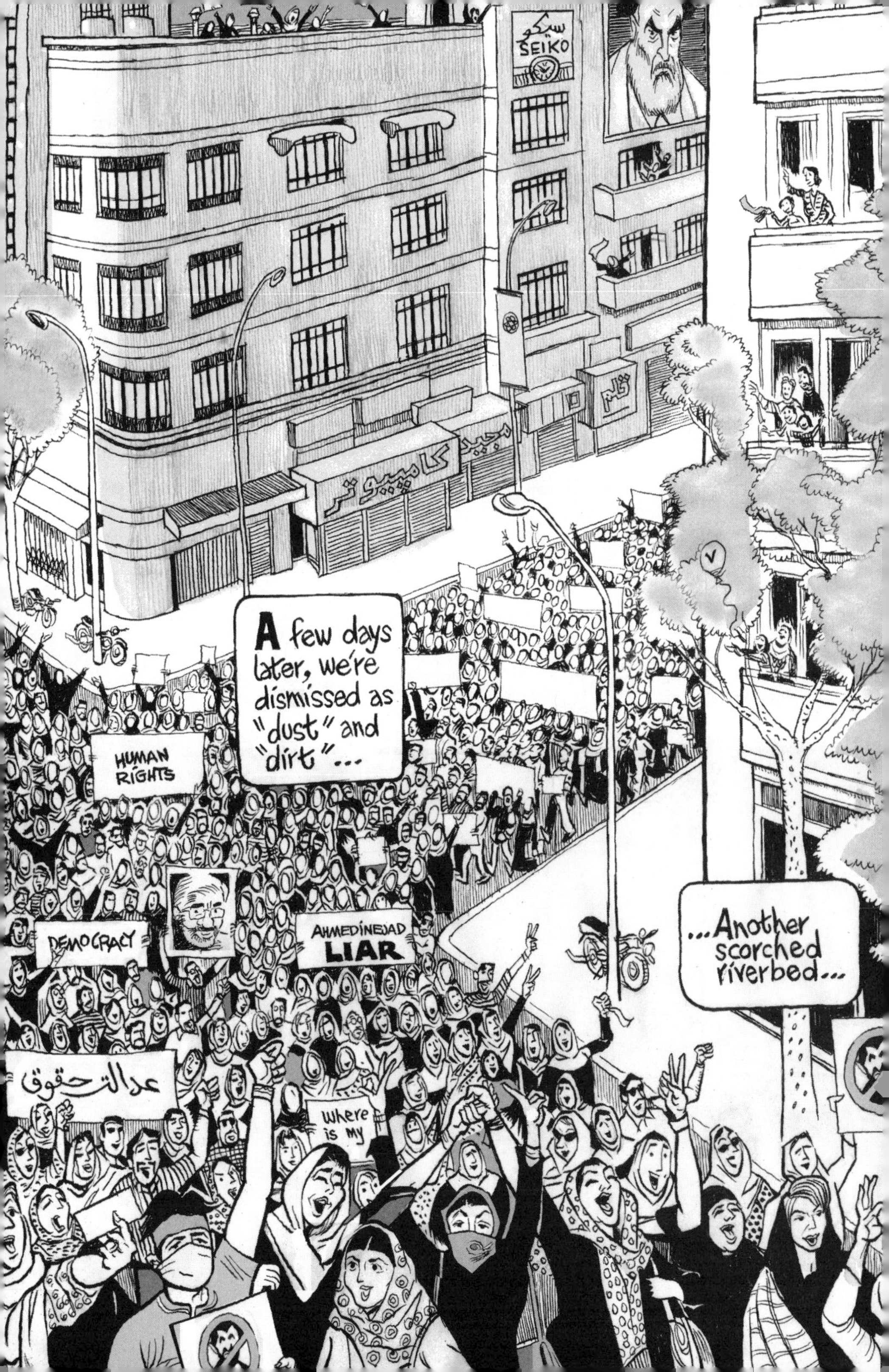

SEIKO
سیکو
A few days later, we're dismissed as "dust" and "dirt"...
HUMAN RIGHTS
DEMOCRACY
AHMEDINEJAD LIAR
...Another scorched riverbed...
عدالت حقوق
Where is my

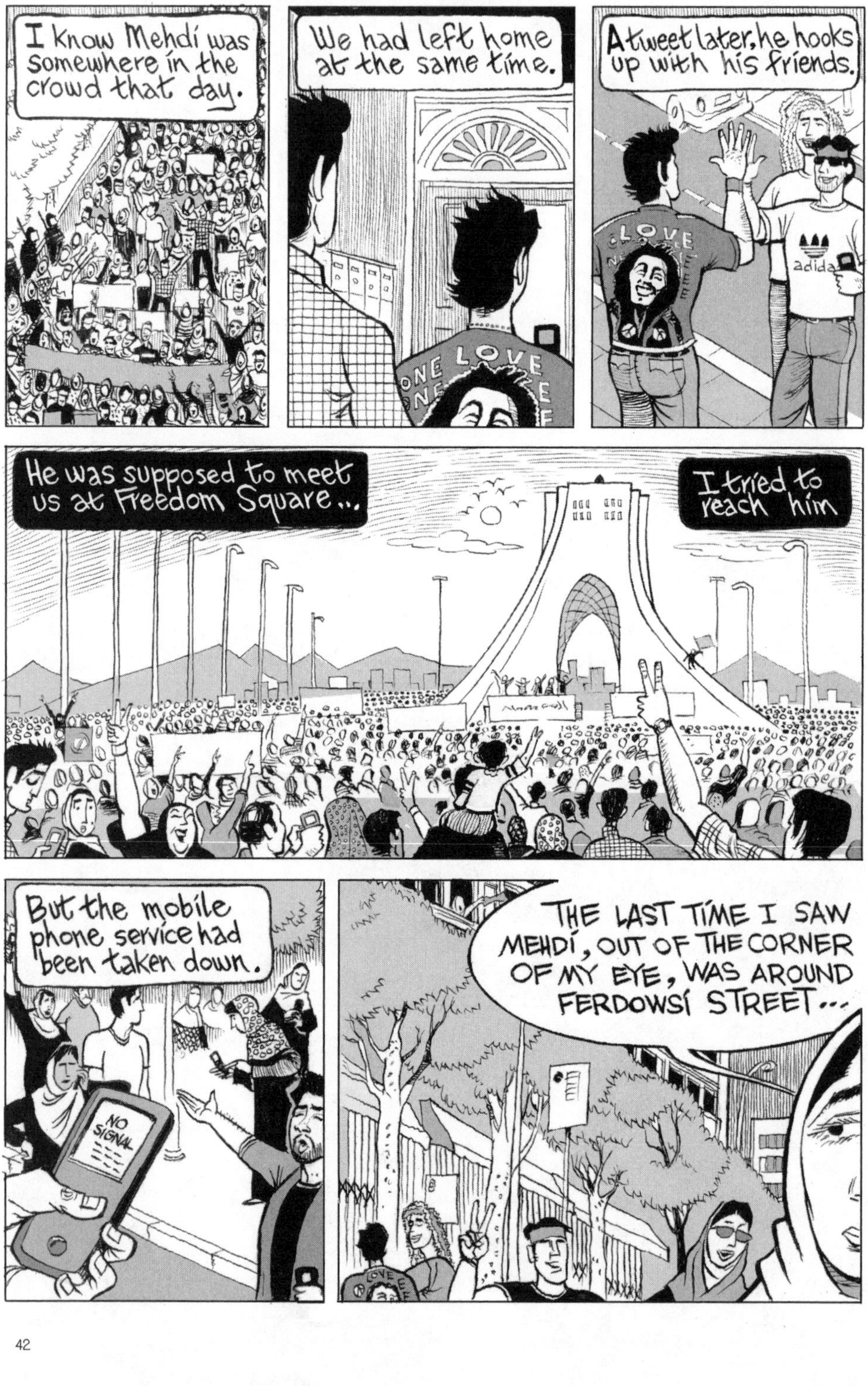
I know Mehdi was somewhere in the crowd that day.
We had left home at the same time.
ONE LOVE
A tweet later, he hooks up with his friends.
LOVE
adidas
He was supposed to meet us at Freedom Square...
I tried to reach him
But the mobile phone service had been taken down.
NO SIGNAL
THE LAST TIME I SAW MEHDI, OUT OF THE CORNER OF MY EYE, WAS AROUND FERDOWSI STREET...
LOVE

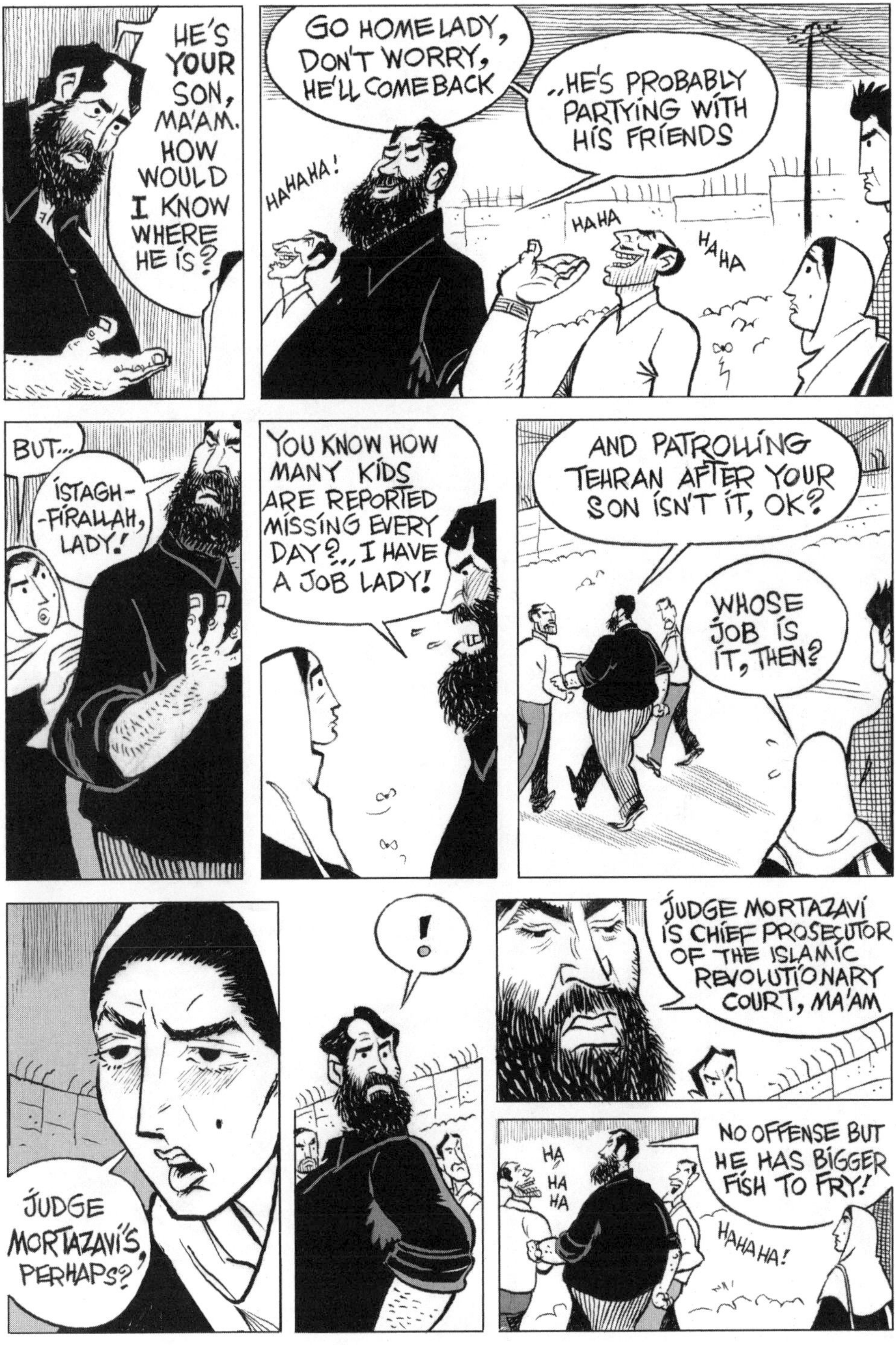
HE'S YOUR SON, MA'AM. HOW WOULD I KNOW WHERE HE IS?
GO HOME LADY, DON'T WORRY, HE'LL COME BACK
..HE'S PROBABLY PARTYING WITH HIS FRIENDS
HAHAHA!
HAHA
HAHA
BUT...
ISTAGH-FIRALLAH, LADY!
YOU KNOW HOW MANY KIDS ARE REPORTED MISSING EVERY DAY?.. I HAVE A JOB LADY!
AND PATROLLING TEHRAN AFTER YOUR SON ISN'T IT, OK?
WHOSE JOB IS IT, THEN?
JUDGE MORTAZAVI'S, PERHAPS?
!
JUDGE MORTAZAVI IS CHIEF PROSECUTOR OF THE ISLAMIC REVOLUTIONARY COURT, MA'AM
NO OFFENSE BUT HE HAS BIGGER FISH TO FRY!
HA HA HA
HAHAHA!

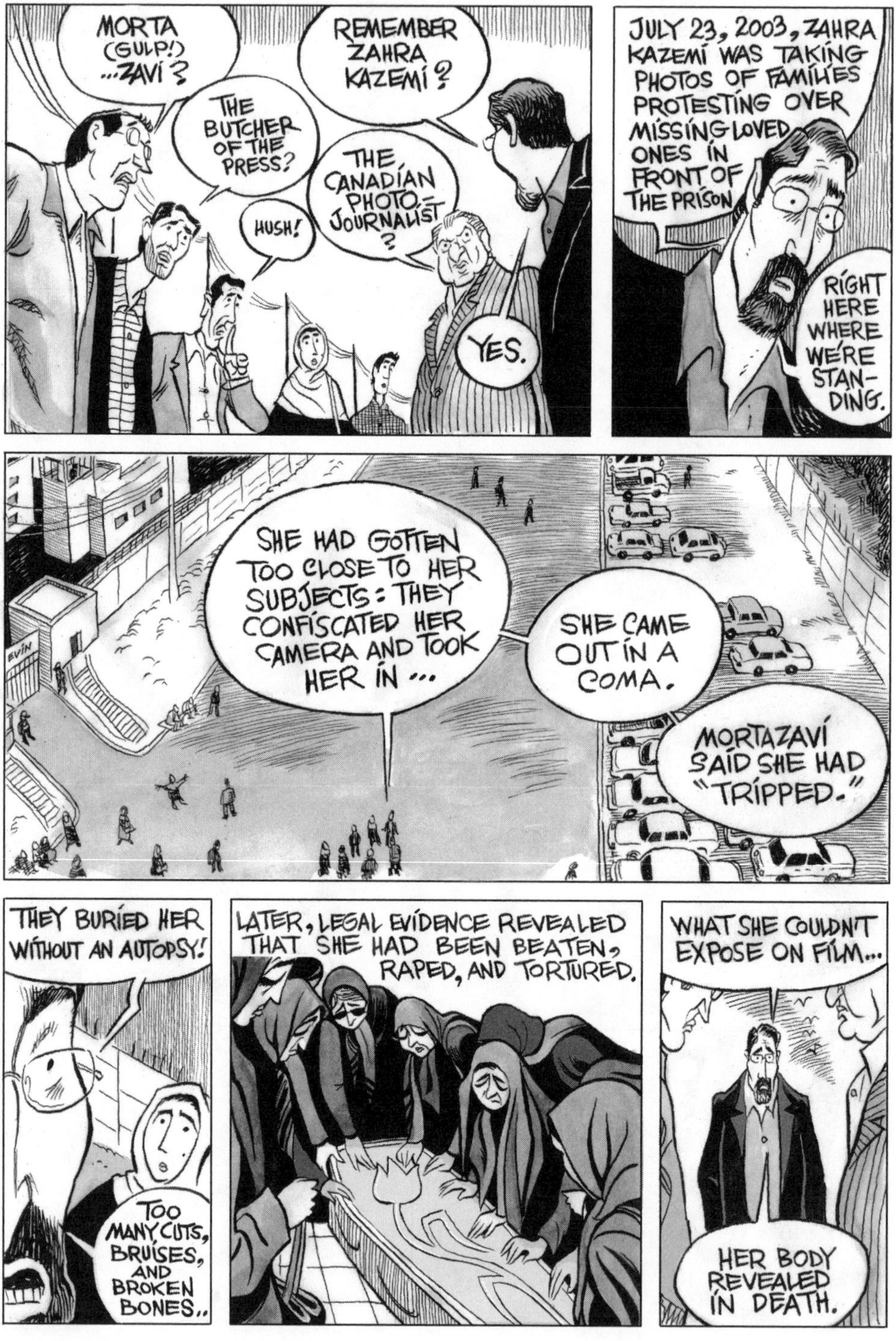
MORTA (GULP!) ...ZAVÍ?
REMEMBER ZAHRA KAZEMÍ?
THE BUTCHER OF THE PRESS?
THE CANADÍAN PHOTO-JOURNALIST?
HUSH!
YES.
JULY 23, 2003, ZAHRA KAZEMÍ WAS TAKÍNG PHOTOS OF FAMÍLÍES PROTESTÍNG OVER MÍSSÍNG LOVED ONES ÍN FRONT OF THE PRÍSON
RÍGHT HERE WHERE WE'RE STAN-DÍNG.
EVÍN
SHE HAD GOTTEN TOO CLOSE TO HER SUBJECTS: THEY CONFÍSCATED HER CAMERA AND TOOK HER ÍN ...
SHE CAME OUT ÍN A COMA.
MORTAZAVÍ SAÍD SHE HAD "TRÍPPED."
THEY BURÍED HER WÍTHOUT AN AUTOPSY!
TOO MANY CUTS, BRUÍSES, AND BROKEN BONES..
LATER, LEGAL EVÍDENCE REVEALED THAT SHE HAD BEEN BEATEN, RAPED, AND TORTURED.
WHAT SHE COULDN'T EXPOSE ON FÍLM...
HER BODY REVEALED ÍN DEATH.

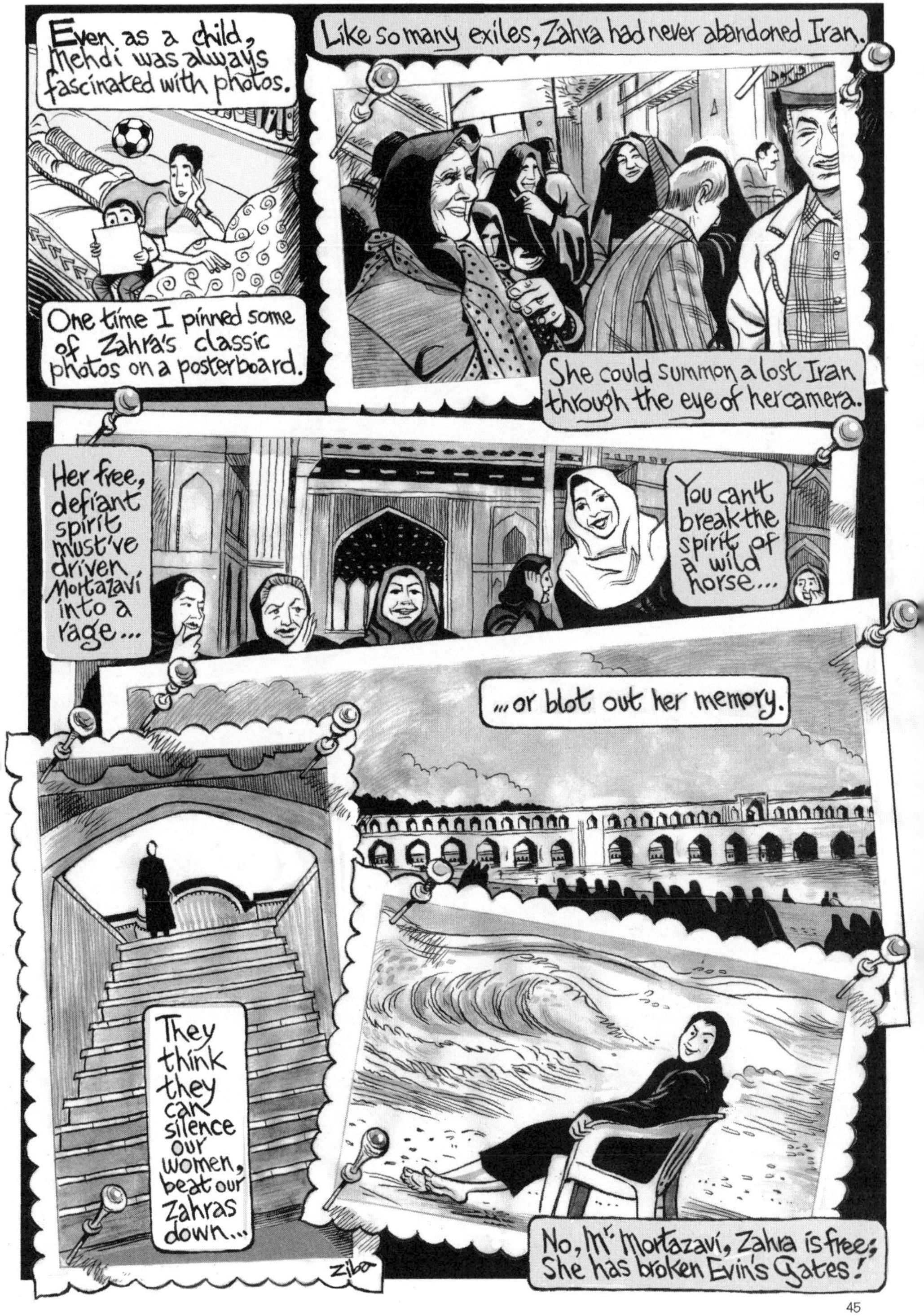

Even as a child, Mehdi was always fascinated with photos.
One time I pinned some of Zahra's classic photos on a posterboard.
Like so many exiles, Zahra had never abandoned Iran.
She could summon a lost Iran through the eye of her camera.
Her free, defiant spirit must've driven Mortazavi into a rage...
You can't break the spirit of a wild horse...
...or blot out her memory.
They think they can silence our women, beat our Zahras down...
No, Mr. Mortazavi, Zahra is free; She has broken Evin's Gates!
Zibo

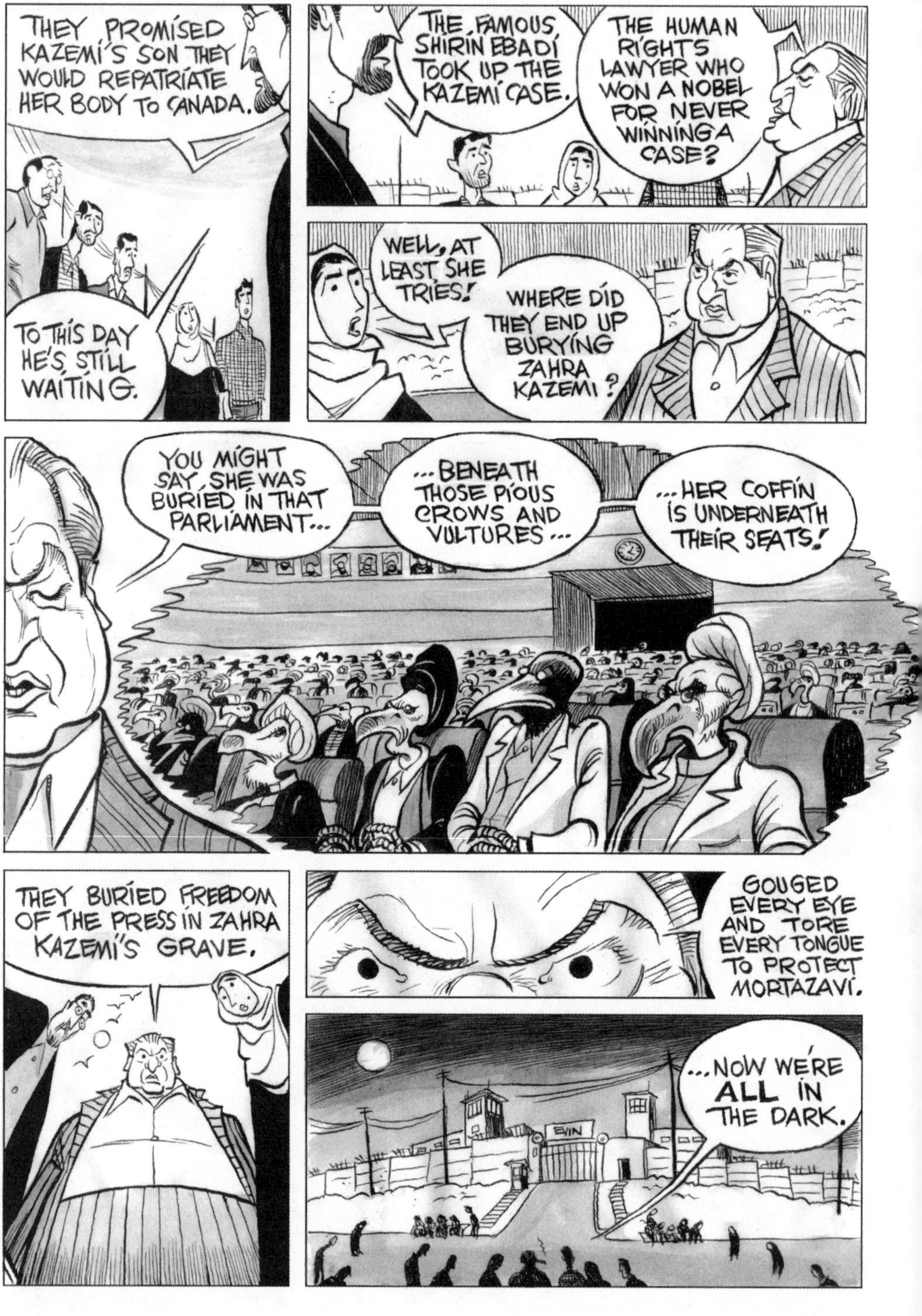
THEY PROMISED KAZEMI'S SON THEY WOULD REPATRIATE HER BODY TO CANADA.
TO THIS DAY HE'S STILL WAITING.
THE FAMOUS SHIRIN EBADI TOOK UP THE KAZEMI CASE.
THE HUMAN RIGHTS LAWYER WHO WON A NOBEL FOR NEVER WINNING A CASE?
WELL, AT LEAST SHE TRIES!
WHERE DID THEY END UP BURYING ZAHRA KAZEMI?
YOU MIGHT SAY SHE WAS BURIED IN THAT PARLIAMENT...
...BENEATH THOSE PIOUS CROWS AND VULTURES...
...HER COFFIN IS UNDERNEATH THEIR SEATS!
THEY BURIED FREEDOM OF THE PRESS IN ZAHRA KAZEMI'S GRAVE.
GOUGED EVERY EYE AND TORE EVERY TONGUE TO PROTECT MORTAZAVI.
EVIN
...NOW WE'RE ALL IN THE DARK.

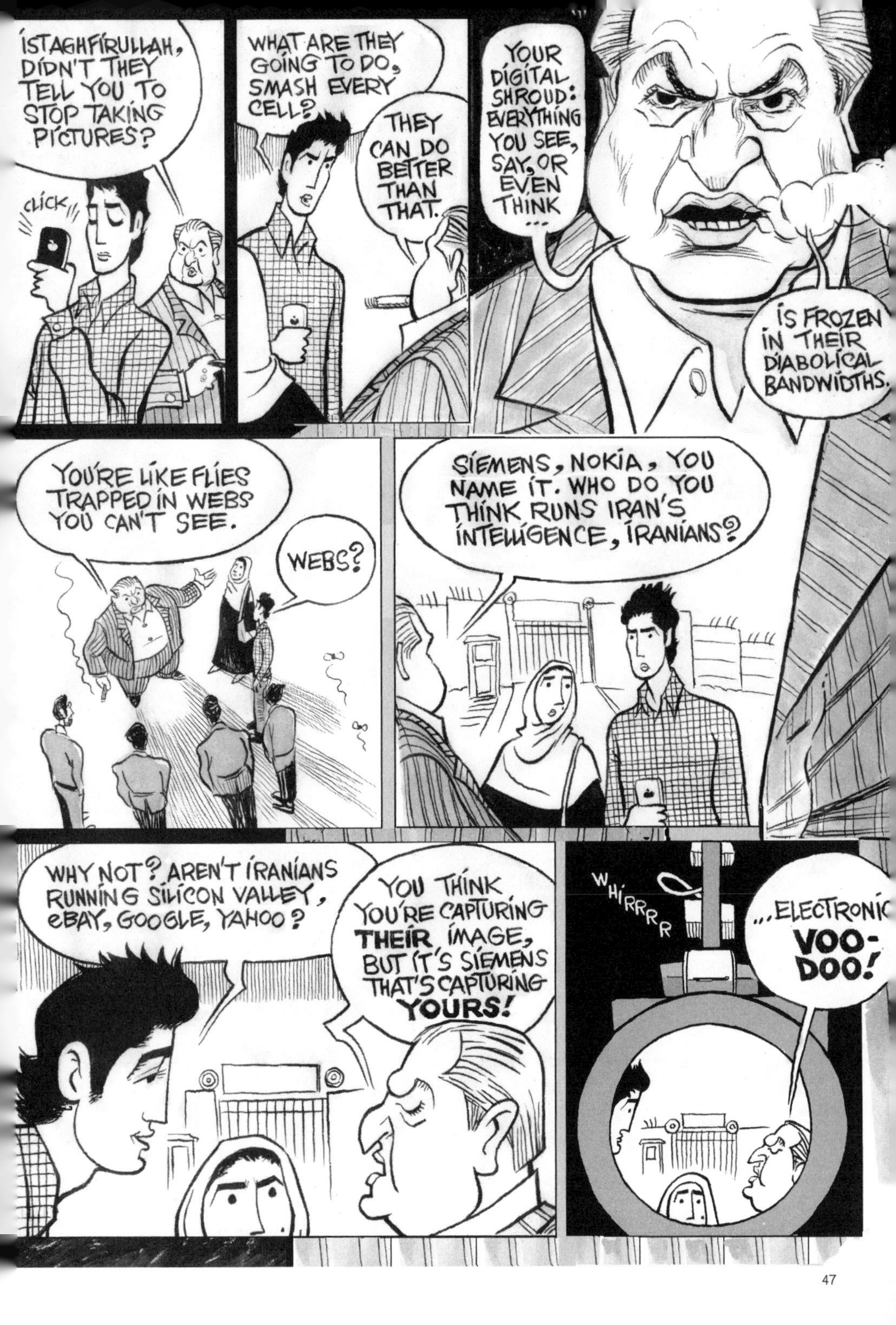
ISTAGHFIRULLAH, DIDN'T THEY TELL YOU TO STOP TAKING PICTURES?
CLICK
WHAT ARE THEY GOING TO DO, SMASH EVERY CELL?
THEY CAN DO BETTER THAN THAT.
YOUR DIGITAL SHROUD: EVERYTHING YOU SEE, SAY, OR EVEN THINK ...
IS FROZEN IN THEIR DIABOLICAL BANDWIDTHS.
YOU'RE LIKE FLIES TRAPPED IN WEBS YOU CAN'T SEE.
WEBS?
SIEMENS, NOKIA, YOU NAME IT. WHO DO YOU THINK RUNS IRAN'S INTELLIGENCE, IRANIANS?
WHY NOT? AREN'T IRANIANS RUNNING SILICON VALLEY, eBAY, GOOGLE, YAHOO?
YOU THINK YOU'RE CAPTURING THEIR IMAGE, BUT IT'S SIEMENS THAT'S CAPTURING YOURS!
WHIRRRR
...ELECTRONIC VOO-DOO!

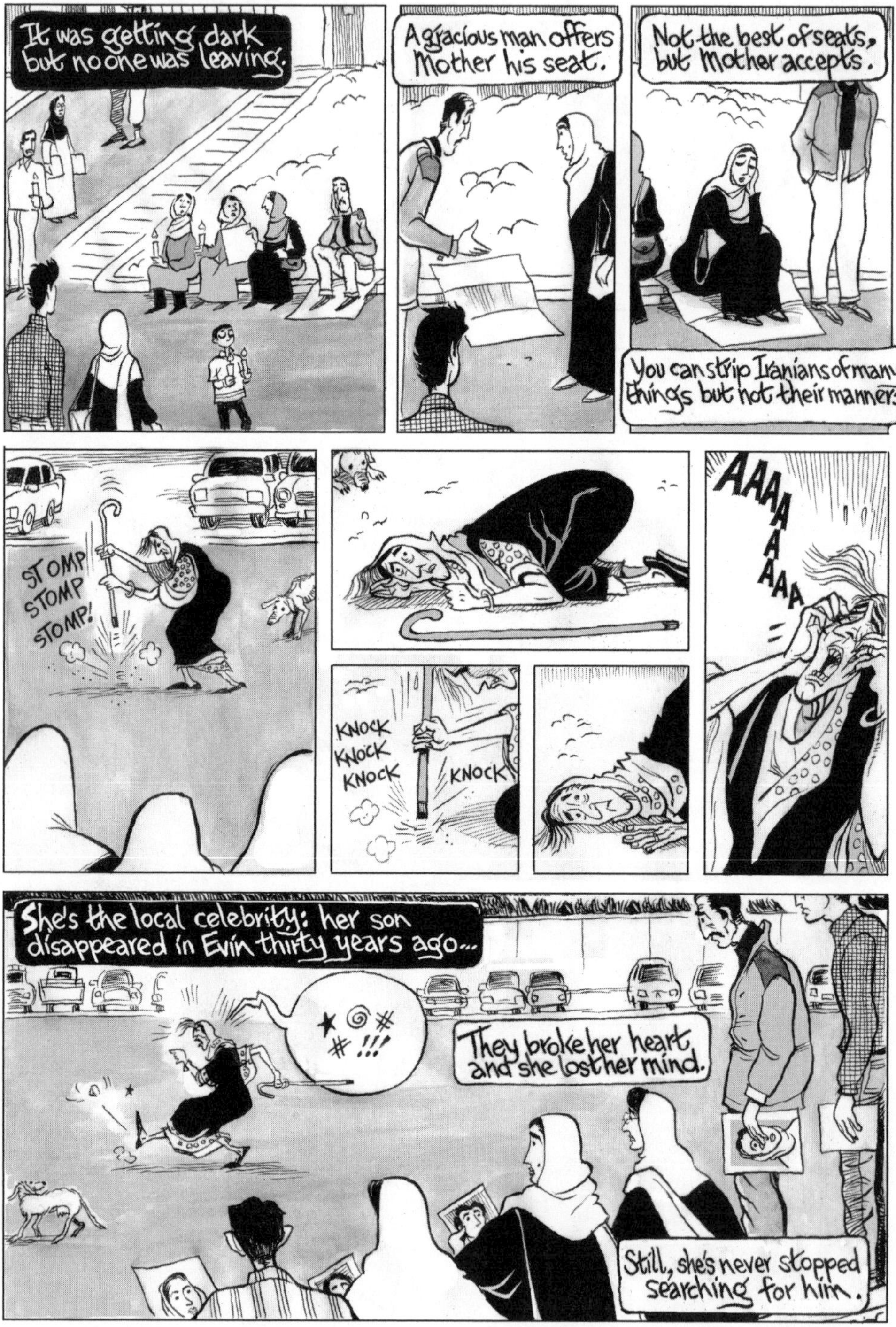
It was getting dark but no one was leaving.
A gracious man offers Mother his seat.
Not the best of seats, but Mother accepts.
You can strip Iranians of many things but not their manners.
STOMP STOMP STOMP!
AAAAAAAAA
KNOCK KNOCK KNOCK
KNOCK
She's the local celebrity: her son disappeared in Evin thirty years ago...
★ @ # # !!!
They broke her heart and she lost her mind.
Still, she's never stopped searching for him.

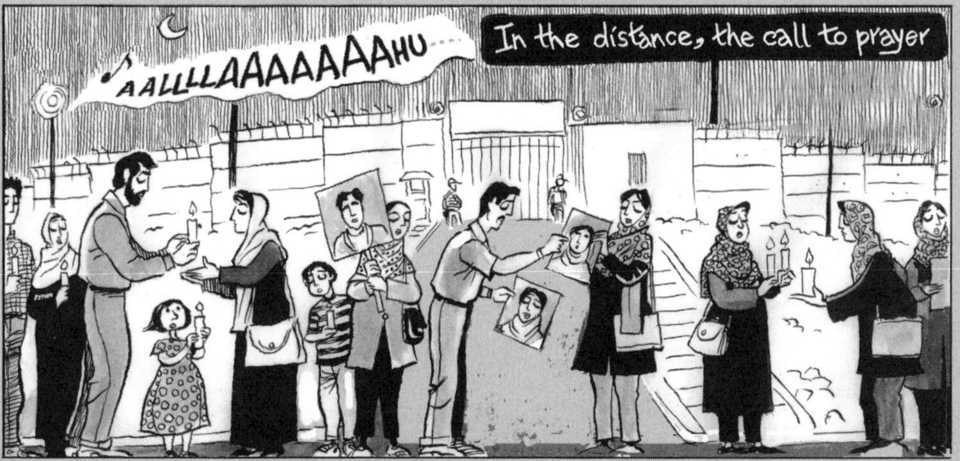
In the distance, the call to prayer
AALLLLAAAAAAAHU

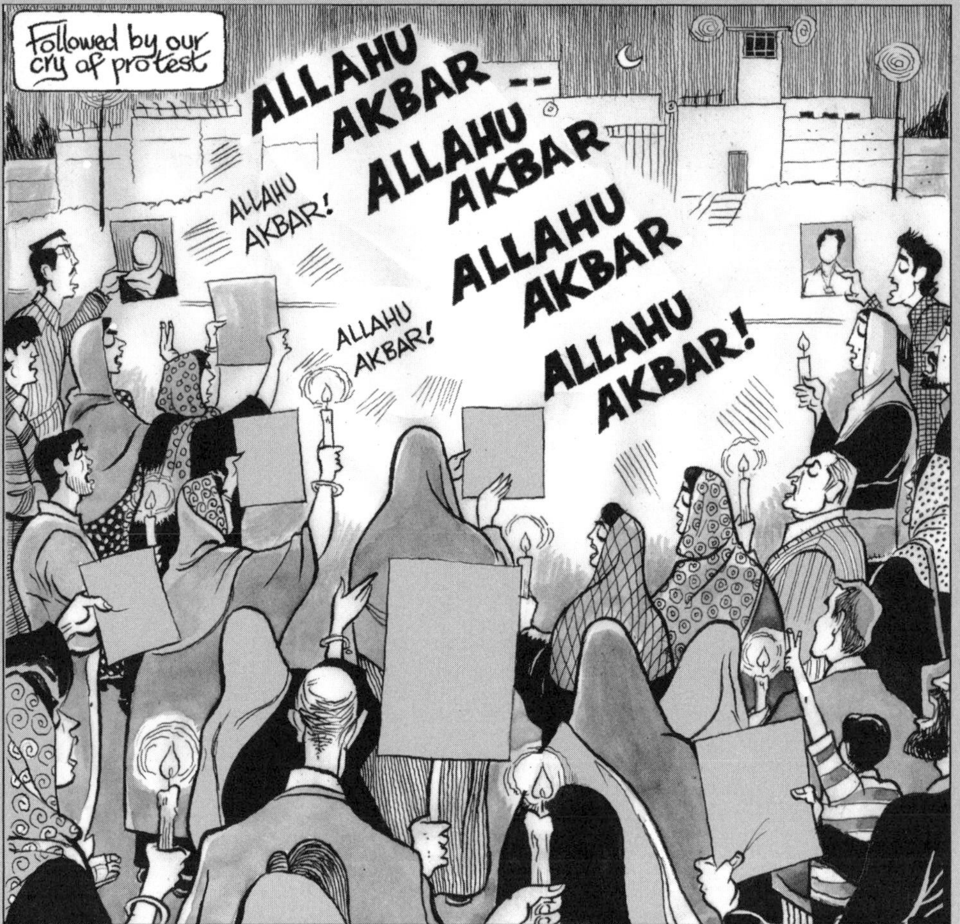
Followed by our cry of protest
ALLAHU AKBAR
ALLAHU AKBAR
ALLAHU AKBAR!
ALLAHU AKBAR
ALLAHU AKBAR!
ALLAHU AKBAR
ALLAHU AKBAR!

THE LECTURE

CHAPTER THREE

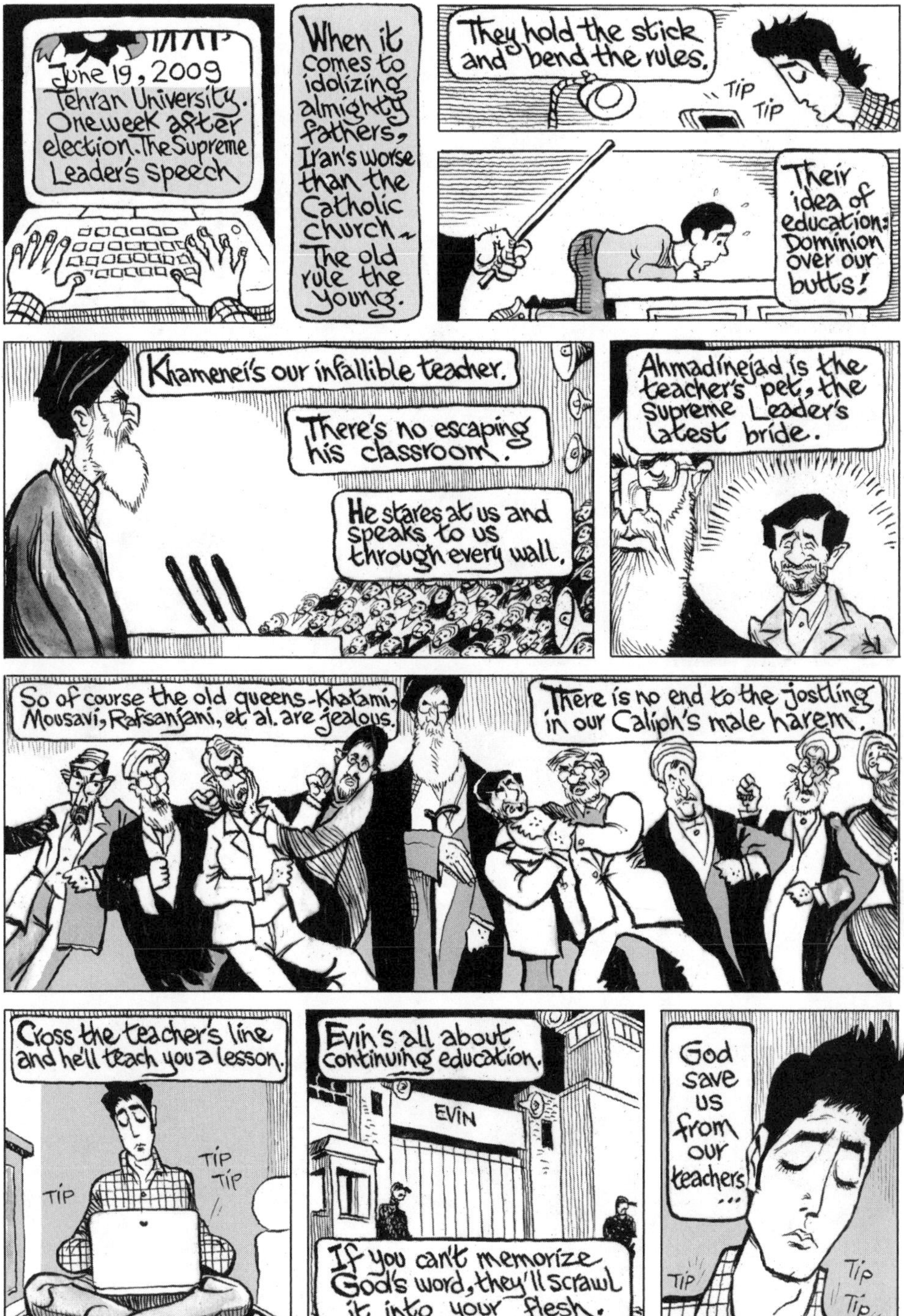
June 19, 2009
Tehran University. One week after election. The Supreme Leader's speech
When it comes to idolizing almighty fathers, Iran's worse than the Catholic church. The old rule the young.
They hold the stick and bend the rules.
TIP
TIP
Their idea of education: Dominion over our butts!
Khamenei's our infallible teacher.
There's no escaping his classroom.
He stares at us and speaks to us through every wall.
Ahmadinejad is the teacher's pet, the Supreme Leader's latest bride.
So of course the old queens - Khatami, Mousavi, Rafsanjani, et al. are jealous.
There is no end to the jostling in our Caliph's male harem.
Cross the teacher's line and he'll teach you a lesson.
TIP
TIP
TIP
Evin's all about continuing education.
EVIN
If you can't memorize God's word, they'll scrawl it into your flesh.
God save us from our teachers...
TIP
Tip
Tip

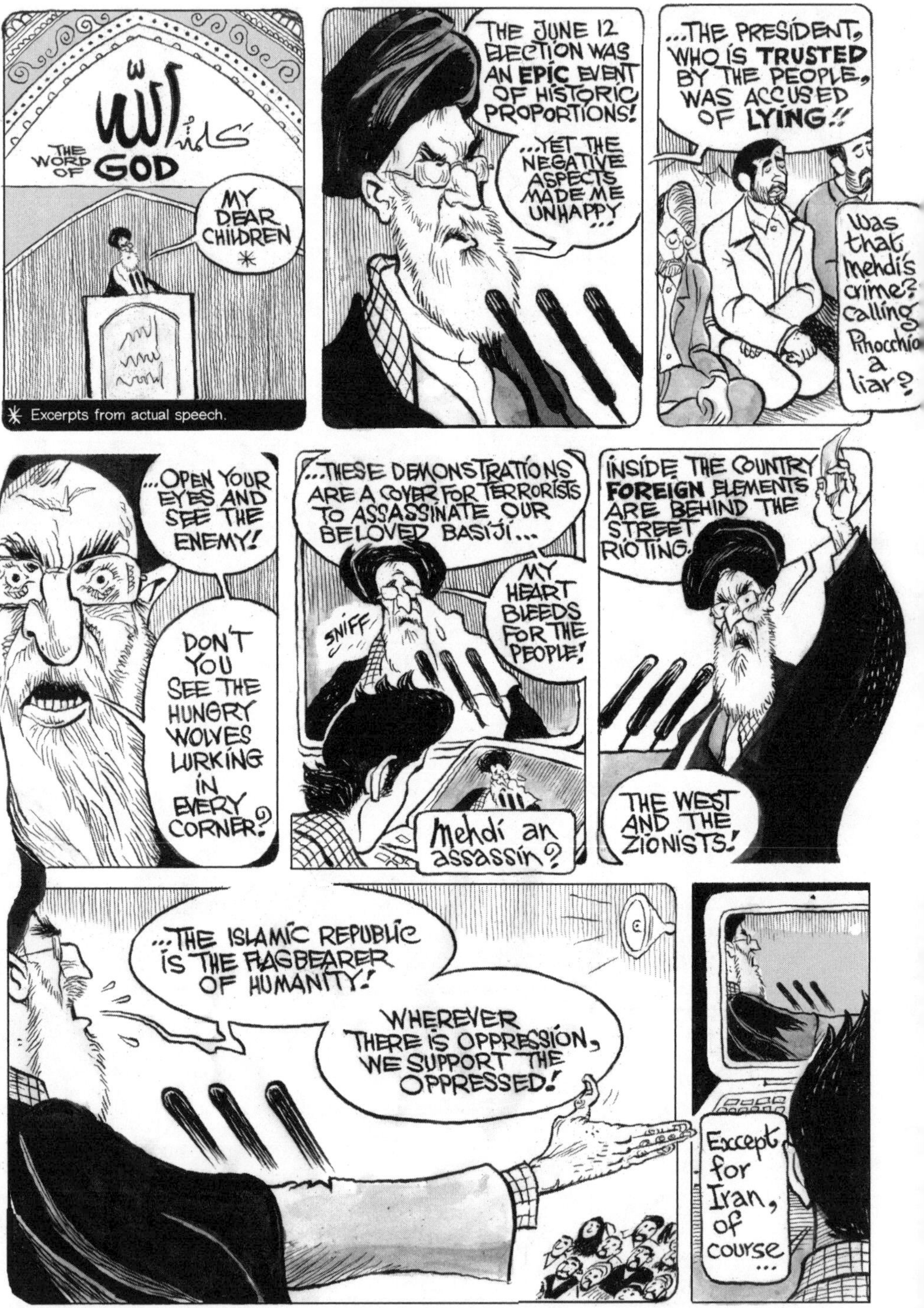
THE WORD OF GOD
MY DEAR CHILDREN *
* Excerpts from actual speech.
THE JUNE 12 ELECTION WAS AN EPIC EVENT OF HISTORIC PROPORTIONS!
...YET THE NEGATIVE ASPECTS MADE ME UNHAPPY...
...THE PRESIDENT, WHO IS TRUSTED BY THE PEOPLE, WAS ACCUSED OF LYING!!
Was that Mehdi's crime? calling Pinocchio a liar?
...OPEN YOUR EYES AND SEE THE ENEMY!
DON'T YOU SEE THE HUNGRY WOLVES LURKING IN EVERY CORNER?
...THESE DEMONSTRATIONS ARE A COVER FOR TERRORISTS TO ASSASSINATE OUR BELOVED BASIJI...
SNIFF
MY HEART BLEEDS FOR THE PEOPLE!
Mehdi an assassin?
INSIDE THE COUNTRY FOREIGN ELEMENTS ARE BEHIND THE STREET RIOTING.
THE WEST AND THE ZIONISTS!
...THE ISLAMIC REPUBLIC IS THE FLAGBEARER OF HUMANITY!
WHEREVER THERE IS OPPRESSION, WE SUPPORT THE OPPRESSED!
Except for Iran, of course...

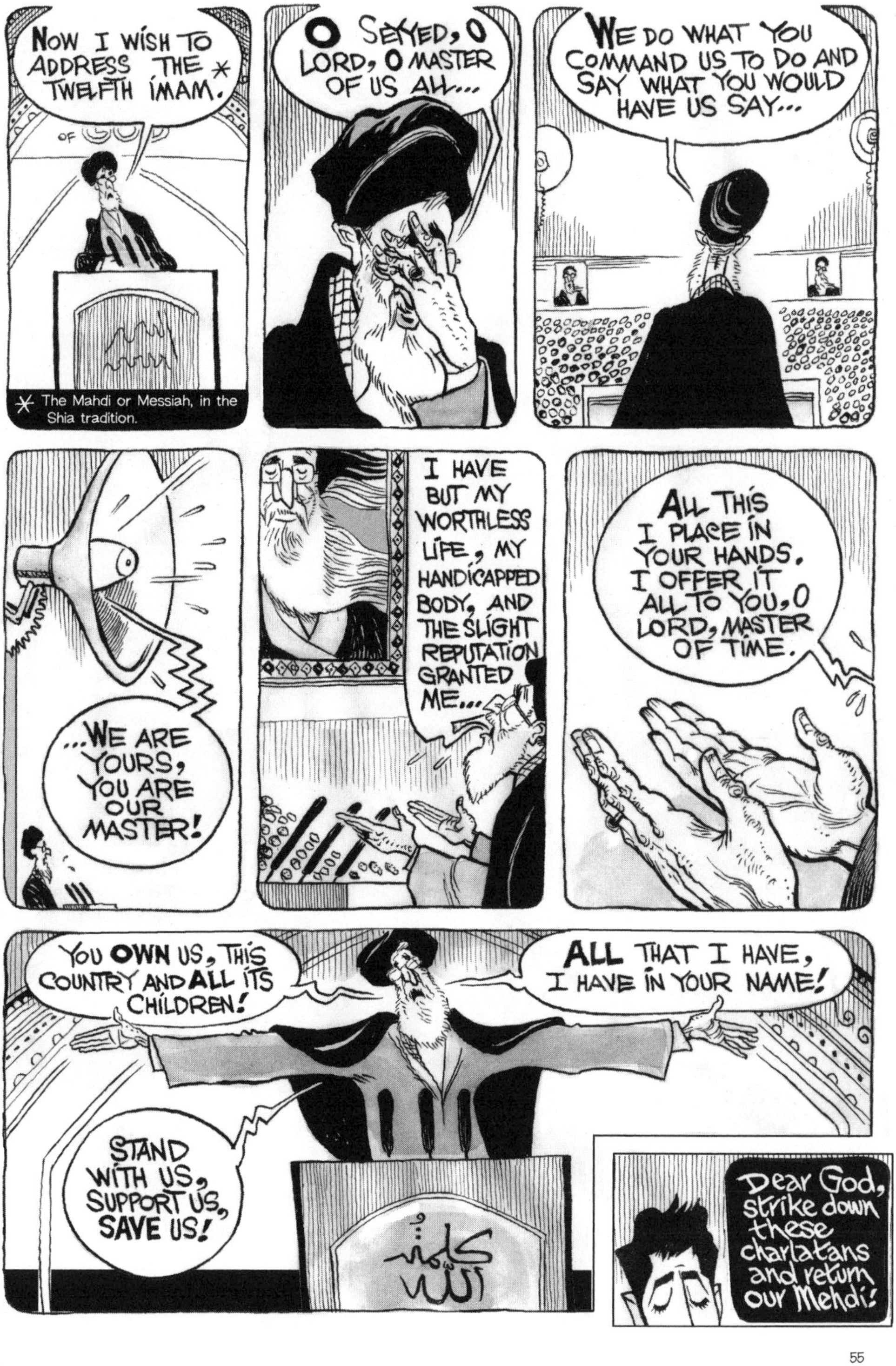
NOW I WISH TO ADDRESS THE TWELFTH IMAM.*
* The Mahdi or Messiah, in the Shia tradition.
O SEYYED, O LORD, O MASTER OF US ALL...
WE DO WHAT YOU COMMAND US TO DO AND SAY WHAT YOU WOULD HAVE US SAY...
...WE ARE YOURS, YOU ARE OUR MASTER!
I HAVE BUT MY WORTHLESS LIFE, MY HANDICAPPED BODY, AND THE SLIGHT REPUTATION GRANTED ME...
ALL THIS I PLACE IN YOUR HANDS. I OFFER IT ALL TO YOU, O LORD, MASTER OF TIME.
YOU OWN US, THIS COUNTRY AND ALL ITS CHILDREN!
ALL THAT I HAVE, I HAVE IN YOUR NAME!
STAND WITH US, SUPPORT US, SAVE US!
Dear God, strike down these charlatans and return our Mehdi!

THE PEOPLE'S PRESS

CHAPTER FOUR

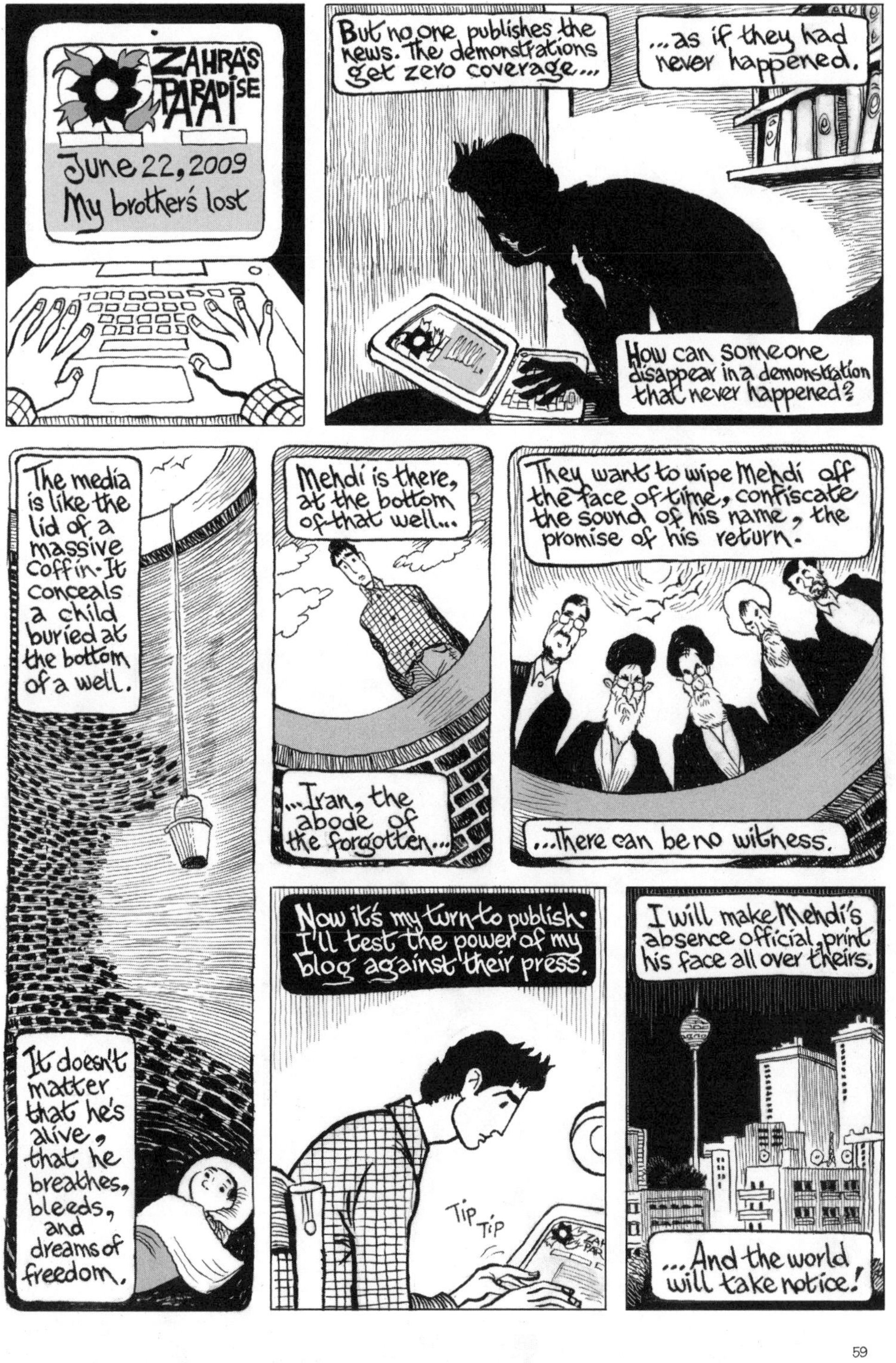
ZAHRA'S PARADISE
June 22, 2009
My brother's lost
But no one publishes the news. The demonstrations get zero coverage...
...as if they had never happened.
How can someone disappear in a demonstration that never happened?
The media is like the lid of a massive coffin. It conceals a child buried at the bottom of a well.
It doesn't matter that he's alive, that he breathes, bleeds, and dreams of freedom.
Mehdi is there, at the bottom of that well...
...Iran, the abode of the forgotten...
They want to wipe Mehdi off the face of time, confiscate the sound of his name, the promise of his return.
...There can be no witness.
Now it's my turn to publish. I'll test the power of my blog against their press.
Tip Tip
I will make Mehdi's absence official, print his face all over theirs.
...And the world will take notice!

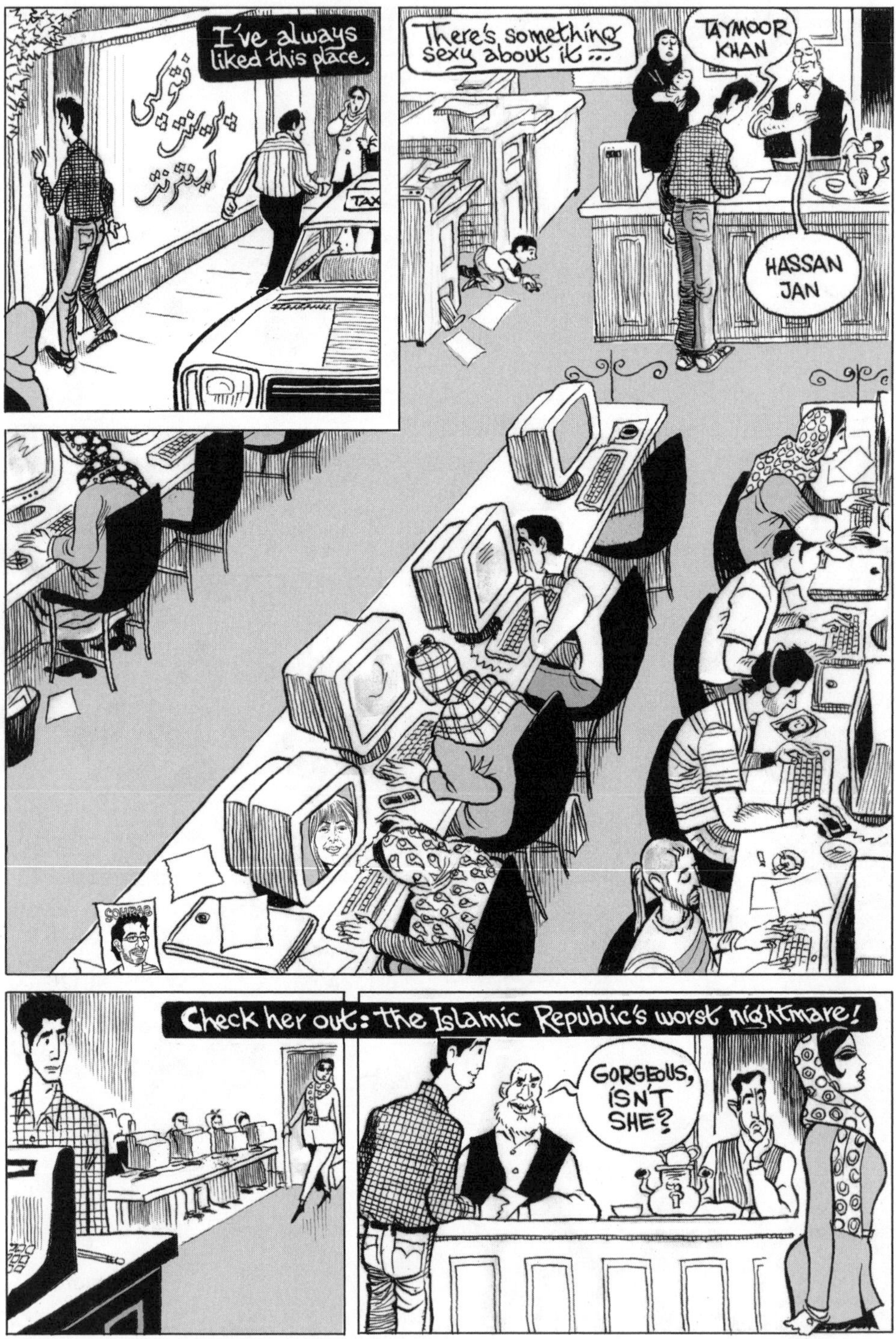

I've always liked this place.
فتوکپی
پرینت
اینترنت
There's something sexy about it...
TAYMOOR KHAN
HASSAN JAN
SOHRAB
Check her out: the Islamic Republic's worst nightmare!
GORGEOUS, ISN'T SHE?

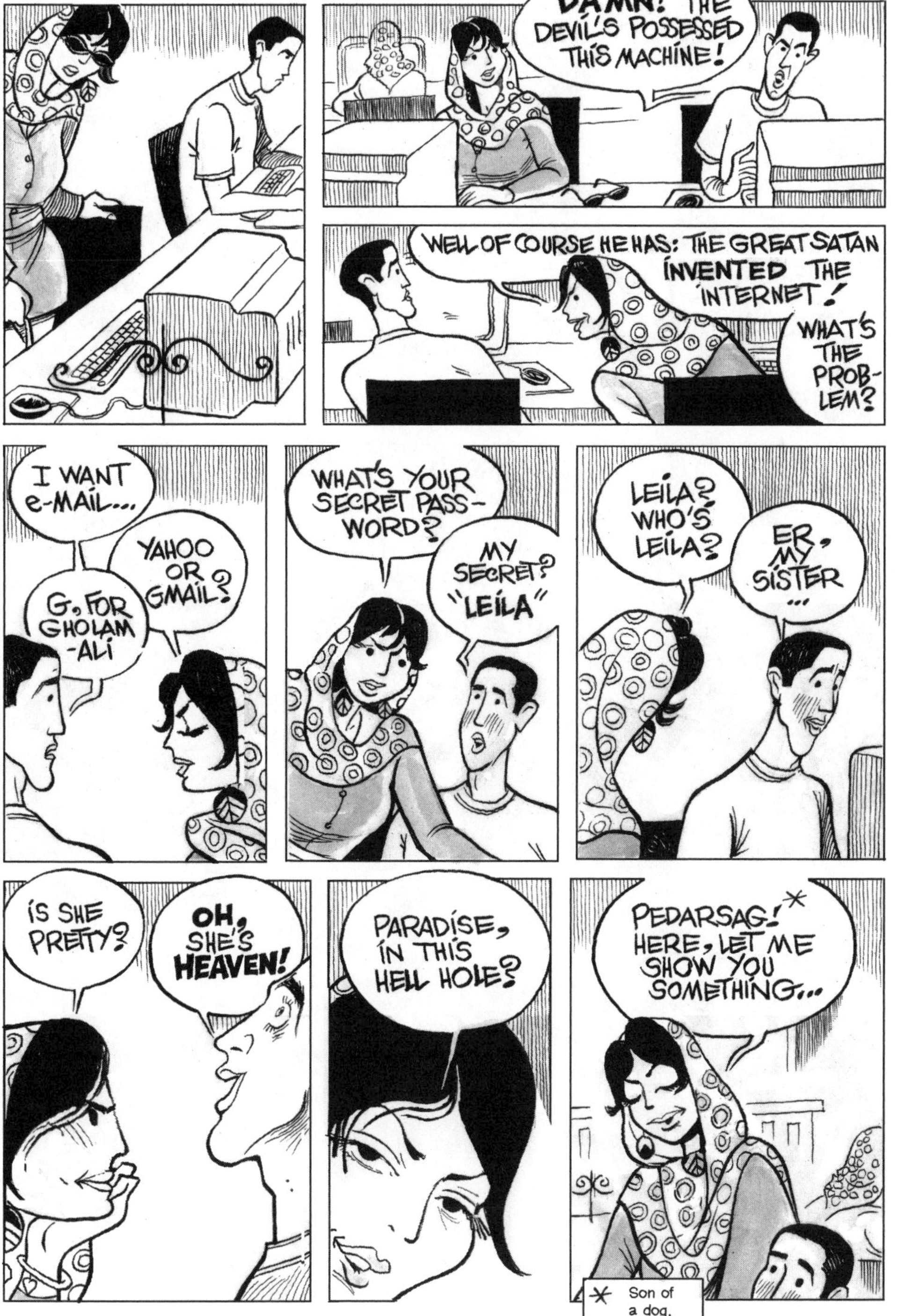
DAMN! THE DEVIL'S POSSESSED THIS MACHINE!
WELL OF COURSE HE HAS: THE GREAT SATAN INVENTED THE INTERNET!
WHAT'S THE PROB-LEM?
I WANT e-MAIL...
YAHOO OR GMAIL?
G. FOR GHOLAM-ALI
WHAT'S YOUR SECRET PASS-WORD?
MY SECRET? "LEILA"
LEILA? WHO'S LEILA?
ER, MY SISTER...
IS SHE PRETTY?
OH, SHE'S HEAVEN!
PARADISE, IN THIS HELL HOLE?
PEDARSAG!* HERE, LET ME SHOW YOU SOMETHING...

* Son of a dog.

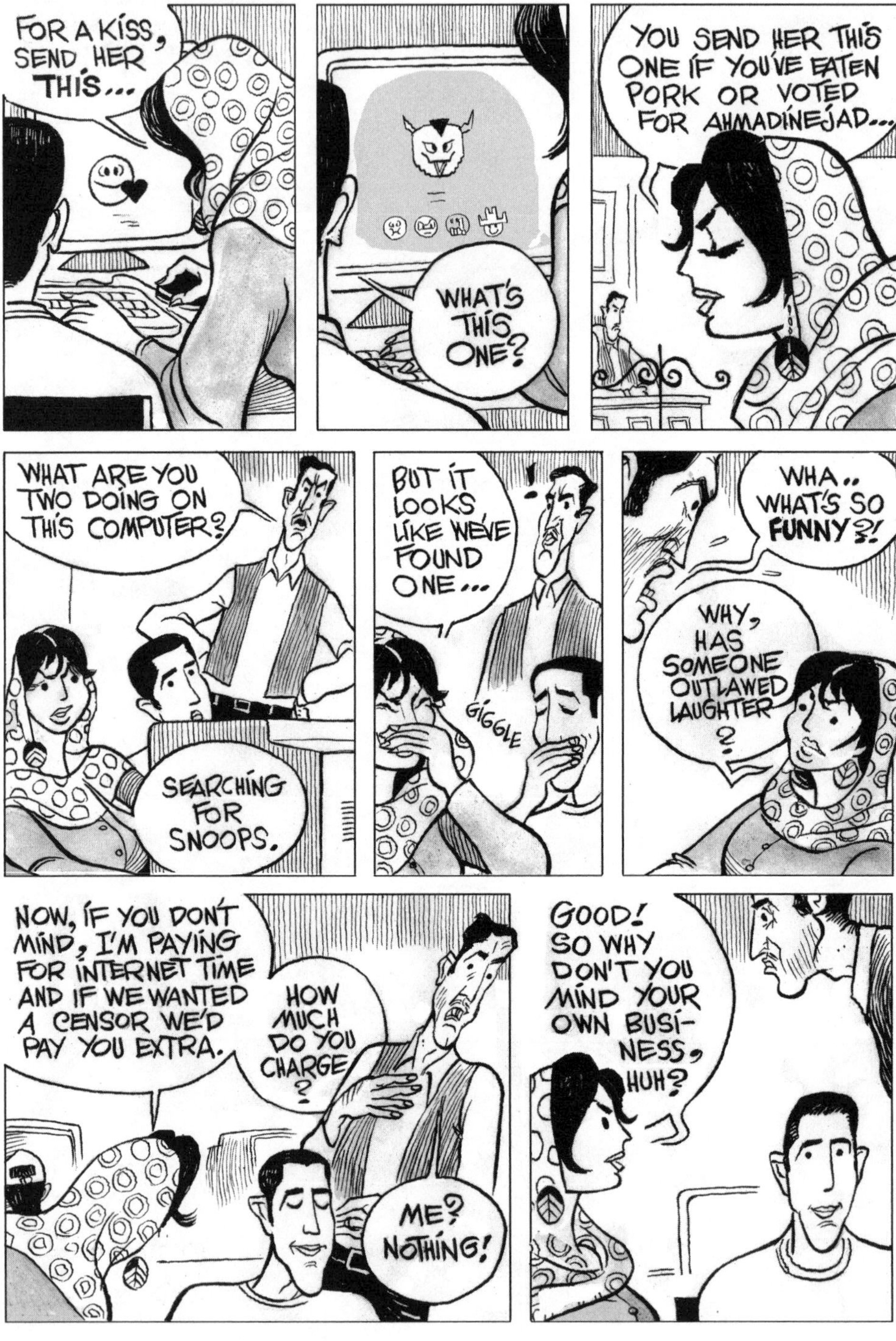
FOR A KISS, SEND HER THIS...
WHAT'S THIS ONE?
YOU SEND HER THIS ONE IF YOU'VE EATEN PORK OR VOTED FOR AHMADINEJAD...
WHAT ARE YOU TWO DOING ON THIS COMPUTER?
SEARCHING FOR SNOOPS.
BUT IT LOOKS LIKE WE'VE FOUND ONE...
GIGGLE
WHA.. WHAT'S SO FUNNY?!
WHY, HAS SOMEONE OUTLAWED LAUGHTER?
NOW, IF YOU DON'T MIND, I'M PAYING FOR INTERNET TIME AND IF WE WANTED A CENSOR WE'D PAY YOU EXTRA.
HOW MUCH DO YOU CHARGE?
ME? NOTHING!
GOOD! SO WHY DON'T YOU MIND YOUR OWN BUSINESS, HUH?

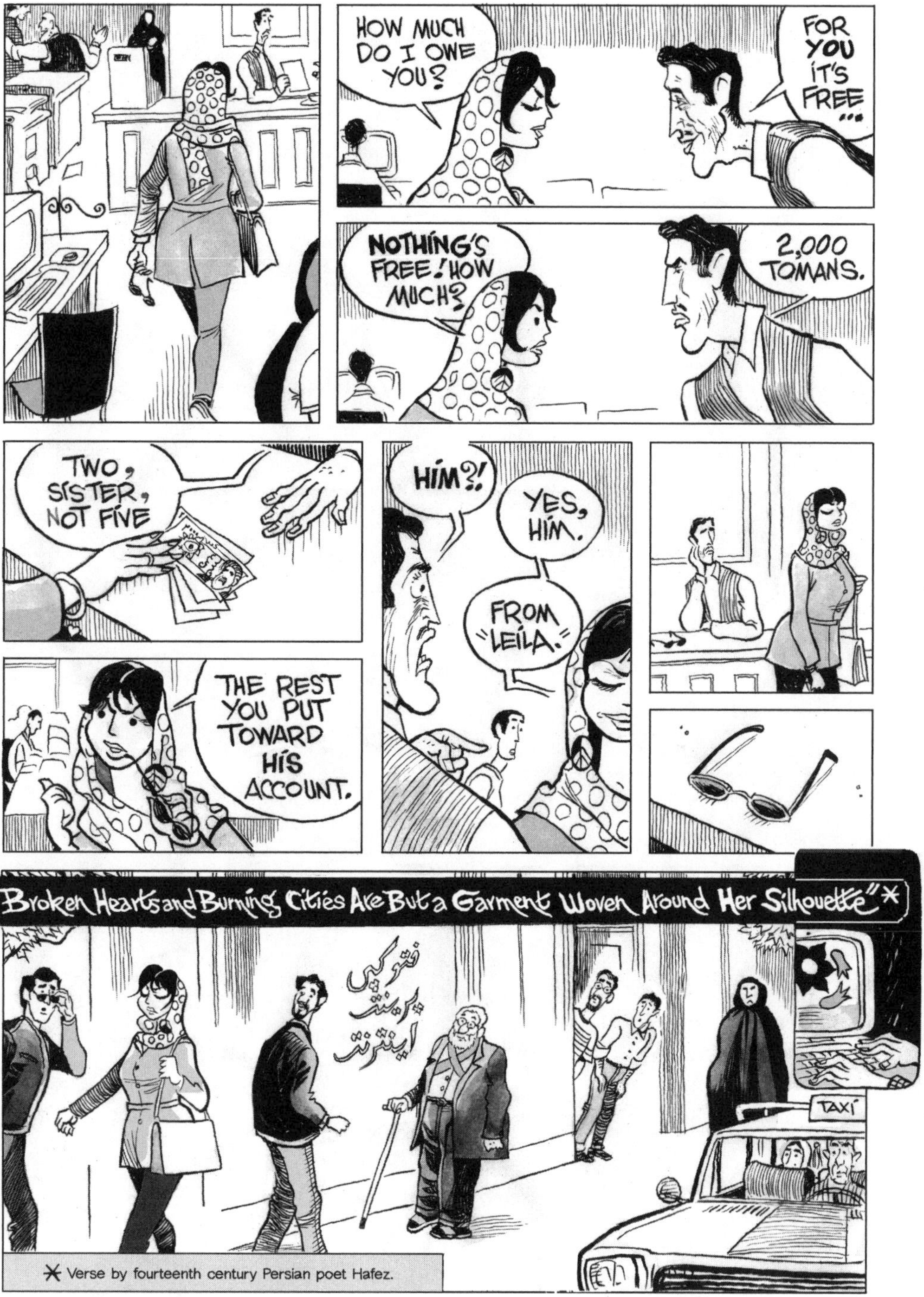
HOW MUCH DO I OWE YOU?
FOR YOU IT'S FREE...
NOTHING'S FREE! HOW MUCH?
2,000 TOMANS.
TWO, SISTER, NOT FIVE
THE REST YOU PUT TOWARD HIS ACCOUNT.
HIM?!
YES, HIM.
FROM LEILA.
"Broken Hearts and Burning Cities Are But a Garment Woven Around Her Silhouette"*
فتوکپی
پرینت
اینترنت
TAXI

* Verse by fourteenth century Persian poet Hafez.

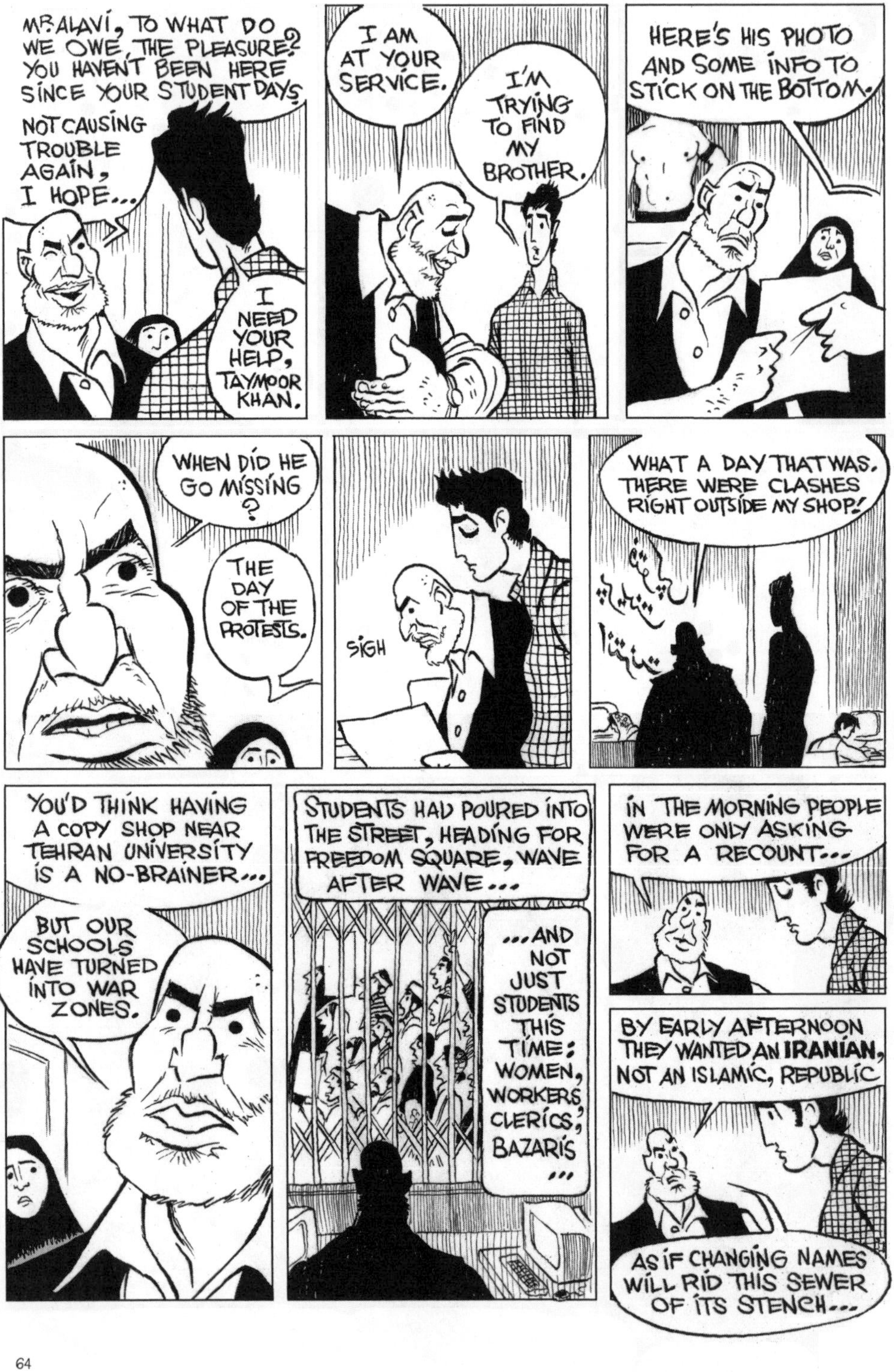
MR. ALAVI, TO WHAT DO WE OWE THE PLEASURE? YOU HAVEN'T BEEN HERE SINCE YOUR STUDENT DAYS.
NOT CAUSING TROUBLE AGAIN, I HOPE...
I NEED YOUR HELP, TAYMOOR KHAN.
I AM AT YOUR SERVICE.
I'M TRYING TO FIND MY BROTHER.
HERE'S HIS PHOTO AND SOME INFO TO STICK ON THE BOTTOM.
WHEN DID HE GO MISSING?
THE DAY OF THE PROTESTS.
SIGH
WHAT A DAY THAT WAS. THERE WERE CLASHES RIGHT OUTSIDE MY SHOP!
YOU'D THINK HAVING A COPY SHOP NEAR TEHRAN UNIVERSITY IS A NO-BRAINER...
BUT OUR SCHOOLS HAVE TURNED INTO WAR ZONES.
STUDENTS HAD POURED INTO THE STREET, HEADING FOR FREEDOM SQUARE, WAVE AFTER WAVE...
...AND NOT JUST STUDENTS THIS TIME: WOMEN, WORKERS, CLERICS, BAZARIS...
IN THE MORNING PEOPLE WERE ONLY ASKING FOR A RECOUNT...
BY EARLY AFTERNOON THEY WANTED AN IRANIAN, NOT AN ISLAMIC, REPUBLIC
AS IF CHANGING NAMES WILL RID THIS SEWER OF ITS STENCH...

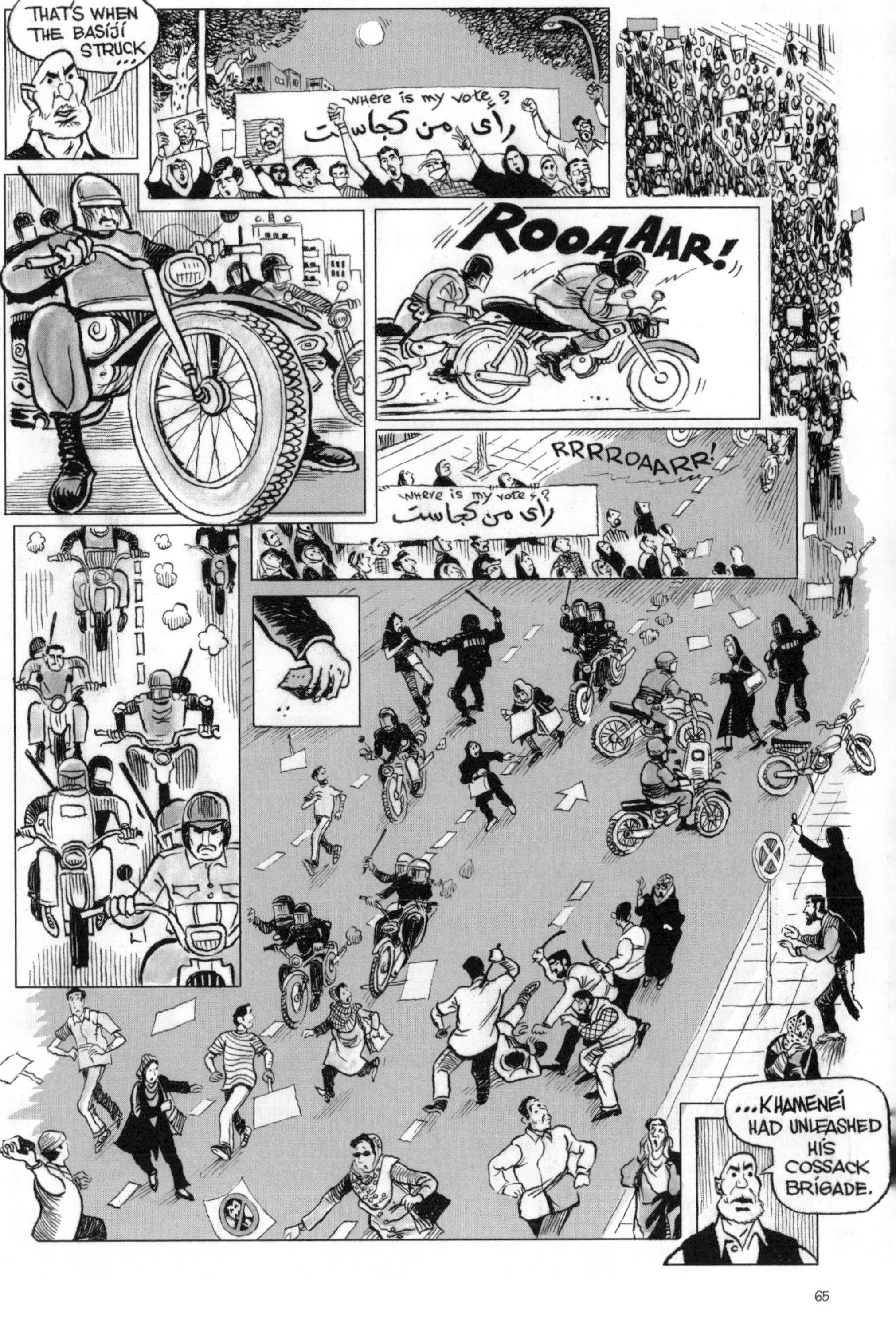
THAT'S WHEN THE BASÍJÍ STRUCK...
where is my vote?
رای من کجاست
ROOAAAR!
RRRROAARR!
where is my vote?
رای من کجاست
...KHAMENEI HAD UNLEASHED HIS COSSACK BRIGADE.

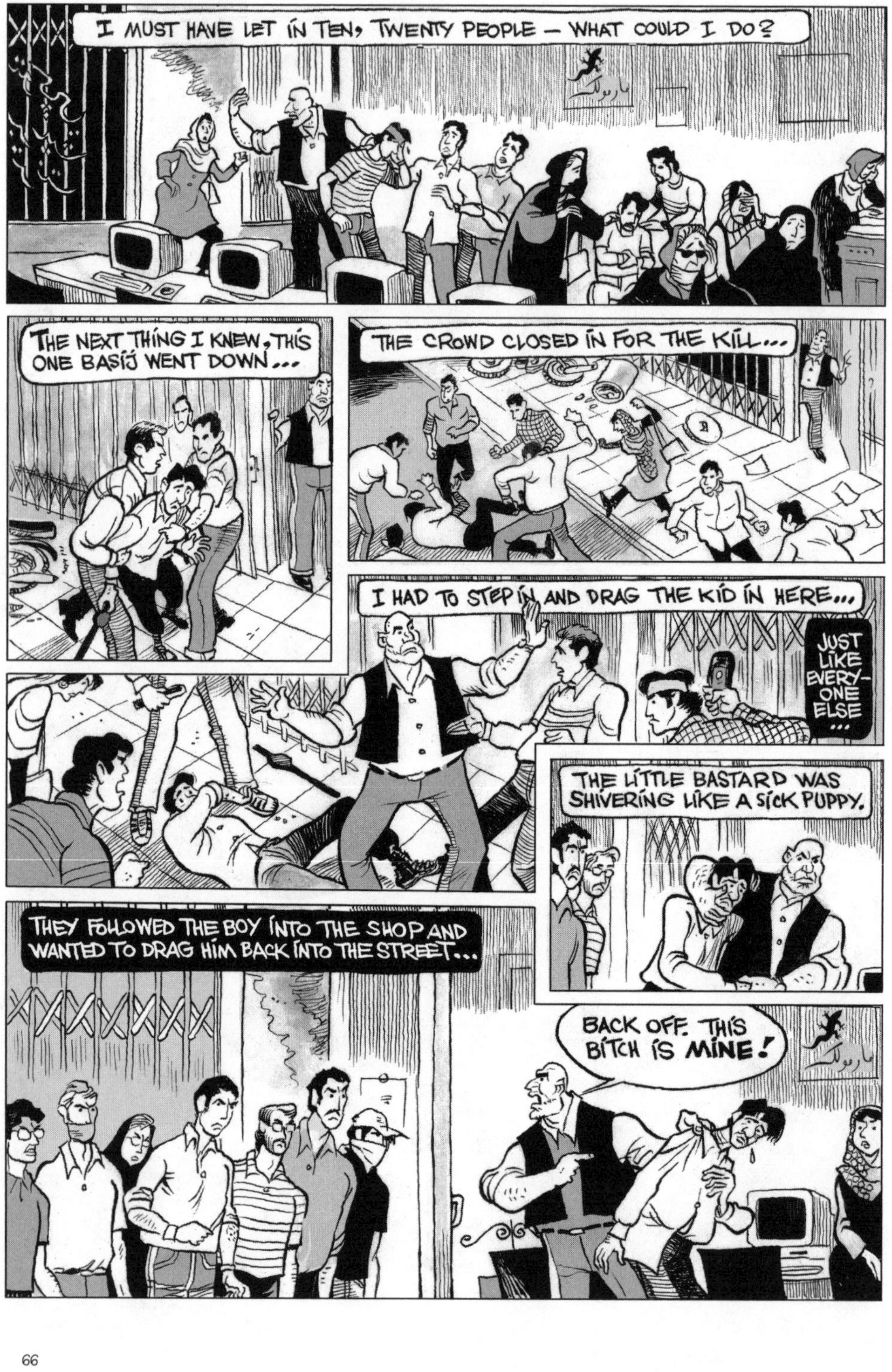
I MUST HAVE LET IN TEN, TWENTY PEOPLE — WHAT COULD I DO?
THE NEXT THING I KNEW, THIS ONE BASIJ WENT DOWN...
THE CROWD CLOSED IN FOR THE KILL...
I HAD TO STEP IN AND DRAG THE KID IN HERE...
JUST LIKE EVERY-ONE ELSE...
THE LITTLE BASTARD WAS SHIVERING LIKE A SICK PUPPY.
THEY FOLLOWED THE BOY INTO THE SHOP AND WANTED TO DRAG HIM BACK INTO THE STREET...
BACK OFF. THIS BITCH IS MINE!

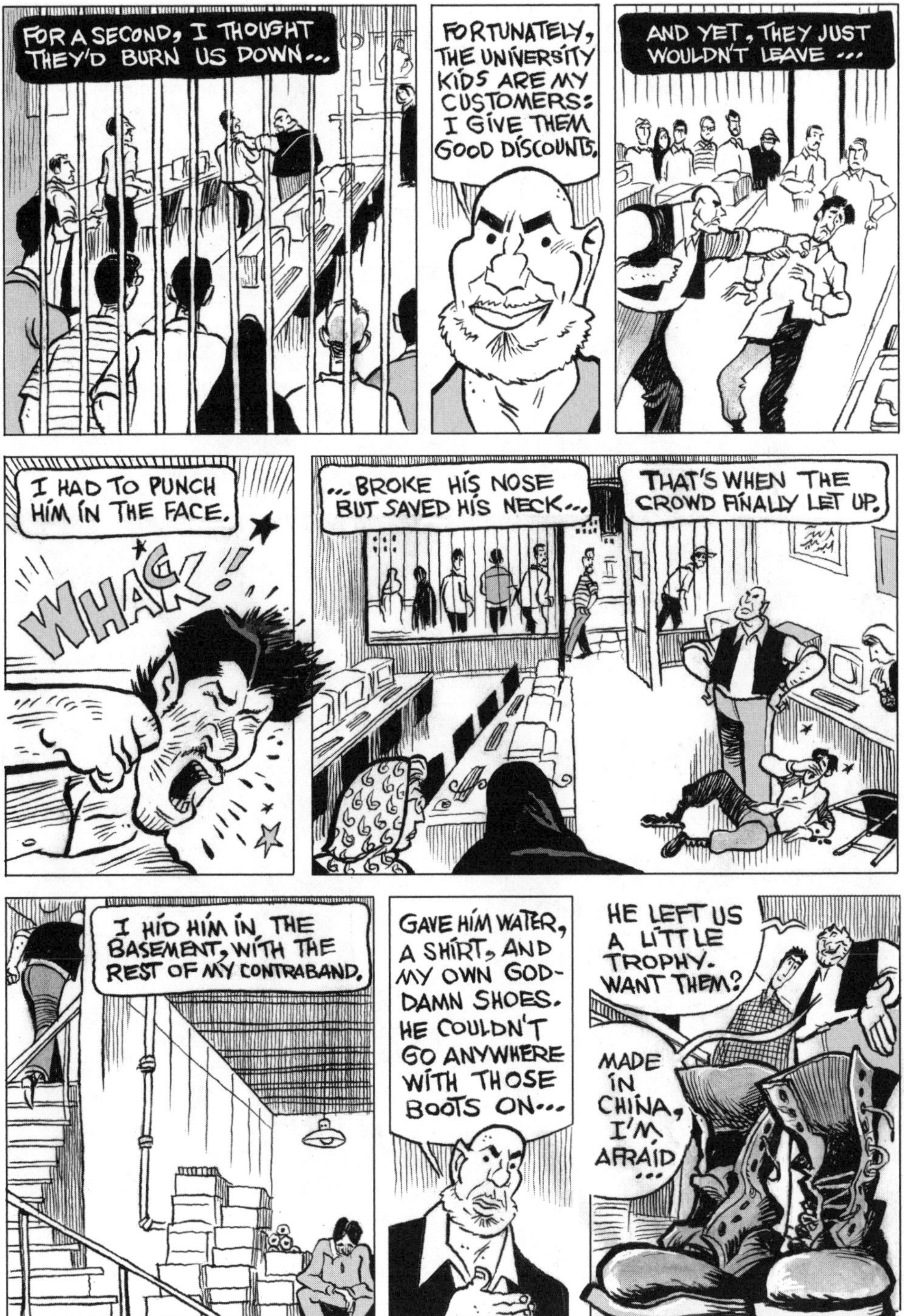
FOR A SECOND, I THOUGHT THEY'D BURN US DOWN...
FORTUNATELY, THE UNIVERSITY KIDS ARE MY CUSTOMERS: I GIVE THEM GOOD DISCOUNTS.
AND YET, THEY JUST WOULDN'T LEAVE...
I HAD TO PUNCH HIM IN THE FACE.
WHACK!
...BROKE HIS NOSE BUT SAVED HIS NECK...
THAT'S WHEN THE CROWD FINALLY LET UP.
I HID HIM IN THE BASEMENT, WITH THE REST OF MY CONTRABAND.
GAVE HIM WATER, A SHIRT, AND MY OWN GOD-DAMN SHOES. HE COULDN'T GO ANYWHERE WITH THOSE BOOTS ON...
HE LEFT US A LITTLE TROPHY. WANT THEM?
MADE IN CHINA, I'M AFRAID...

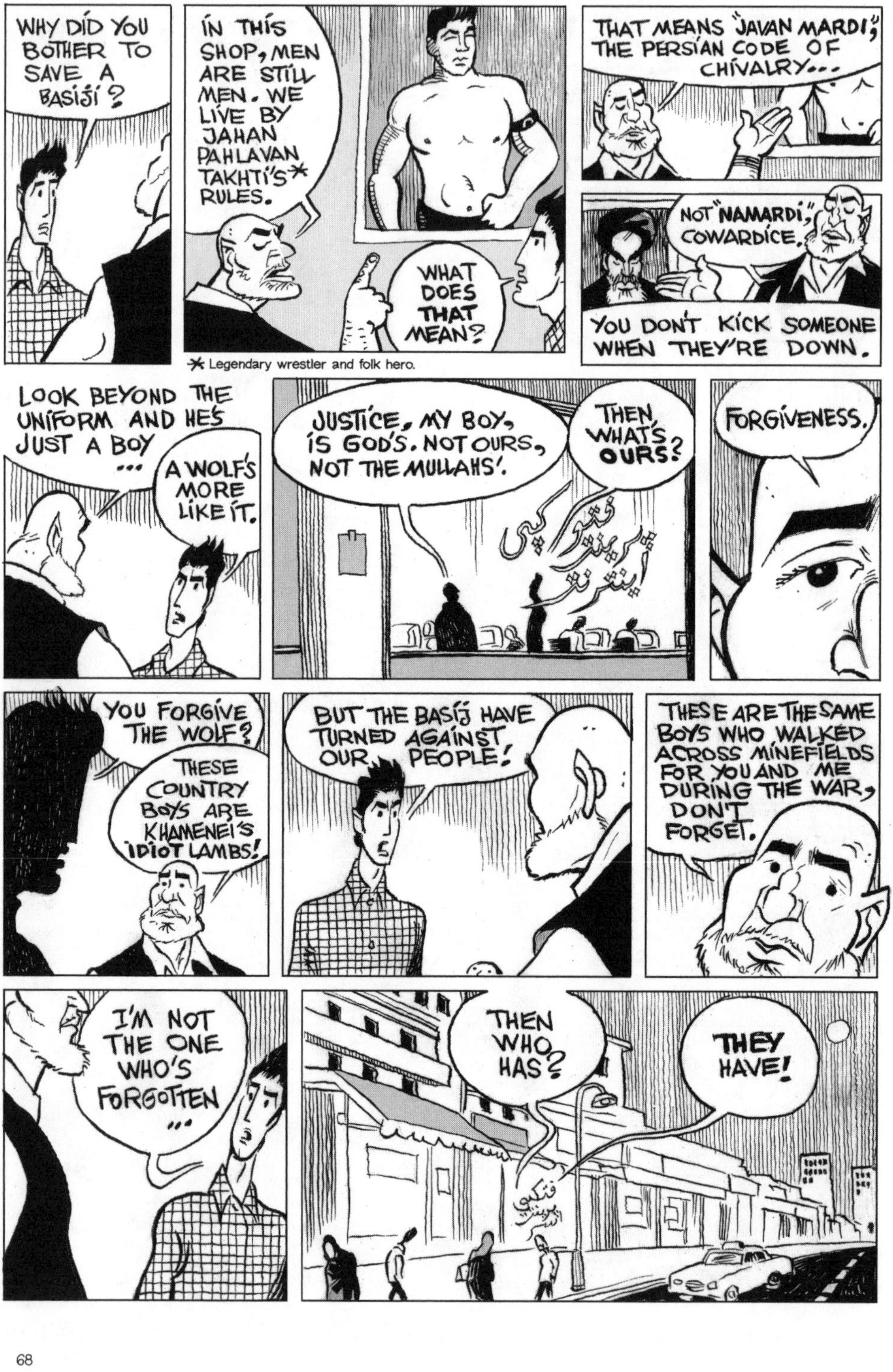
WHY DID YOU BOTHER TO SAVE A BASIJI?
IN THIS SHOP, MEN ARE STILL MEN. WE LIVE BY JAHAN PAHLAVAN TAKHTI'S* RULES.
WHAT DOES THAT MEAN?
THAT MEANS "JAVAN MARDI," THE PERSIAN CODE OF CHIVALRY...
NOT "NAMARDI," COWARDICE.
YOU DON'T KICK SOMEONE WHEN THEY'RE DOWN.
LOOK BEYOND THE UNIFORM AND HE'S JUST A BOY ...
A WOLF'S MORE LIKE IT.
JUSTICE, MY BOY, IS GOD'S. NOT OURS, NOT THE MULLAHS'.
THEN, WHAT'S OURS?
FORGIVENESS.
YOU FORGIVE THE WOLF?
THESE COUNTRY BOYS ARE KHAMENEI'S IDIOT LAMBS!
BUT THE BASIJ HAVE TURNED AGAINST OUR PEOPLE!
THESE ARE THE SAME BOYS WHO WALKED ACROSS MINEFIELDS FOR YOU AND ME DURING THE WAR, DON'T FORGET.
I'M NOT THE ONE WHO'S FORGOTTEN ...
THEN WHO HAS?
THEY HAVE!

* Legendary wrestler and folk hero.

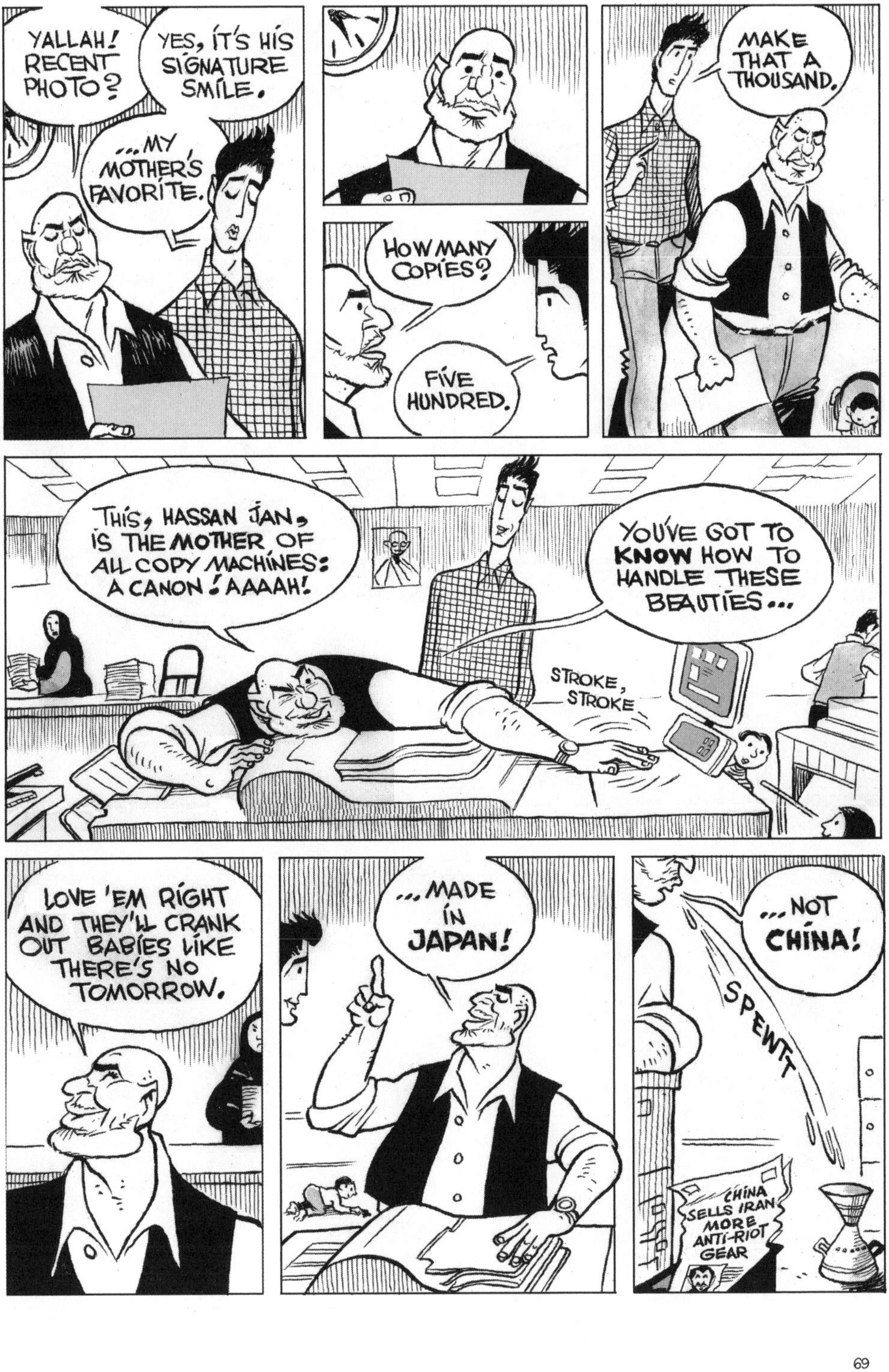
YALLAH! RECENT PHOTO?
YES, IT'S HIS SIGNATURE SMILE.
...MY MOTHER'S FAVORITE.
HOW MANY COPIES?
FIVE HUNDRED.
MAKE THAT A THOUSAND.
THIS, HASSAN JAN, IS THE MOTHER OF ALL COPY MACHINES: A CANON! AAAAH!
YOU'VE GOT TO KNOW HOW TO HANDLE THESE BEAUTIES...
STROKE, STROKE
LOVE 'EM RIGHT AND THEY'LL CRANK OUT BABIES LIKE THERE'S NO TOMORROW.
...MADE IN JAPAN!
...NOT CHINA!
SPEWTT
CHINA SELLS IRAN MORE ANTI-RIOT GEAR

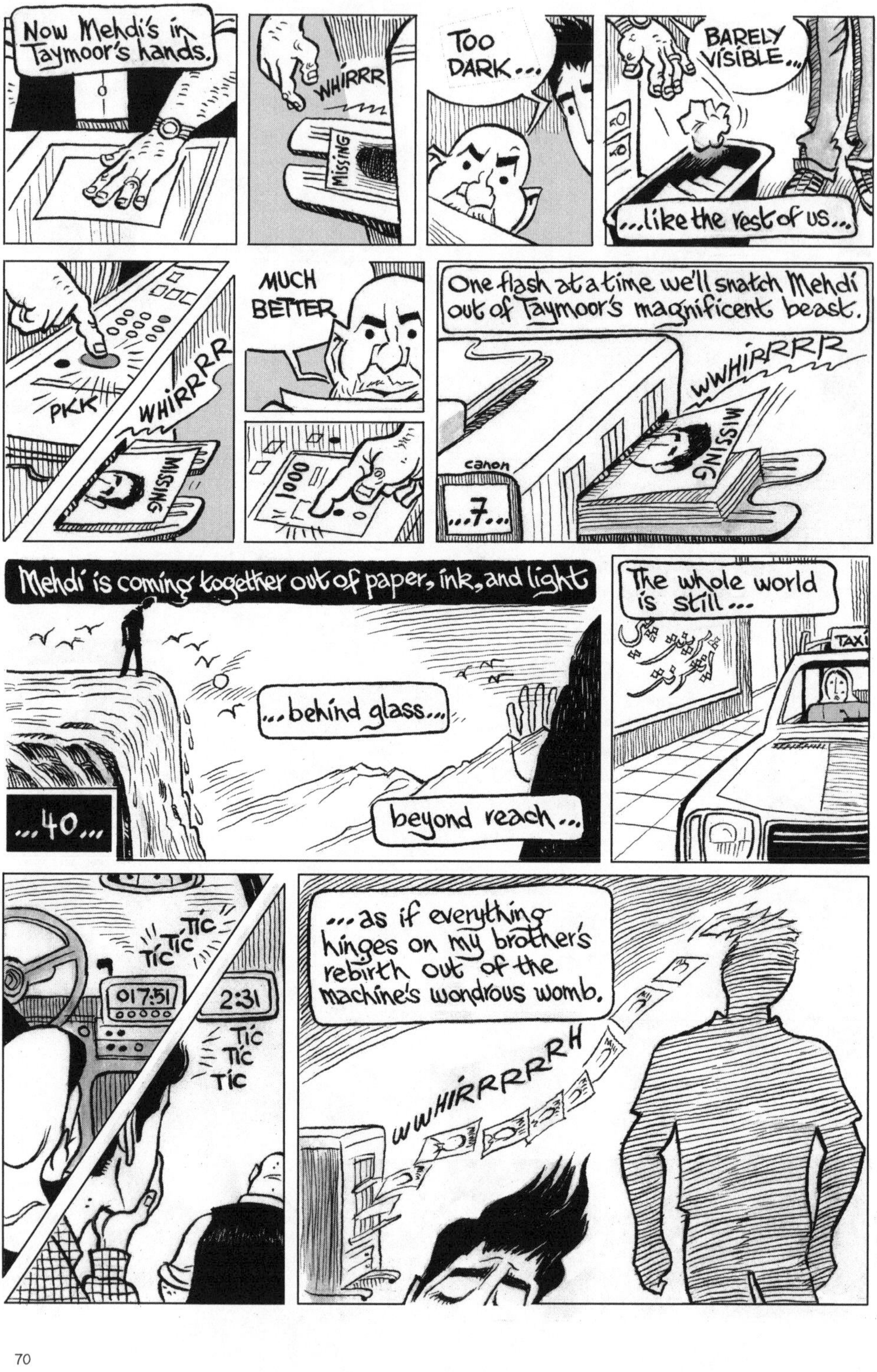
Now Mehdi's in Taymoor's hands.
WHIRRR
MISSING
TOO DARK...
BARELY VISIBLE...
...like the rest of us...
PKK
WHIRRR
MISSING
MUCH BETTER
One flash at a time we'll snatch Mehdi out of Taymoor's magnificent beast.
WWHIRRRR
MISSING
canon
...7...
Mehdi is coming together out of paper, ink, and light
...behind glass...
beyond reach...
...40...
The whole world is still...
TAXI
TIC TIC TIC
017:51
2:31
TIC TIC TIC
...as if everything hinges on my brother's rebirth out of the machine's wondrous womb.
WWHIRRRRRH

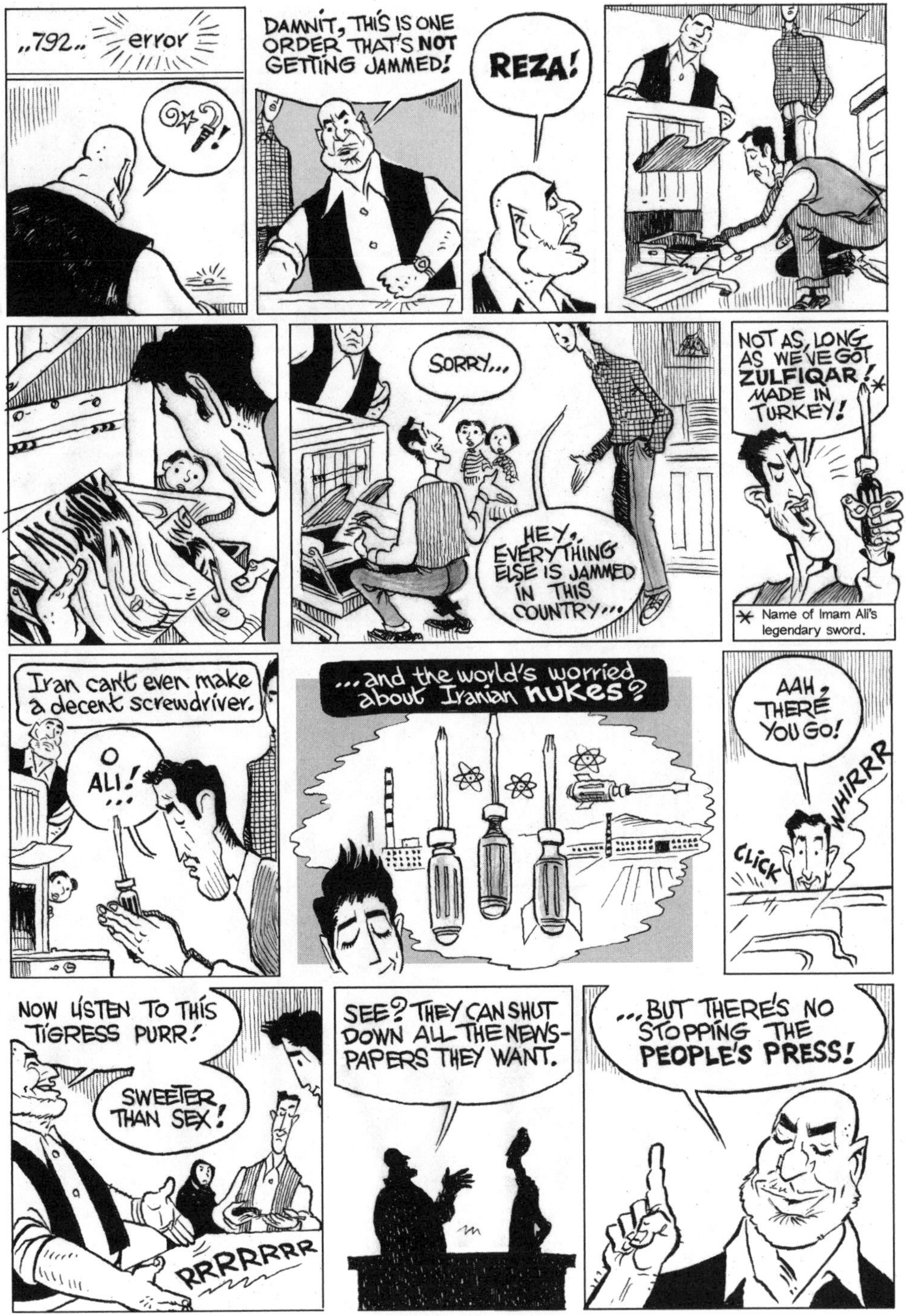
..792.. error
DAMNIT, THIS IS ONE ORDER THAT'S NOT GETTING JAMMED!
REZA!
SORRY...
HEY, EVERYTHING ELSE IS JAMMED IN THIS COUNTRY...
NOT AS LONG AS WE'VE GOT ZULFIQAR!* MADE IN TURKEY!
* Name of Imam Ali's legendary sword.
Iran can't even make a decent screwdriver.
O ALI! ...
...and the world's worried about Iranian nukes?
AAH, THERE YOU GO!
WHIRRR
CLICK
NOW LISTEN TO THIS TIGRESS PURR!
SWEETER THAN SEX!
RRRRRRR
SEE? THEY CAN SHUT DOWN ALL THE NEWSPAPERS THEY WANT.
...BUT THERE'S NO STOPPING THE PEOPLE'S PRESS!

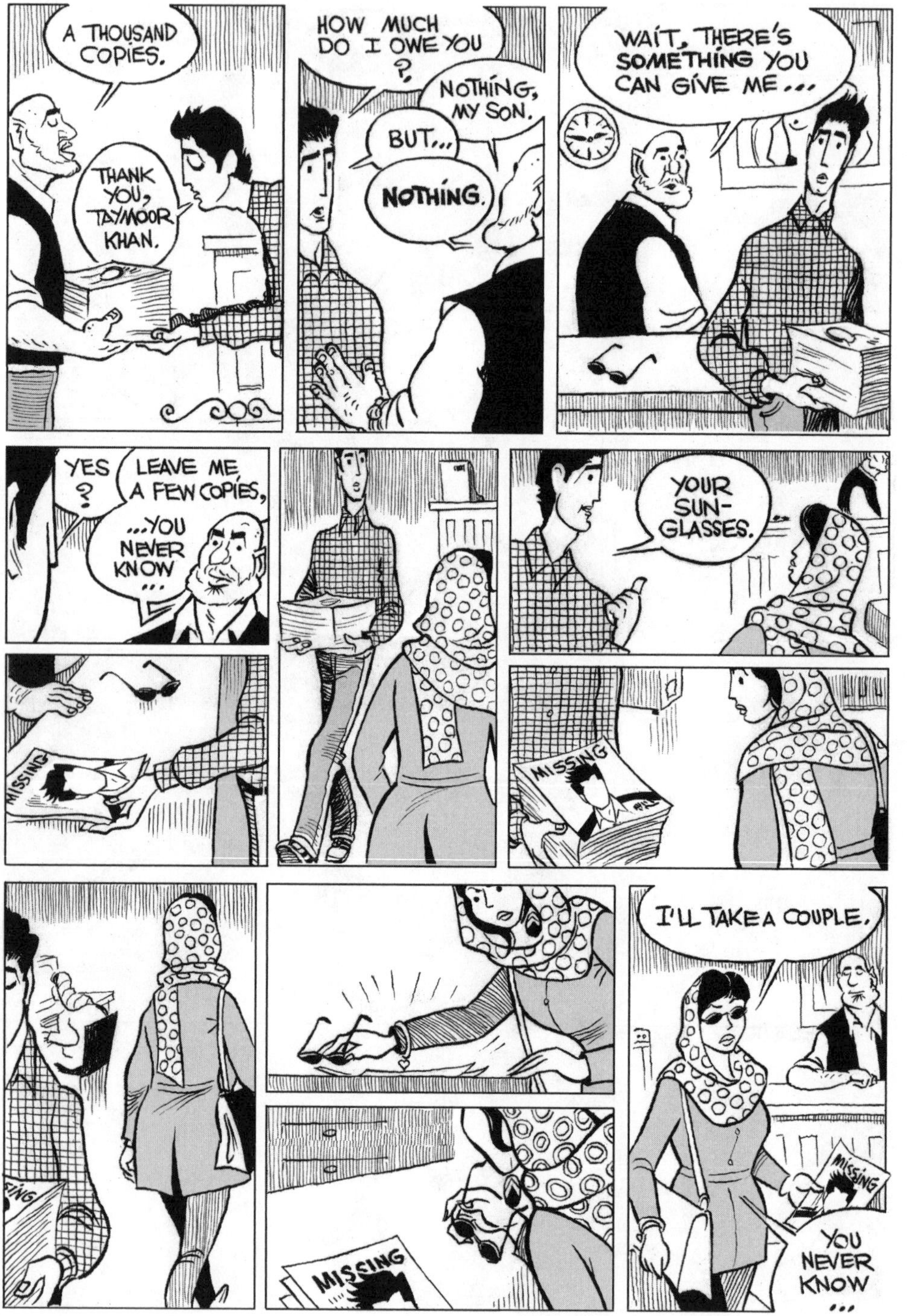
A THOUSAND COPIES.
THANK YOU, TAYMOOR KHAN.
HOW MUCH DO I OWE YOU ?
NOTHING, MY SON.
BUT...
NOTHING.
WAIT, THERE'S SOMETHING YOU CAN GIVE ME...
YES ?
LEAVE ME A FEW COPIES,
...YOU NEVER KNOW ...
YOUR SUN-GLASSES.
MISSING
MISSING
MISSING
I'LL TAKE A COUPLE.
MISSING
YOU NEVER KNOW ...

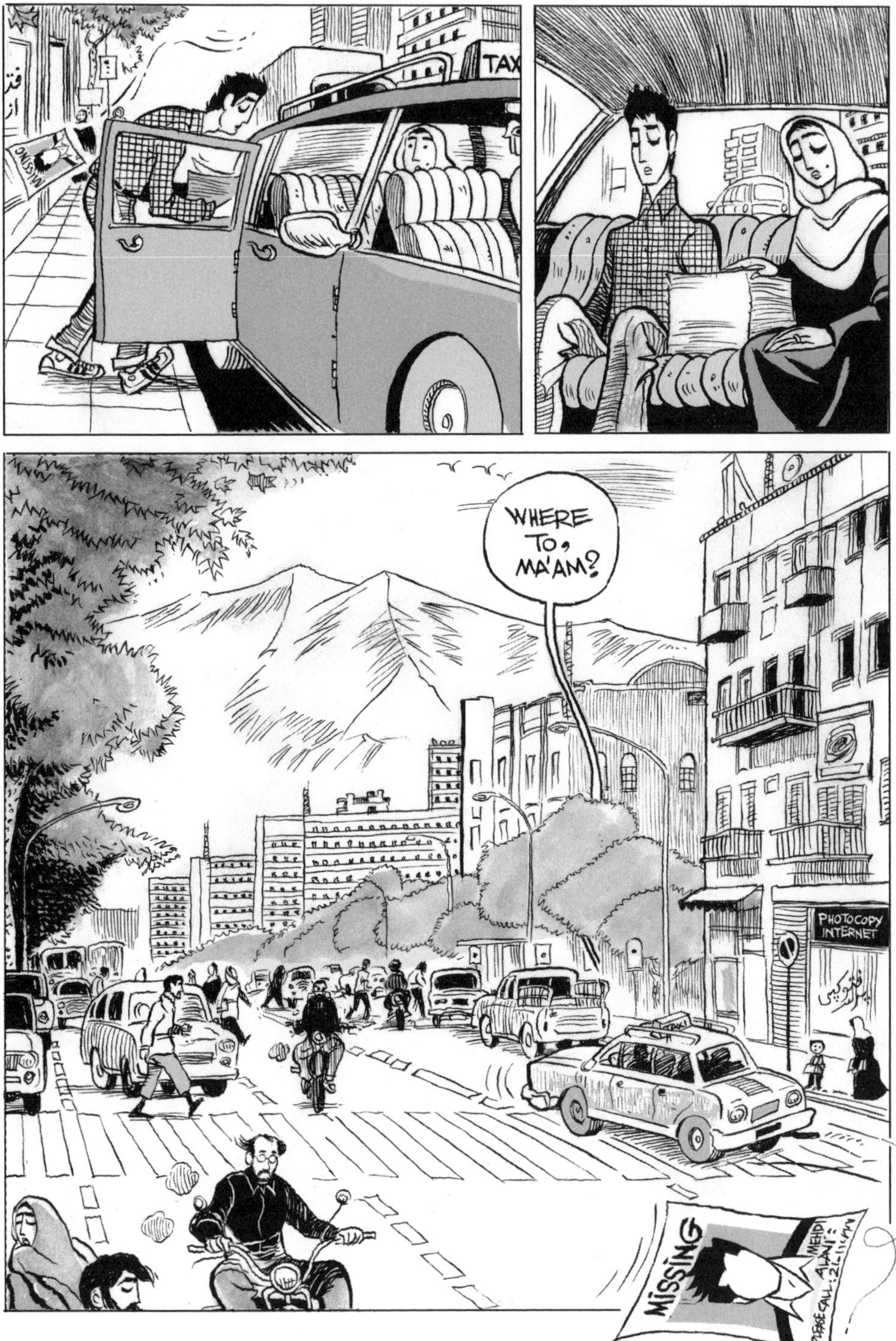
TAX
WHERE TO, MA'AM?
PHOTOCOPY
INTERNET
MISSING
MEHDI ALANI

WATERMELON JUICE

CHAPTER FIVE

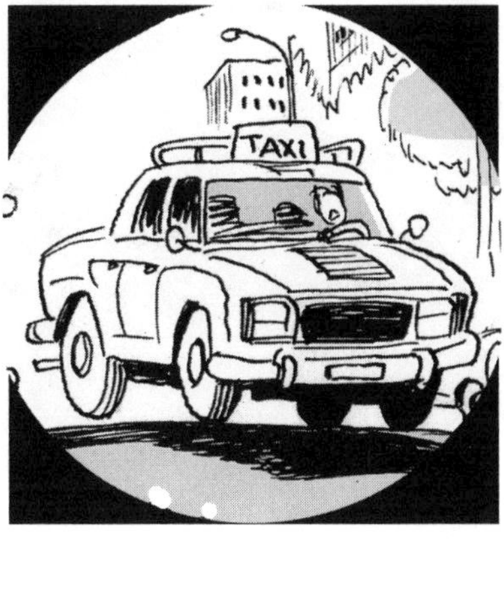
TAXI

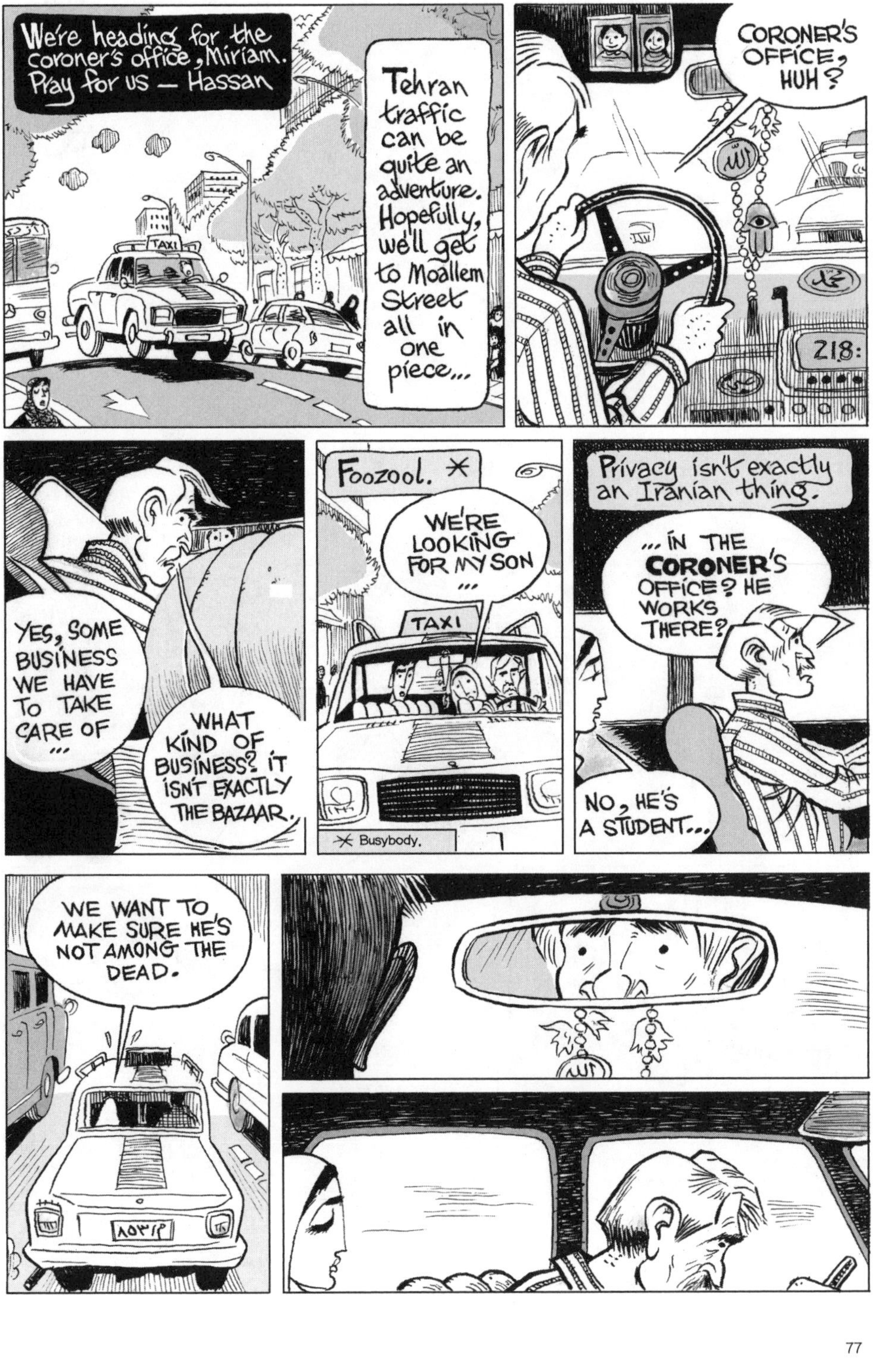

We're heading for the coroner's office, Miriam. Pray for us — Hassan
Tehran traffic can be quite an adventure. Hopefully, we'll get to Moallem Street all in one piece...
TAXI
CORONER'S OFFICE, HUH?
218:
YES, SOME BUSINESS WE HAVE TO TAKE CARE OF ...
WHAT KIND OF BUSINESS? IT ISN'T EXACTLY THE BAZAAR.
Foozool. *
WE'RE LOOKING FOR MY SON ...
TAXI
* Busybody.
Privacy isn't exactly an Iranian thing.
... IN THE CORONER'S OFFICE? HE WORKS THERE?
NO, HE'S A STUDENT...
WE WANT TO MAKE SURE HE'S NOT AMONG THE DEAD.

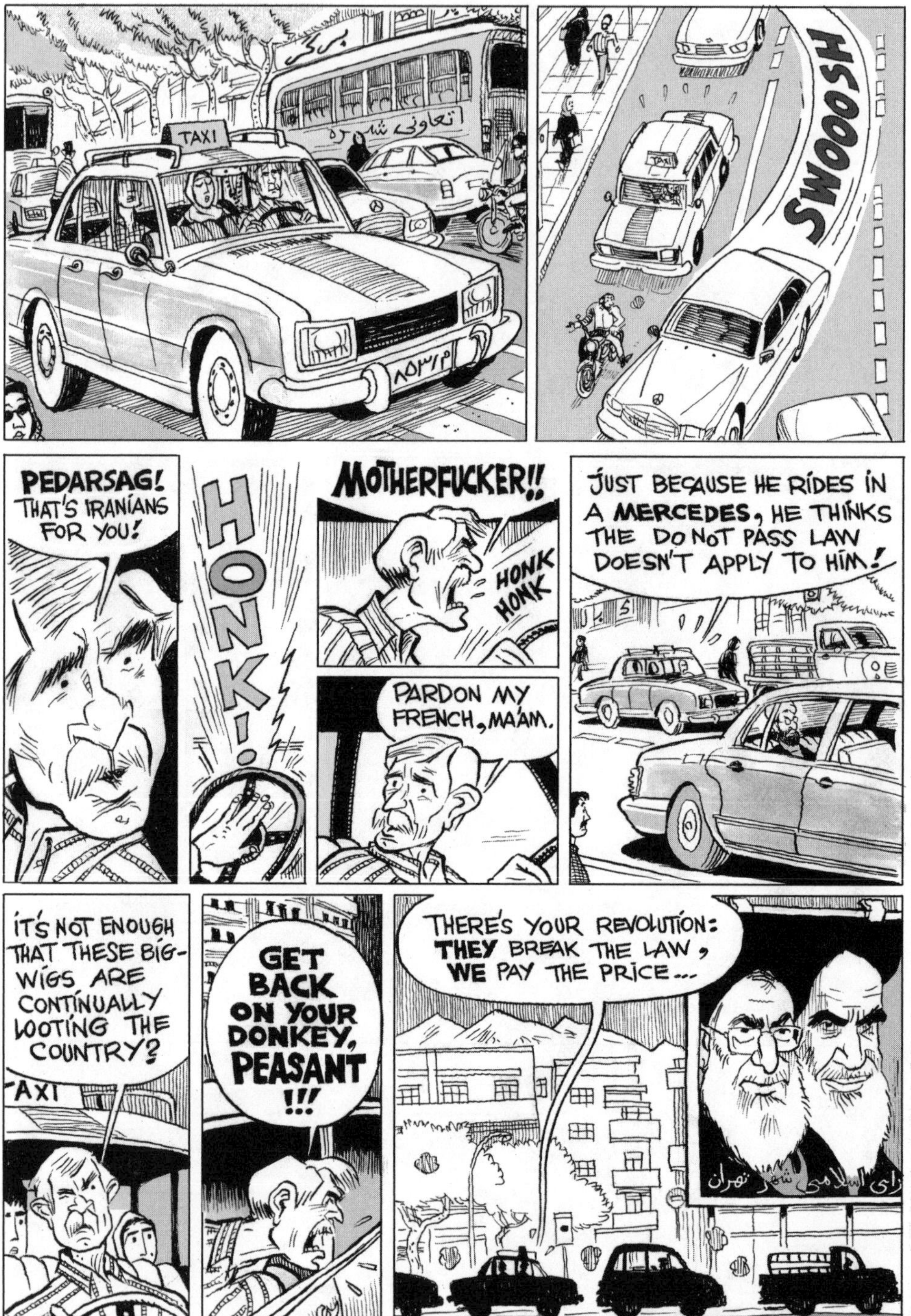
TAXI
SWOOOSH
PEDARSAG! THAT'S IRANIANS FOR YOU!
HONK!
MOTHERFUCKER!!
HONK HONK
PARDON MY FRENCH, MA'AM.
JUST BECAUSE HE RIDES IN A MERCEDES, HE THINKS THE DO NOT PASS LAW DOESN'T APPLY TO HIM!
IT'S NOT ENOUGH THAT THESE BIG-WIGS ARE CONTINUALLY LOOTING THE COUNTRY?
TAXI
GET BACK ON YOUR DONKEY, PEASANT!!!
THERE'S YOUR REVOLUTION: THEY BREAK THE LAW, WE PAY THE PRICE...

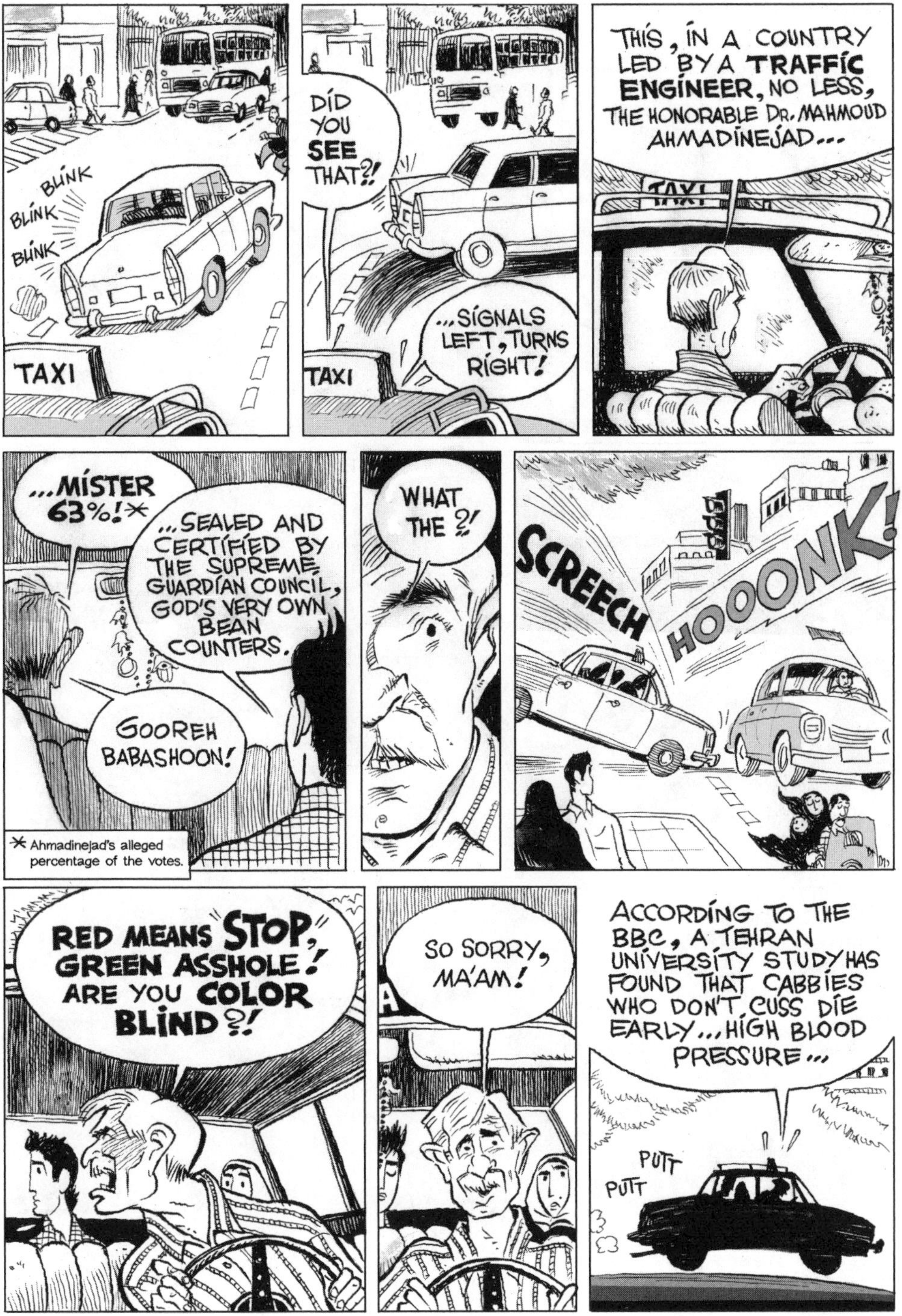
BLINK
BLINK
BLINK
TAXI
DID YOU SEE THAT?!
...SIGNALS LEFT, TURNS RIGHT!
TAXI
THIS, IN A COUNTRY LED BY A TRAFFIC ENGINEER, NO LESS, THE HONORABLE DR. MAHMOUD AHMADINEJAD...
TAXI
...MISTER 63%!*
...SEALED AND CERTIFIED BY THE SUPREME GUARDIAN COUNCIL, GOD'S VERY OWN BEAN COUNTERS.
GOOREH BABASHOON!
* Ahmadinejad's alleged percentage of the votes.
WHAT THE ?!
SCREECH
HOOONK!
RED MEANS STOP, GREEN ASSHOLE! ARE YOU COLOR BLIND?!
SO SORRY, MA'AM!
ACCORDING TO THE BBC, A TEHRAN UNIVERSITY STUDY HAS FOUND THAT CABBIES WHO DON'T CUSS DIE EARLY... HIGH BLOOD PRESSURE...
PUTT
PUTT

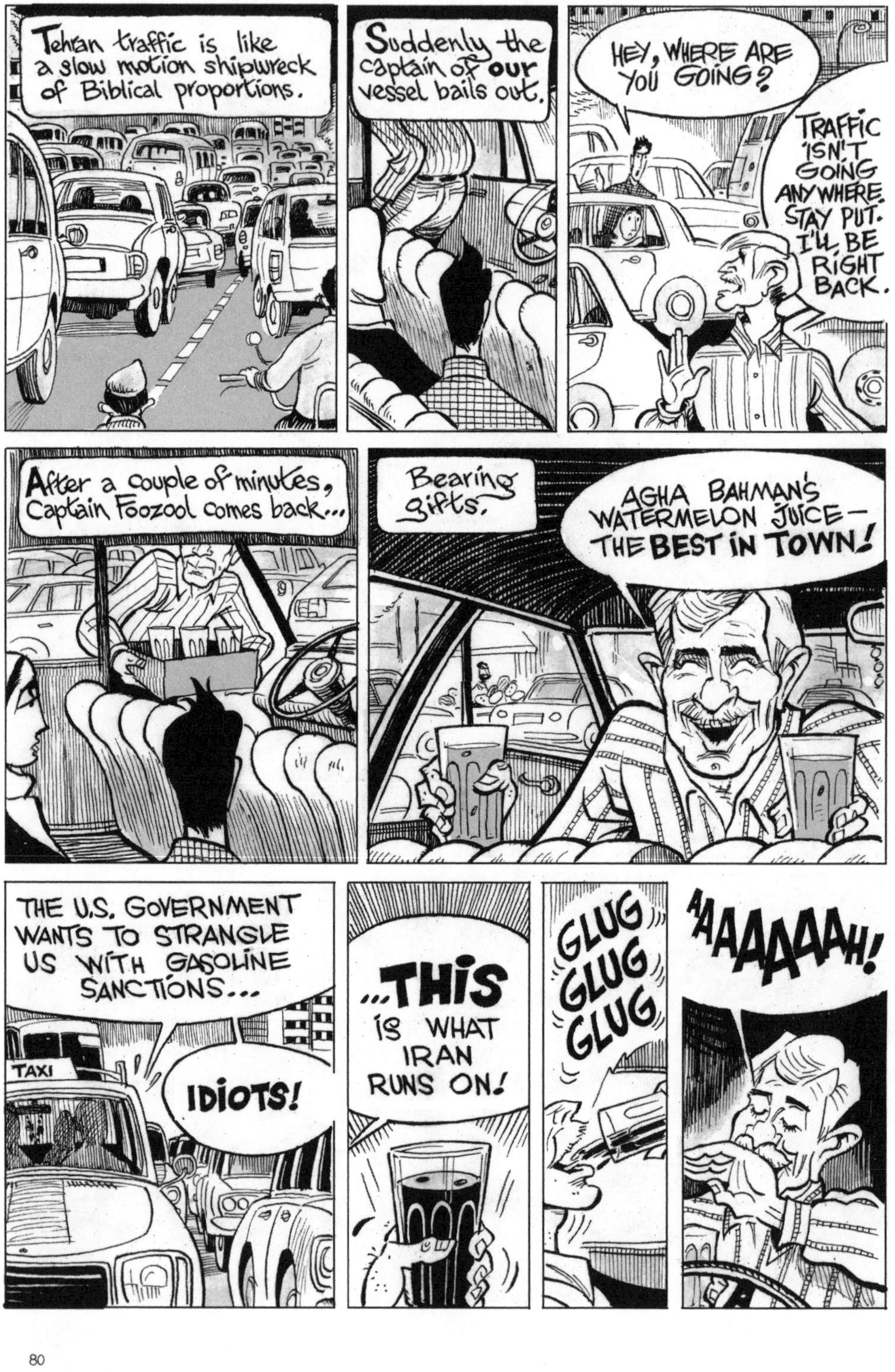
Tehran traffic is like a slow motion shipwreck of Biblical proportions.
Suddenly the captain of our vessel bails out.
HEY, WHERE ARE YOU GOING?
TRAFFIC ISN'T GOING ANYWHERE. STAY PUT. I'LL BE RIGHT BACK.
After a couple of minutes, Captain Foozool comes back...
Bearing gifts.
AGHA BAHMAN'S WATERMELON JUICE— THE BEST IN TOWN!
THE U.S. GOVERNMENT WANTS TO STRANGLE US WITH GASOLINE SANCTIONS...
TAXI
IDIOTS!
...THIS IS WHAT IRAN RUNS ON!
GLUG GLUG GLUG
AAAAAAAH!

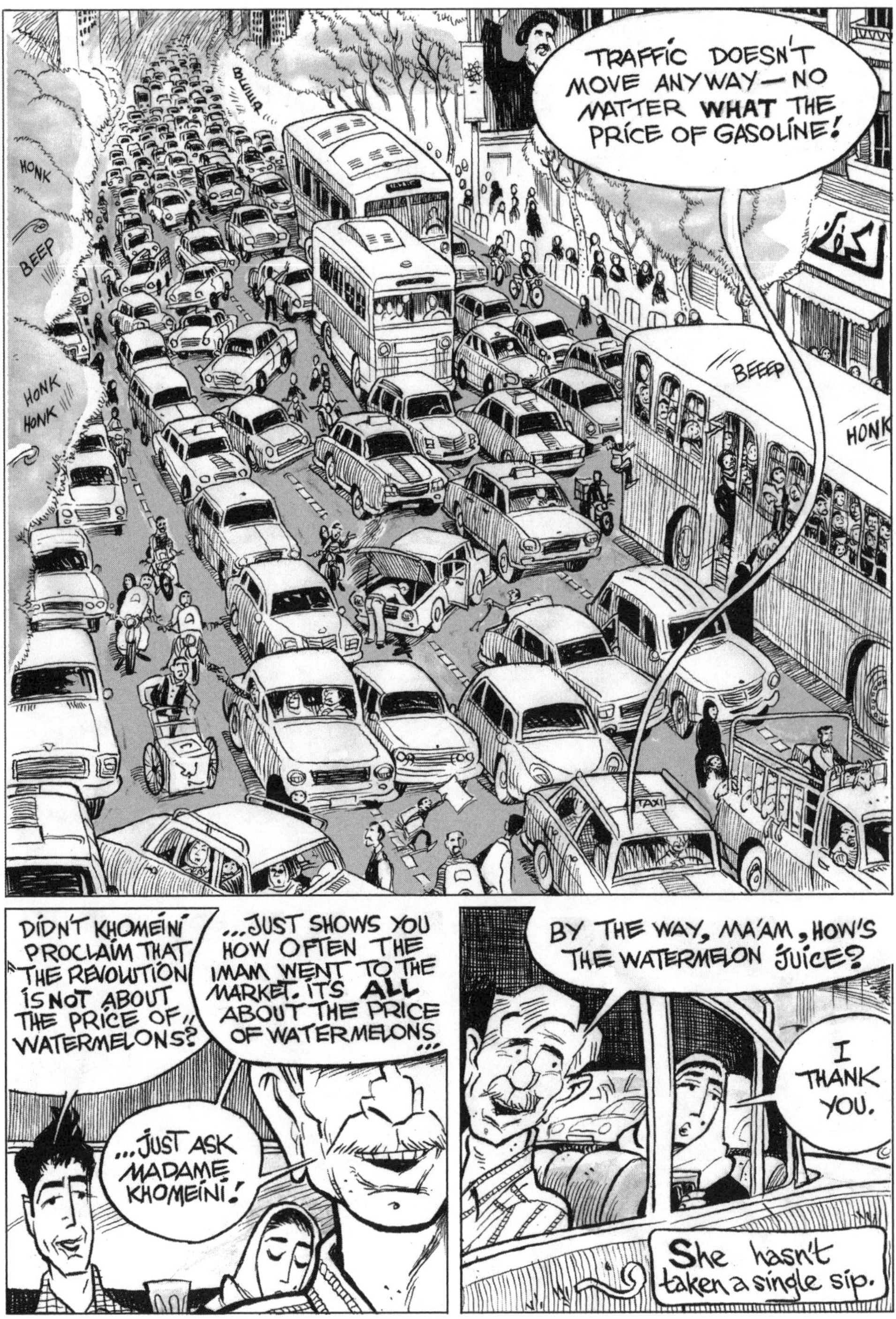
TRAFFIC DOESN'T MOVE ANYWAY—NO MATTER **WHAT** THE PRICE OF GASOLINE!
HONK
BEEP
HONK HONK
BEEEP
HONK
DIDN'T KHOMEINI PROCLAIM THAT "THE REVOLUTION IS **NOT** ABOUT THE PRICE OF WATERMELONS"?
...JUST SHOWS YOU HOW OFTEN THE IMAM WENT TO THE MARKET. IT'S **ALL** ABOUT THE PRICE OF WATERMELONS...
...JUST ASK MADAME KHOMEINI!
BY THE WAY, MA'AM, HOW'S THE WATERMELON JUICE?
I THANK YOU.
She hasn't taken a single sip.

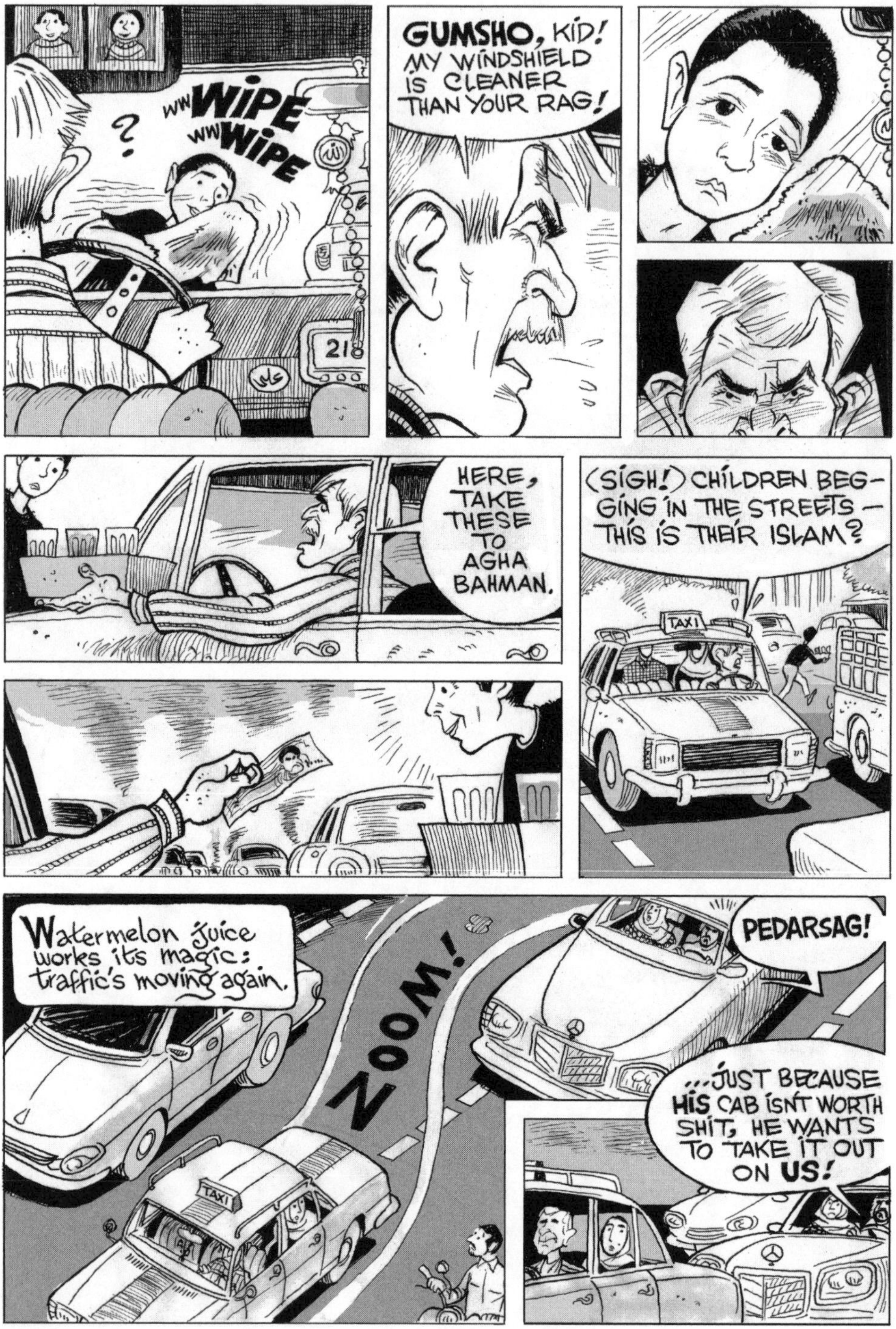
WWWIPE WWWIPE
?
GUMSHO, KID! MY WINDSHIELD IS CLEANER THAN YOUR RAG!
HERE, TAKE THESE TO AGHA BAHMAN.
(SIGH!) CHILDREN BEGGING IN THE STREETS — THIS IS THEIR ISLAM?
TAXI
Watermelon juice works its magic: traffic's moving again.
ZOOM!
PEDARSAG!
TAXI
...JUST BECAUSE HIS CAB ISN'T WORTH SHIT, HE WANTS TO TAKE IT OUT ON US!

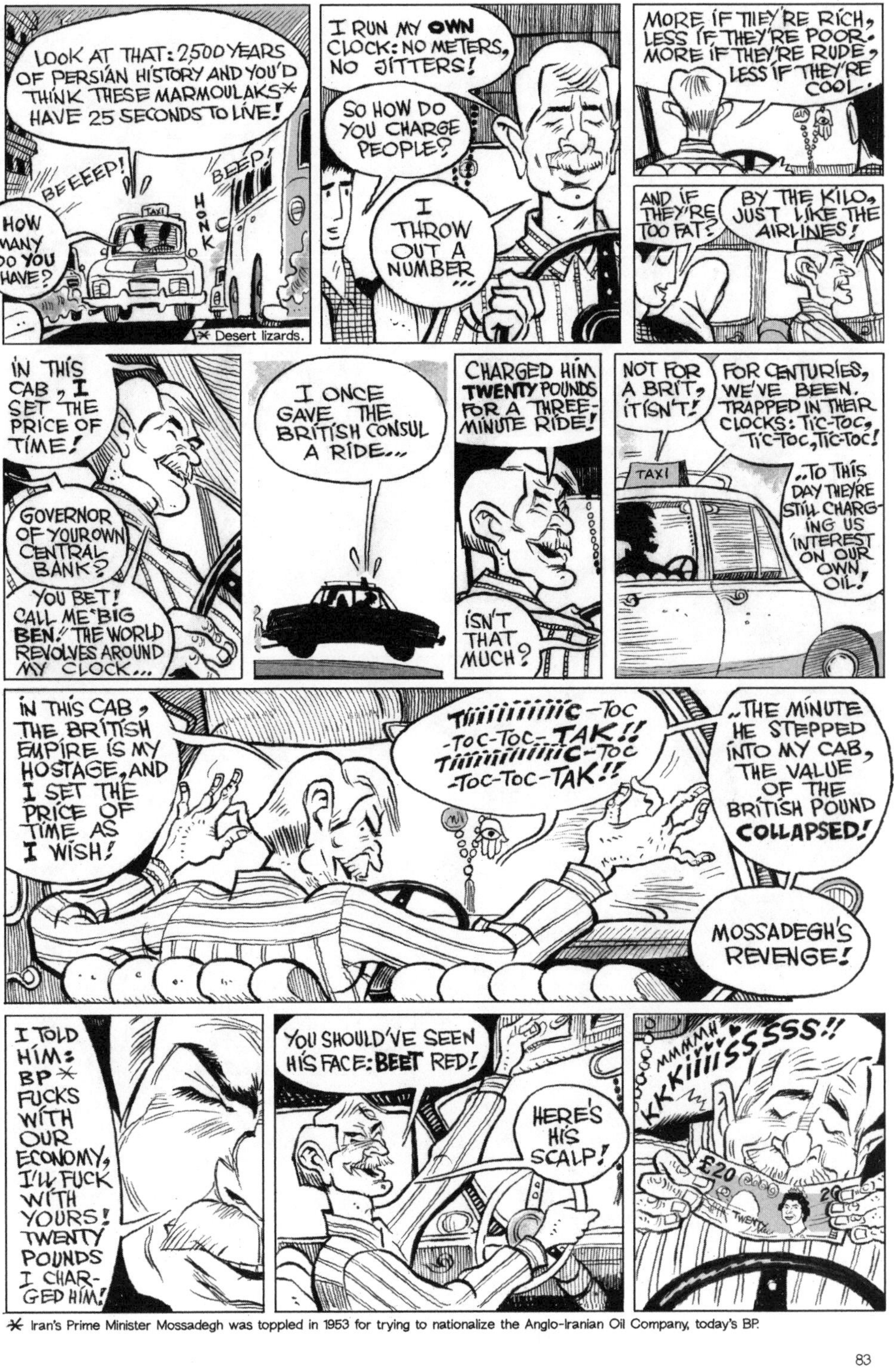
LOOK AT THAT: 2,500 YEARS OF PERSIAN HISTORY AND YOU'D THINK THESE MARMOULAKS* HAVE 25 SECONDS TO LIVE!
BEEEEP!
BEEP!
HONK
TAXI
HOW MANY DO YOU HAVE?
* Desert lizards.
I RUN MY OWN CLOCK: NO METERS, NO JITTERS!
SO HOW DO YOU CHARGE PEOPLE?
I THROW OUT A NUMBER...
MORE IF THEY'RE RICH, LESS IF THEY'RE POOR. MORE IF THEY'RE RUDE, LESS IF THEY'RE COOL.
AND IF THEY'RE TOO FAT?
BY THE KILO, JUST LIKE THE AIRLINES!
IN THIS CAB, I SET THE PRICE OF TIME!
GOVERNOR OF YOUR OWN CENTRAL BANK?
YOU BET! CALL ME "BIG BEN!" THE WORLD REVOLVES AROUND MY CLOCK...
I ONCE GAVE THE BRITISH CONSUL A RIDE...
CHARGED HIM TWENTY POUNDS FOR A THREE-MINUTE RIDE!
ISN'T THAT MUCH?
NOT FOR A BRIT, IT ISN'T!
FOR CENTURIES, WE'VE BEEN TRAPPED IN THEIR CLOCKS: TIC-TOC, TIC-TOC, TIC-TOC!
TAXI
...TO THIS DAY THEY'RE STILL CHARGING US INTEREST ON OUR OWN OIL!
IN THIS CAB, THE BRITISH EMPIRE IS MY HOSTAGE, AND I SET THE PRICE OF TIME AS I WISH!
TIIIIIIIIIIC-TOC-TOC-TOC-TAK!! TIIIIIIIIIIC-TOC-TOC-TOC-TAK!!
...THE MINUTE HE STEPPED INTO MY CAB, THE VALUE OF THE BRITISH POUND COLLAPSED!
MOSSADEGH'S REVENGE!
I TOLD HIM: BP* FUCKS WITH OUR ECONOMY, I'LL FUCK WITH YOURS! TWENTY POUNDS I CHARGED HIM!
YOU SHOULD'VE SEEN HIS FACE: BEET RED!
HERE'S HIS SCALP!
MMMMH KKKIIIISSSSSS!!
£20
TWENTY

* Iran's Prime Minister Mossadegh was toppled in 1953 for trying to nationalize the Anglo-Iranian Oil Company, today's BP.

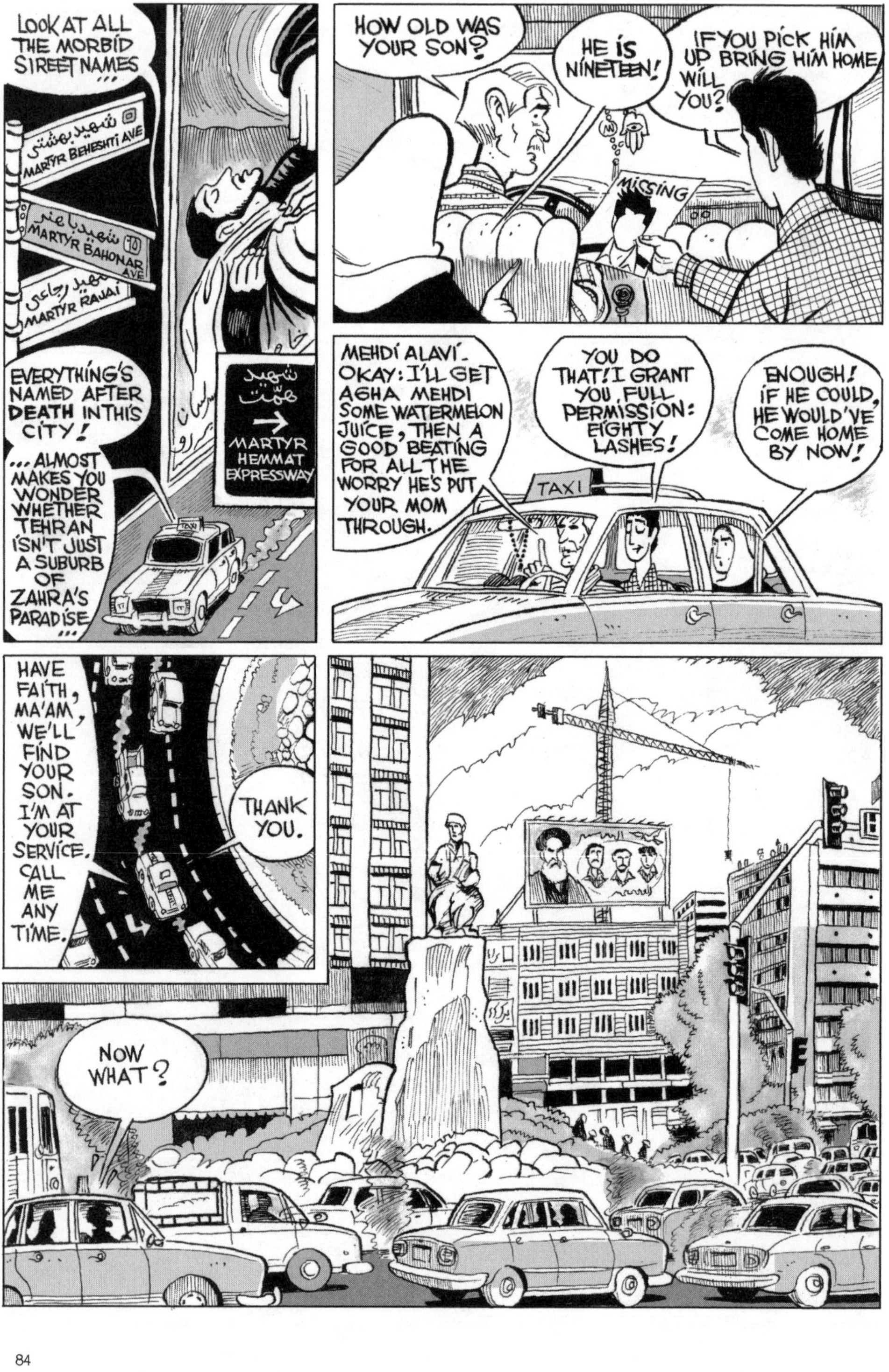
LOOK AT ALL THE MORBID STREET NAMES...
شهيد بهشتى
MARTYR BEHESHTI AVE
شهيد باهنر
MARTYR BAHONAR AVE
شهيد رجائى
MARTYR RAJAI
EVERYTHING'S NAMED AFTER DEATH IN THIS CITY!
...ALMOST MAKES YOU WONDER WHETHER TEHRAN ISN'T JUST A SUBURB OF ZAHRA'S PARADISE...
MARTYR HEMMAT EXPRESSWAY
HOW OLD WAS YOUR SON?
HE IS NINETEEN!
IF YOU PICK HIM UP BRING HIM HOME, WILL YOU?
MISSING
MEHDI ALAVI. OKAY: I'LL GET AGHA MEHDI SOME WATERMELON JUICE, THEN A GOOD BEATING FOR ALL THE WORRY HE'S PUT YOUR MOM THROUGH.
YOU DO THAT! I GRANT YOU FULL PERMISSION: EIGHTY LASHES!
ENOUGH! IF HE COULD, HE WOULD'VE COME HOME BY NOW!
TAXI
HAVE FAITH, MA'AM, WE'LL FIND YOUR SON. I'M AT YOUR SERVICE. CALL ME ANY TIME.
THANK YOU.
NOW WHAT?

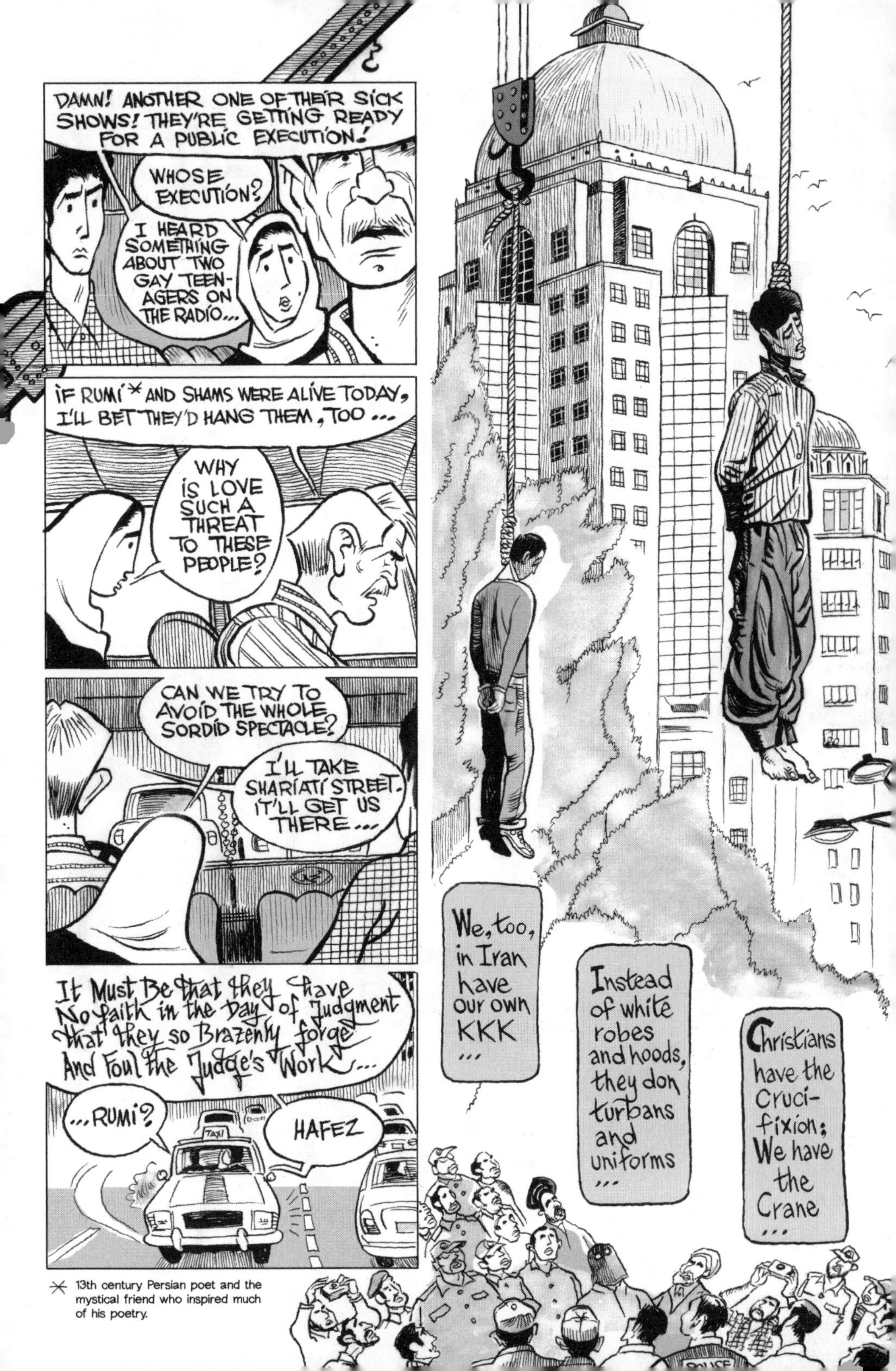
DAMN! ANOTHER ONE OF THEIR SICK SHOWS! THEY'RE GETTING READY FOR A PUBLIC EXECUTION!
WHOSE EXECUTION?
I HEARD SOMETHING ABOUT TWO GAY TEEN-AGERS ON THE RADIO...
IF RUMI* AND SHAMS WERE ALIVE TODAY, I'LL BET THEY'D HANG THEM, TOO...
WHY IS LOVE SUCH A THREAT TO THESE PEOPLE?
CAN WE TRY TO AVOID THE WHOLE SORDID SPECTACLE?
I'LL TAKE SHARIATI STREET. IT'LL GET US THERE...
It Must Be that they have No faith in the Day of Judgment that they so Brazenly forge And Foul the Judge's Work...
...RUMI?
HAFEZ
We, too, in Iran have our own KKK...
Instead of white robes and hoods, they don turbans and uniforms...
Christians have the Cruci-fixion; We have the Crane...

* 13th century Persian poet and the mystical friend who inspired much of his poetry.

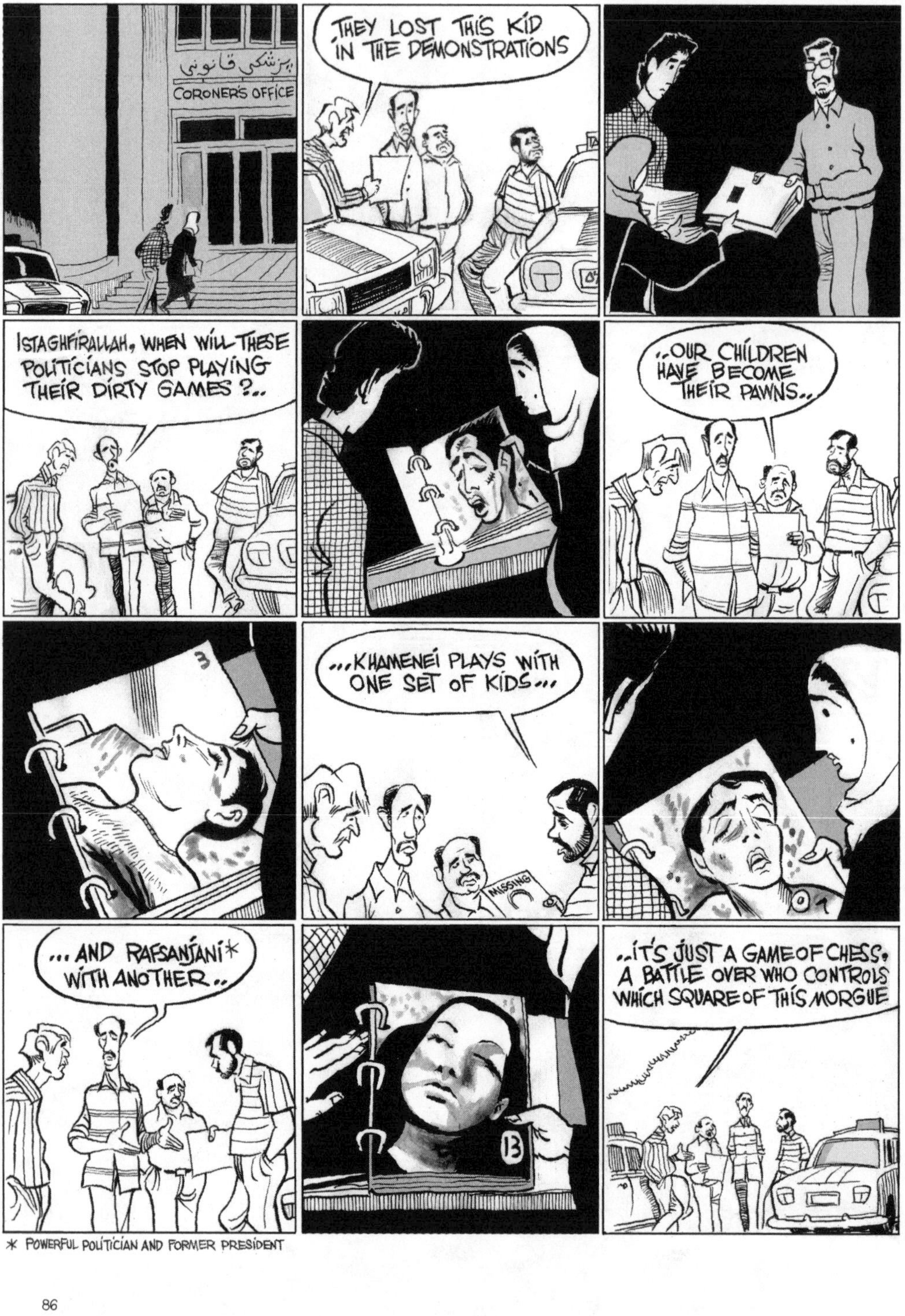
پزشکی قانونی
CORONER'S OFFICE
THEY LOST THIS KID IN THE DEMONSTRATIONS
ISTAGHFIRALLAH, WHEN WILL THESE POLITICIANS STOP PLAYING THEIR DIRTY GAMES ?..
..OUR CHILDREN HAVE BECOME THEIR PAWNS..
...KHAMENEI PLAYS WITH ONE SET OF KIDS...
MISSING
... AND RAFSANJANI* WITH ANOTHER..
13
..IT'S JUST A GAME OF CHESS, A BATTLE OVER WHO CONTROLS WHICH SQUARE OF THIS MORGUE

* POWERFUL POLITICIAN AND FORMER PRESIDENT

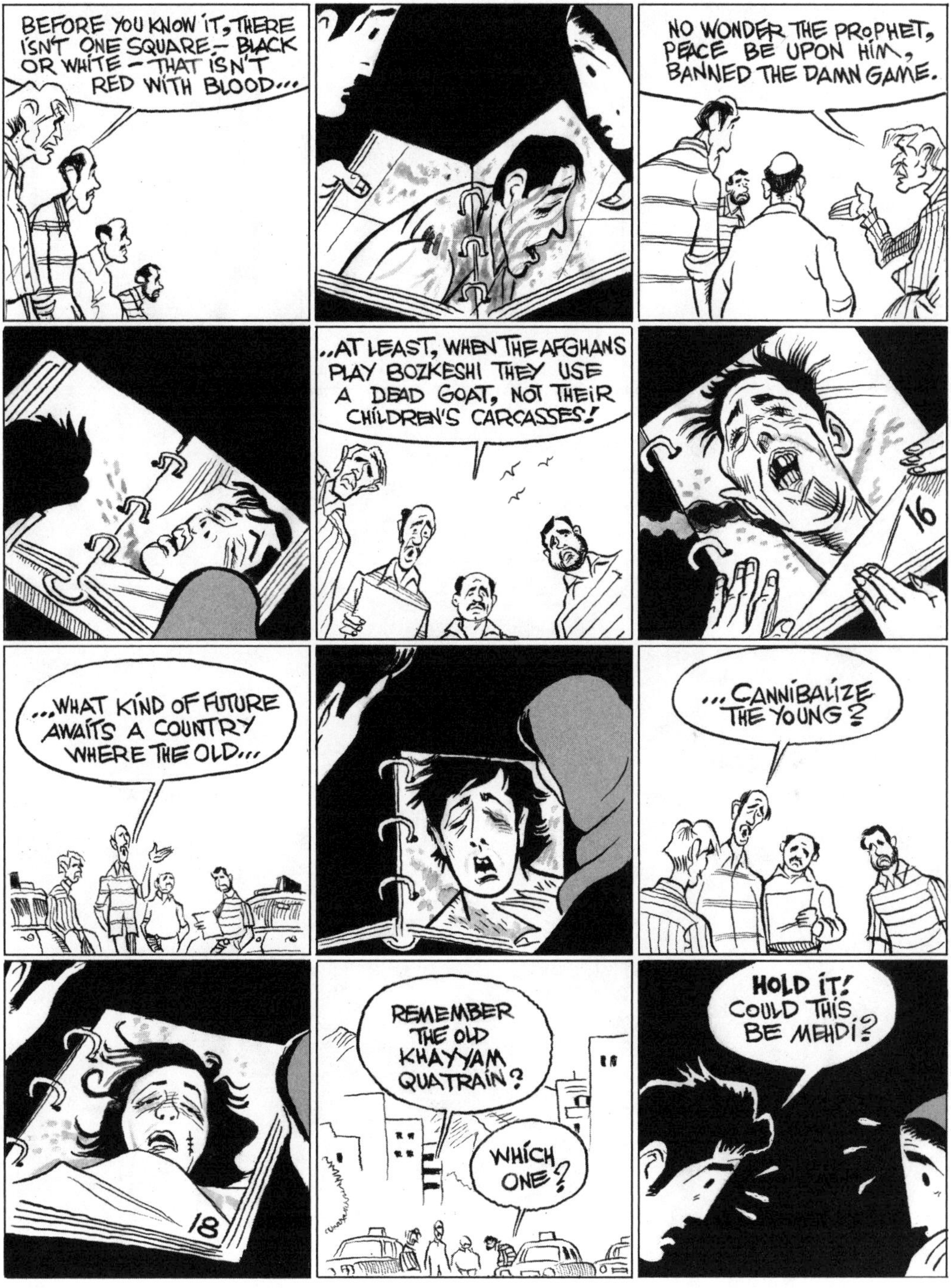
BEFORE YOU KNOW IT, THERE ISN'T ONE SQUARE – BLACK OR WHITE – THAT ISN'T RED WITH BLOOD...
NO WONDER THE PROPHET, PEACE BE UPON HIM, BANNED THE DAMN GAME.
..AT LEAST, WHEN THE AFGHANS PLAY BOZKESHI THEY USE A DEAD GOAT, NOT THEIR CHILDREN'S CARCASSES!
16
...WHAT KIND OF FUTURE AWAITS A COUNTRY WHERE THE OLD...
...CANNIBALIZE THE YOUNG?
18
REMEMBER THE OLD KHAYYAM QUATRAIN?
WHICH ONE?
HOLD IT! COULD THIS BE MEHDI?

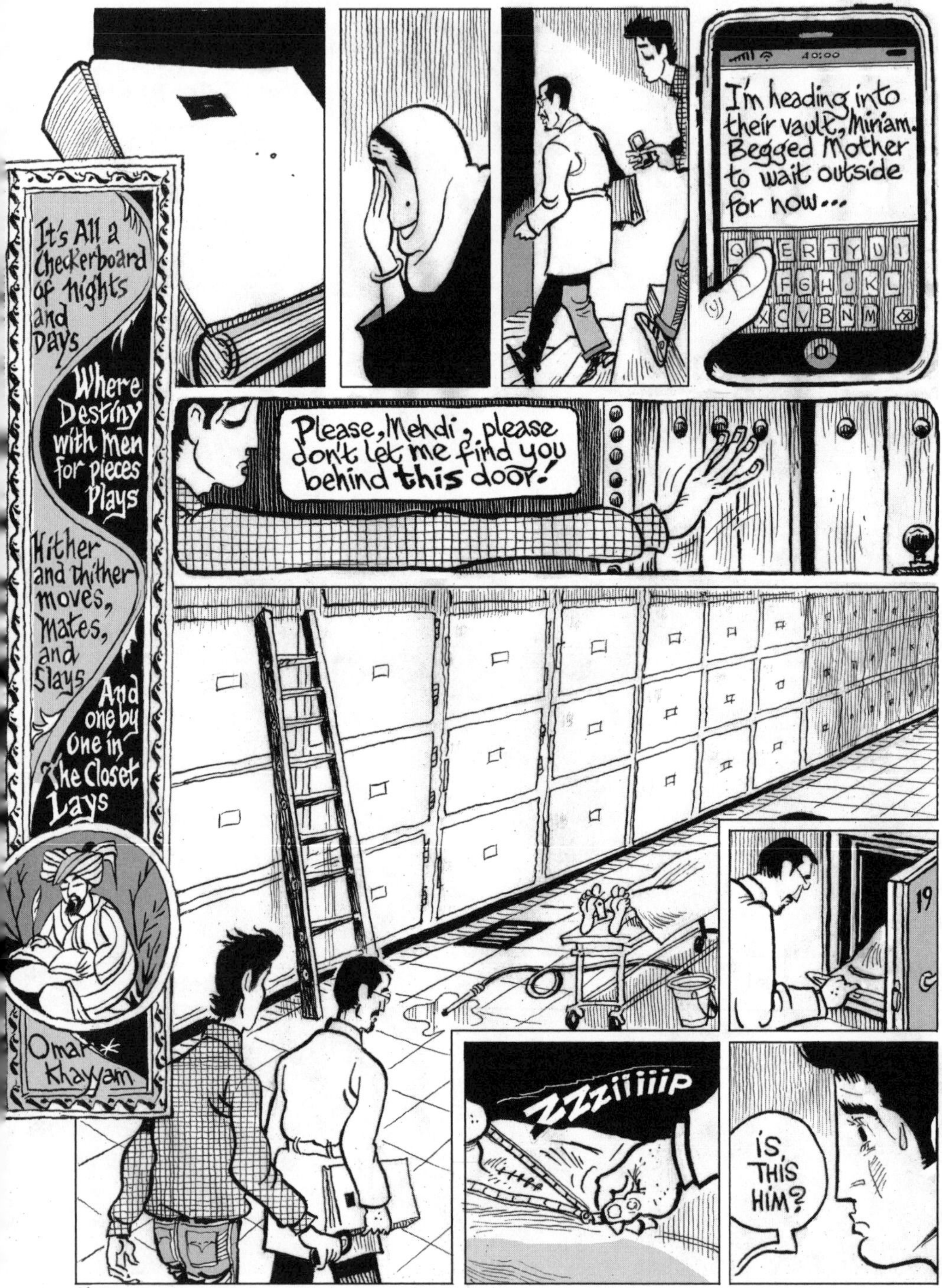
It's All a Checkerboard of nights and Days Where Destiny with Men for pieces Plays Hither and thither moves, Mates, and Slays And one by One in The Closet Lays
Omar* Khayyam
I'm heading into their vault, Miriam. Begged Mother to wait outside for now...
Please, Mehdi, please don't let me find you behind this door!
19
ZZZiiiiiP
IS THIS HIM?

* 12th century poet and mathematician.

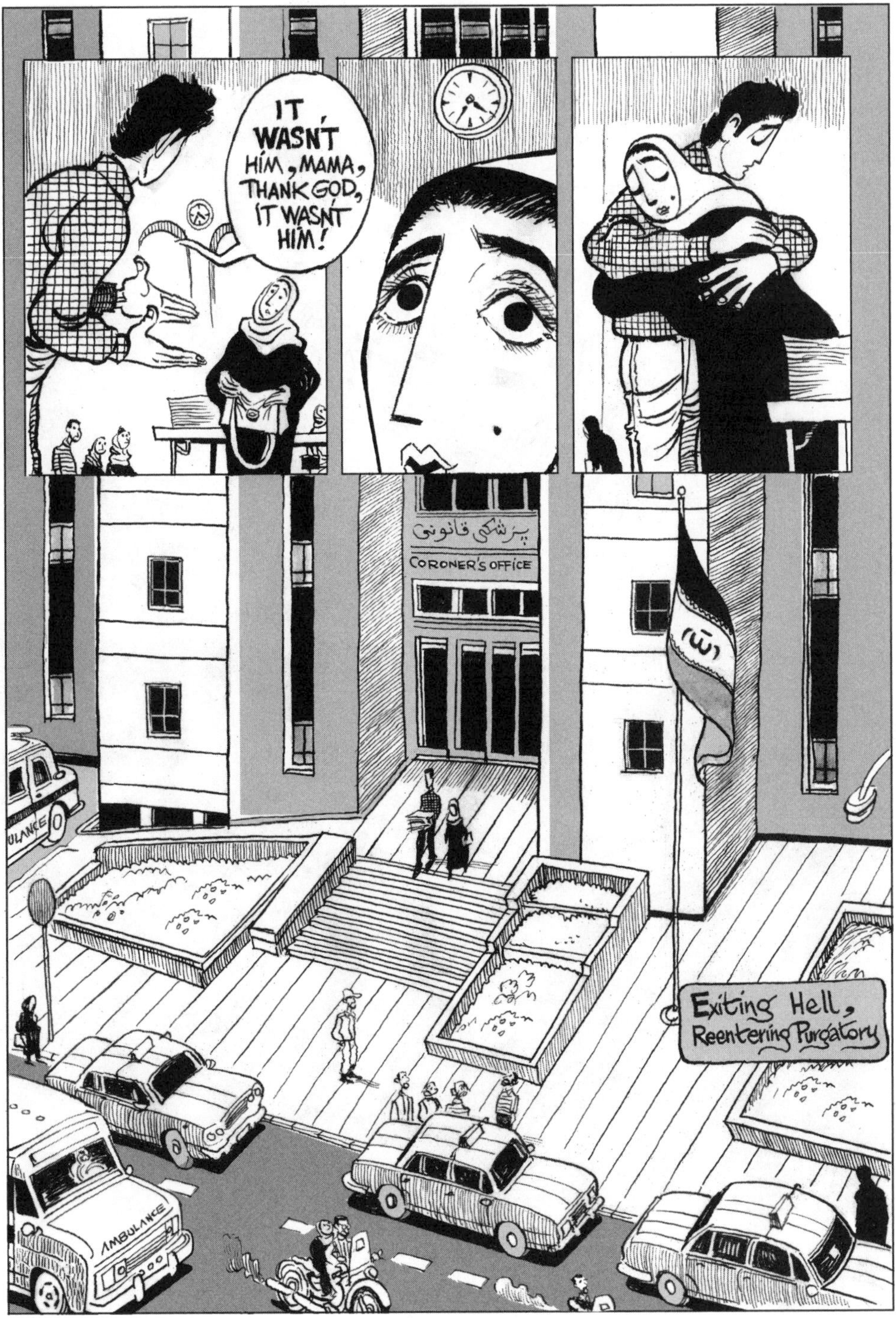
IT WASN'T HIM, MAMA, THANK GOD, IT WASN'T HIM!
پزشکی قانونی
CORONER'S OFFICE
Exiting Hell, Reentering Purgatory
AMBULANCE
ULANCE

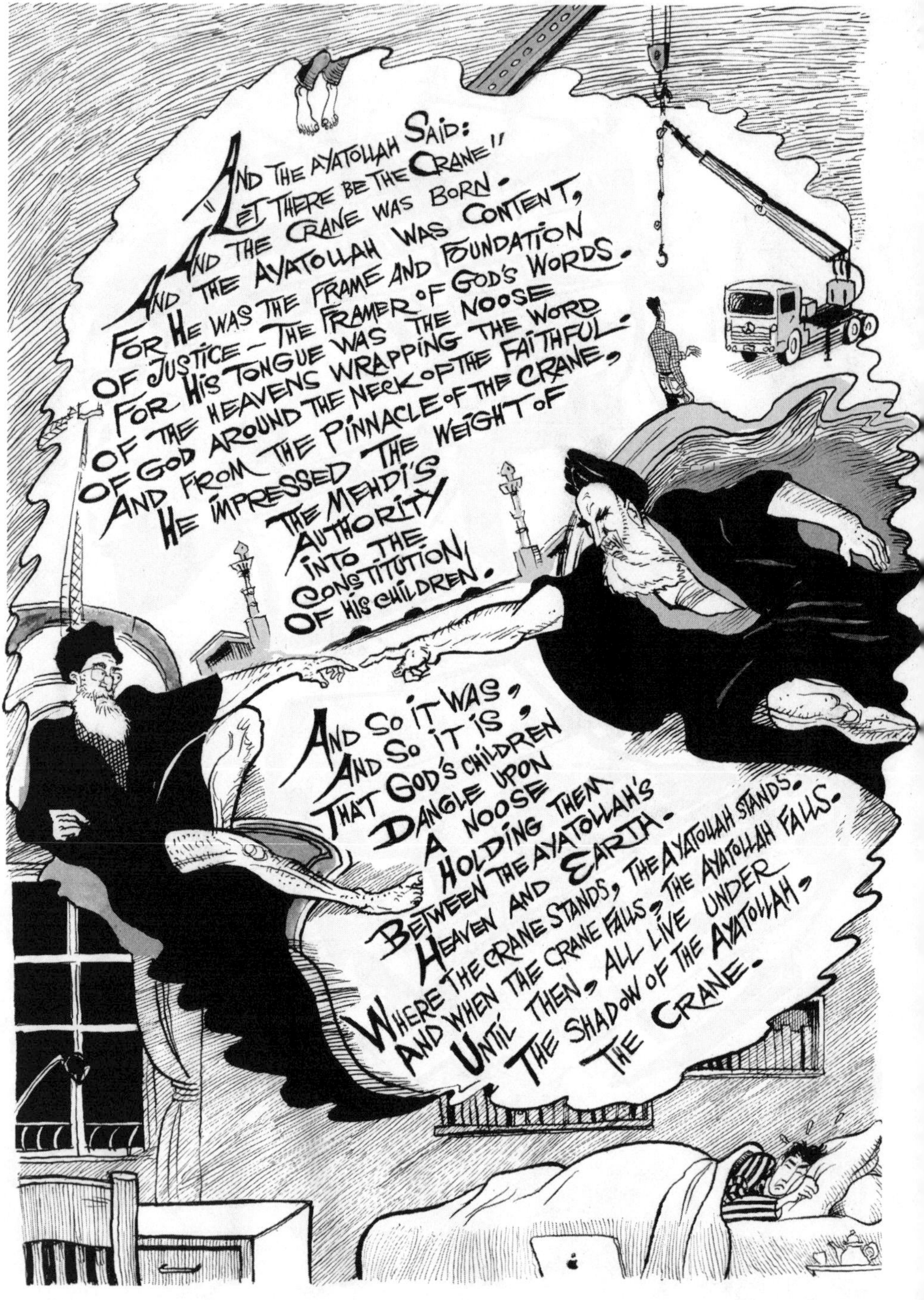
And the Ayatollah said:
"Let there be the Crane"
And the Crane was born.
And the Ayatollah was content,
For He was the frame and foundation
of justice - the framer of God's words.
For His tongue was the noose
of the heavens wrapping the word
of God around the neck of the faithful.
And from the pinnacle of the crane,
He impressed the weight of
the Mehdi's
authority
into the
constitution
of his children.
And so it was,
And so it is,
That God's children
Dangle upon
A noose
Holding them
Between the Ayatollah's
Heaven and Earth.
Where the crane stands, the Ayatollah stands.
And when the crane falls, the Ayatollah falls.
Until then, all live under
the shadow of the Ayatollah.
The crane.

MEHDI'S ROOM
CHAPTER SIX

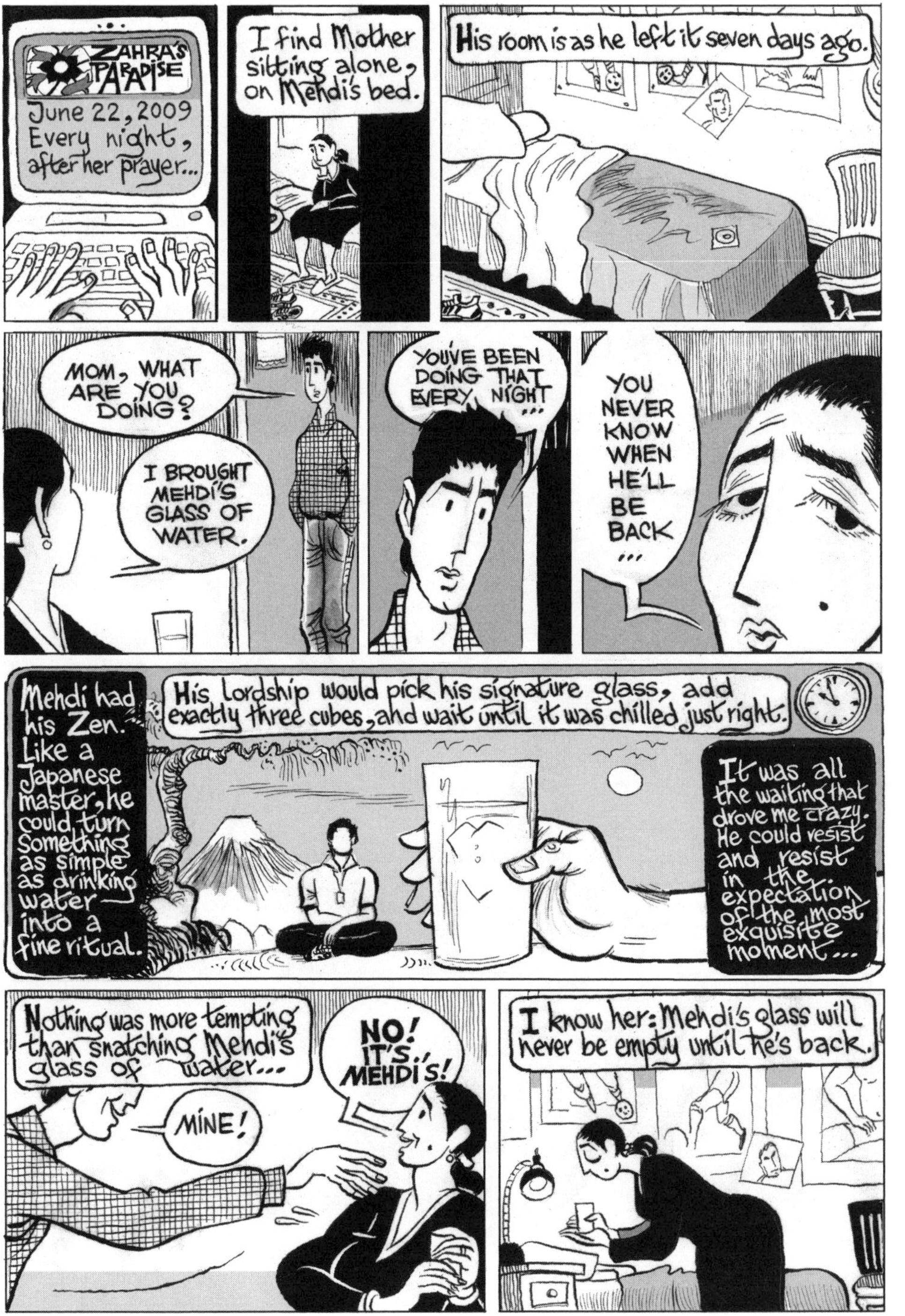
ZAHRA'S PARADISE
June 22, 2009
Every night, after her prayer...
I find Mother sitting alone, on Mehdi's bed.
His room is as he left it seven days ago.
MOM, WHAT ARE YOU DOING?
I BROUGHT MEHDI'S GLASS OF WATER.
YOU'VE BEEN DOING THAT EVERY NIGHT...
YOU NEVER KNOW WHEN HE'LL BE BACK...
Mehdi had his Zen. Like a Japanese master, he could turn something as simple as drinking water into a fine ritual.
His lordship would pick his signature glass, add exactly three cubes, and wait until it was chilled just right.
It was all the waiting that drove me crazy. He could resist and resist in the expectation of the most exquisite moment...
Nothing was more tempting than snatching Mehdi's glass of water...
MINE!
NO! IT'S MEHDI'S!
I know her: Mehdi's glass will never be empty until he's back.

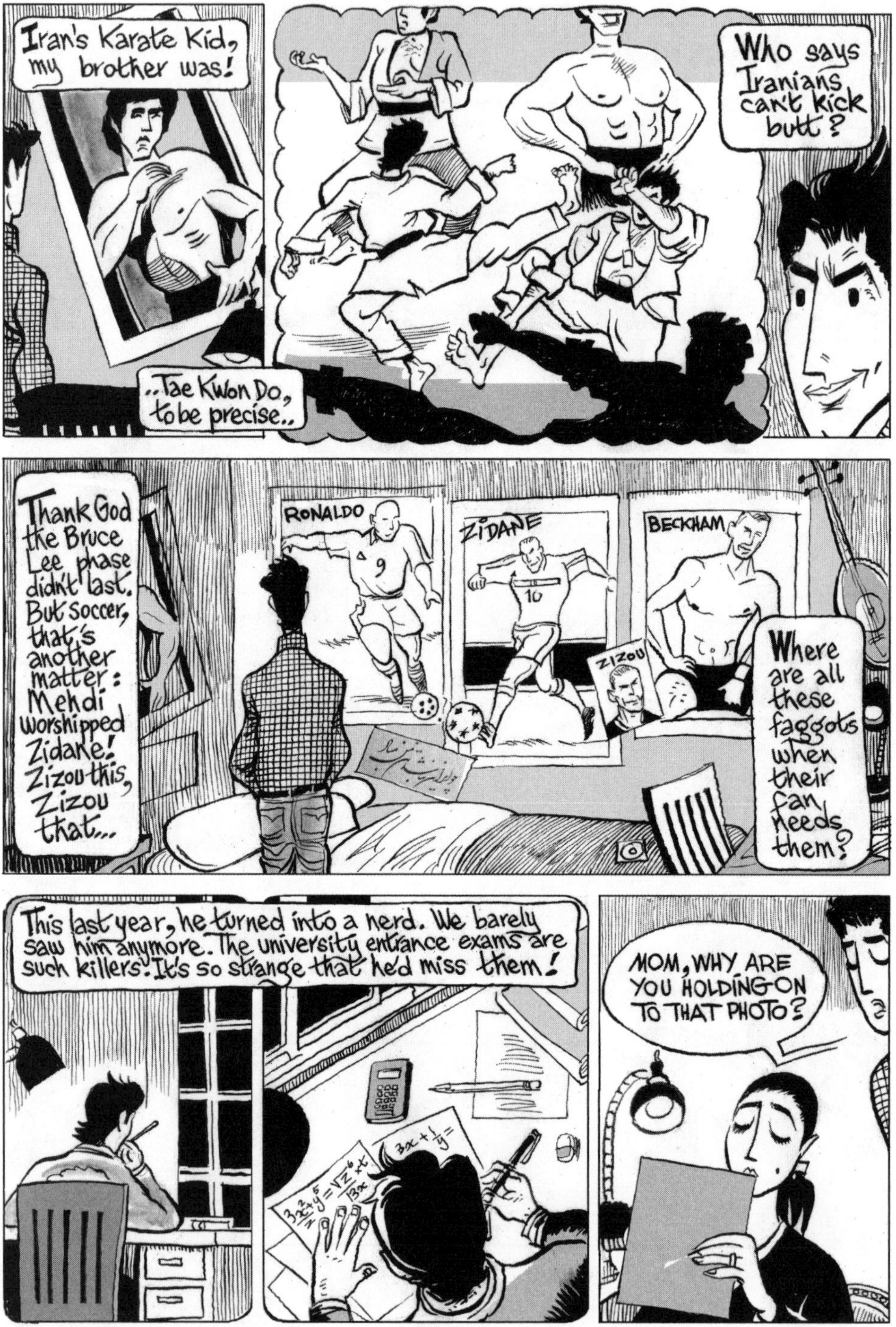

Iran's Karate Kid, my brother was!
..Tae Kwon Do, to be precise..
Who says Iranians can't kick butt?
Thank God the Bruce Lee phase didn't last. But soccer, that's another matter: Mehdi worshipped Zidane! Zizou this, Zizou that...
RONALDO
ZIDANE
BECKHAM
ZIZOU
Where are all these faggots when their fan needs them?
This last year, he turned into a nerd. We barely saw him anymore. The university entrance exams are such killers. It's so strange that he'd miss them!
MOM, WHY ARE YOU HOLDING ON TO THAT PHOTO?

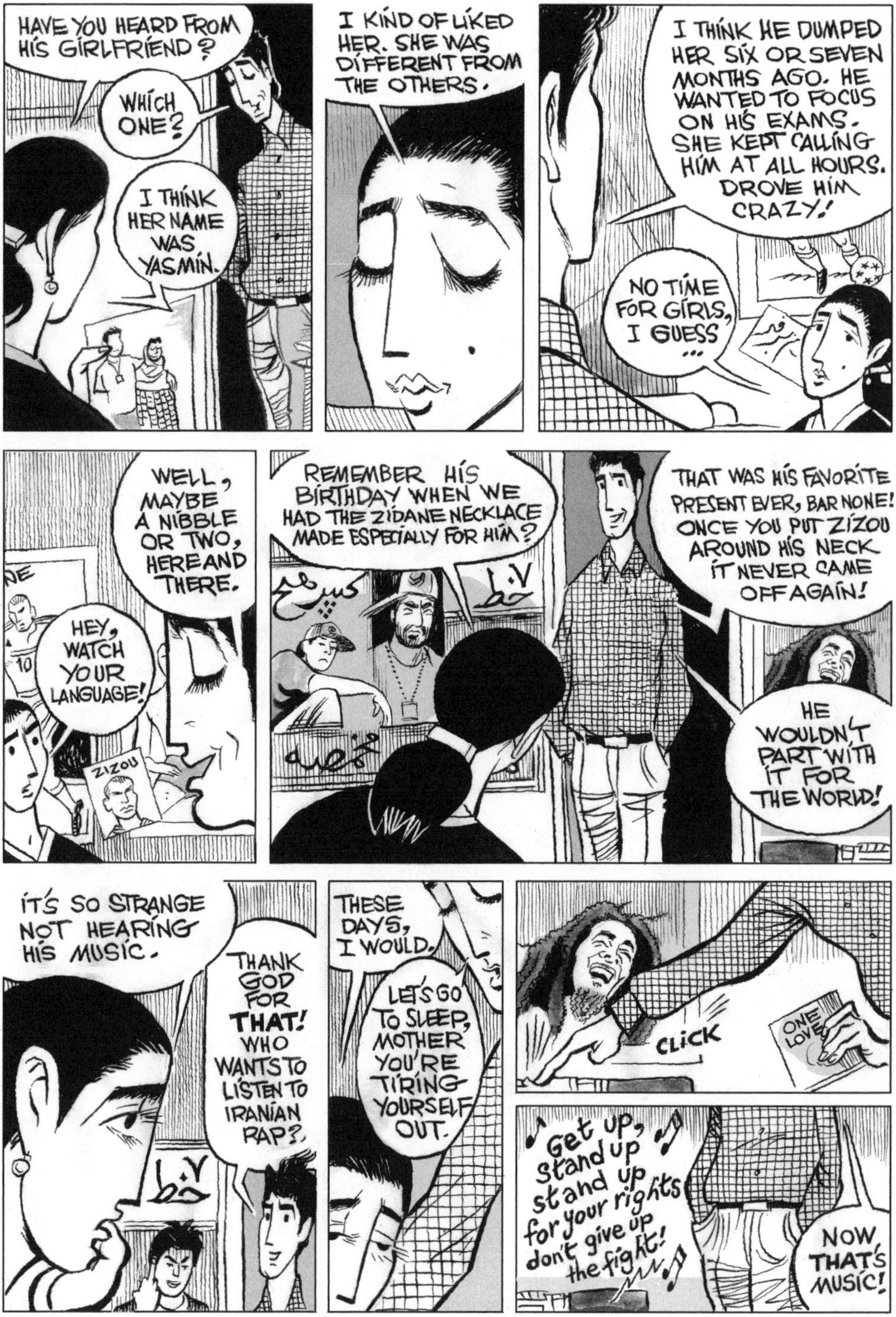

HAVE YOU HEARD FROM HIS GIRLFRIEND?
WHICH ONE?
I THINK HER NAME WAS YASMIN.
I KIND OF LIKED HER. SHE WAS DIFFERENT FROM THE OTHERS.
I THINK HE DUMPED HER SIX OR SEVEN MONTHS AGO. HE WANTED TO FOCUS ON HIS EXAMS. SHE KEPT CALLING HIM AT ALL HOURS. DROVE HIM CRAZY!
NO TIME FOR GIRLS, I GUESS...
WELL, MAYBE A NIBBLE OR TWO, HERE AND THERE.
HEY, WATCH YOUR LANGUAGE!
ZIZOU
REMEMBER HIS BIRTHDAY WHEN WE HAD THE ZIDANE NECKLACE MADE ESPECIALLY FOR HIM?
THAT WAS HIS FAVORITE PRESENT EVER, BAR NONE! ONCE YOU PUT ZIZOU AROUND HIS NECK IT NEVER CAME OFF AGAIN!
HE WOULDN'T PART WITH IT FOR THE WORLD!
IT'S SO STRANGE NOT HEARING HIS MUSIC.
THANK GOD FOR THAT! WHO WANTS TO LISTEN TO IRANIAN RAP?
THESE DAYS, I WOULD.
LET'S GO TO SLEEP, MOTHER. YOU'RE TIRING YOURSELF OUT.
CLICK
ONE LOVE
Get up, stand up stand up for your rights don't give up the fight!
NOW THAT'S MUSIC!

THE REVOLUTIONARY COURT

CHAPTER SEVEN

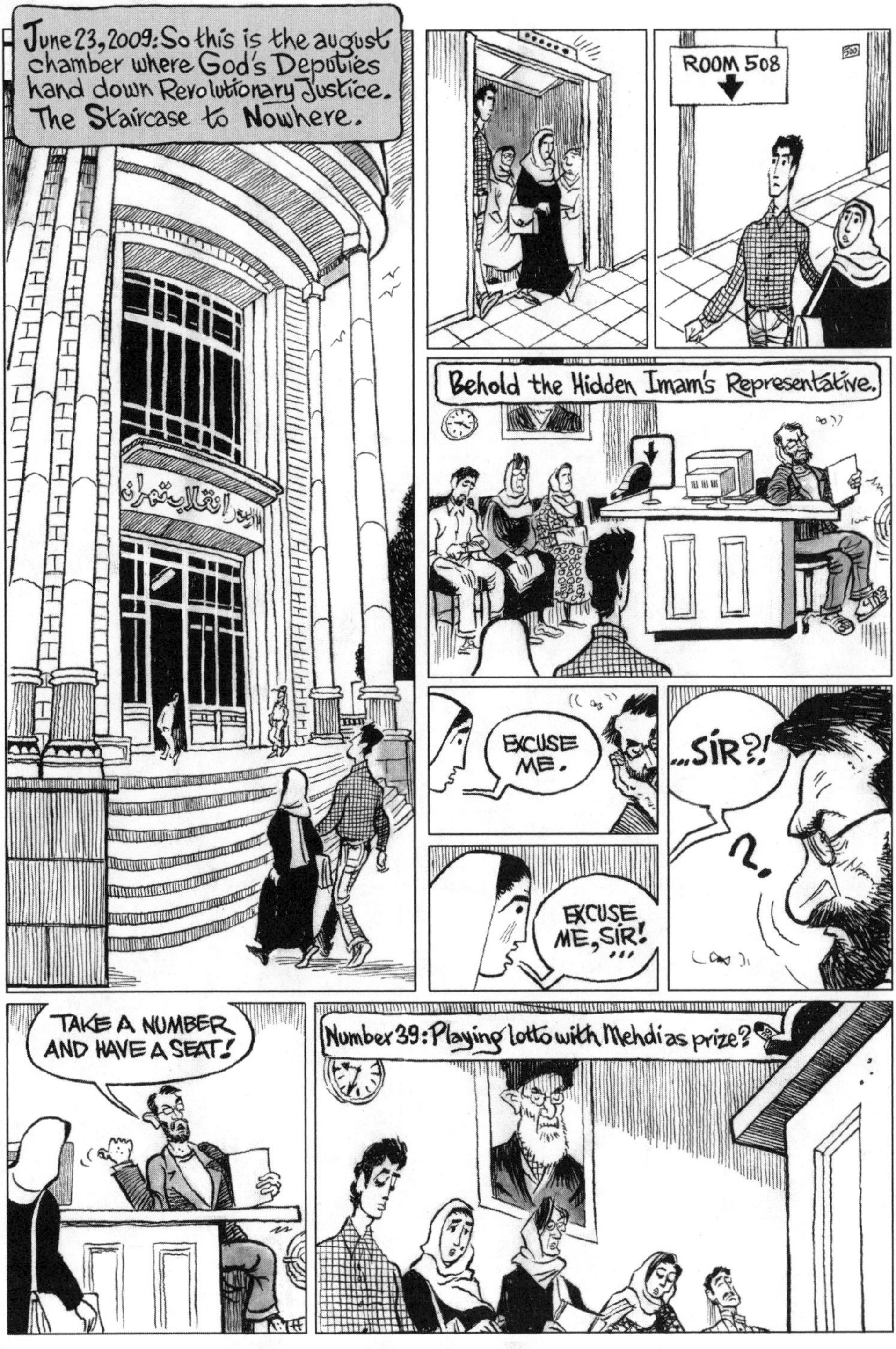
June 23, 2009: So this is the august chamber where God's Deputies hand down Revolutionary Justice. The Staircase to Nowhere.
ROOM 508
Behold the Hidden Imam's Representative.
EXCUSE ME.
...SIR?!
EXCUSE ME, SIR! ...
TAKE A NUMBER AND HAVE A SEAT!
Number 39: Playing lotto with Mehdi as prize?

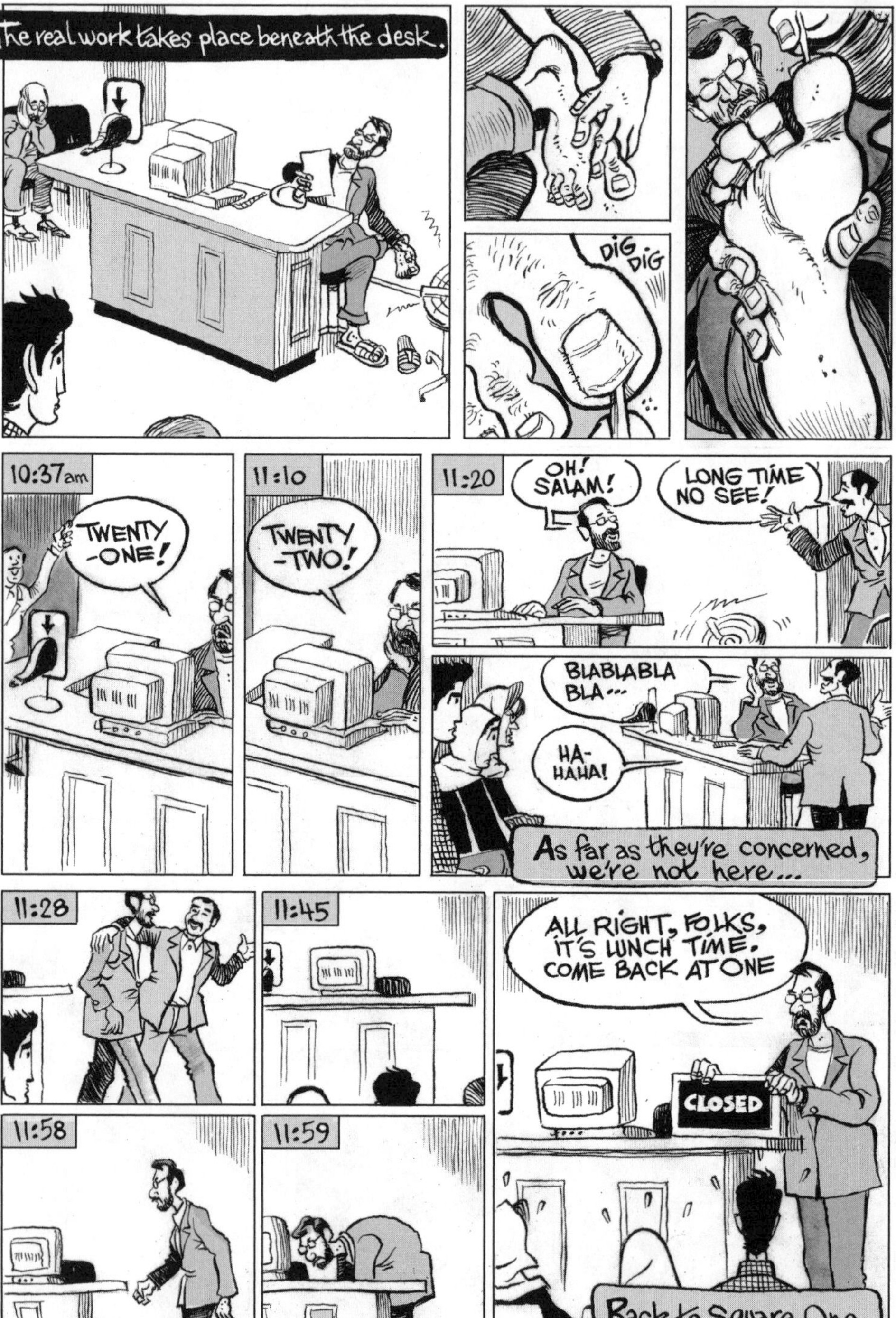
The real work takes place beneath the desk.
DIG DIG
10:37am
TWENTY -ONE!
11:10
TWENTY -TWO!
11:20
OH! SALAM!
LONG TIME NO SEE!
BLABLABLA BLA...
HA-HAHA!
As far as they're concerned, we're not here...
11:28
11:45
11:58
11:59
ALL RIGHT, FOLKS, IT'S LUNCH TIME. COME BACK AT ONE
CLOSED
Back to Square One...

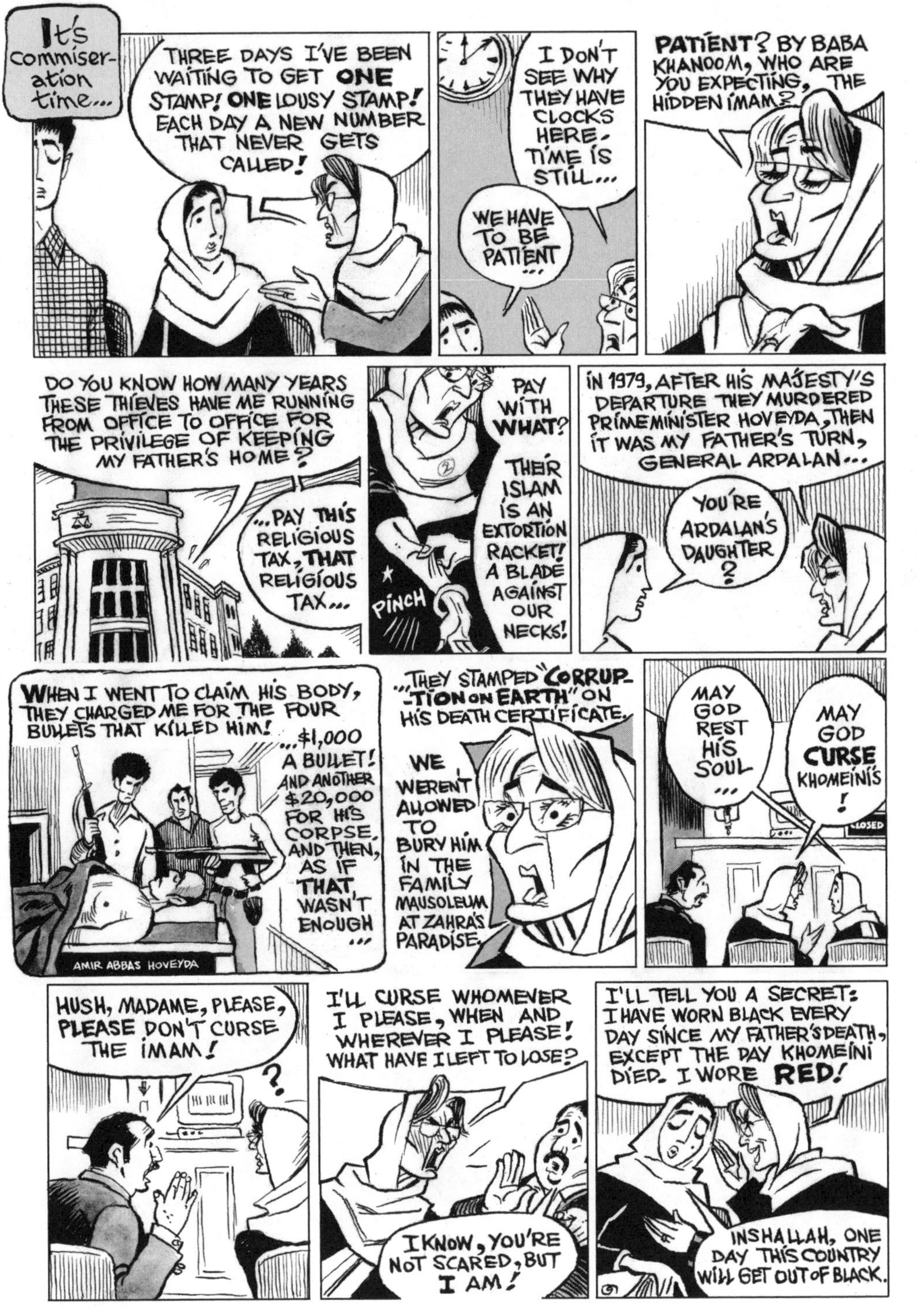
It's commiseration time...
THREE DAYS I'VE BEEN WAITING TO GET ONE STAMP! ONE LOUSY STAMP! EACH DAY A NEW NUMBER THAT NEVER GETS CALLED!
I DON'T SEE WHY THEY HAVE CLOCKS HERE. TIME IS STILL...
WE HAVE TO BE PATIENT...
PATIENT? BY BABA KHANOOM, WHO ARE YOU EXPECTING, THE HIDDEN IMAM?
DO YOU KNOW HOW MANY YEARS THESE THIEVES HAVE ME RUNNING FROM OFFICE TO OFFICE FOR THE PRIVILEGE OF KEEPING MY FATHER'S HOME?
...PAY THIS RELIGIOUS TAX, THAT RELIGIOUS TAX...
PAY WITH WHAT?
THEIR ISLAM IS AN EXTORTION RACKET! A BLADE AGAINST OUR NECKS!
PINCH
IN 1979, AFTER HIS MAJESTY'S DEPARTURE THEY MURDERED PRIME MINISTER HOVEYDA, THEN IT WAS MY FATHER'S TURN, GENERAL ARDALAN...
YOU'RE ARDALAN'S DAUGHTER?
WHEN I WENT TO CLAIM HIS BODY, THEY CHARGED ME FOR THE FOUR BULLETS THAT KILLED HIM!
...$1,000 A BULLET! AND ANOTHER $20,000 FOR HIS CORPSE. AND THEN, AS IF THAT WASN'T ENOUGH...
AMIR ABBAS HOVEYDA
...THEY STAMPED "CORRUPTION ON EARTH" ON HIS DEATH CERTIFICATE.
WE WEREN'T ALLOWED TO BURY HIM IN THE FAMILY MAUSOLEUM AT ZAHRA'S PARADISE.
MAY GOD REST HIS SOUL...
MAY GOD CURSE KHOMEINI'S!
CLOSED
HUSH, MADAME, PLEASE, PLEASE DON'T CURSE THE IMAM!
?
I'LL CURSE WHOMEVER I PLEASE, WHEN AND WHEREVER I PLEASE! WHAT HAVE I LEFT TO LOSE?
I KNOW, YOU'RE NOT SCARED, BUT I AM!
I'LL TELL YOU A SECRET: I HAVE WORN BLACK EVERY DAY SINCE MY FATHER'S DEATH, EXCEPT THE DAY KHOMEINI DIED. I WORE RED!
INSHALLAH, ONE DAY THIS COUNTRY WILL GET OUT OF BLACK.

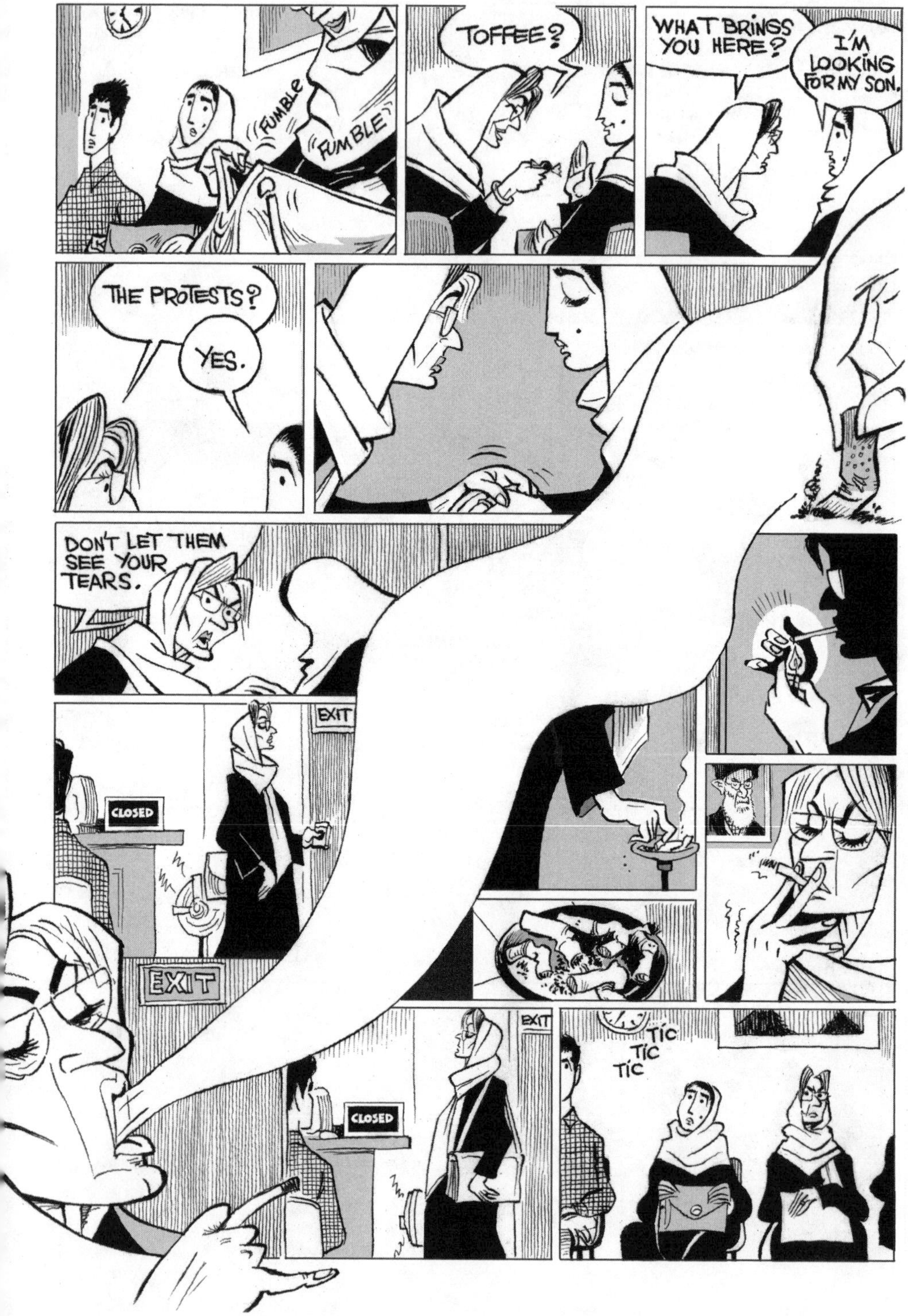
FUMBLE
FUMBLE
TOFFEE?
WHAT BRINGS YOU HERE?
I'M LOOKING FOR MY SON.
THE PROTESTS?
YES.
DON'T LET THEM SEE YOUR TEARS.
EXIT
CLOSED
EXIT
EXIT
CLOSED
TIC
TIC
TIC

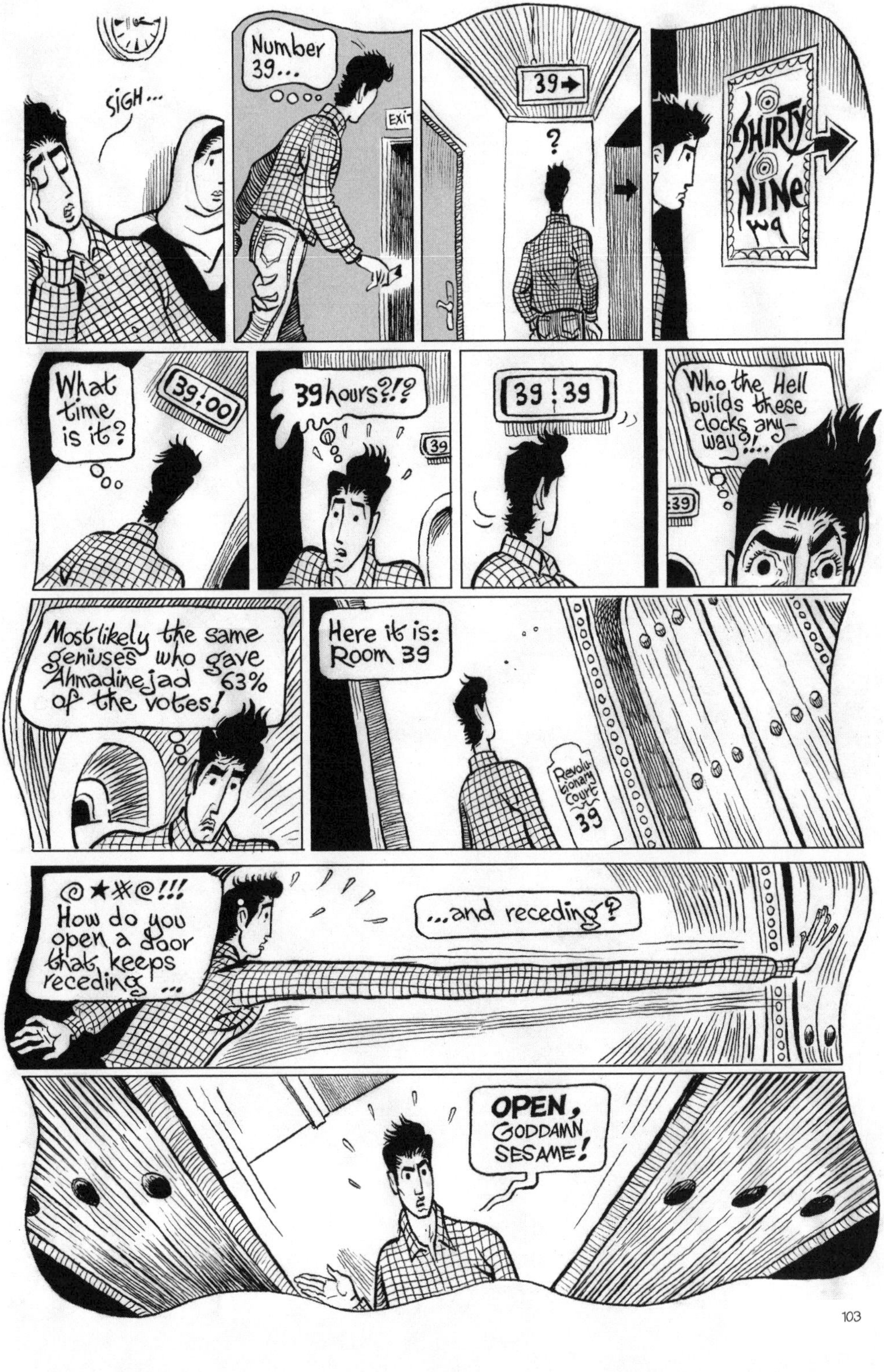
SIGH...
Number 39...
EXIT
39
?
THIRTY NINE
٣٩
What time is it?
39:00
39 hours?!?
39
39:39
Who the Hell builds these clocks anyway?!...
39
Most likely the same geniuses who gave Ahmadinejad 63% of the votes!
Here it is: Room 39
Revolutionary Court 39
@★#@!!! How do you open a door that keeps receding...
...and receding?
OPEN, GODDAMN SESAME!

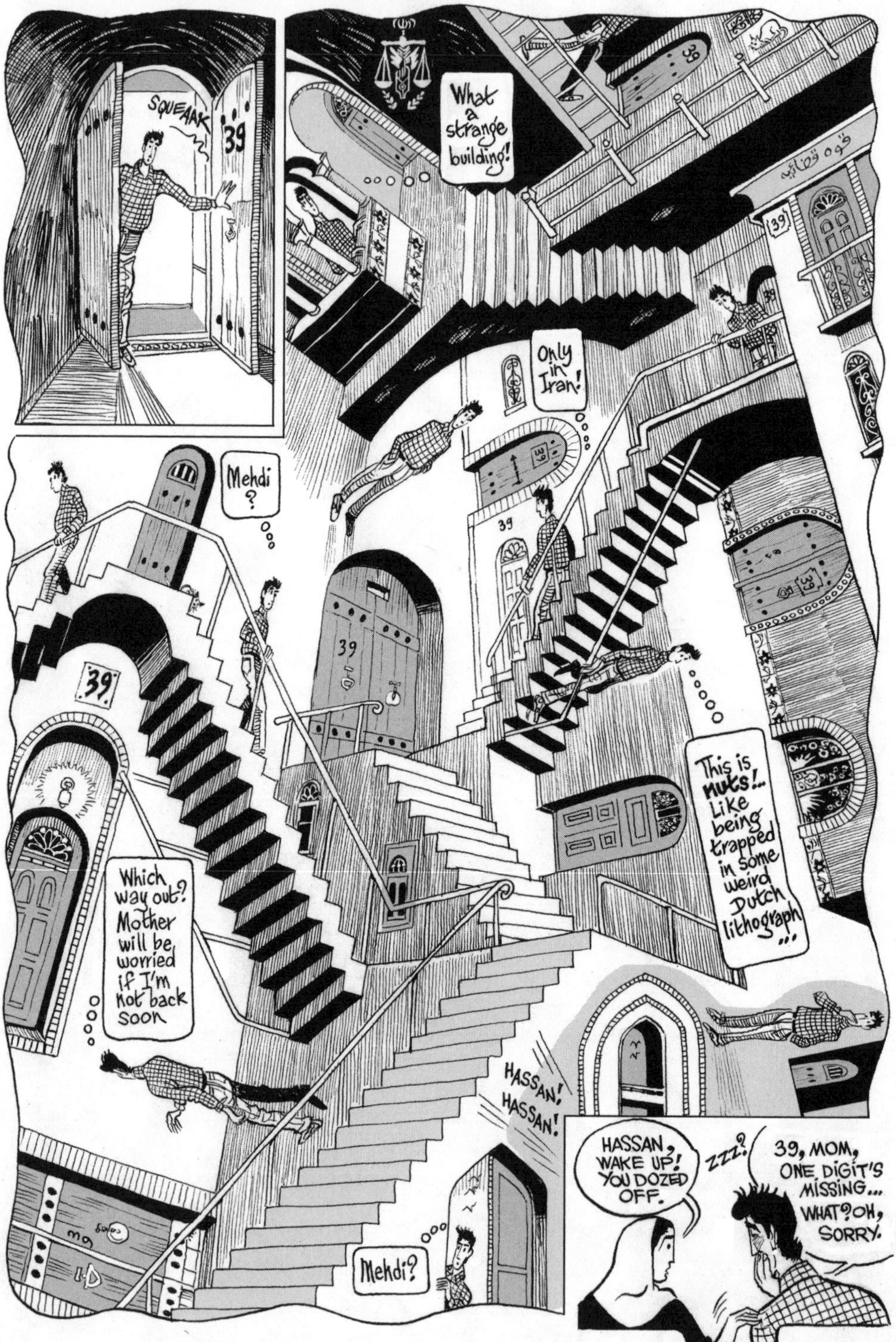
SQUEAAK
39
What a strange building!
Only in Iran!
Mehdi?
Which way out? Mother will be worried if I'm not back soon
This is nuts!... Like being trapped in some weird Dutch lithograph...
HASSAN! HASSAN!
Mehdi?
HASSAN, WAKE UP! YOU DOZED OFF.
ZZZ?
39, MOM, ONE DIGIT'S MISSING... WHAT? OH, SORRY.

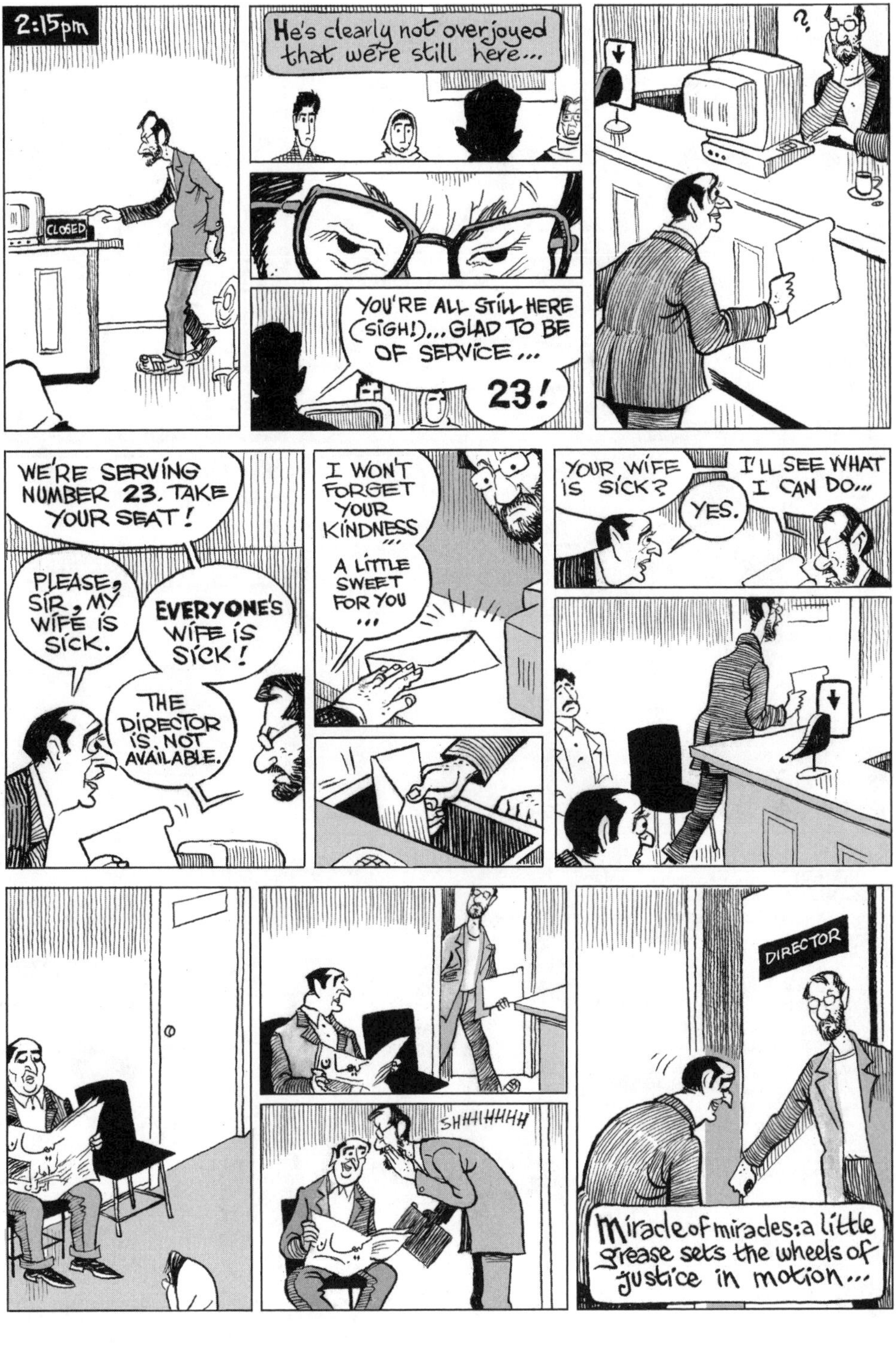
2:15pm
CLOSED
He's clearly not overjoyed that we're still here...
YOU'RE ALL STILL HERE (SIGH!)... GLAD TO BE OF SERVICE...
23!
WE'RE SERVING NUMBER 23. TAKE YOUR SEAT!
PLEASE, SIR, MY WIFE IS SICK.
EVERYONE'S WIFE IS SICK!
THE DIRECTOR IS NOT AVAILABLE.
I WON'T FORGET YOUR KINDNESS...
A LITTLE SWEET FOR YOU...
YOUR WIFE IS SICK?
YES.
I'LL SEE WHAT I CAN DO...
SHHHHHHH
DIRECTOR
Miracle of miracles: a little grease sets the wheels of justice in motion...

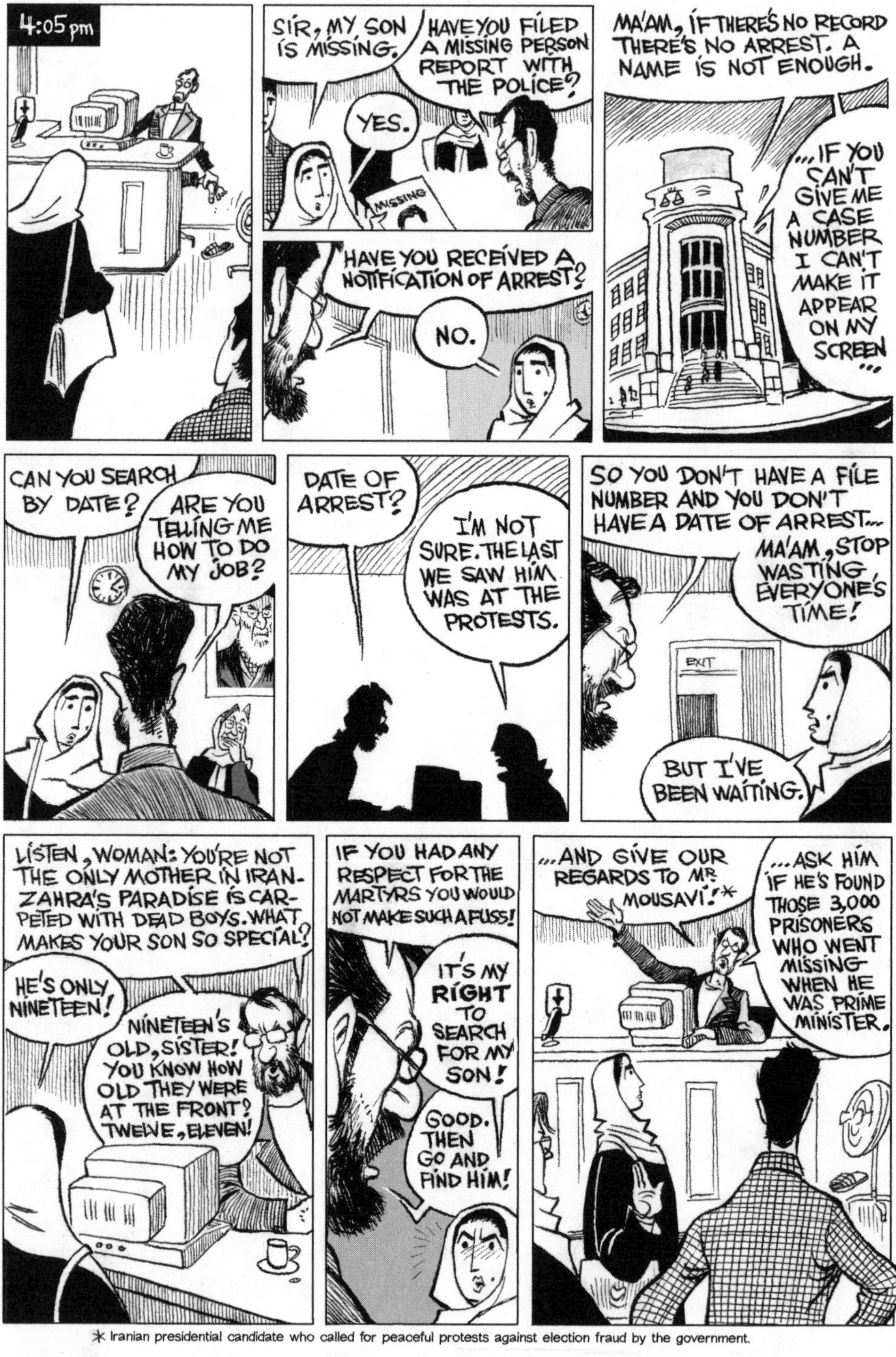
4:05 pm
SIR, MY SON IS MISSING.
HAVE YOU FILED A MISSING PERSON REPORT WITH THE POLICE?
YES.
MISSING
HAVE YOU RECEIVED A NOTIFICATION OF ARREST?
NO.
MA'AM, IF THERE'S NO RECORD THERE'S NO ARREST. A NAME IS NOT ENOUGH.
...IF YOU CAN'T GIVE ME A CASE NUMBER I CAN'T MAKE IT APPEAR ON MY SCREEN...
CAN YOU SEARCH BY DATE?
ARE YOU TELLING ME HOW TO DO MY JOB?
DATE OF ARREST?
I'M NOT SURE. THE LAST WE SAW HIM WAS AT THE PROTESTS.
SO YOU DON'T HAVE A FILE NUMBER AND YOU DON'T HAVE A DATE OF ARREST...
MA'AM, STOP WASTING EVERYONE'S TIME!
EXIT
BUT I'VE BEEN WAITING.
LISTEN, WOMAN: YOU'RE NOT THE ONLY MOTHER IN IRAN. ZAHRA'S PARADISE IS CARPETED WITH DEAD BOYS. WHAT MAKES YOUR SON SO SPECIAL?
HE'S ONLY NINETEEN!
NINETEEN'S OLD, SISTER! YOU KNOW HOW OLD THEY WERE AT THE FRONT? TWELVE, ELEVEN!
IF YOU HAD ANY RESPECT FOR THE MARTYRS YOU WOULD NOT MAKE SUCH A FUSS!
IT'S MY **RIGHT** TO SEARCH FOR MY SON!
GOOD. THEN GO AND FIND HIM!
...AND GIVE OUR REGARDS TO MR. MOUSAVI!*
...ASK HIM IF HE'S FOUND THOSE 3,000 PRISONERS WHO WENT MISSING WHEN HE WAS PRIME MINISTER.

* Iranian presidential candidate who called for peaceful protests against election fraud by the government.

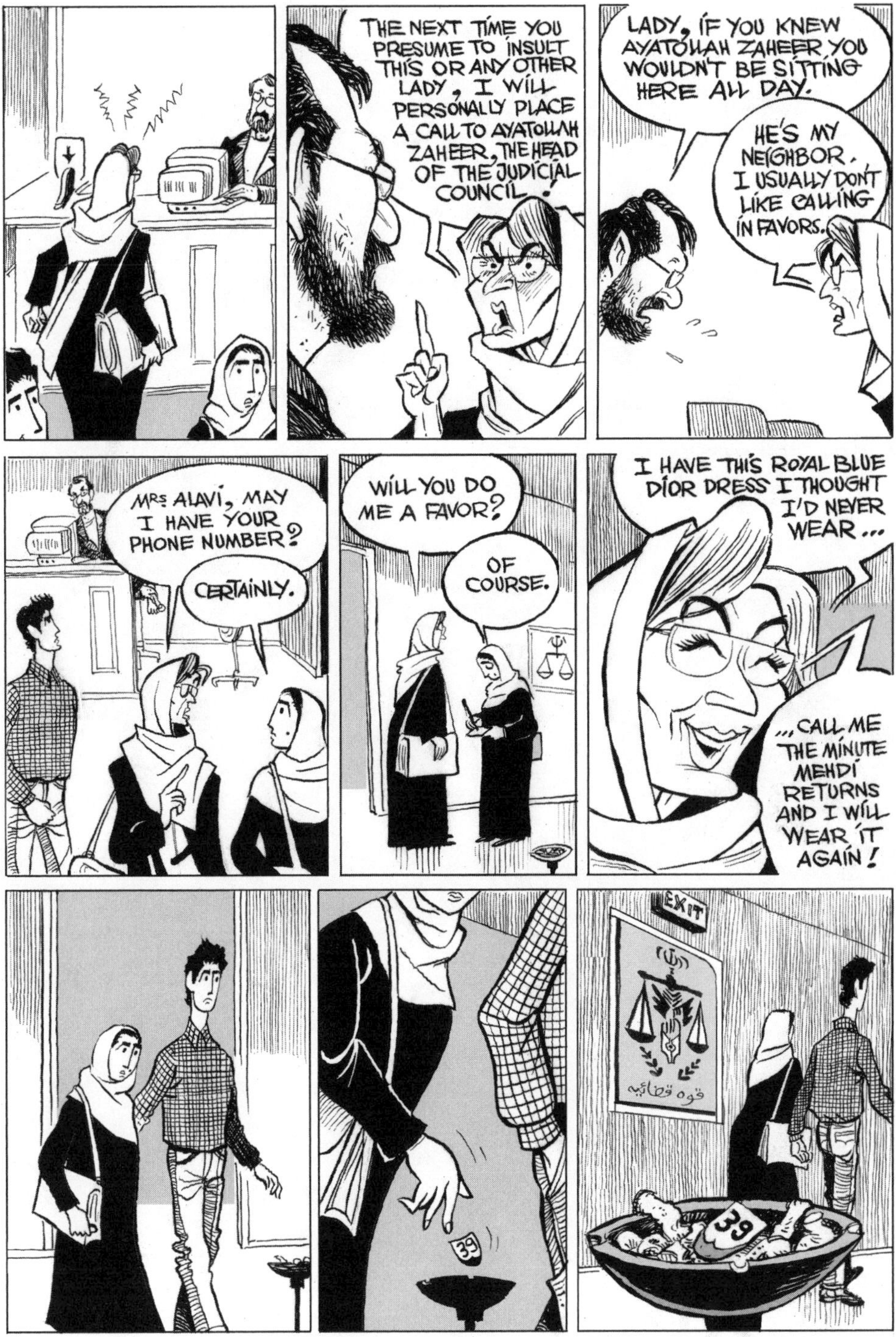
THE NEXT TIME YOU PRESUME TO INSULT THIS OR ANY OTHER LADY, I WILL PERSONALLY PLACE A CALL TO AYATOLLAH ZAHEER, THE HEAD OF THE JUDICIAL COUNCIL!
LADY, IF YOU KNEW AYATOLLAH ZAHEER YOU WOULDN'T BE SITTING HERE ALL DAY.
HE'S MY NEIGHBOR. I USUALLY DON'T LIKE CALLING IN FAVORS.
MRS. ALAVI, MAY I HAVE YOUR PHONE NUMBER?
CERTAINLY.
WILL YOU DO ME A FAVOR?
OF COURSE.
I HAVE THIS ROYAL BLUE DIOR DRESS I THOUGHT I'D NEVER WEAR...
...CALL ME THE MINUTE MEHDI RETURNS AND I WILL WEAR IT AGAIN!
EXIT
قوه قضائیه
39

THE MALEK QUR'AN

CHAPTER EIGHT

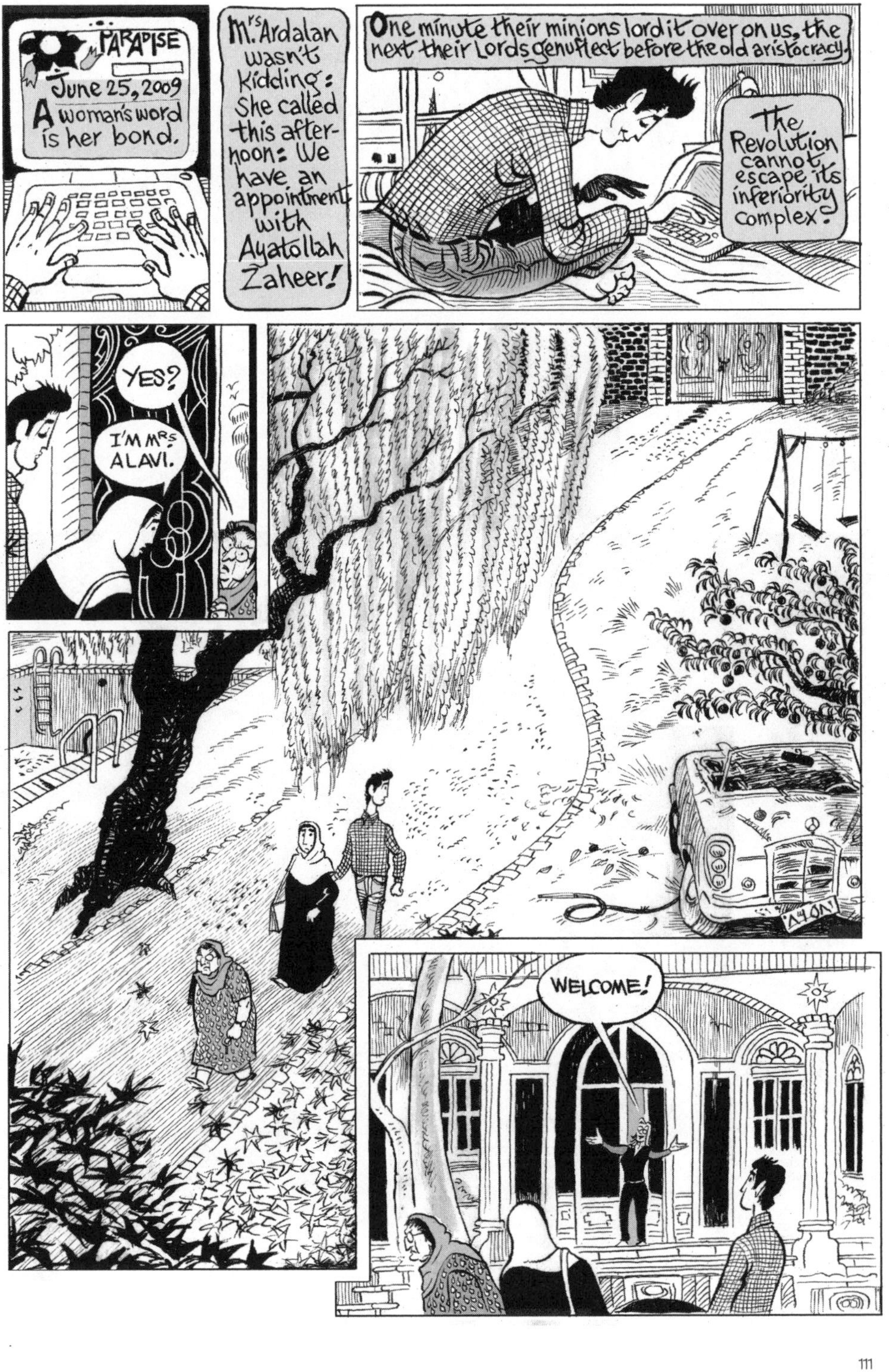
PARADISE
June 25, 2009
A woman's word is her bond.
Mrs. Ardalan wasn't kidding: She called this afternoon: We have an appointment with Ayatollah Zaheer!
One minute their minions lord it over on us, the next their Lords genuflect before the old aristocracy.
The Revolution cannot escape its inferiority complex!
YES?
I'M MRS ALAVI.
WELCOME!

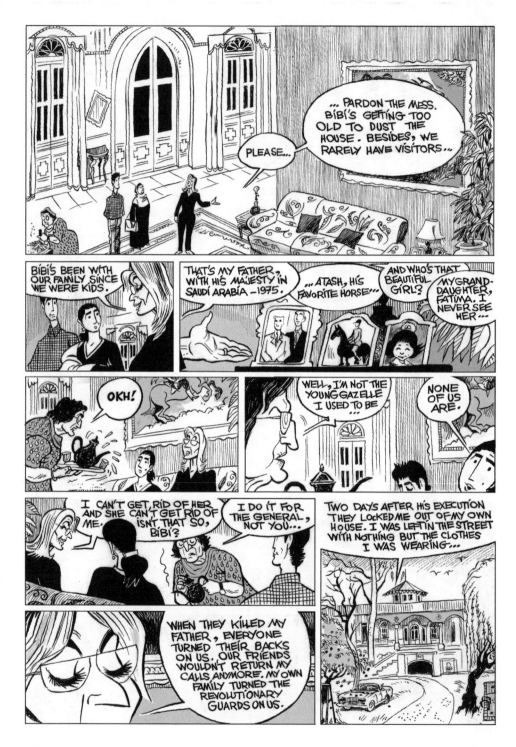

... PARDON THE MESS. BIBI'S GETTING TOO OLD TO DUST THE HOUSE. BESIDES, WE RARELY HAVE VISITORS...

PLEASE...

BIBI'S BEEN WITH OUR FAMILY SINCE WE WERE KIDS.

THAT'S MY FATHER WITH HIS MAJESTY IN SAUDI ARABIA - 1975.

... ATASH, HIS FAVORITE HORSE...

AND WHO'S THAT BEAUTIFUL GIRL?

MY GRAND-DAUGHTER, FATIMA. I NEVER SEE HER...

OKH!

WELL, I'M NOT THE YOUNG GAZELLE I USED TO BE...

NONE OF US ARE.

I CAN'T GET RID OF HER AND SHE CAN'T GET RID OF ME. ISN'T THAT SO, BIBI?

I DO IT FOR THE GENERAL, NOT YOU...

TWO DAYS AFTER HIS EXECUTION THEY LOCKED ME OUT OF MY OWN HOUSE. I WAS LEFT IN THE STREET WITH NOTHING BUT THE CLOTHES I WAS WEARING...

WHEN THEY KILLED MY FATHER, EVERYONE TURNED THEIR BACKS ON US. OUR FRIENDS WOULDN'T RETURN MY CALLS ANYMORE. MY OWN FAMILY TURNED THE REVOLUTIONARY GUARDS ON US.

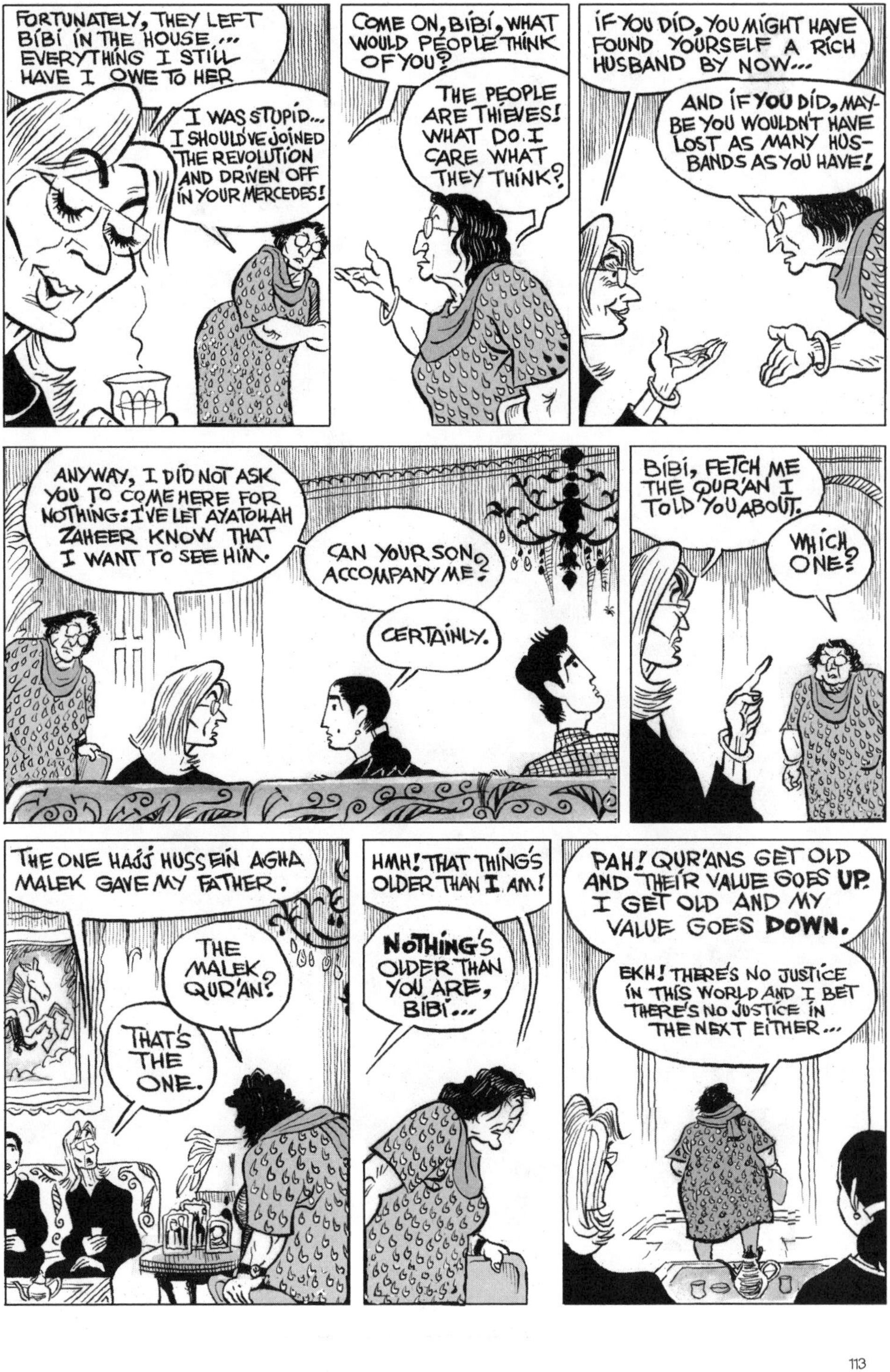
FORTUNATELY, THEY LEFT BÍBÍ IN THE HOUSE ... EVERYTHING I STILL HAVE I OWE TO HER
I WAS STUPID... I SHOULD'VE JOINED THE REVOLUTION AND DRIVEN OFF IN YOUR MERCEDES!
COME ON, BÍBÍ, WHAT WOULD PEOPLE THINK OF YOU?
THE PEOPLE ARE THIEVES! WHAT DO I CARE WHAT THEY THINK?
IF YOU DID, YOU MIGHT HAVE FOUND YOURSELF A RICH HUSBAND BY NOW...
AND IF YOU DID, MAYBE YOU WOULDN'T HAVE LOST AS MANY HUSBANDS AS YOU HAVE!
ANYWAY, I DID NOT ASK YOU TO COME HERE FOR NOTHING: I'VE LET AYATOLLAH ZAHEER KNOW THAT I WANT TO SEE HIM.
CAN YOUR SON ACCOMPANY ME?
CERTAINLY.
BÍBÍ, FETCH ME THE QUR'AN I TOLD YOU ABOUT.
WHICH ONE?
THE ONE HAJJ HUSSEIN AGHA MALEK GAVE MY FATHER.
THE MALEK QUR'AN?
THAT'S THE ONE.
HMH! THAT THING'S OLDER THAN I AM!
NOTHING'S OLDER THAN YOU ARE, BÍBÍ...
PAH! QUR'ANS GET OLD AND THEIR VALUE GOES UP. I GET OLD AND MY VALUE GOES DOWN.
EKH! THERE'S NO JUSTICE IN THIS WORLD AND I BET THERE'S NO JUSTICE IN THE NEXT EITHER...

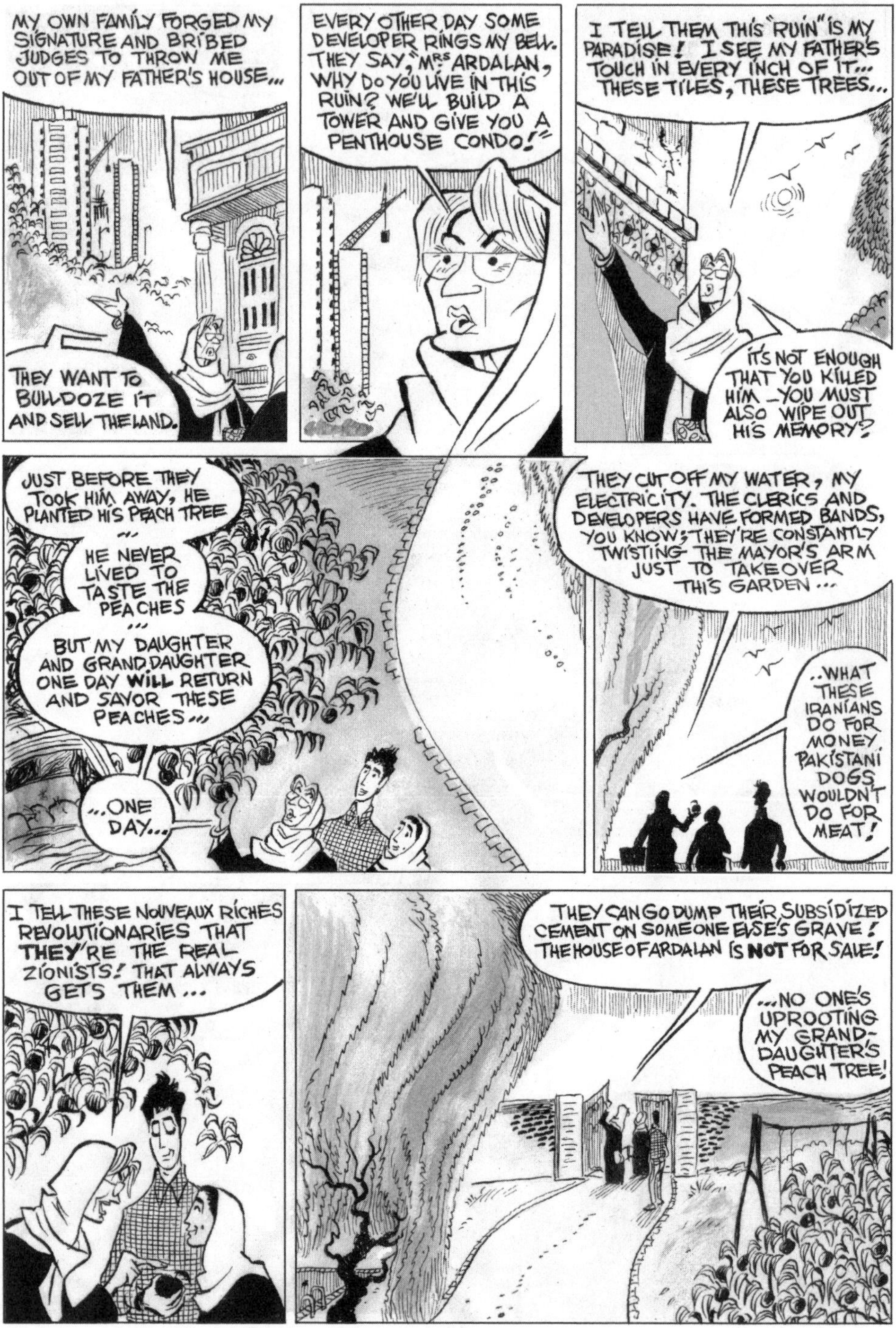
MY OWN FAMILY FORGED MY SIGNATURE AND BRIBED JUDGES TO THROW ME OUT OF MY FATHER'S HOUSE...
THEY WANT TO BULLDOZE IT AND SELL THE LAND.
EVERY OTHER DAY SOME DEVELOPER RINGS MY BELL. THEY SAY, "MRS ARDALAN, WHY DO YOU LIVE IN THIS RUIN? WE'LL BUILD A TOWER AND GIVE YOU A PENTHOUSE CONDO!"
I TELL THEM THIS "RUIN" IS MY PARADISE! I SEE MY FATHER'S TOUCH IN EVERY INCH OF IT... THESE TILES, THESE TREES...
IT'S NOT ENOUGH THAT YOU KILLED HIM —YOU MUST ALSO WIPE OUT HIS MEMORY?
JUST BEFORE THEY TOOK HIM AWAY, HE PLANTED HIS PEACH TREE ...
HE NEVER LIVED TO TASTE THE PEACHES ...
BUT MY DAUGHTER AND GRANDDAUGHTER ONE DAY **WILL** RETURN AND SAVOR THESE PEACHES...
...ONE DAY...
THEY CUT OFF MY WATER, MY ELECTRICITY. THE CLERICS AND DEVELOPERS HAVE FORMED BANDS, YOU KNOW; THEY'RE CONSTANTLY TWISTING THE MAYOR'S ARM JUST TO TAKE OVER THIS GARDEN ...
..WHAT THESE IRANIANS DO FOR MONEY, PAKISTANI DOGS WOULDN'T DO FOR MEAT!
I TELL THESE NOUVEAUX RICHES REVOLUTIONARIES THAT **THEY**'RE THE REAL ZIONISTS! THAT ALWAYS GETS THEM ...
THEY CAN GO DUMP THEIR SUBSIDIZED CEMENT ON SOMEONE ELSE'S GRAVE! THE HOUSE OF ARDALAN IS **NOT** FOR SALE!
...NO ONE'S UPROOTING MY GRAND-DAUGHTER'S PEACH TREE!

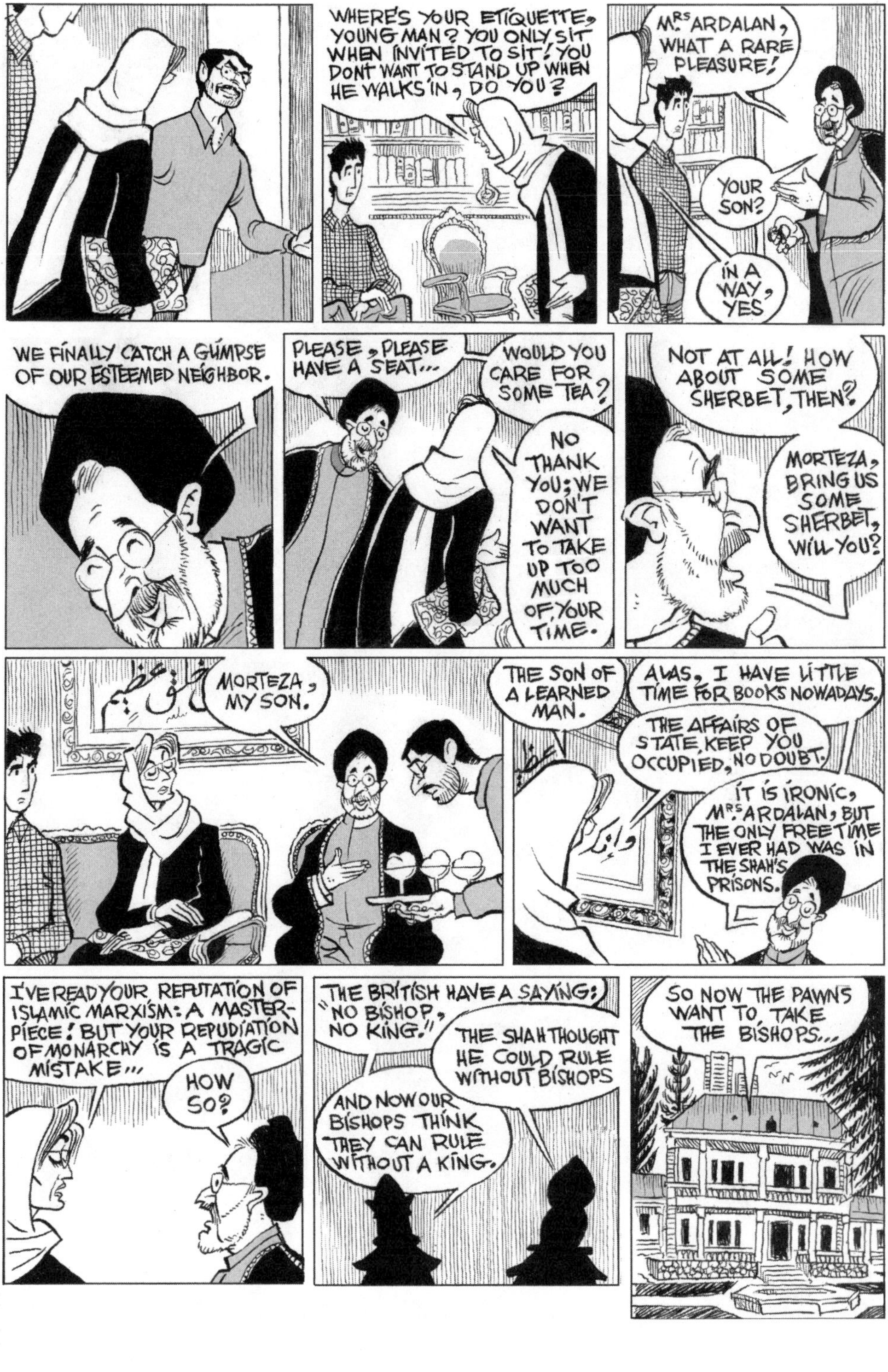
WHERE'S YOUR ETIQUETTE, YOUNG MAN? YOU ONLY SIT WHEN INVITED TO SIT! YOU DONT WANT TO STAND UP WHEN HE WALKS IN, DO YOU?
MRS. ARDALAN, WHAT A RARE PLEASURE!
YOUR SON?
IN A WAY, YES
WE FINALLY CATCH A GLIMPSE OF OUR ESTEEMED NEIGHBOR.
PLEASE, PLEASE HAVE A SEAT...
WOULD YOU CARE FOR SOME TEA?
NO THANK YOU; WE DON'T WANT TO TAKE UP TOO MUCH OF YOUR TIME.
NOT AT ALL! HOW ABOUT SOME SHERBET, THEN?
MORTEZA, BRING US SOME SHERBET, WILL YOU?
MORTEZA, MY SON.
THE SON OF A LEARNED MAN.
ALAS, I HAVE LITTLE TIME FOR BOOKS NOWADAYS.
THE AFFAIRS OF STATE KEEP YOU OCCUPIED, NO DOUBT.
IT IS IRONIC, MRS. ARDALAN, BUT THE ONLY FREE TIME I EVER HAD WAS IN THE SHAH'S PRISONS.
I'VE READ YOUR REFUTATION OF ISLAMIC MARXISM: A MASTERPIECE! BUT YOUR REPUDIATION OF MONARCHY IS A TRAGIC MISTAKE...
HOW SO?
THE BRITISH HAVE A SAYING: "NO BISHOP, NO KING."
THE SHAH THOUGHT HE COULD RULE WITHOUT BISHOPS
AND NOW OUR BISHOPS THINK THEY CAN RULE WITHOUT A KING.
SO NOW THE PAWNS WANT TO TAKE THE BISHOPS...

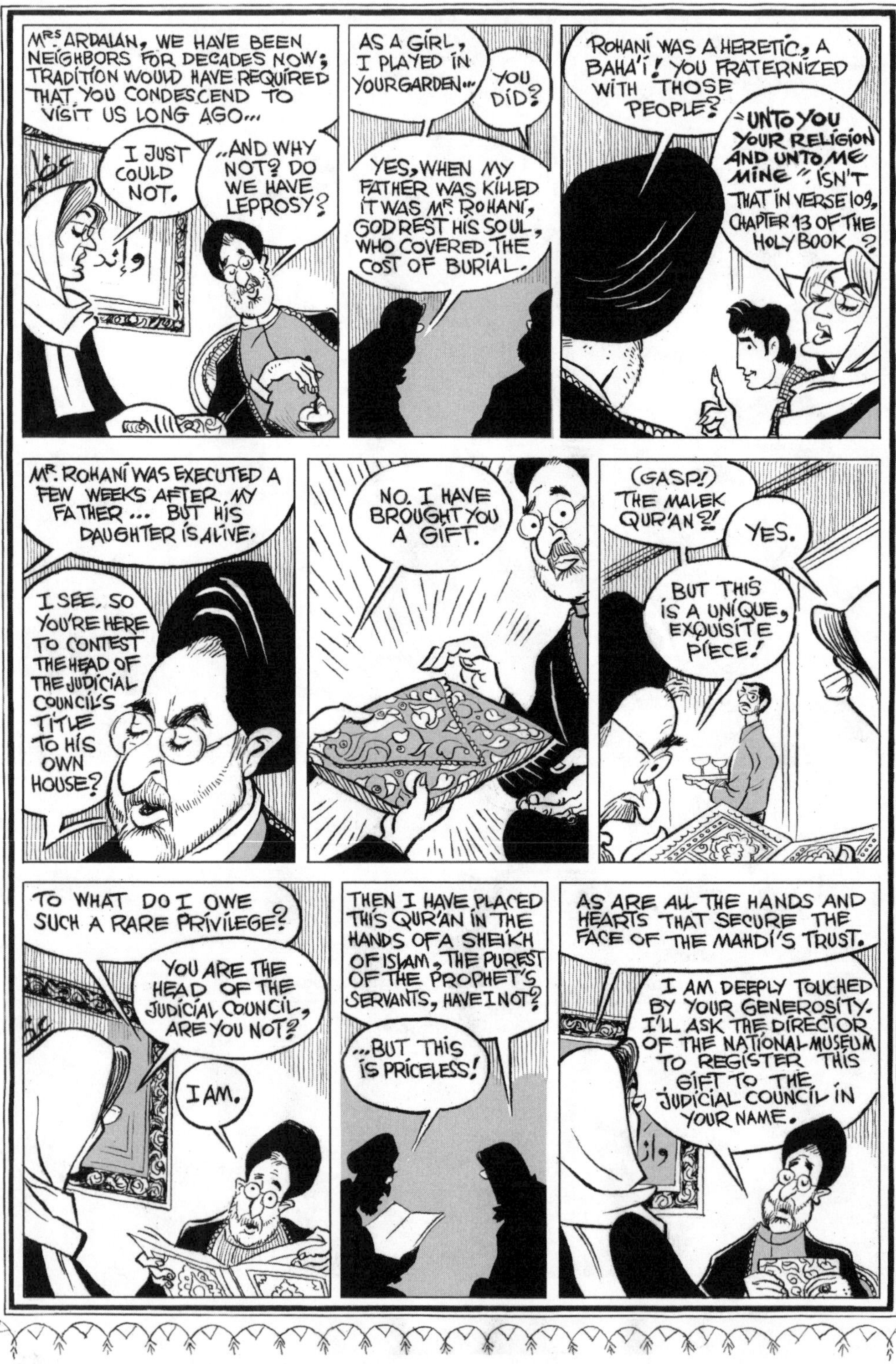
MRS. ARDALAN, WE HAVE BEEN NEIGHBORS FOR DECADES NOW; TRADITION WOULD HAVE REQUIRED THAT YOU CONDESCEND TO VISIT US LONG AGO...
I JUST COULD NOT.
...AND WHY NOT? DO WE HAVE LEPROSY?
AS A GIRL, I PLAYED IN YOUR GARDEN...
YOU DID?
YES, WHEN MY FATHER WAS KILLED IT WAS MR. ROHANI, GOD REST HIS SOUL, WHO COVERED THE COST OF BURIAL.
ROHANI WAS A HERETIC, A BAHA'I! YOU FRATERNIZED WITH THOSE PEOPLE?
"UNTO YOU YOUR RELIGION AND UNTO ME MINE." ISN'T THAT IN VERSE 109, CHAPTER 13 OF THE HOLY BOOK?
MR. ROHANI WAS EXECUTED A FEW WEEKS AFTER MY FATHER... BUT HIS DAUGHTER IS ALIVE.
I SEE. SO YOU'RE HERE TO CONTEST THE HEAD OF THE JUDICIAL COUNCIL'S TITLE TO HIS OWN HOUSE?
NO. I HAVE BROUGHT YOU A GIFT.
(GASP!) THE MALEK QUR'AN?!
YES.
BUT THIS IS A UNIQUE, EXQUISITE PIECE!
TO WHAT DO I OWE SUCH A RARE PRIVILEGE?
YOU ARE THE HEAD OF THE JUDICIAL COUNCIL, ARE YOU NOT?
I AM.
THEN I HAVE PLACED THIS QUR'AN IN THE HANDS OF A SHEIKH OF ISLAM, THE PUREST OF THE PROPHET'S SERVANTS, HAVE I NOT?
...BUT THIS IS PRICELESS!
AS ARE ALL THE HANDS AND HEARTS THAT SECURE THE FACE OF THE MAHDI'S TRUST.
I AM DEEPLY TOUCHED BY YOUR GENEROSITY. I'LL ASK THE DIRECTOR OF THE NATIONAL MUSEUM TO REGISTER THIS GIFT TO THE JUDICIAL COUNCIL IN YOUR NAME.

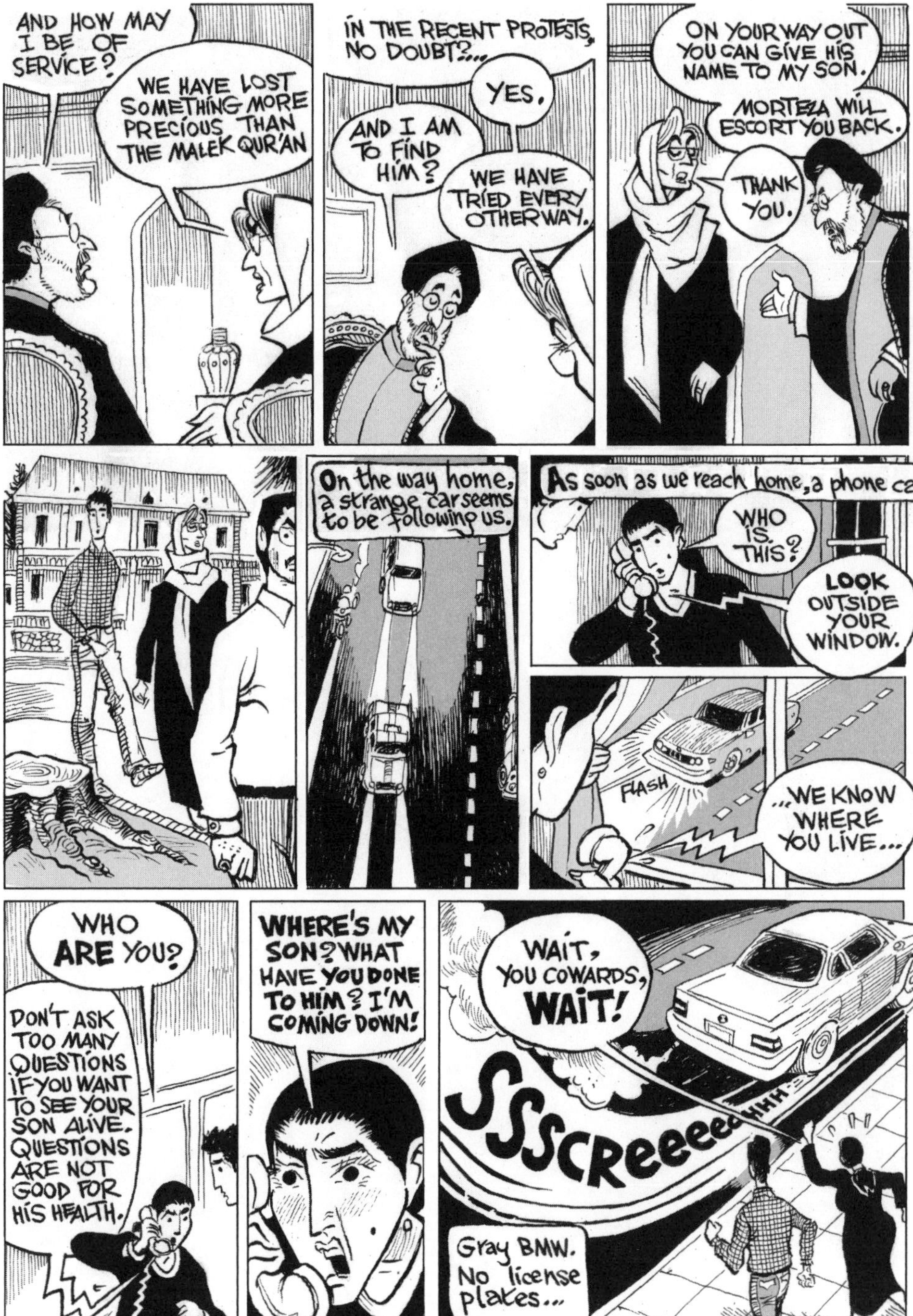
AND HOW MAY I BE OF SERVICE?
WE HAVE LOST SOMETHING MORE PRECIOUS THAN THE MALEK QUR'AN
IN THE RECENT PROTESTS, NO DOUBT?...
YES.
AND I AM TO FIND HIM?
WE HAVE TRIED EVERY OTHER WAY.
ON YOUR WAY OUT YOU CAN GIVE HIS NAME TO MY SON.
MORTEZA WILL ESCORT YOU BACK.
THANK YOU.
On the way home, a strange car seems to be following us.
As soon as we reach home, a phone call.
WHO IS THIS?
LOOK OUTSIDE YOUR WINDOW.
FLASH
...WE KNOW WHERE YOU LIVE...
WHO ARE YOU?
DON'T ASK TOO MANY QUESTIONS IF YOU WANT TO SEE YOUR SON ALIVE. QUESTIONS ARE NOT GOOD FOR HIS HEALTH.
WHERE'S MY SON? WHAT HAVE YOU DONE TO HIM? I'M COMING DOWN!
WAIT, YOU COWARDS, WAIT!
SSSCREEEEEHHH
Gray BMW. No license plates...

KAHRIZAK

CHAPTER NINE

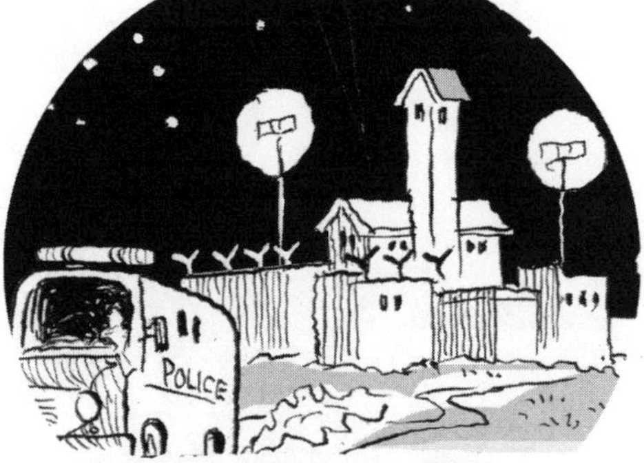
POLICE

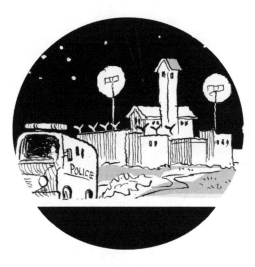

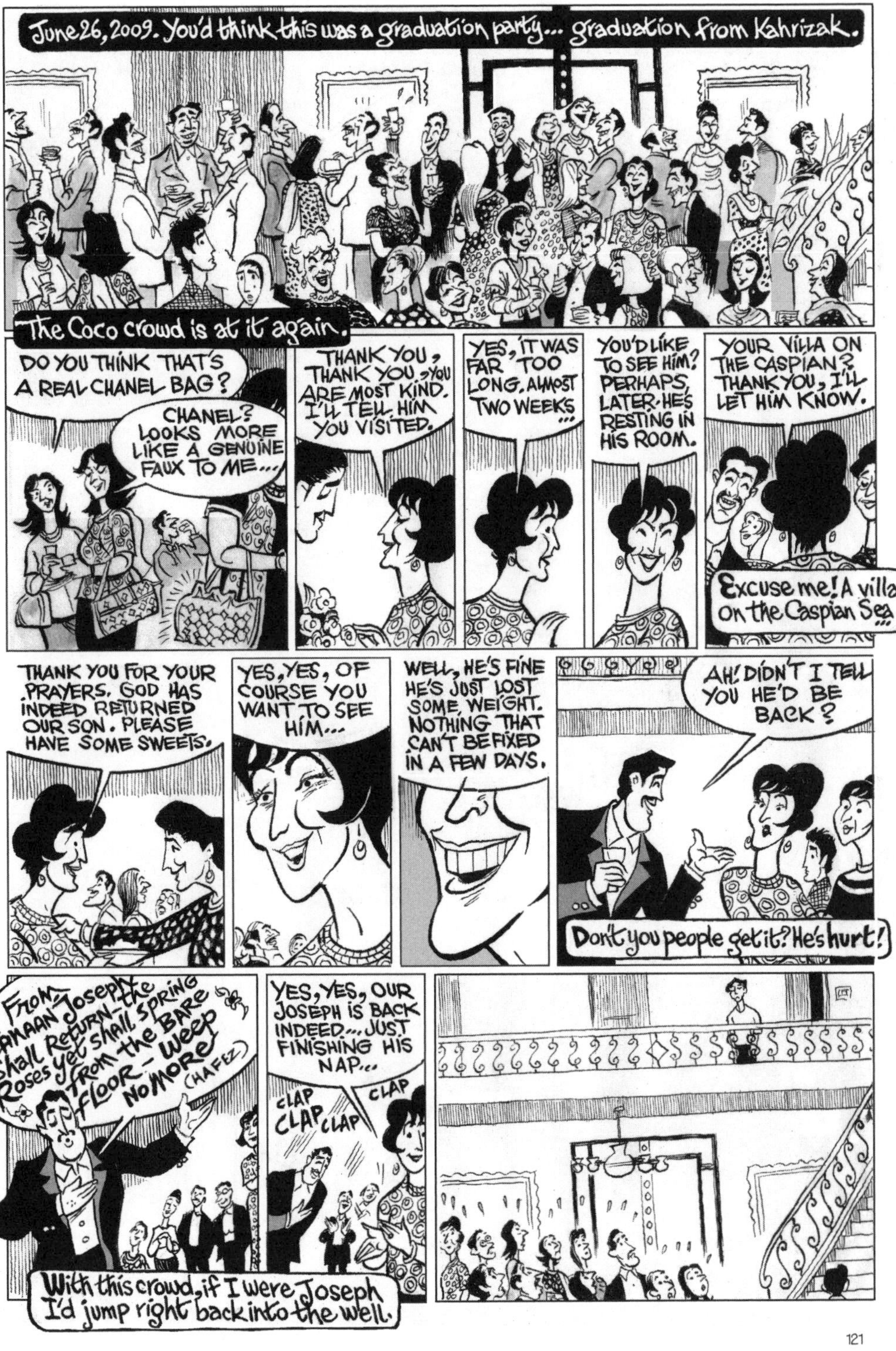
June 26, 2009. You'd think this was a graduation party... graduation from Kahrizak.
The Coco crowd is at it again.
DO YOU THINK THAT'S A REAL CHANEL BAG?
CHANEL? LOOKS MORE LIKE A GENUINE FAUX TO ME...
THANK YOU, THANK YOU, YOU ARE MOST KIND. I'LL TELL HIM YOU VISITED.
YES, IT WAS FAR TOO LONG. ALMOST TWO WEEKS...
YOU'D LIKE TO SEE HIM? PERHAPS, LATER. HE'S RESTING IN HIS ROOM.
YOUR VILLA ON THE CASPIAN? THANK YOU, I'LL LET HIM KNOW.
Excuse me! A villa on the Caspian Sea...
THANK YOU FOR YOUR PRAYERS. GOD HAS INDEED RETURNED OUR SON. PLEASE HAVE SOME SWEETS.
YES, YES, OF COURSE YOU WANT TO SEE HIM...
WELL, HE'S FINE HE'S JUST LOST SOME WEIGHT. NOTHING THAT CAN'T BE FIXED IN A FEW DAYS.
AH! DIDN'T I TELL YOU HE'D BE BACK?
Don't you people get it? He's hurt!
FROM CANAAN JOSEPH THE SHALL RETURN SPRING ROSES YET SHALL SPRING FROM THE BARE FLOOR - WEEP NO MORE (HAFEZ)
With this crowd, if I were Joseph I'd jump right back into the well.
YES, YES, OUR JOSEPH IS BACK INDEED... JUST FINISHING HIS NAP...
CLAP CLAP CLAP
CLAP

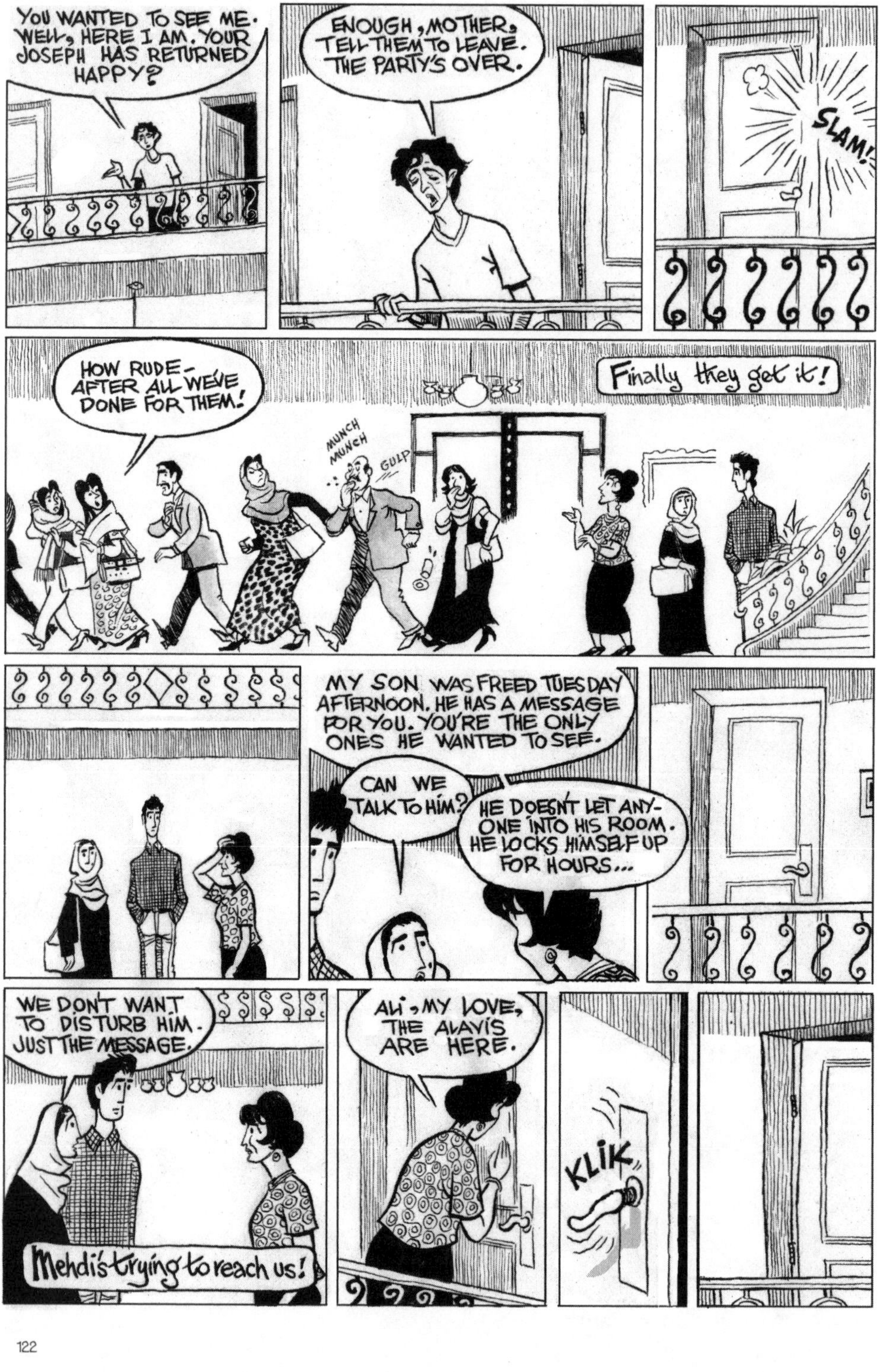

YOU WANTED TO SEE ME. WELL, HERE I AM. YOUR JOSEPH HAS RETURNED HAPPY?
ENOUGH, MOTHER. TELL THEM TO LEAVE. THE PARTY'S OVER.
SLAM!
HOW RUDE- AFTER ALL WE'VE DONE FOR THEM!
Finally they get it!
MUNCH MUNCH
GULP
MY SON WAS FREED TUESDAY AFTERNOON. HE HAS A MESSAGE FOR YOU. YOU'RE THE ONLY ONES HE WANTED TO SEE.
CAN WE TALK TO HIM?
HE DOESN'T LET ANYONE INTO HIS ROOM. HE LOCKS HIMSELF UP FOR HOURS...
WE DON'T WANT TO DISTURB HIM. JUST THE MESSAGE.
Mehdi's trying to reach us!
ALI, MY LOVE, THE ALAVIS ARE HERE.
KLIK

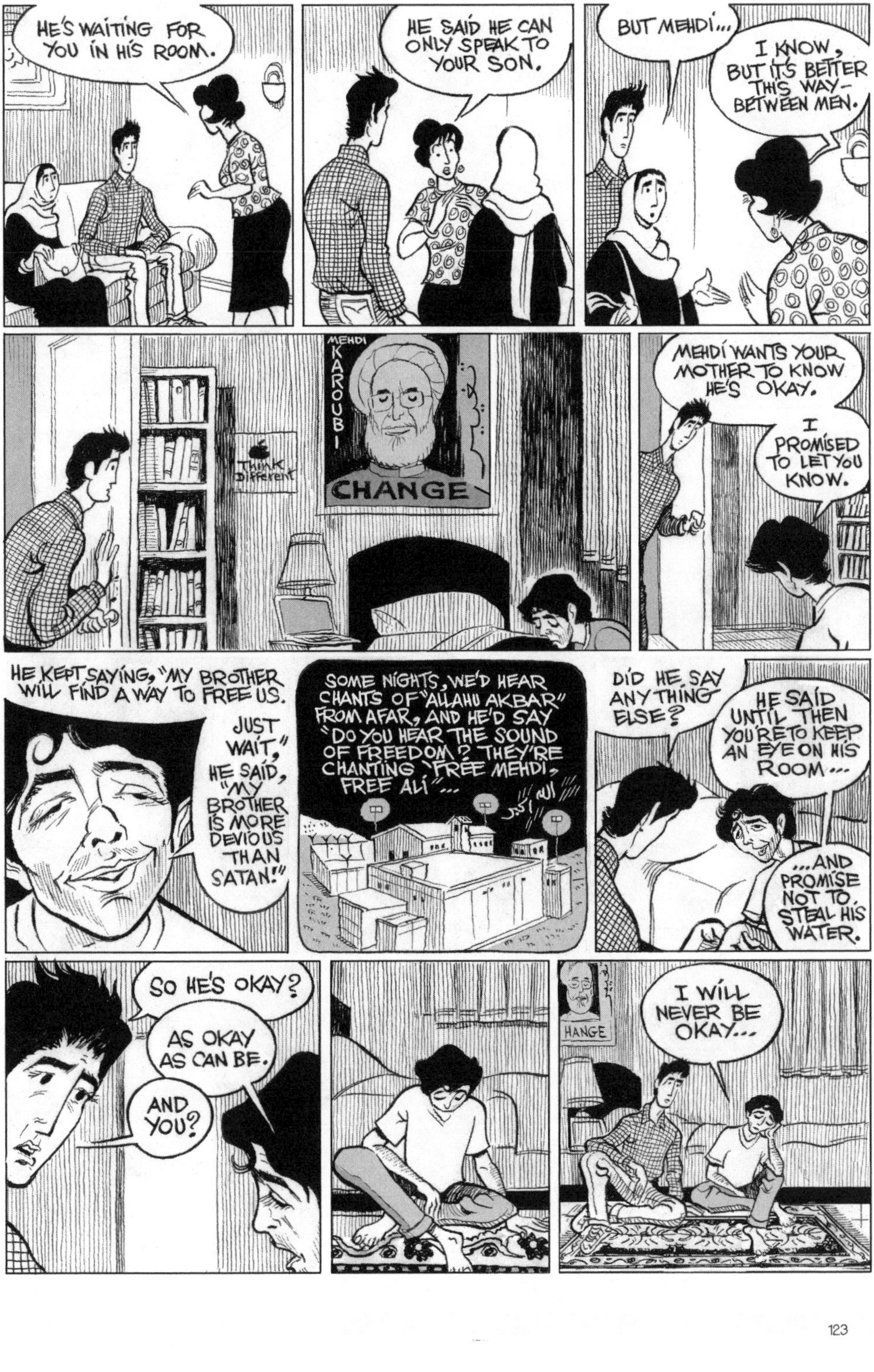
HE'S WAITING FOR YOU IN HIS ROOM.
HE SAID HE CAN ONLY SPEAK TO YOUR SON.
BUT MEHDI...
I KNOW, BUT IT'S BETTER THIS WAY- BETWEEN MEN.
MEHDI KAROUBI
Think Different
CHANGE
MEHDI WANTS YOUR MOTHER TO KNOW HE'S OKAY.
I PROMISED TO LET YOU KNOW.
HE KEPT SAYING, "MY BROTHER WILL FIND A WAY TO FREE US.
JUST WAIT," HE SAID, "MY BROTHER IS MORE DEVIOUS THAN SATAN!"
SOME NIGHTS, WE'D HEAR CHANTS OF "ALLAHU AKBAR" FROM AFAR, AND HE'D SAY "DO YOU HEAR THE SOUND OF FREEDOM? THEY'RE CHANTING 'FREE MEHDI, FREE ALI'"...
DID HE SAY ANYTHING ELSE?
HE SAID UNTIL THEN YOU'RE TO KEEP AN EYE ON HIS ROOM...
...AND PROMISE NOT TO STEAL HIS WATER.
SO HE'S OKAY?
AS OKAY AS CAN BE.
AND YOU?
HANGE
I WILL NEVER BE OKAY...

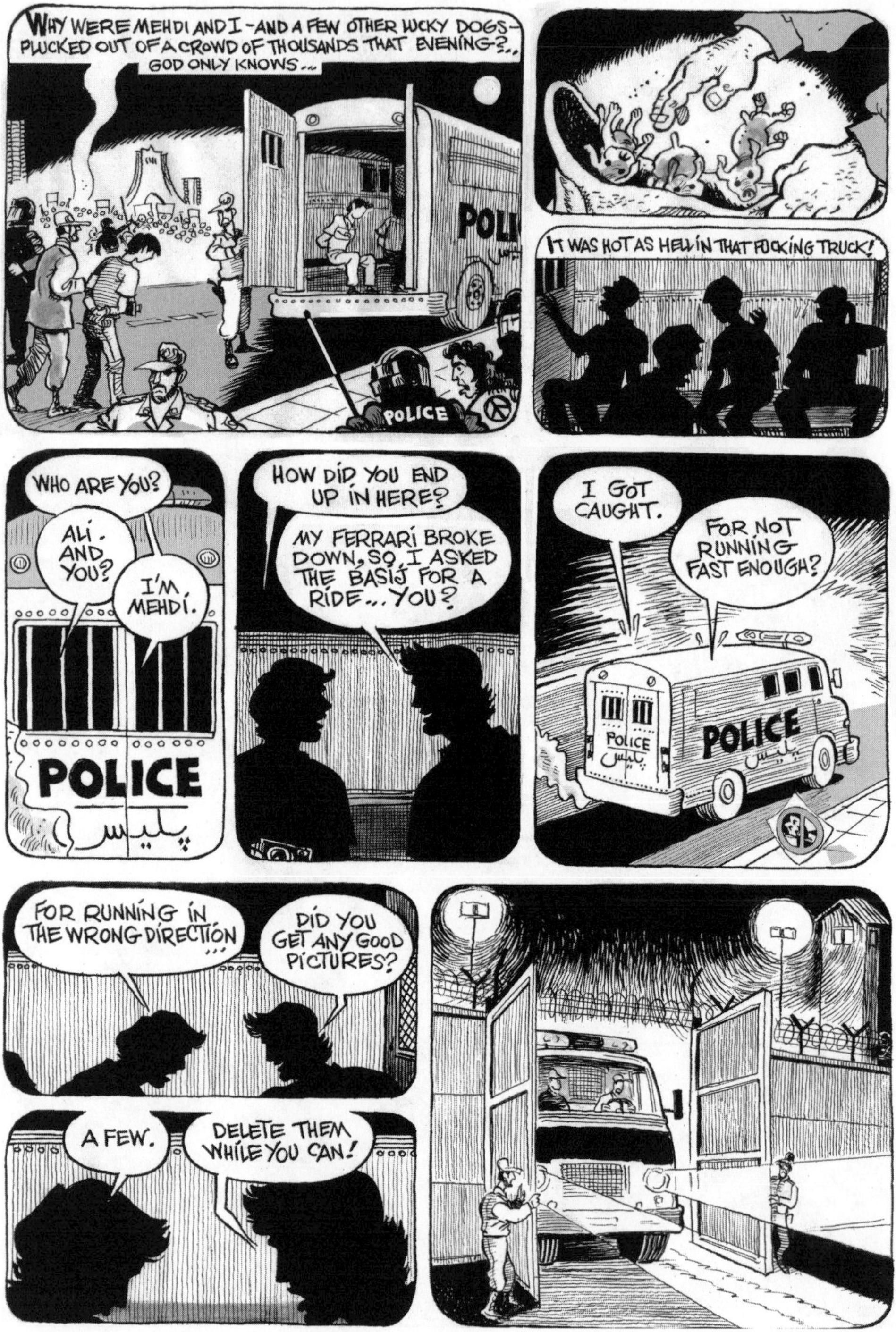
WHY WERE MEHDI AND I - AND A FEW OTHER LUCKY DOGS - PLUCKED OUT OF A CROWD OF THOUSANDS THAT EVENING?..
GOD ONLY KNOWS...
POLICE
IT WAS HOT AS HELL IN THAT FUCKING TRUCK!
WHO ARE YOU?
ALI. AND YOU?
I'M MEHDI.
POLICE
پلیس
HOW DID YOU END UP IN HERE?
MY FERRARI BROKE DOWN, SO, I ASKED THE BASIJ FOR A RIDE... YOU?
I GOT CAUGHT.
FOR NOT RUNNING FAST ENOUGH?
POLICE
پلیس
FOR RUNNING IN THE WRONG DIRECTION...
DID YOU GET ANY GOOD PICTURES?
A FEW.
DELETE THEM WHILE YOU CAN!

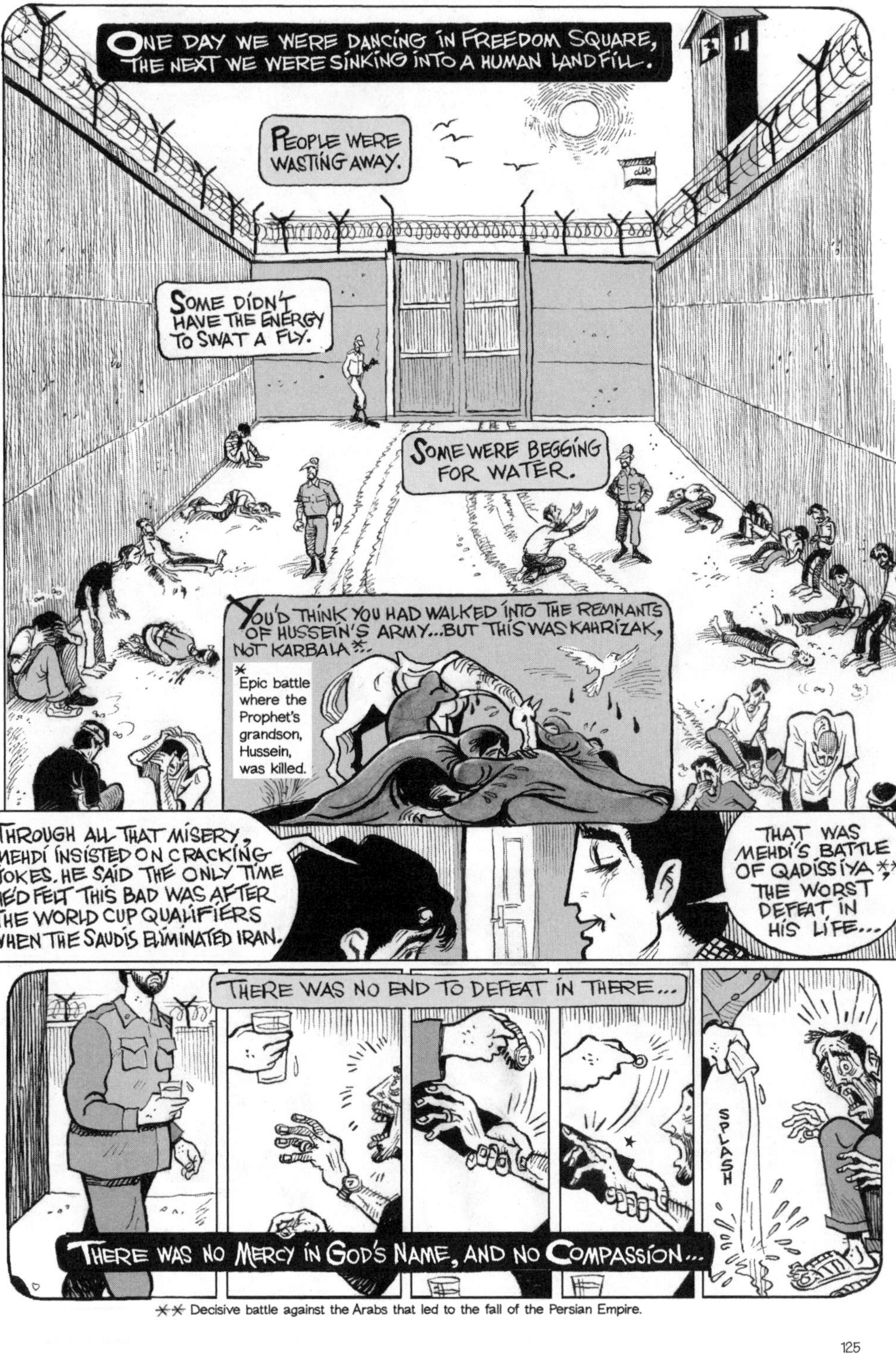
ONE DAY WE WERE DANCING IN FREEDOM SQUARE, THE NEXT WE WERE SINKING INTO A HUMAN LANDFILL.
PEOPLE WERE WASTING AWAY.
SOME DIDN'T HAVE THE ENERGY TO SWAT A FLY.
SOME WERE BEGGING FOR WATER.
YOU'D THINK YOU HAD WALKED INTO THE REMNANTS OF HUSSEIN'S ARMY...BUT THIS WAS KAHRIZAK, NOT KARBALA*.
* Epic battle where the Prophet's grandson, Hussein, was killed.
THROUGH ALL THAT MISERY, MEHDI INSISTED ON CRACKING JOKES. HE SAID THE ONLY TIME HE'D FELT THIS BAD WAS AFTER THE WORLD CUP QUALIFIERS WHEN THE SAUDIS ELIMINATED IRAN.
THAT WAS MEHDI'S BATTLE OF QADISSIYA**, THE WORST DEFEAT IN HIS LIFE...
THERE WAS NO END TO DEFEAT IN THERE...
SPLASH
THERE WAS NO MERCY IN GOD'S NAME, AND NO COMPASSION...

** Decisive battle against the Arabs that led to the fall of the Persian Empire.

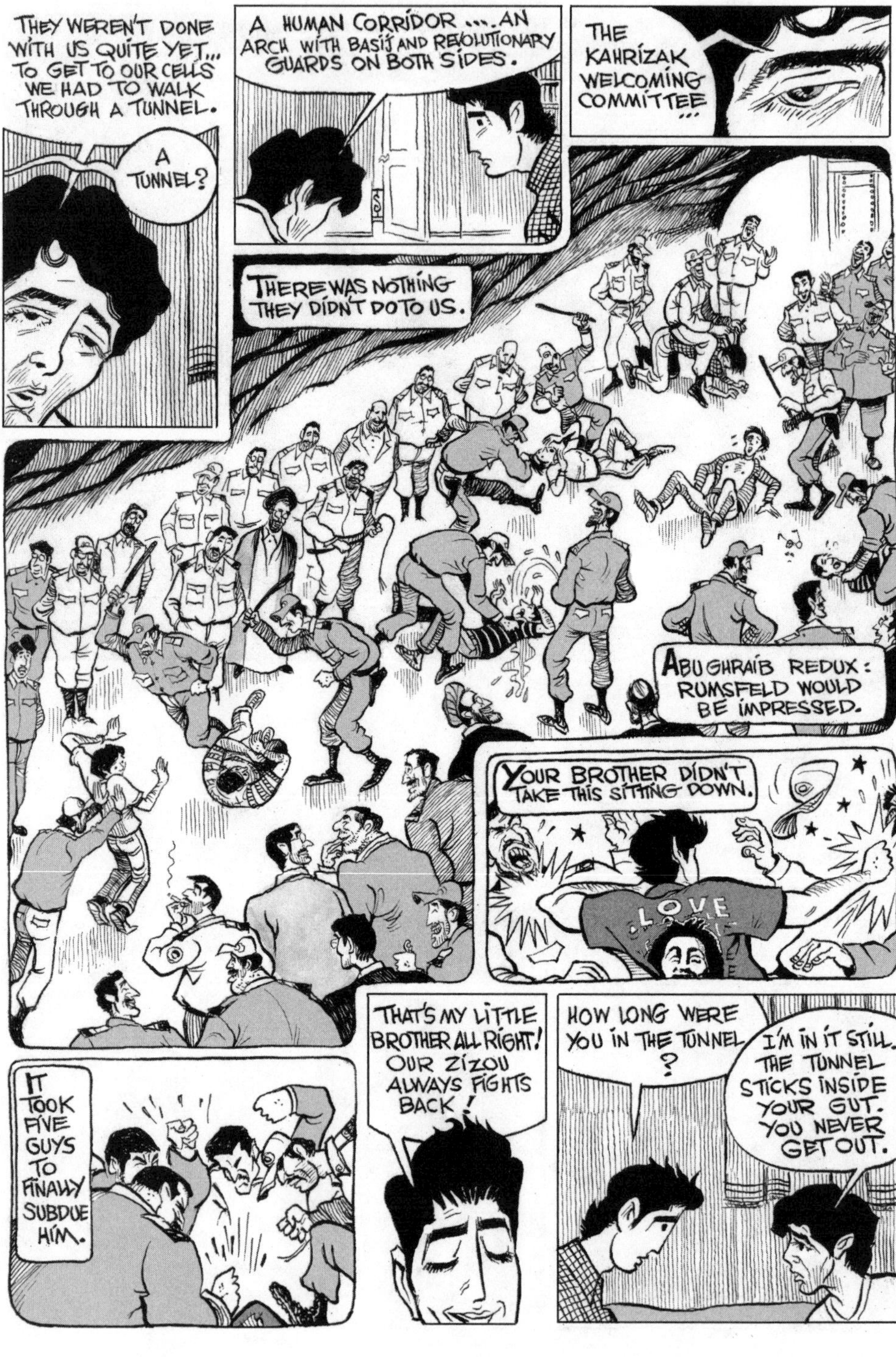
THEY WEREN'T DONE WITH US QUITE YET... TO GET TO OUR CELLS WE HAD TO WALK THROUGH A TUNNEL.
A TUNNEL?
A HUMAN CORRIDOR ....AN ARCH WITH BASIJ AND REVOLUTIONARY GUARDS ON BOTH SIDES.
THE KAHRIZAK WELCOMING COMMITTEE ...
THERE WAS NOTHING THEY DIDN'T DO TO US.
ABU GHRAIB REDUX: RUMSFELD WOULD BE IMPRESSED.
YOUR BROTHER DIDN'T TAKE THIS SITTING DOWN.
LOVE
IT TOOK FIVE GUYS TO FINALLY SUBDUE HIM.
THAT'S MY LITTLE BROTHER ALL RIGHT! OUR ZIZOU ALWAYS FIGHTS BACK!
HOW LONG WERE YOU IN THE TUNNEL?
I'M IN IT STILL. THE TUNNEL STICKS INSIDE YOUR GUT. YOU NEVER GET OUT.

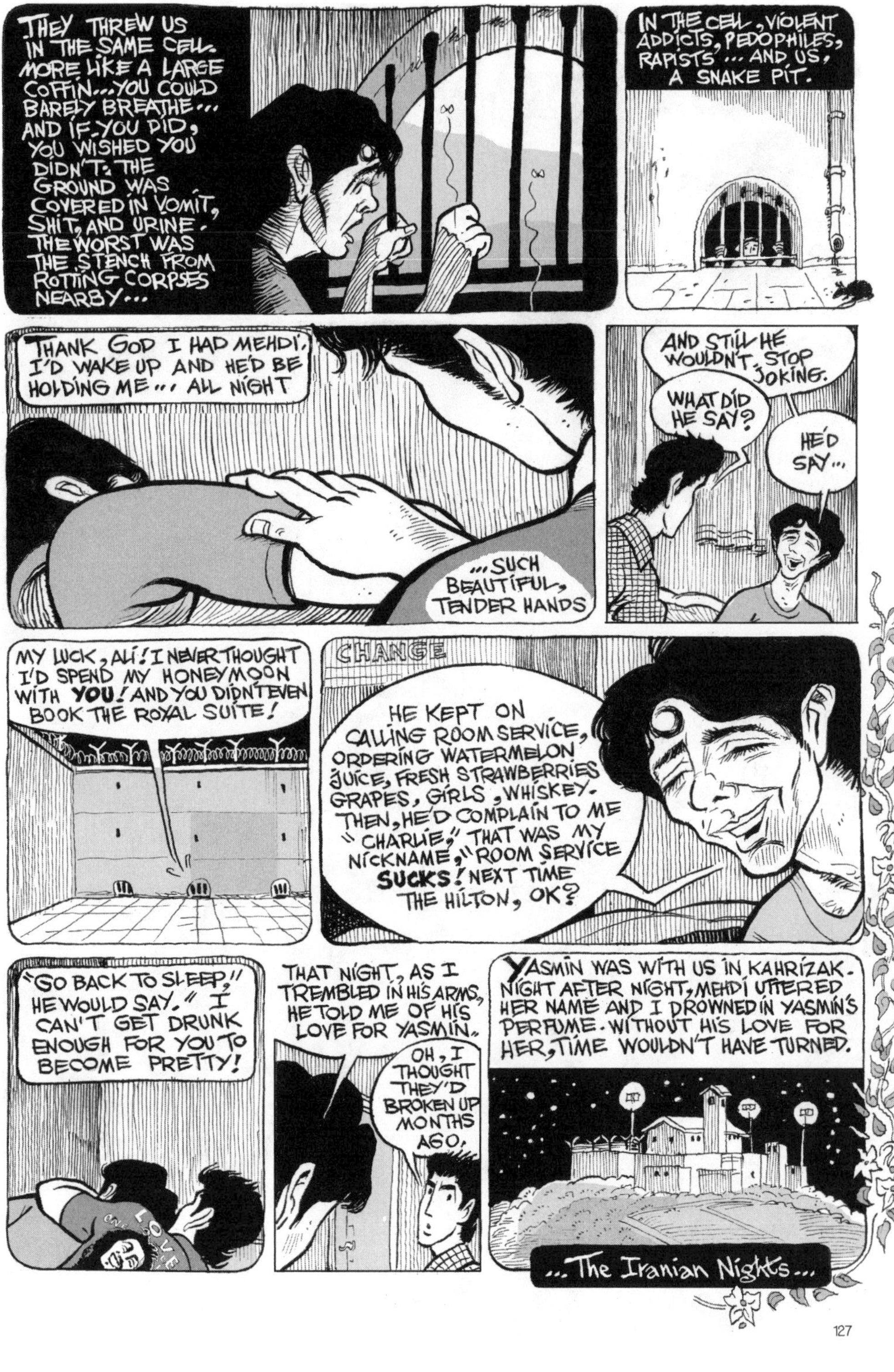
THEY THREW US IN THE SAME CELL. MORE LIKE A LARGE COFFIN... YOU COULD BARELY BREATHE... AND IF YOU DID, YOU WISHED YOU DIDN'T. THE GROUND WAS COVERED IN VOMIT, SHIT, AND URINE. THE WORST WAS THE STENCH FROM ROTTING CORPSES NEARBY...
IN THE CELL, VIOLENT ADDICTS, PEDOPHILES, RAPISTS ... AND US, A SNAKE PIT.
THANK GOD I HAD MEHDI. I'D WAKE UP AND HE'D BE HOLDING ME... ALL NIGHT
...SUCH BEAUTIFUL, TENDER HANDS
AND STILL HE WOULDN'T STOP JOKING.
WHAT DID HE SAY?
HE'D SAY...
MY LUCK, ALI! I NEVER THOUGHT I'D SPEND MY HONEYMOON WITH YOU! AND YOU DIDN'T EVEN BOOK THE ROYAL SUITE!
CHANGE
HE KEPT ON CALLING ROOM SERVICE, ORDERING WATERMELON JUICE, FRESH STRAWBERRIES GRAPES, GIRLS, WHISKEY. THEN, HE'D COMPLAIN TO ME "CHARLIE," THAT WAS MY NICKNAME, "ROOM SERVICE SUCKS! NEXT TIME THE HILTON, OK?
"GO BACK TO SLEEP," HE WOULD SAY. "I CAN'T GET DRUNK ENOUGH FOR YOU TO BECOME PRETTY!
LOVE
THAT NIGHT, AS I TREMBLED IN HIS ARMS, HE TOLD ME OF HIS LOVE FOR YASMIN.
OH, I THOUGHT THEY'D BROKEN UP MONTHS AGO.
YASMIN WAS WITH US IN KAHRIZAK. NIGHT AFTER NIGHT, MEHDI UTTERED HER NAME AND I DROWNED IN YASMIN'S PERFUME. WITHOUT HIS LOVE FOR HER, TIME WOULDN'T HAVE TURNED.
...The Iranian Nights...

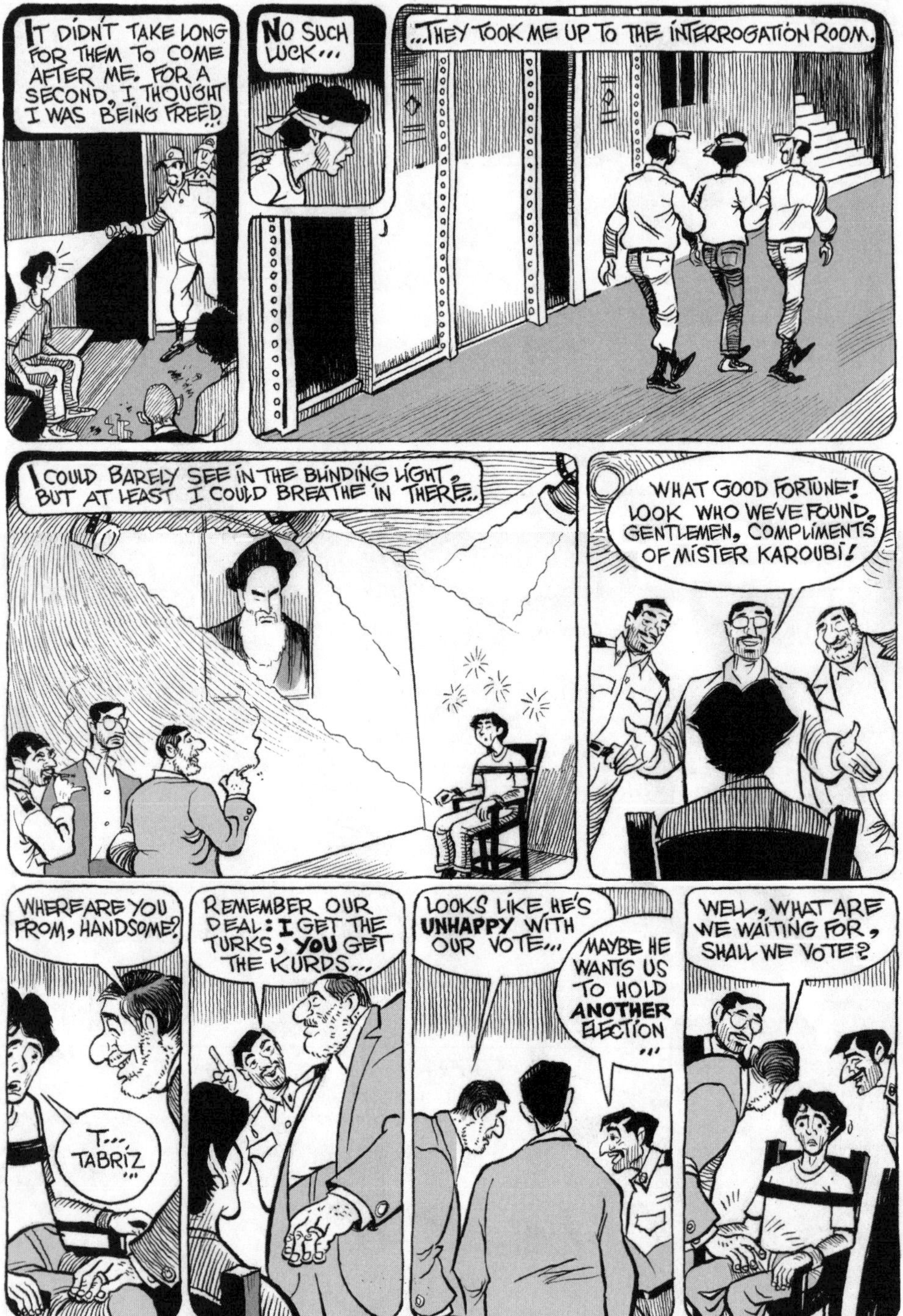
IT DIDN'T TAKE LONG FOR THEM TO COME AFTER ME. FOR A SECOND, I THOUGHT I WAS BEING FREED...
NO SUCH LUCK...
...THEY TOOK ME UP TO THE INTERROGATION ROOM.
I COULD BARELY SEE IN THE BLINDING LIGHT, BUT AT LEAST I COULD BREATHE IN THERE...
WHAT GOOD FORTUNE! LOOK WHO WE'VE FOUND, GENTLEMEN, COMPLIMENTS OF MISTER KAROUBI!
WHERE ARE YOU FROM, HANDSOME?
T... TABRIZ...
REMEMBER OUR DEAL: I GET THE TURKS, YOU GET THE KURDS...
LOOKS LIKE HE'S UNHAPPY WITH OUR VOTE...
MAYBE HE WANTS US TO HOLD ANOTHER ELECTION...
WELL, WHAT ARE WE WAITING FOR, SHALL WE VOTE?

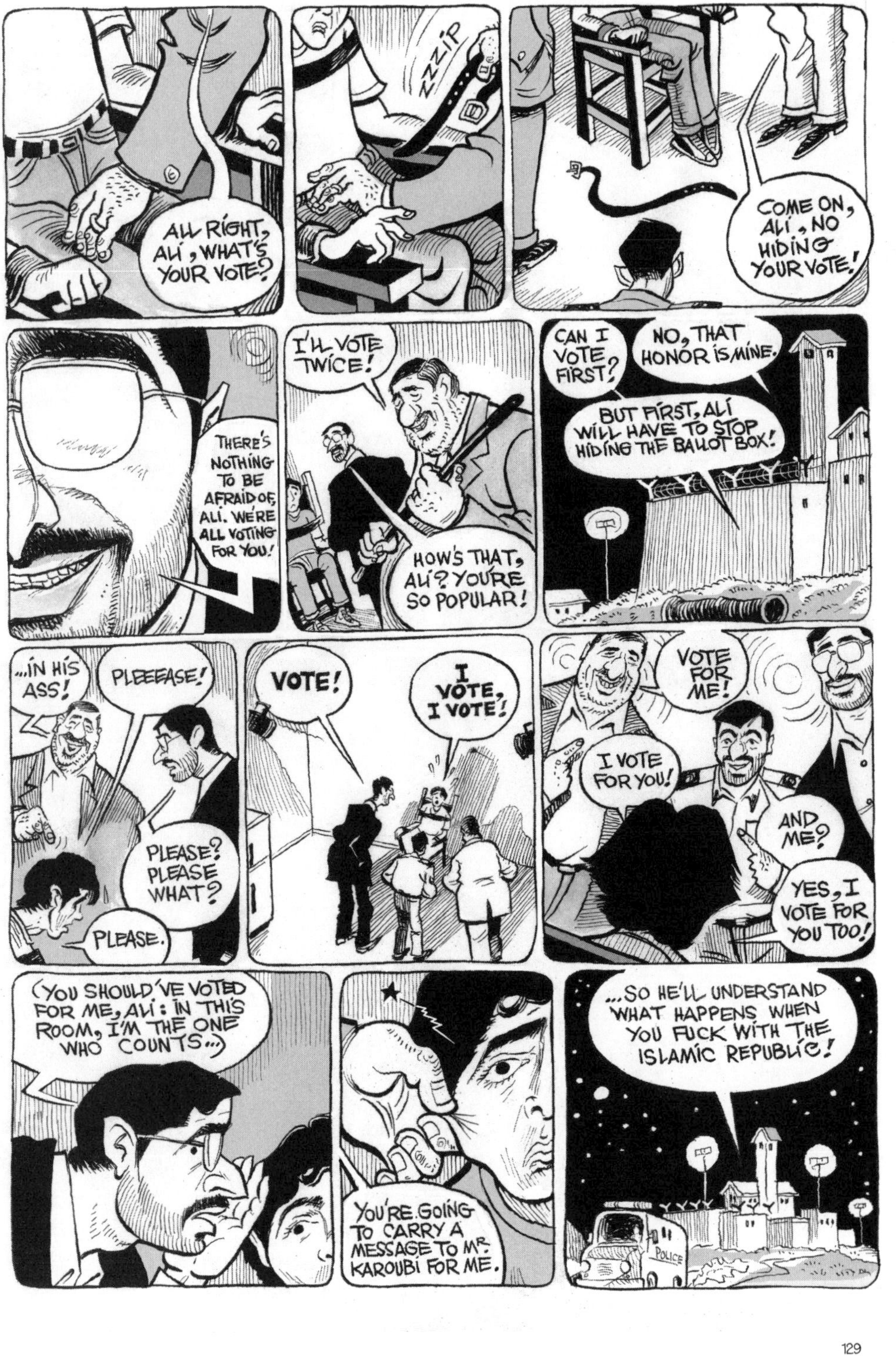

ALL RIGHT, ALÍ, WHAT'S YOUR VOTE?
ZZZIP
COME ON, ALÍ, NO HIDING YOUR VOTE!
THERE'S NOTHING TO BE AFRAID OF, ALÍ. WE'RE ALL VOTING FOR YOU!
I'LL VOTE TWICE!
HOW'S THAT, ALÍ? YOU'RE SO POPULAR!
CAN I VOTE FIRST?
NO, THAT HONOR IS MINE.
BUT FIRST, ALÍ WILL HAVE TO STOP HIDING THE BALLOT BOX!
...IN HIS ASS!
PLEEEASE!
PLEASE? PLEASE WHAT?
PLEASE.
VOTE!
I VOTE, I VOTE!
VOTE FOR ME!
I VOTE FOR YOU!
AND ME?
YES, I VOTE FOR YOU TOO!
(YOU SHOULD'VE VOTED FOR ME, ALÍ: IN THIS ROOM, I'M THE ONE WHO COUNTS...)
YOU'RE GOING TO CARRY A MESSAGE TO MR. KAROUBI FOR ME.
...SO HE'LL UNDERSTAND WHAT HAPPENS WHEN YOU FUCK WITH THE ISLAMIC REPUBLIC!
POLICE

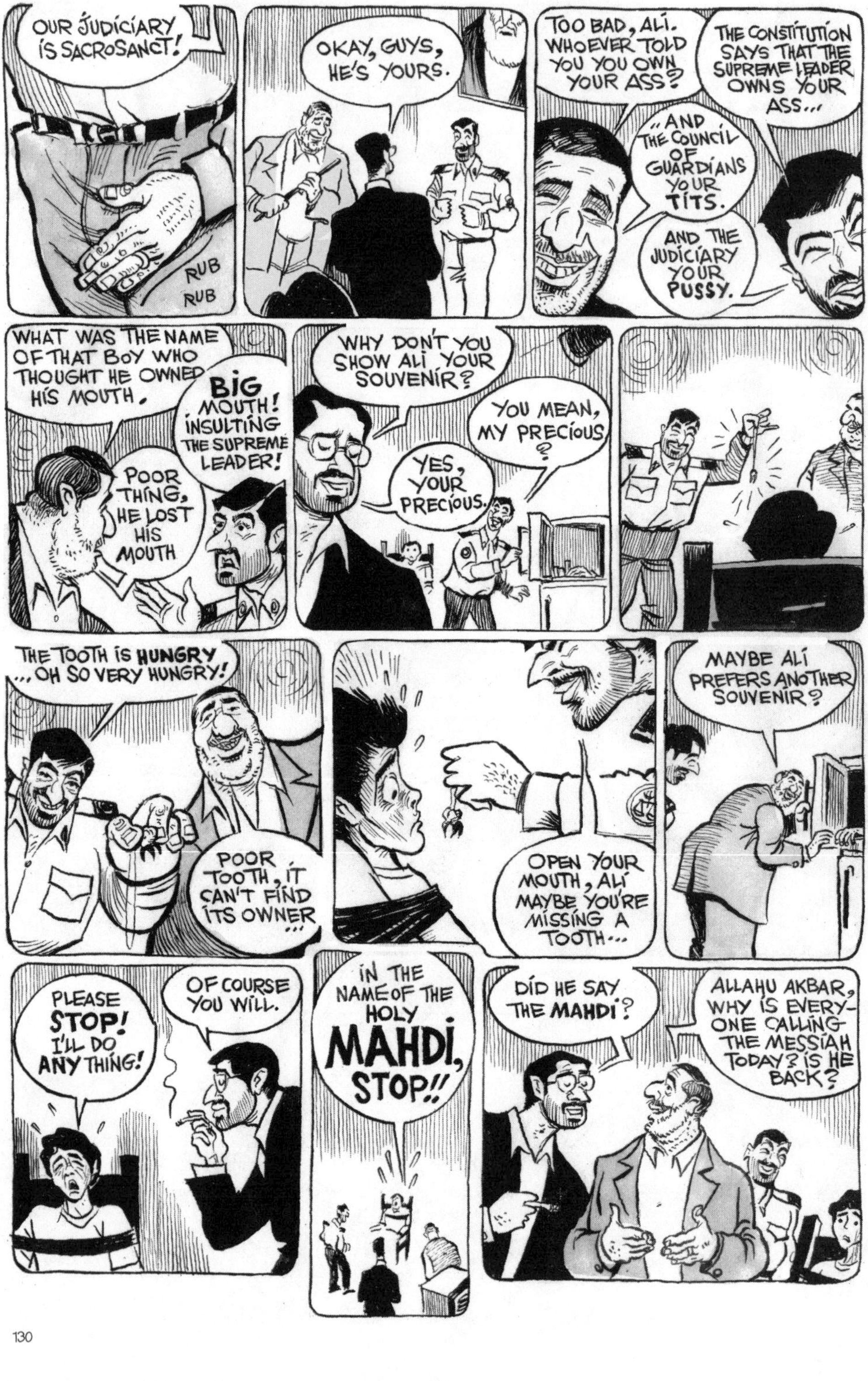
OUR JUDICIARY IS SACROSANCT!
RUB RUB
OKAY, GUYS, HE'S YOURS.
TOO BAD, ALI. WHOEVER TOLD YOU YOU OWN YOUR ASS?
THE CONSTITUTION SAYS THAT THE SUPREME LEADER OWNS YOUR ASS...
...AND THE COUNCIL OF GUARDIANS YOUR TITS.
AND THE JUDICIARY YOUR PUSSY.
WHAT WAS THE NAME OF THAT BOY WHO THOUGHT HE OWNED HIS MOUTH.
BIG MOUTH! INSULTING THE SUPREME LEADER!
POOR THING, HE LOST HIS MOUTH
WHY DON'T YOU SHOW ALI YOUR SOUVENIR?
YOU MEAN, MY PRECIOUS?
YES, YOUR PRECIOUS.
THE TOOTH IS HUNGRY ...OH SO VERY HUNGRY!
POOR TOOTH, IT CAN'T FIND ITS OWNER...
OPEN YOUR MOUTH, ALI MAYBE YOU'RE MISSING A TOOTH...
MAYBE ALI PREFERS ANOTHER SOUVENIR?
PLEASE STOP! I'LL DO ANYTHING!
OF COURSE YOU WILL.
IN THE NAME OF THE HOLY MAHDI, STOP!!
DID HE SAY THE MAHDI?
ALLAHU AKBAR, WHY IS EVERYONE CALLING THE MESSIAH TODAY? IS HE BACK?

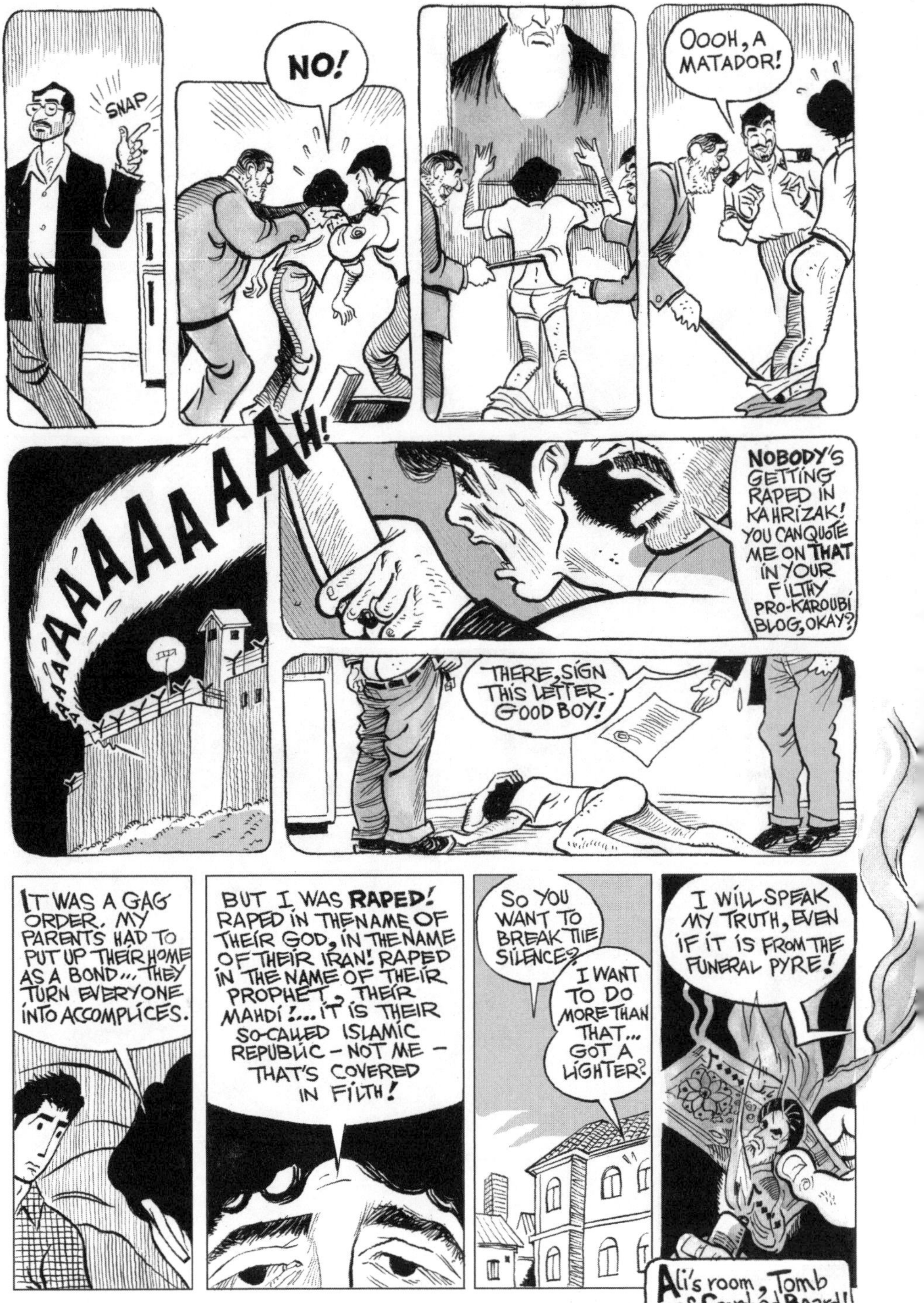
SNAP
NO!
OOOH, A MATADOR!
AAAAAAAAAAAAH!
NOBODY'S GETTING RAPED IN KAHRIZAK! YOU CAN QUOTE ME ON THAT IN YOUR FILTHY PRO-KAROUBI BLOG, OKAY?
THERE, SIGN THIS LETTER. GOOD BOY!
IT WAS A GAG ORDER. MY PARENTS HAD TO PUT UP THEIR HOME AS A BOND... THEY TURN EVERYONE INTO ACCOMPLICES.
BUT I WAS RAPED! RAPED IN THE NAME OF THEIR GOD, IN THE NAME OF THEIR IRAN! RAPED IN THE NAME OF THEIR PROPHET, THEIR MAHDI!... IT IS THEIR SO-CALLED ISLAMIC REPUBLIC - NOT ME - THAT'S COVERED IN FILTH!
SO YOU WANT TO BREAK THE SILENCE?
I WANT TO DO MORE THAN THAT... GOT A LIGHTER?
I WILL SPEAK MY TRUTH, EVEN IF IT IS FROM THE FUNERAL PYRE!
Ali's room, Tomb of Scorched Beard!

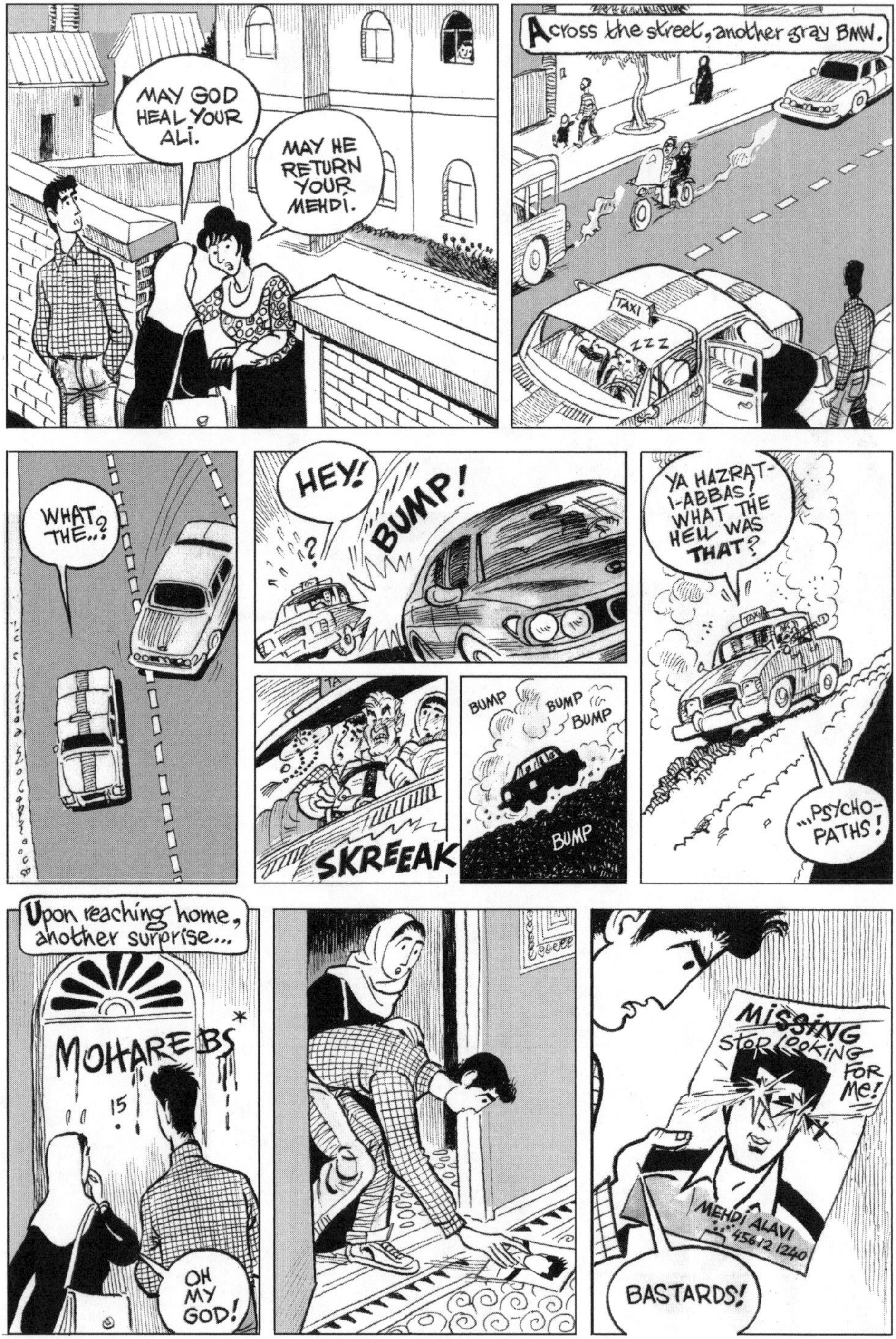
MAY GOD HEAL YOUR ALI.
MAY HE RETURN YOUR MEHDI.
Across the street, another gray BMW.
TAXI
Z Z Z
WHAT THE..?
HEY!
BUMP!
YA HAZRAT-I-ABBAS! WHAT THE HELL WAS THAT?
SKREEAK
BUMP
BUMP
BUMP
BUMP
...PSYCHO-PATHS!
Upon reaching home, another surprise....
MOHAREBS*
15
OH MY GOD!
MISSING
STOP LOOKING FOR ME!
MEHDI ALAVI
45612 1240
BASTARDS!

* Enemies of God.

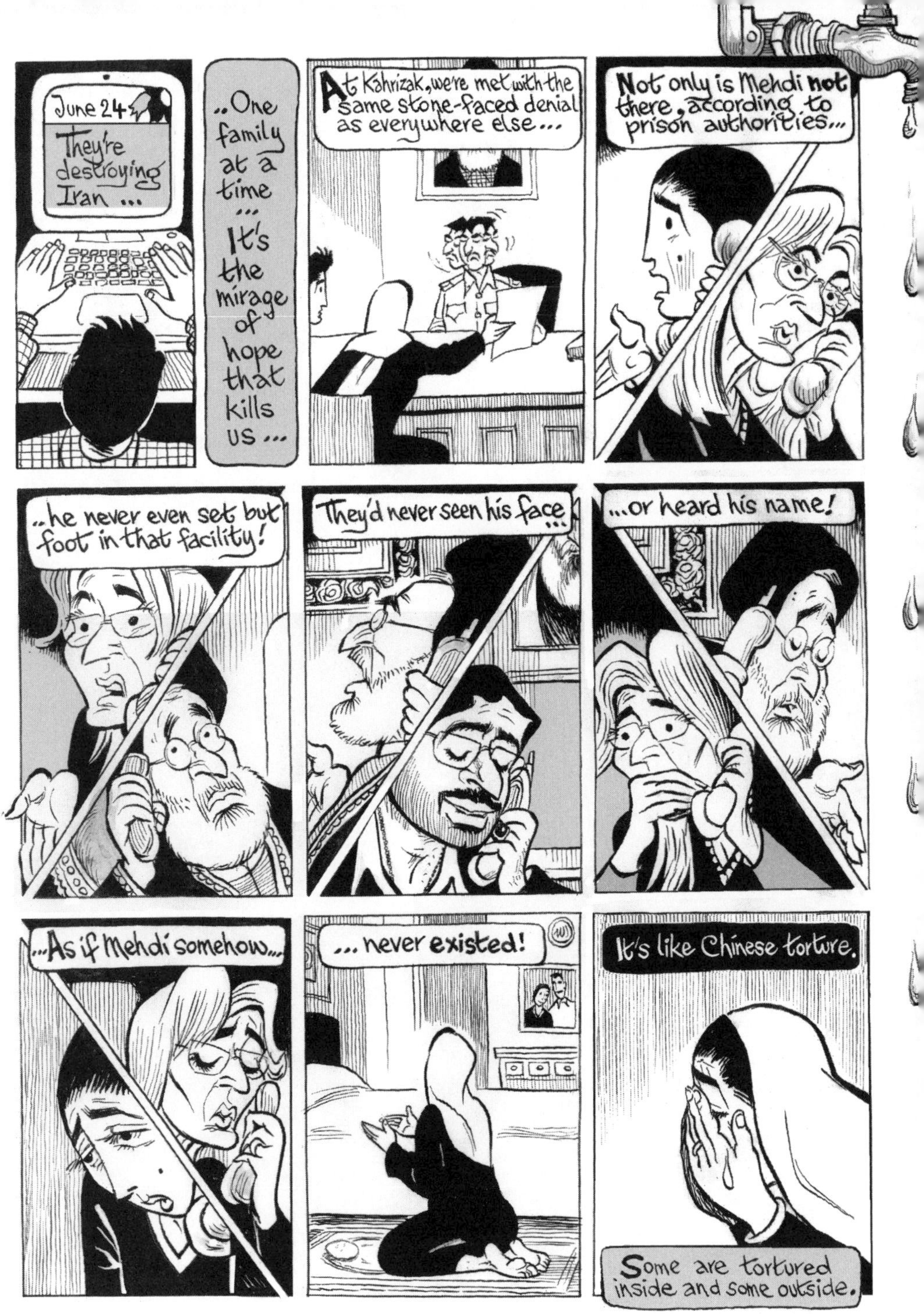
June 24
They're destroying Iran ...
..One family at a time ... It's the mirage of hope that kills us ...
At Kahrizak, we're met with the same stone-faced denial as everywhere else ...
Not only is Mehdi not there, according to prison authorities...
..he never even set foot in that facility!
They'd never seen his face ...
...or heard his name!
...As if Mehdi somehow...
... never existed!
It's like Chinese torture.
Some are tortured inside and some outside.

THE GRIEVING MOTHERS

CHAPTER TEN

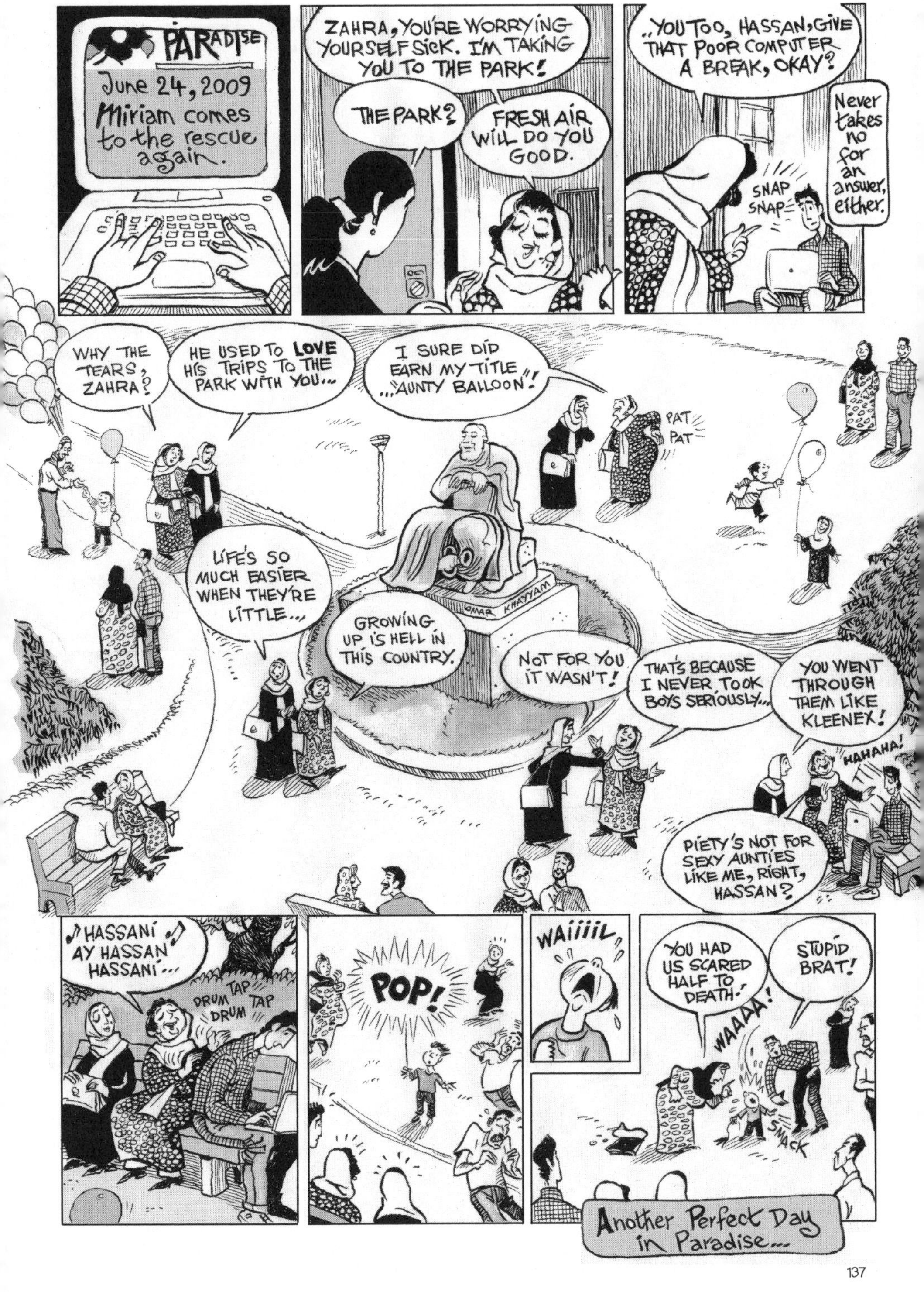
PARADISE
June 24, 2009
Miriam comes to the rescue again.
ZAHRA, YOU'RE WORRYING YOURSELF SICK. I'M TAKING YOU TO THE PARK!
THE PARK?
FRESH AIR WILL DO YOU GOOD.
..YOU TOO, HASSAN, GIVE THAT POOR COMPUTER A BREAK, OKAY?
SNAP SNAP
Never takes no for an answer, either.
WHY THE TEARS, ZAHRA?
HE USED TO LOVE HIS TRIPS TO THE PARK WITH YOU...
I SURE DID EARN MY TITLE ..."AUNTY BALLOON"!
PAT PAT
LIFE'S SO MUCH EASIER WHEN THEY'RE LITTLE...
OMAR KHAYYAM
GROWING UP IS HELL IN THIS COUNTRY.
NOT FOR YOU IT WASN'T!
THAT'S BECAUSE I NEVER TOOK BOYS SERIOUSLY...
YOU WENT THROUGH THEM LIKE KLEENEX!
HAHAHA!
PIETY'S NOT FOR SEXY AUNTIES LIKE ME, RIGHT, HASSAN?
HASSANI AY HASSAN HASSANI...
DRUM TAP DRUM TAP
POP!
WAiiiiiL
YOU HAD US SCARED HALF TO DEATH!
STUPID BRAT!
WAAAA!
SMACK
Another Perfect Day in Paradise...

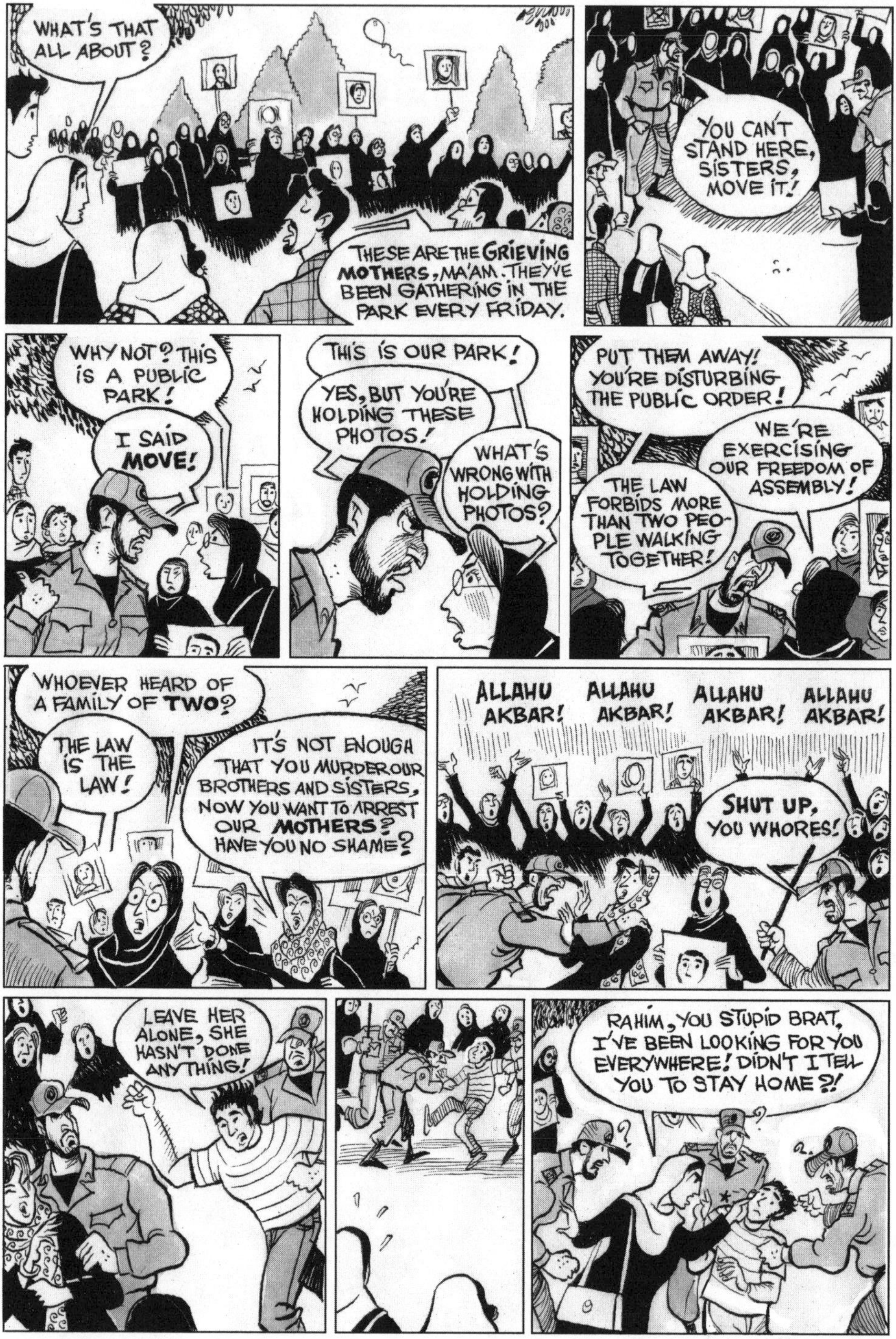
WHAT'S THAT ALL ABOUT?
THESE ARE THE GRIEVING MOTHERS, MA'AM. THEY'VE BEEN GATHERING IN THE PARK EVERY FRIDAY.
YOU CAN'T STAND HERE, SISTERS, MOVE IT!
WHY NOT? THIS IS A PUBLIC PARK!
I SAID MOVE!
THIS IS OUR PARK!
YES, BUT YOU'RE HOLDING THESE PHOTOS!
WHAT'S WRONG WITH HOLDING PHOTOS?
PUT THEM AWAY! YOU'RE DISTURBING THE PUBLIC ORDER!
WE'RE EXERCISING OUR FREEDOM OF ASSEMBLY!
THE LAW FORBIDS MORE THAN TWO PEOPLE WALKING TOGETHER!
WHOEVER HEARD OF A FAMILY OF TWO?
THE LAW IS THE LAW!
IT'S NOT ENOUGH THAT YOU MURDER OUR BROTHERS AND SISTERS, NOW YOU WANT TO ARREST OUR MOTHERS? HAVE YOU NO SHAME?
ALLAHU AKBAR! ALLAHU AKBAR! ALLAHU AKBAR! ALLAHU AKBAR!
SHUT UP, YOU WHORES!
LEAVE HER ALONE, SHE HASN'T DONE ANYTHING!
RAHIM, YOU STUPID BRAT, I'VE BEEN LOOKING FOR YOU EVERYWHERE! DIDN'T I TELL YOU TO STAY HOME?!

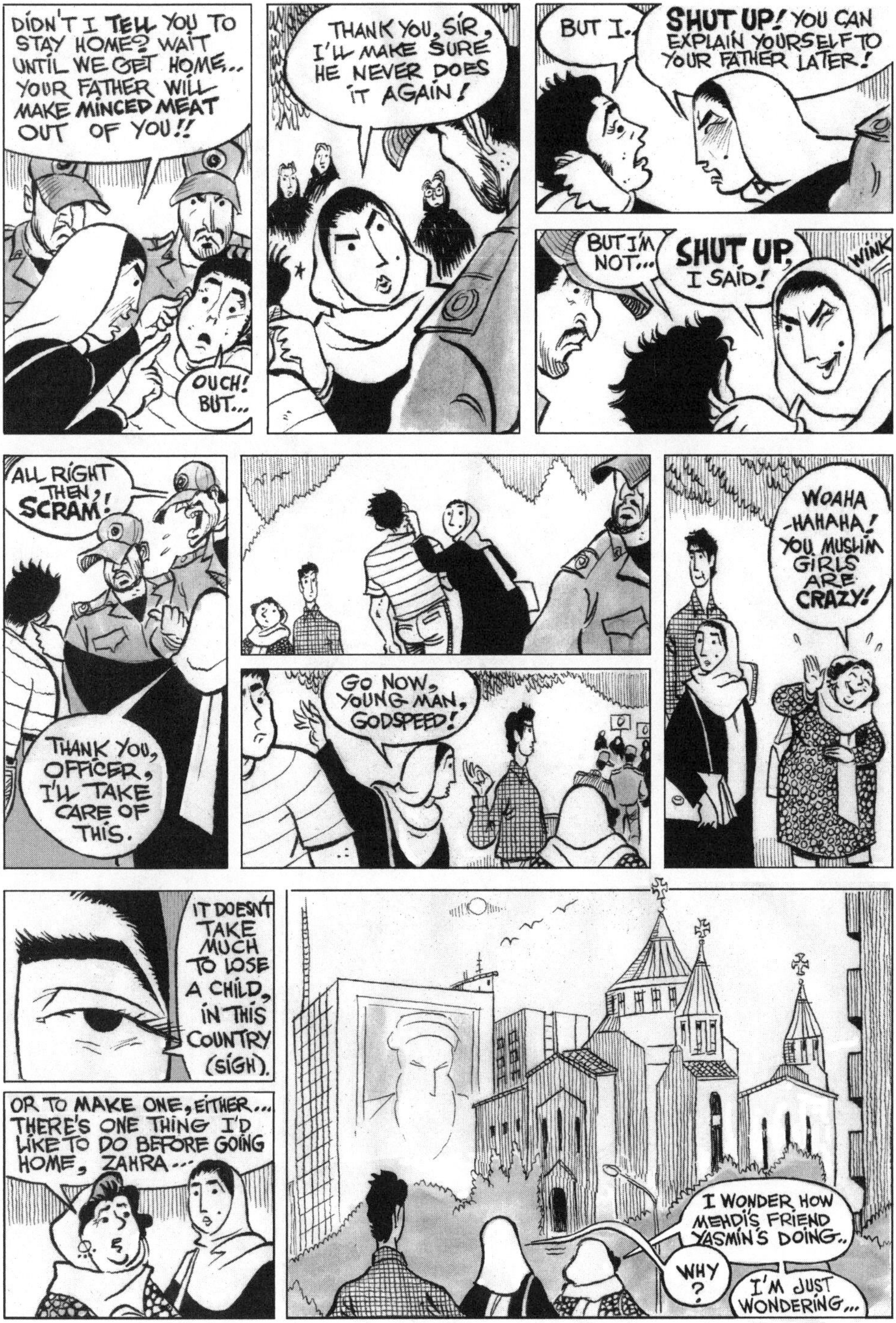
DIDN'T I TELL YOU TO STAY HOME? WAIT UNTIL WE GET HOME... YOUR FATHER WILL MAKE MINCED MEAT OUT OF YOU!!
OUCH! BUT...
THANK YOU, SIR, I'LL MAKE SURE HE NEVER DOES IT AGAIN!
BUT I...
SHUT UP! YOU CAN EXPLAIN YOURSELF TO YOUR FATHER LATER!
BUT I'M NOT...
SHUT UP, I SAID!
WINK
ALL RIGHT THEN, SCRAM!
THANK YOU, OFFICER, I'LL TAKE CARE OF THIS.
GO NOW, YOUNG MAN, GODSPEED!
WOAHA -HAHAHA! YOU MUSLIM GIRLS ARE CRAZY!
IT DOESN'T TAKE MUCH TO LOSE A CHILD, IN THIS COUNTRY (SIGH).
OR TO MAKE ONE, EITHER... THERE'S ONE THING I'D LIKE TO DO BEFORE GOING HOME, ZAHRA...
I WONDER HOW MEHDI'S FRIEND YASMIN'S DOING..
WHY?
I'M JUST WONDERING...

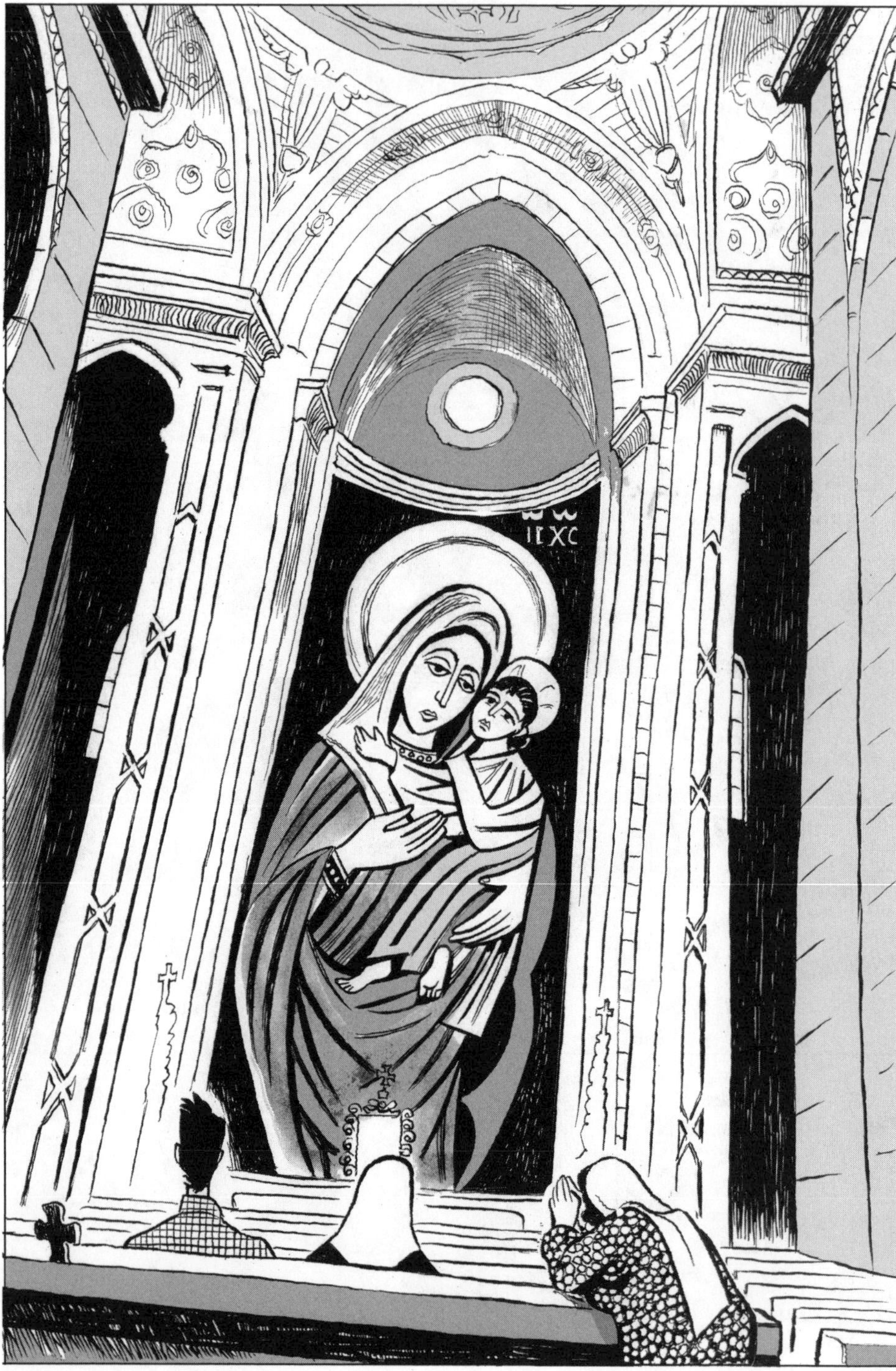
IC XC

THE HOUSE OF SIN

CHAPTER ELEVEN

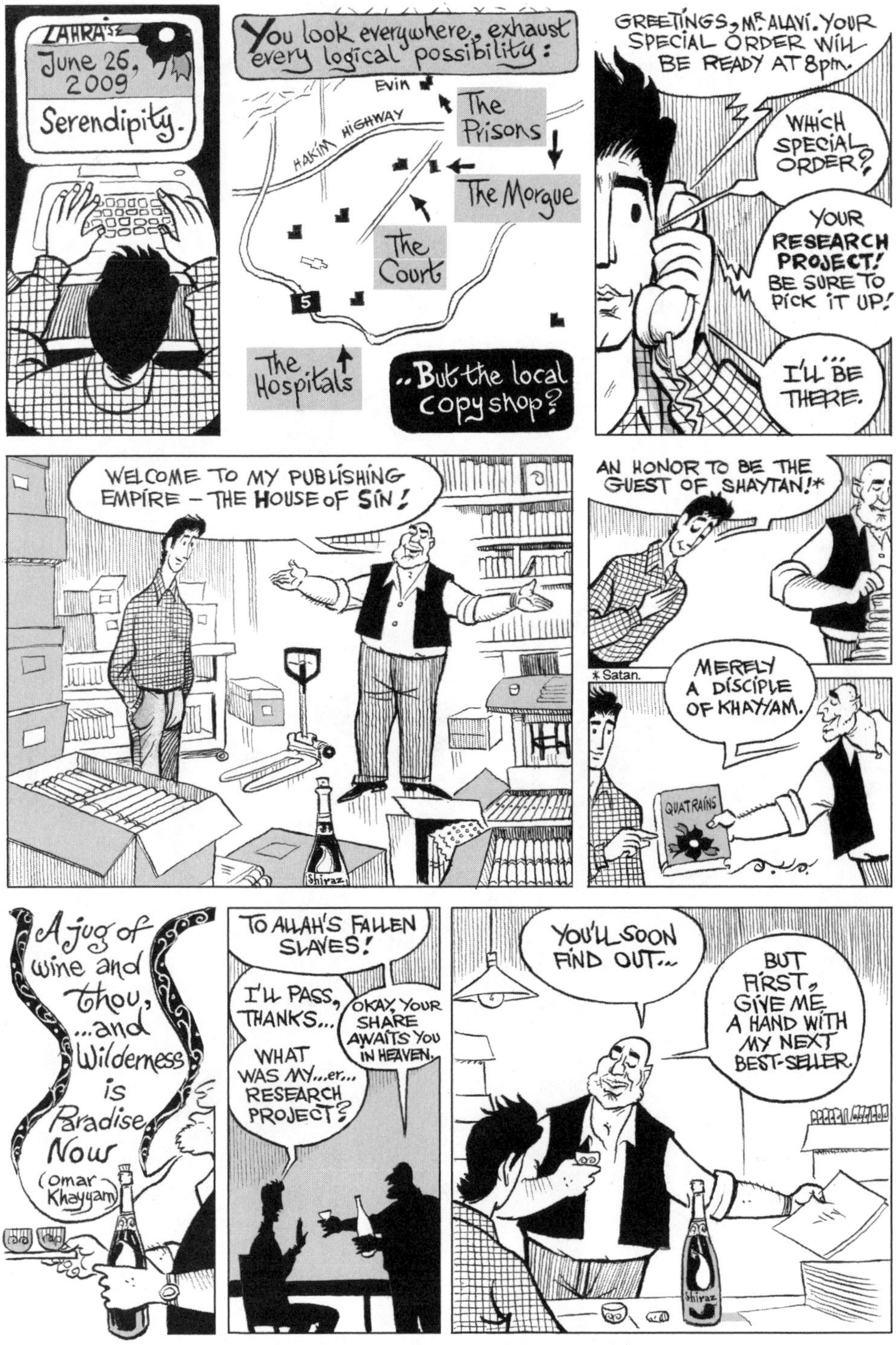
Zahra's
June 26, 2009
Serendipity.
You look everywhere, exhaust every logical possibility:
Evin
Hakim Highway
The Prisons
The Morgue
The Court
5
The Hospitals
..But the local copy shop?
GREETINGS, MR. ALAVI. YOUR SPECIAL ORDER WILL BE READY AT 8pm.
WHICH SPECIAL ORDER?
YOUR RESEARCH PROJECT! BE SURE TO PICK IT UP!
... I'LL BE THERE.
WELCOME TO MY PUBLISHING EMPIRE – THE HOUSE OF SIN!
Shiraz
AN HONOR TO BE THE GUEST OF SHAYTAN!*
* Satan.
MERELY A DISCIPLE OF KHAYYAM.
QUATRAINS
A jug of wine and thou, ...and Wilderness is Paradise Now
(Omar Khayyam)
TO ALLAH'S FALLEN SLAVES!
I'LL PASS, THANKS...
OKAY, YOUR SHARE AWAITS YOU IN HEAVEN.
WHAT WAS MY...er... RESEARCH PROJECT?
YOU'LL SOON FIND OUT...
BUT FIRST, GIVE ME A HAND WITH MY NEXT BEST-SELLER.
Shiraz

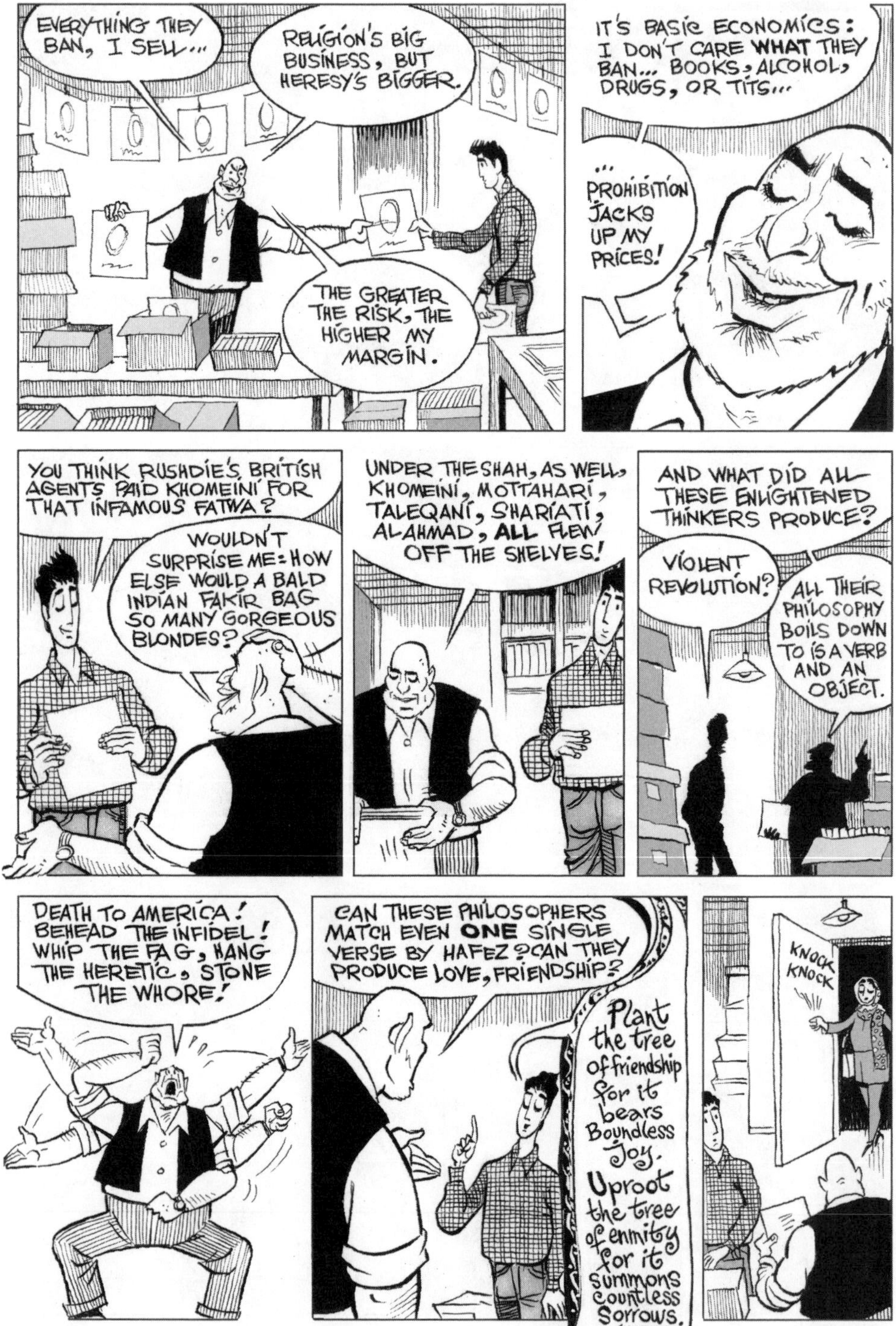
EVERYTHING THEY BAN, I SELL...
RELIGION'S BIG BUSINESS, BUT HERESY'S BIGGER.
THE GREATER THE RISK, THE HIGHER MY MARGIN.
IT'S BASIC ECONOMICS: I DON'T CARE WHAT THEY BAN... BOOKS, ALCOHOL, DRUGS, OR TITS...
... PROHIBITION JACKS UP MY PRICES!
YOU THINK RUSHDIE'S BRITISH AGENTS PAID KHOMEINI FOR THAT INFAMOUS FATWA?
WOULDN'T SURPRISE ME: HOW ELSE WOULD A BALD INDIAN FAKIR BAG SO MANY GORGEOUS BLONDES?
UNDER THE SHAH, AS WELL, KHOMEINI, MOTTAHARI, TALEQANI, SHARIATI, ALAHMAD, ALL FLEW OFF THE SHELVES!
AND WHAT DID ALL THESE ENLIGHTENED THINKERS PRODUCE?
VIOLENT REVOLUTION?
ALL THEIR PHILOSOPHY BOILS DOWN TO IS A VERB AND AN OBJECT.
DEATH TO AMERICA! BEHEAD THE INFIDEL! WHIP THE FAG, HANG THE HERETIC, STONE THE WHORE!
CAN THESE PHILOSOPHERS MATCH EVEN ONE SINGLE VERSE BY HAFEZ? CAN THEY PRODUCE LOVE, FRIENDSHIP?
Plant the tree of friendship for it bears Boundless Joy. Uproot the tree of enmity for it summons countless Sorrows. (HAFEZ)
KNOCK KNOCK

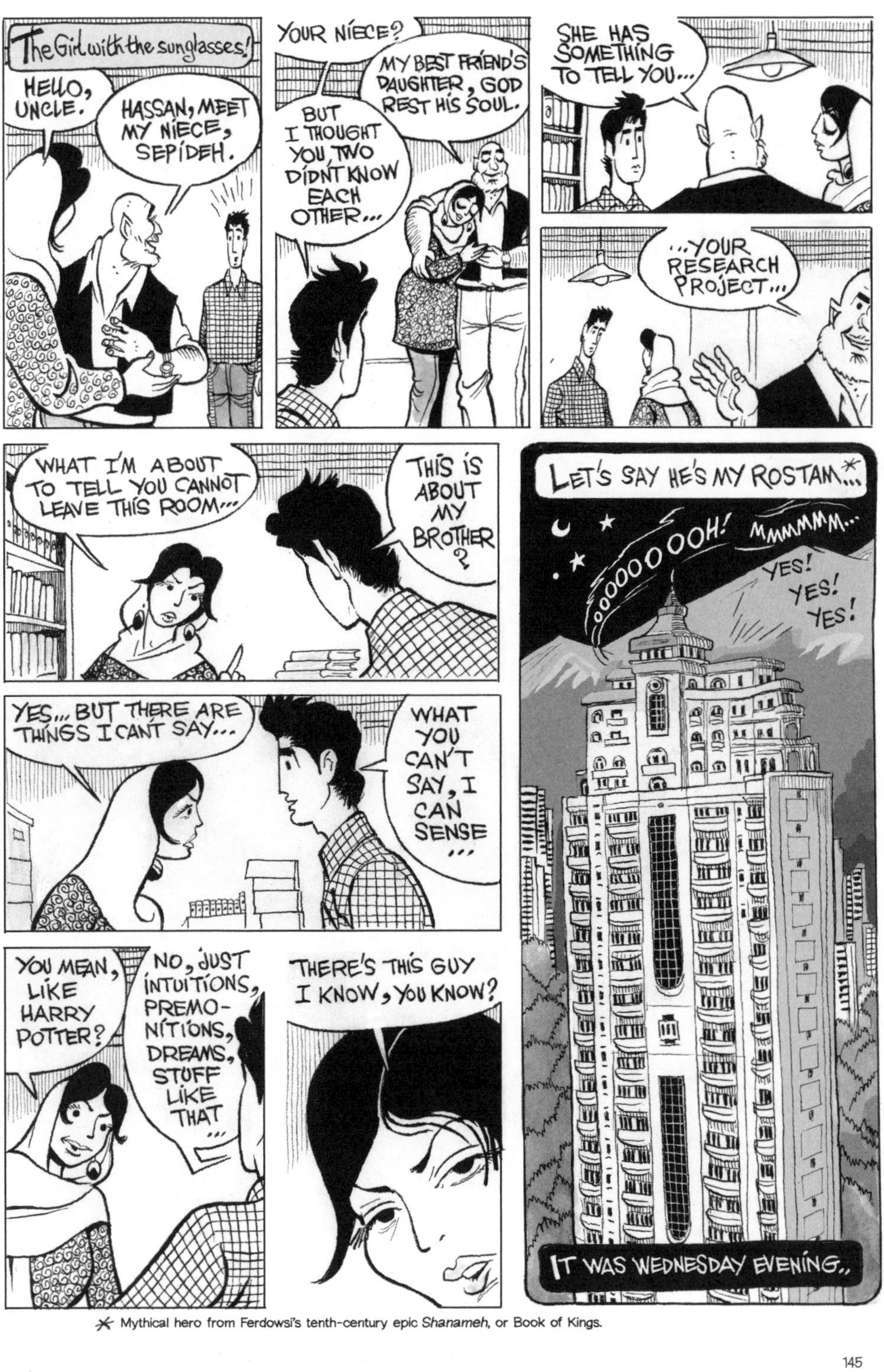
The Girl with the sunglasses!
HELLO, UNCLE.
HASSAN, MEET MY NIECE, SEPIDEH.
YOUR NIECE?
MY BEST FRIEND'S DAUGHTER, GOD REST HIS SOUL.
BUT I THOUGHT YOU TWO DIDN'T KNOW EACH OTHER...
SHE HAS SOMETHING TO TELL YOU...
...YOUR RESEARCH PROJECT...
WHAT I'M ABOUT TO TELL YOU CANNOT LEAVE THIS ROOM...
THIS IS ABOUT MY BROTHER?
YES... BUT THERE ARE THINGS I CAN'T SAY...
WHAT YOU CAN'T SAY, I CAN SENSE...
YOU MEAN, LIKE HARRY POTTER?
NO, JUST INTUITIONS, PREMO-NITIONS, DREAMS, STUFF LIKE THAT...
THERE'S THIS GUY I KNOW, YOU KNOW?
LET'S SAY HE'S MY ROSTAM*...
OOOOOOOOH!
MMMMMM...
YES! YES! YES!
IT WAS WEDNESDAY EVENING..

* Mythical hero from Ferdowsi's tenth-century epic *Shanameh*, or Book of Kings.

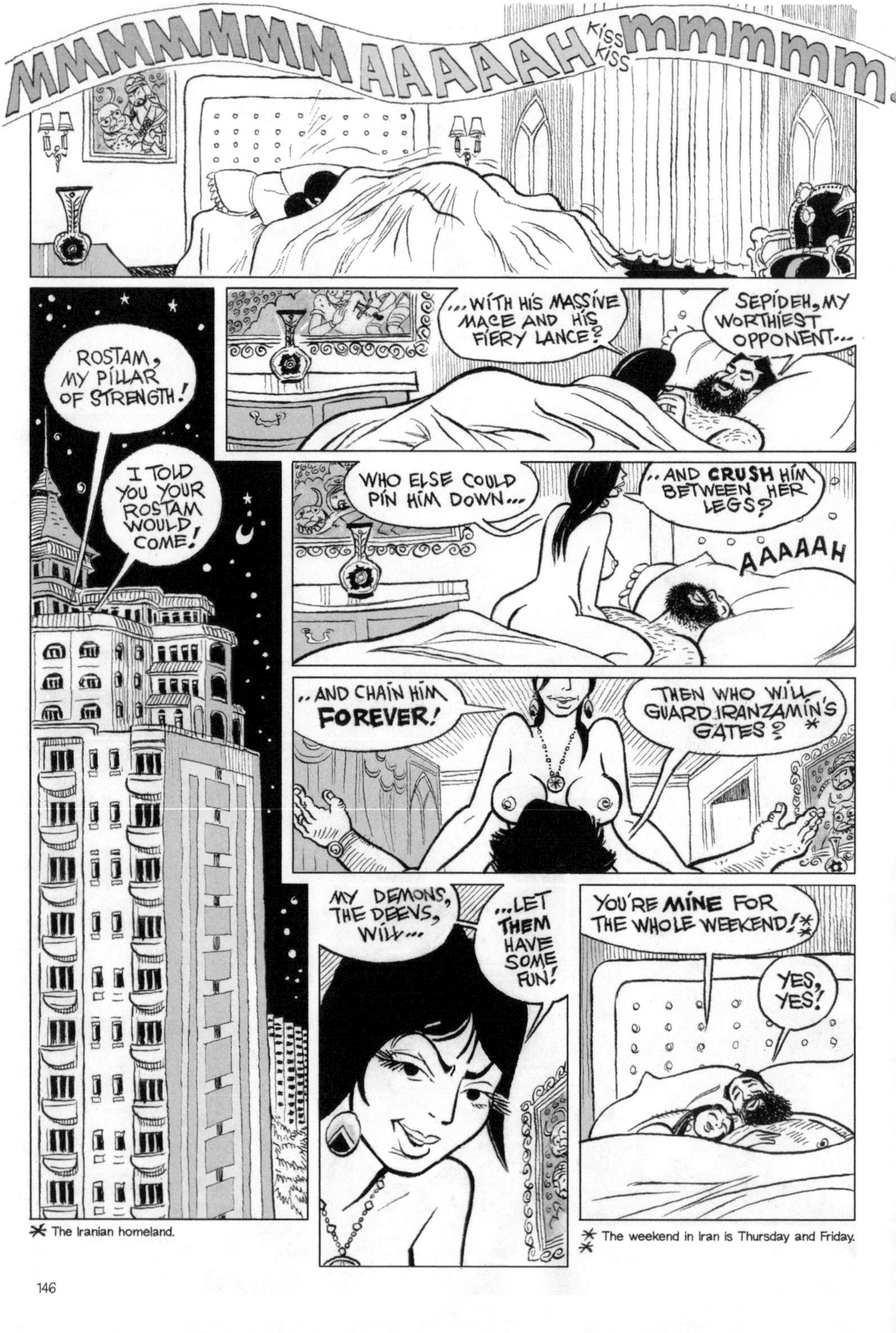

MMMMMMMAAAAAAH
KISS KISS
mmmmm
ROSTAM, MY PILLAR OF STRENGTH!
I TOLD YOU YOUR ROSTAM WOULD COME!
...WITH HIS MASSIVE MACE AND HIS FIERY LANCE?
SEPIDEH, MY WORTHIEST OPPONENT...
WHO ELSE COULD PIN HIM DOWN...
...AND CRUSH HIM BETWEEN HER LEGS?
AAAAAH
..AND CHAIN HIM FOREVER!
THEN WHO WILL GUARD IRANZAMIN'S GATES? *
MY DEMONS, THE DEEVS, WILL...
...LET THEM HAVE SOME FUN!
YOU'RE MINE FOR THE WHOLE WEEKEND! **
YES, YES!

* The Iranian homeland.

** The weekend in Iran is Thursday and Friday.

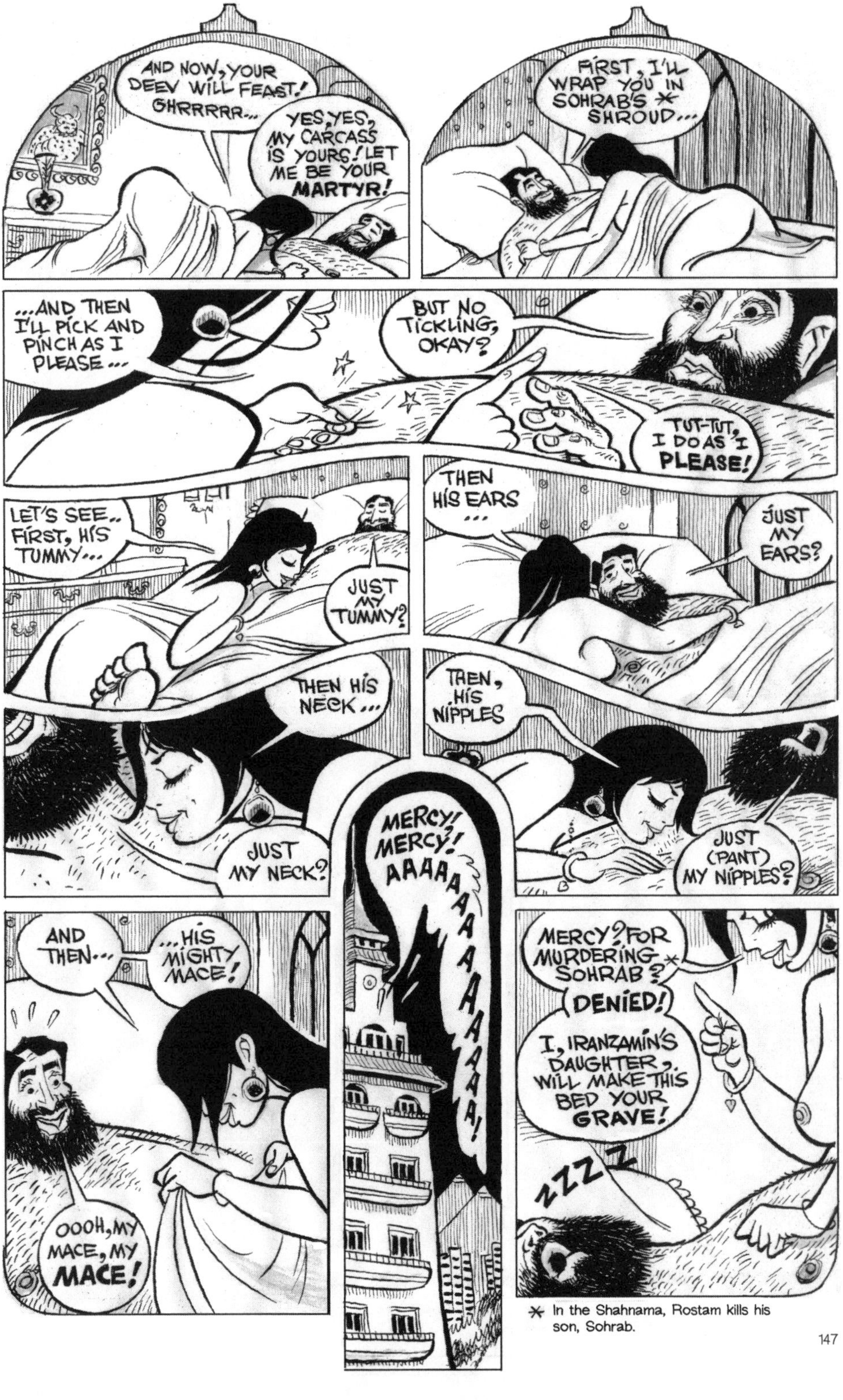
AND NOW, YOUR DEEV WILL FEAST! GHRRRRR...
YES, YES, MY CARCASS IS YOURS! LET ME BE YOUR MARTYR!
FIRST, I'LL WRAP YOU IN SOHRAB'S * SHROUD...
...AND THEN I'LL PICK AND PINCH AS I PLEASE...
BUT NO TICKLING, OKAY?
TUT-TUT, I DO AS I PLEASE!
LET'S SEE.. FIRST, HIS TUMMY...
JUST MY TUMMY?
THEN HIS EARS ...
JUST MY EARS?
THEN HIS NECK...
JUST MY NECK?
THEN, HIS NIPPLES
JUST (PANT) MY NIPPLES?
MERCY! MERCY! AAAAAAAAAAAAAAAA!
AND THEN...
...HIS MIGHTY MACE!
OOOH, MY MACE, MY MACE!
MERCY? FOR MURDERING SOHRAB? *
DENIED!
I, IRANZAMIN'S DAUGHTER, WILL MAKE THIS BED YOUR GRAVE!
ZZZZ

* In the Shahnama, Rostam kills his son, Sohrab.

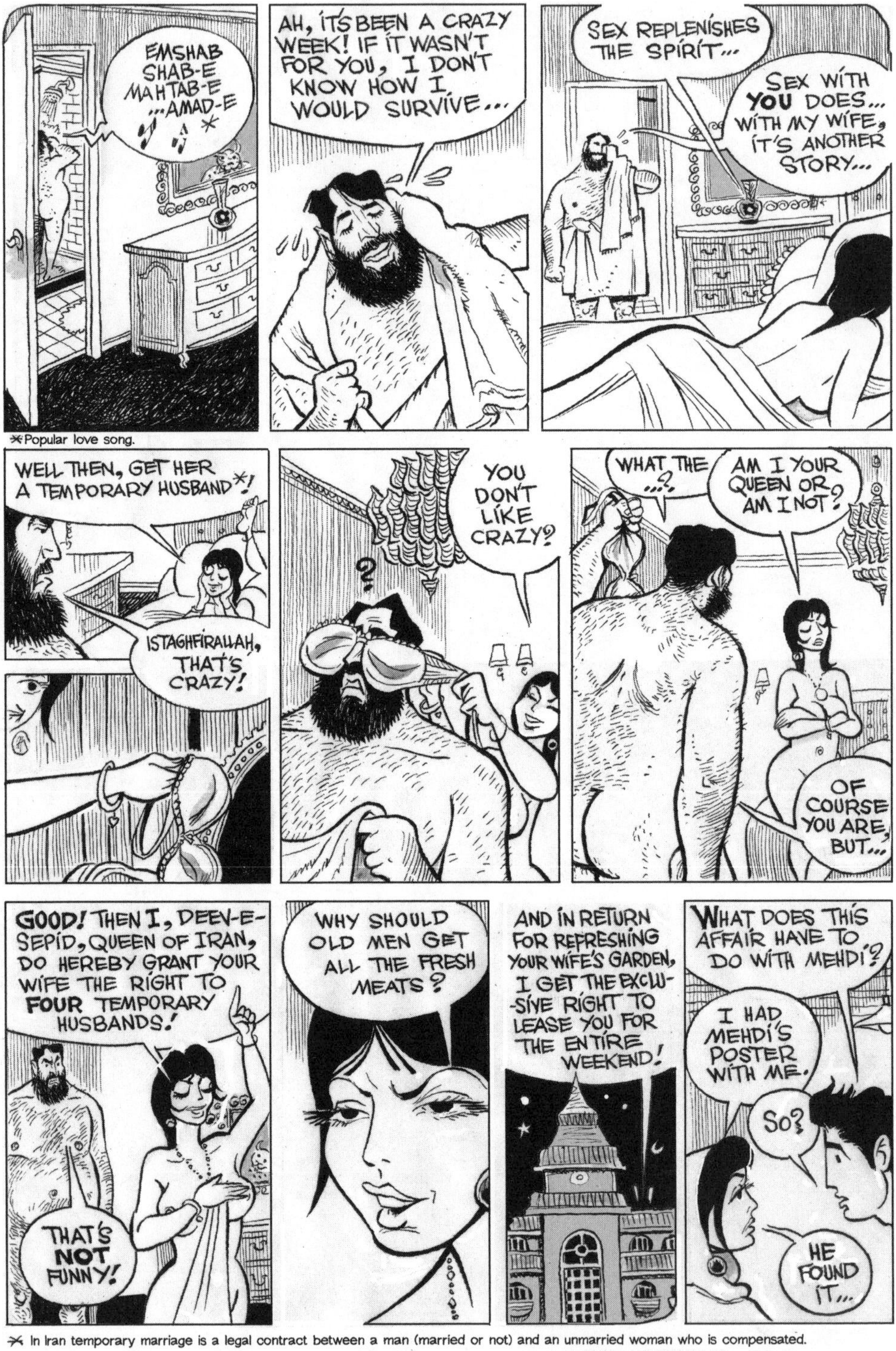
EMSHAB SHAB-E MAHTAB-E ...AMAD-E *
AH, IT'S BEEN A CRAZY WEEK! IF IT WASN'T FOR YOU, I DON'T KNOW HOW I WOULD SURVIVE...
SEX REPLENISHES THE SPIRIT...
SEX WITH **YOU** DOES... WITH MY WIFE, IT'S ANOTHER STORY...
*Popular love song.
WELL THEN, GET HER A TEMPORARY HUSBAND*!
ISTAGHFIRALLAH, THAT'S CRAZY!
YOU DON'T LIKE CRAZY?
WHAT THE ...?
AM I YOUR QUEEN OR AM I NOT?
OF COURSE YOU ARE, BUT...
GOOD! THEN I, DEEV-E-SEPID, QUEEN OF IRAN, DO HEREBY GRANT YOUR WIFE THE RIGHT TO **FOUR** TEMPORARY HUSBANDS!
THAT'S **NOT** FUNNY!
WHY SHOULD OLD MEN GET ALL THE FRESH MEATS?
AND IN RETURN FOR REFRESHING YOUR WIFE'S GARDEN, I GET THE EXCLU-SIVE RIGHT TO LEASE YOU FOR THE ENTIRE WEEKEND!
WHAT DOES THIS AFFAIR HAVE TO DO WITH MEHDI?
I HAD MEHDI'S POSTER WITH ME.
SO?
HE FOUND IT...

* In Iran temporary marriage is a legal contract between a man (married or not) and an unmarried woman who is compensated.

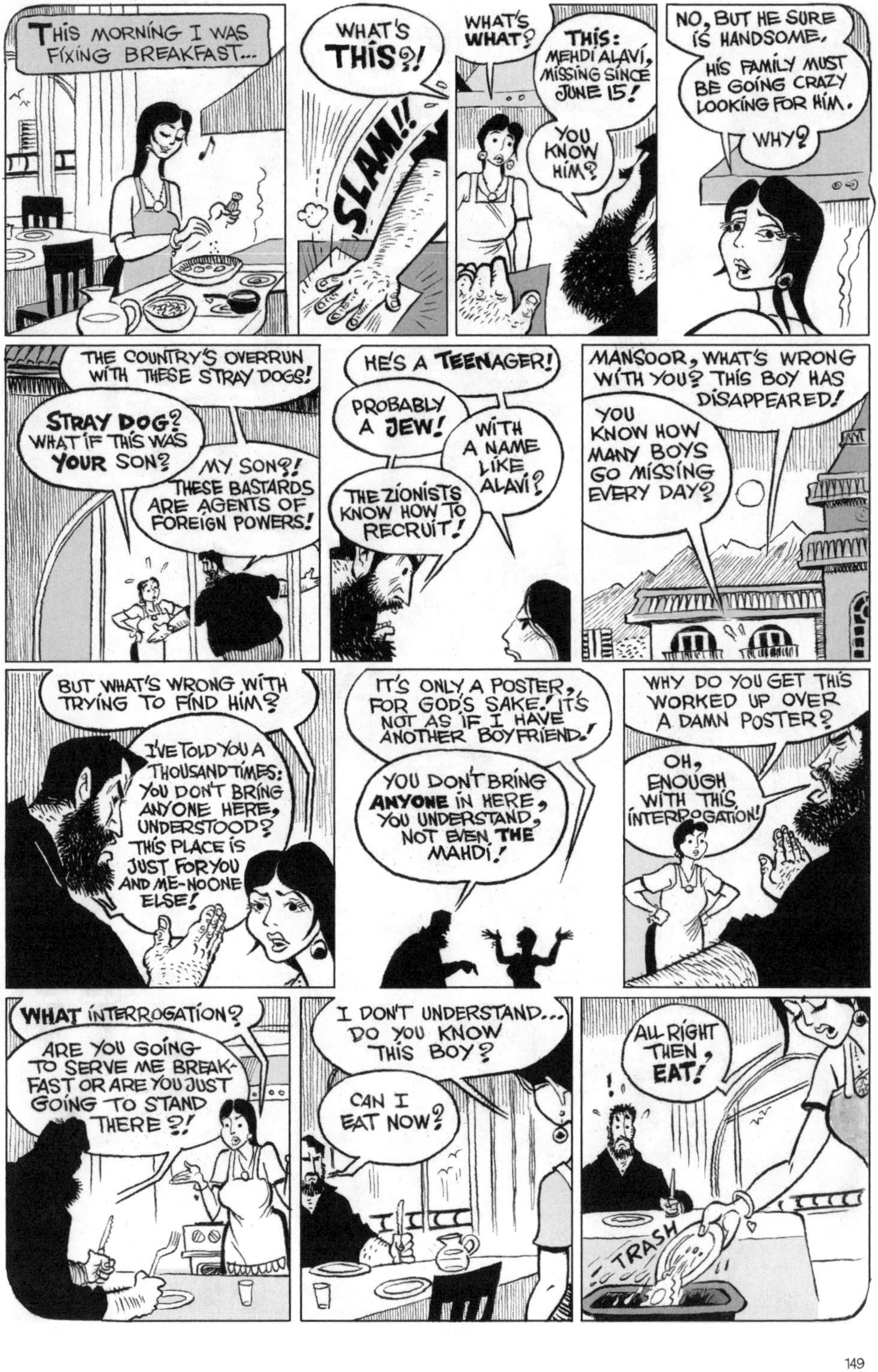
THIS MORNING I WAS FIXING BREAKFAST...
WHAT'S THIS?!
SLAM!!
WHAT'S WHAT?
THIS: MEHDI ALAVI, MISSING SINCE JUNE 15!
YOU KNOW HIM?
NO, BUT HE SURE IS HANDSOME.
HIS FAMILY MUST BE GOING CRAZY LOOKING FOR HIM.
WHY?
THE COUNTRY'S OVERRUN WITH THESE STRAY DOGS!
STRAY DOG? WHAT IF THIS WAS YOUR SON?
MY SON?! THESE BASTARDS ARE AGENTS OF FOREIGN POWERS!
HE'S A TEENAGER!
PROBABLY A JEW!
WITH A NAME LIKE ALAVI?
THE ZIONISTS KNOW HOW TO RECRUIT!
MANSOOR, WHAT'S WRONG WITH YOU? THIS BOY HAS DISAPPEARED!
YOU KNOW HOW MANY BOYS GO MISSING EVERY DAY?
BUT WHAT'S WRONG WITH TRYING TO FIND HIM?
I'VE TOLD YOU A THOUSAND TIMES: YOU DON'T BRING ANYONE HERE, UNDERSTOOD? THIS PLACE IS JUST FOR YOU AND ME-NOONE ELSE!
IT'S ONLY A POSTER, FOR GOD'S SAKE! IT'S NOT AS IF I HAVE ANOTHER BOYFRIEND!
YOU DON'T BRING ANYONE IN HERE, YOU UNDERSTAND, NOT EVEN THE MAHDI!
WHY DO YOU GET THIS WORKED UP OVER A DAMN POSTER?
OH, ENOUGH WITH THIS INTERROGATION!
WHAT INTERROGATION?
ARE YOU GOING TO SERVE ME BREAKFAST OR ARE YOU JUST GOING TO STAND THERE?!
I DON'T UNDERSTAND... DO YOU KNOW THIS BOY?
CAN I EAT NOW?
ALL RIGHT THEN, EAT!
TRASH

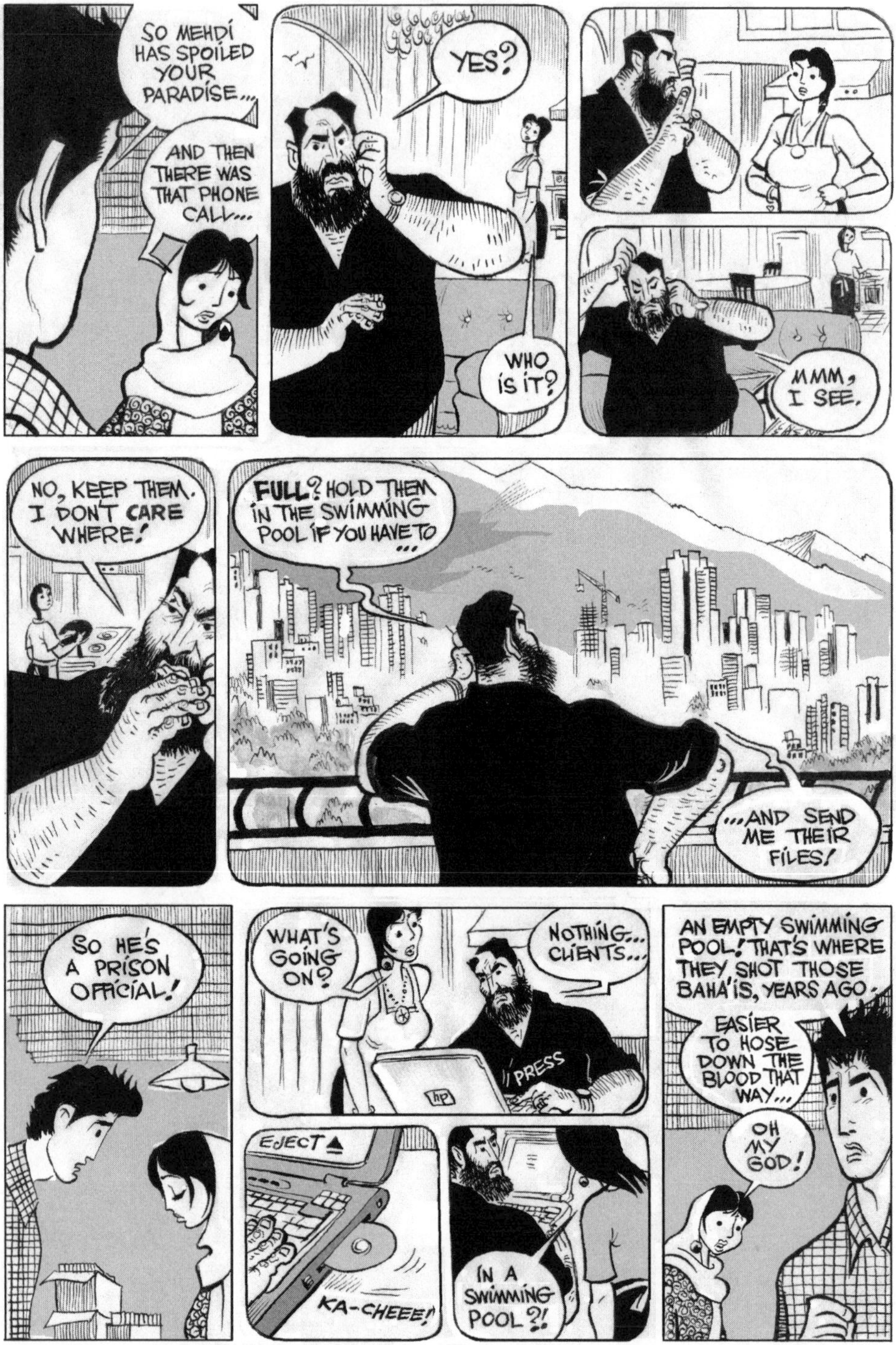
SO MEHDI HAS SPOILED YOUR PARADISE...
AND THEN THERE WAS THAT PHONE CALL...
YES?
WHO IS IT?
MMM, I SEE.
NO, KEEP THEM. I DON'T CARE WHERE!
FULL? HOLD THEM IN THE SWIMMING POOL IF YOU HAVE TO...
...AND SEND ME THEIR FILES!
SO HE'S A PRISON OFFICIAL!
WHAT'S GOING ON?
NOTHING... CLIENTS...
PRESS
EJECT
KA-CHEEE!
IN A SWIMMING POOL?!
AN EMPTY SWIMMING POOL! THAT'S WHERE THEY SHOT THOSE BAHA'IS, YEARS AGO.
EASIER TO HOSE DOWN THE BLOOD THAT WAY...
OH MY GOD!

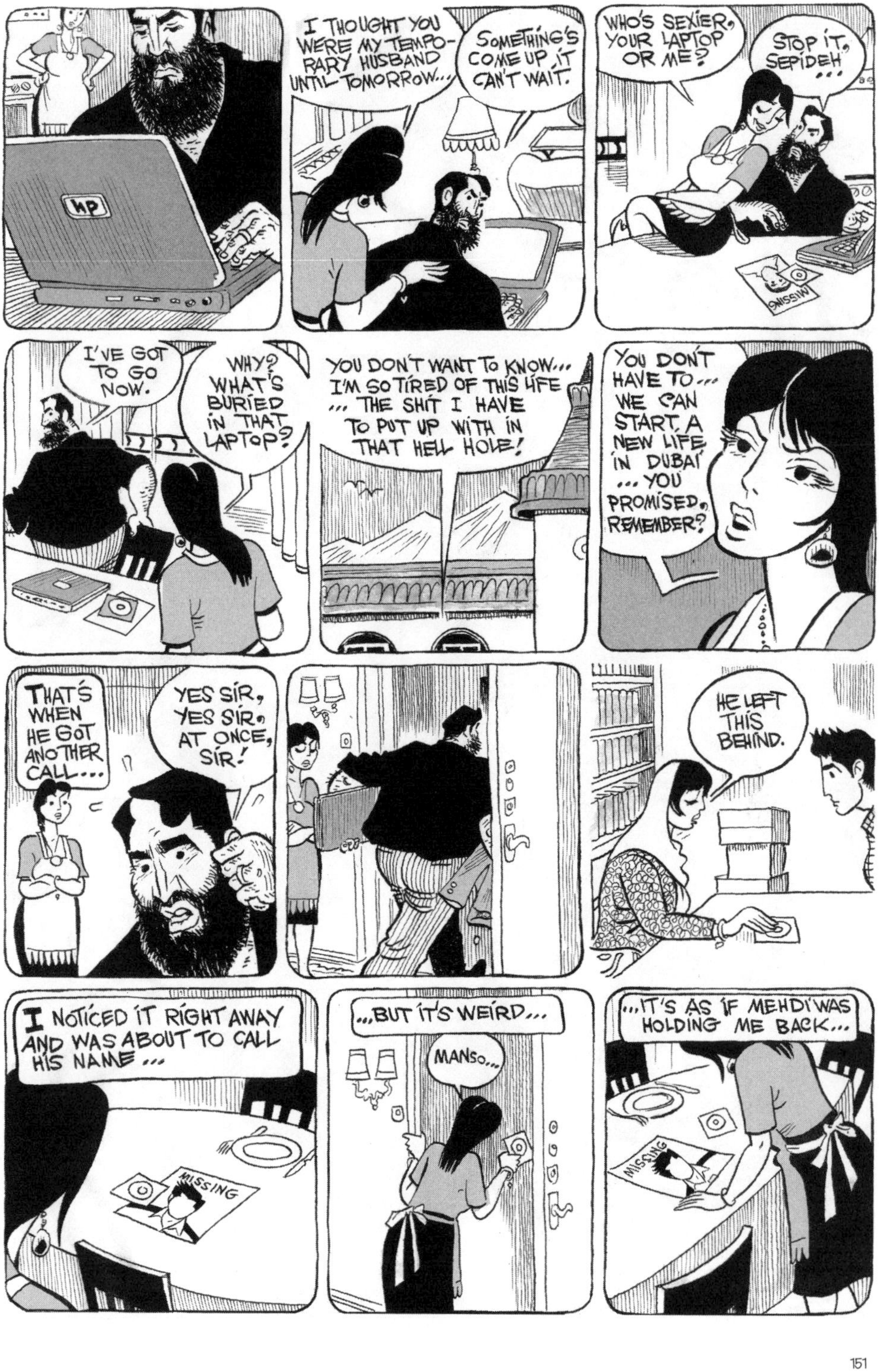
I THOUGHT YOU WERE MY TEMPORARY HUSBAND UNTIL TOMORROW...
SOMETHING'S COME UP. IT CAN'T WAIT.
WHO'S SEXIER, YOUR LAPTOP OR ME?
STOP IT, SEPIDEH...
MISSING
I'VE GOT TO GO NOW.
WHY? WHAT'S BURIED IN THAT LAPTOP?
YOU DON'T WANT TO KNOW... I'M SO TIRED OF THIS LIFE ... THE SHIT I HAVE TO PUT UP WITH IN THAT HELL HOLE!
YOU DON'T HAVE TO... WE CAN START A NEW LIFE IN DUBAI ... YOU PROMISED, REMEMBER?
THAT'S WHEN HE GOT ANOTHER CALL...
YES SIR, YES SIR, AT ONCE, SIR!
HE LEFT THIS BEHIND.
I NOTICED IT RIGHT AWAY AND WAS ABOUT TO CALL HIS NAME ...
MISSING
...BUT IT'S WEIRD...
MANSO...
...IT'S AS IF MEHDI WAS HOLDING ME BACK...
MISSING

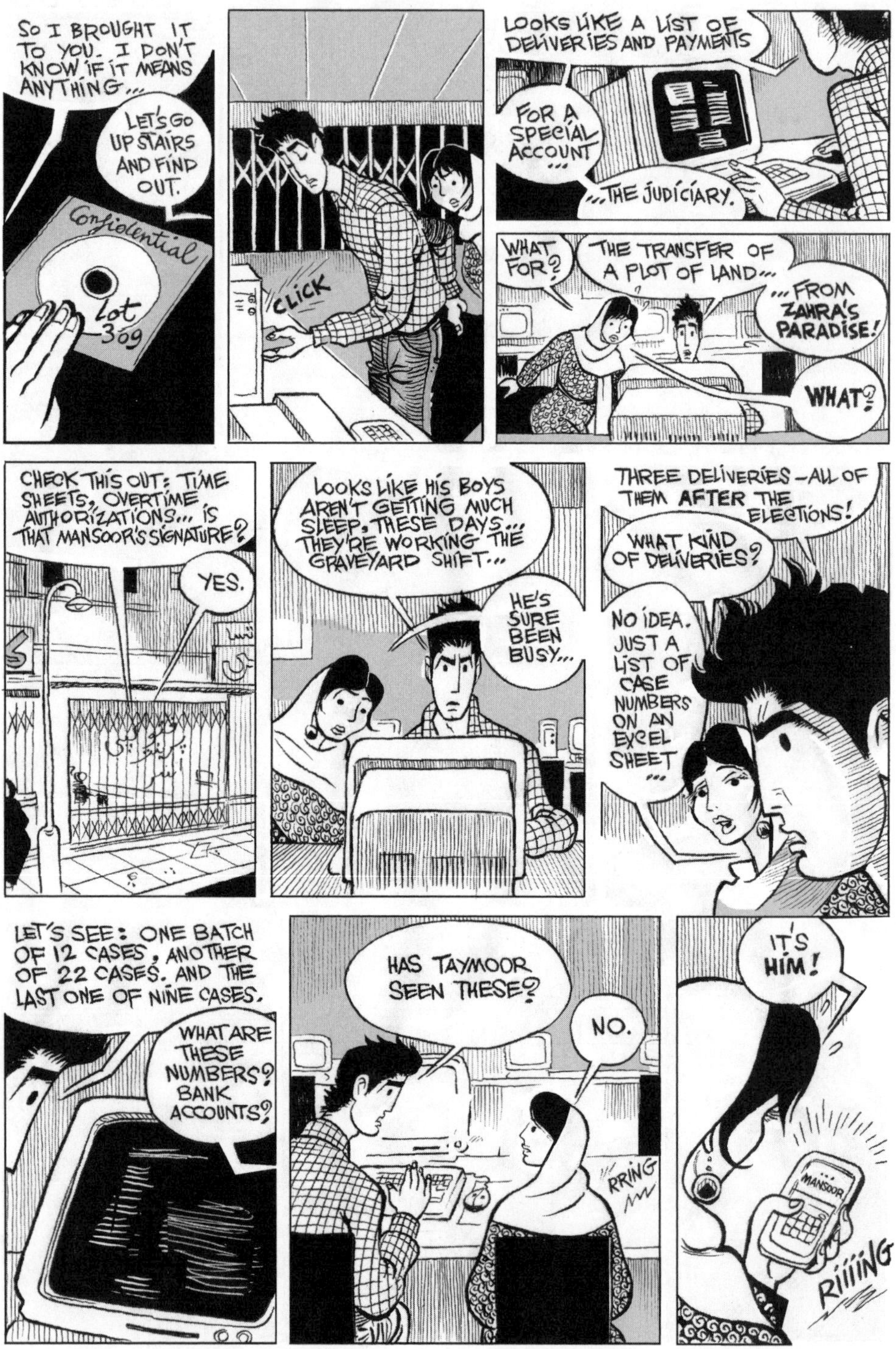
SO I BROUGHT IT TO YOU. I DON'T KNOW IF IT MEANS ANYTHING...
LET'S GO UPSTAIRS AND FIND OUT.
Confidential
Lot 309
CLICK
LOOKS LIKE A LIST OF DELIVERIES AND PAYMENTS
FOR A SPECIAL ACCOUNT...
...THE JUDICIARY.
WHAT FOR?
THE TRANSFER OF A PLOT OF LAND...
...FROM ZAHRA'S PARADISE!
WHAT?
CHECK THIS OUT: TIME SHEETS, OVERTIME AUTHORIZATIONS... IS THAT MANSOOR'S SIGNATURE?
YES.
LOOKS LIKE HIS BOYS AREN'T GETTING MUCH SLEEP, THESE DAYS... THEY'RE WORKING THE GRAVEYARD SHIFT...
HE'S SURE BEEN BUSY...
THREE DELIVERIES—ALL OF THEM AFTER THE ELECTIONS!
WHAT KIND OF DELIVERIES?
NO IDEA. JUST A LIST OF CASE NUMBERS ON AN EXCEL SHEET...
LET'S SEE: ONE BATCH OF 12 CASES, ANOTHER OF 22 CASES. AND THE LAST ONE OF NINE CASES.
WHAT ARE THESE NUMBERS? BANK ACCOUNTS?
HAS TAYMOOR SEEN THESE?
NO.
RRING
IT'S HIM!
MANSOOR
RIIIING

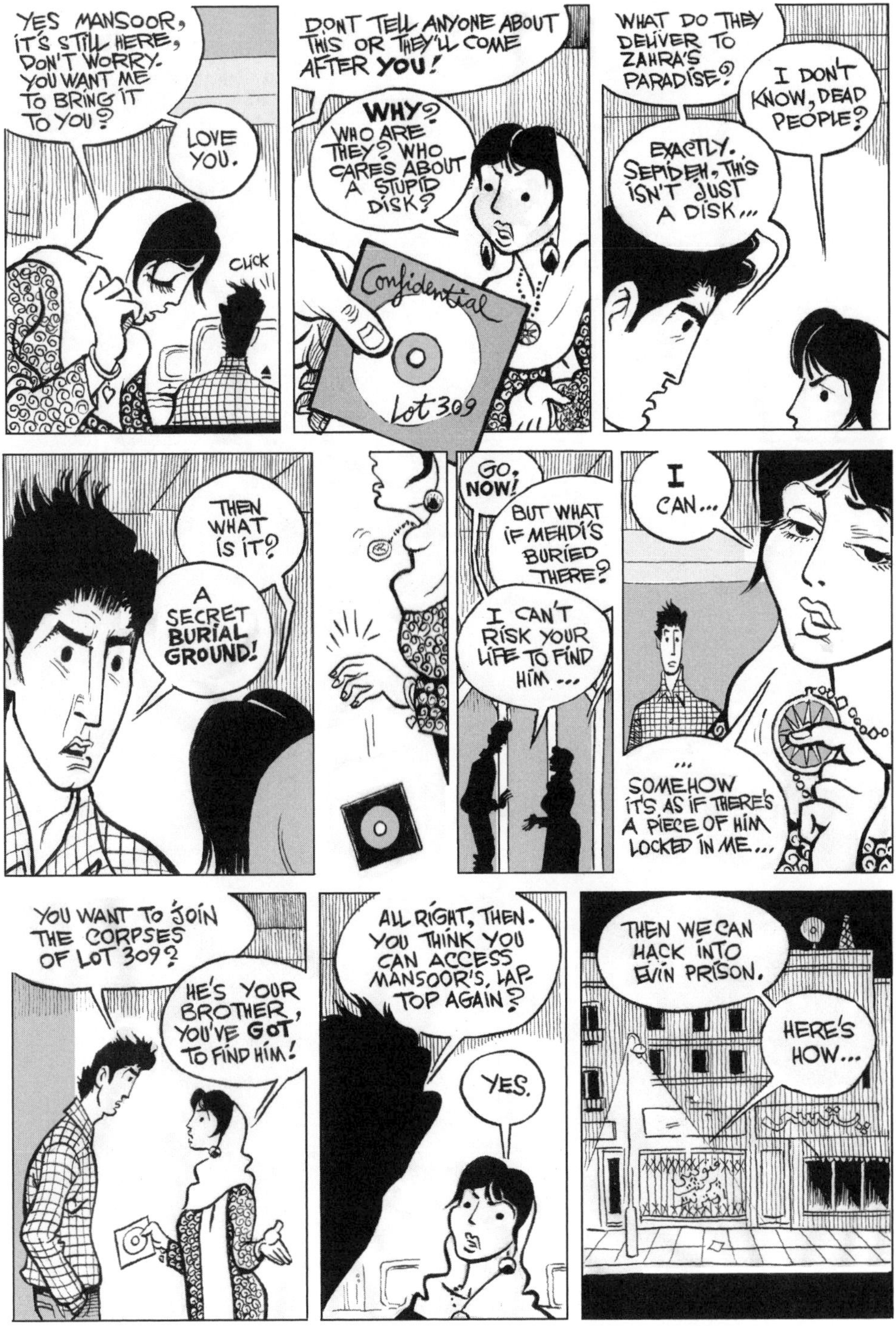

YES MANSOOR, IT'S STILL HERE, DON'T WORRY. YOU WANT ME TO BRING IT TO YOU?
LOVE YOU.
CLICK
DONT TELL ANYONE ABOUT THIS OR THEY'LL COME AFTER **YOU**!
WHY? WHO ARE THEY? WHO CARES ABOUT A STUPID DISK?
Confidential
Lot 309
WHAT DO THEY DELIVER TO ZAHRA'S PARADISE?
I DON'T KNOW, DEAD PEOPLE?
EXACTLY. SEPIDEH, THIS ISN'T JUST A DISK...
THEN WHAT IS IT?
A SECRET **BURIAL GROUND**!
GO, **NOW**!
BUT WHAT IF MEHDI'S BURIED THERE?
I CAN'T RISK YOUR LIFE TO FIND HIM...
I CAN...
...SOMEHOW IT'S AS IF THERE'S A PIECE OF HIM LOCKED IN ME...
YOU WANT TO JOIN THE CORPSES OF LOT 309?
HE'S YOUR BROTHER, YOU'VE **GOT** TO FIND HIM!
ALL RIGHT, THEN. YOU THINK YOU CAN ACCESS MANSOOR'S LAP-TOP AGAIN?
YES.
THEN WE CAN HACK INTO EVIN PRISON.
HERE'S HOW...

LOT 309

CHAPTER TWELVE

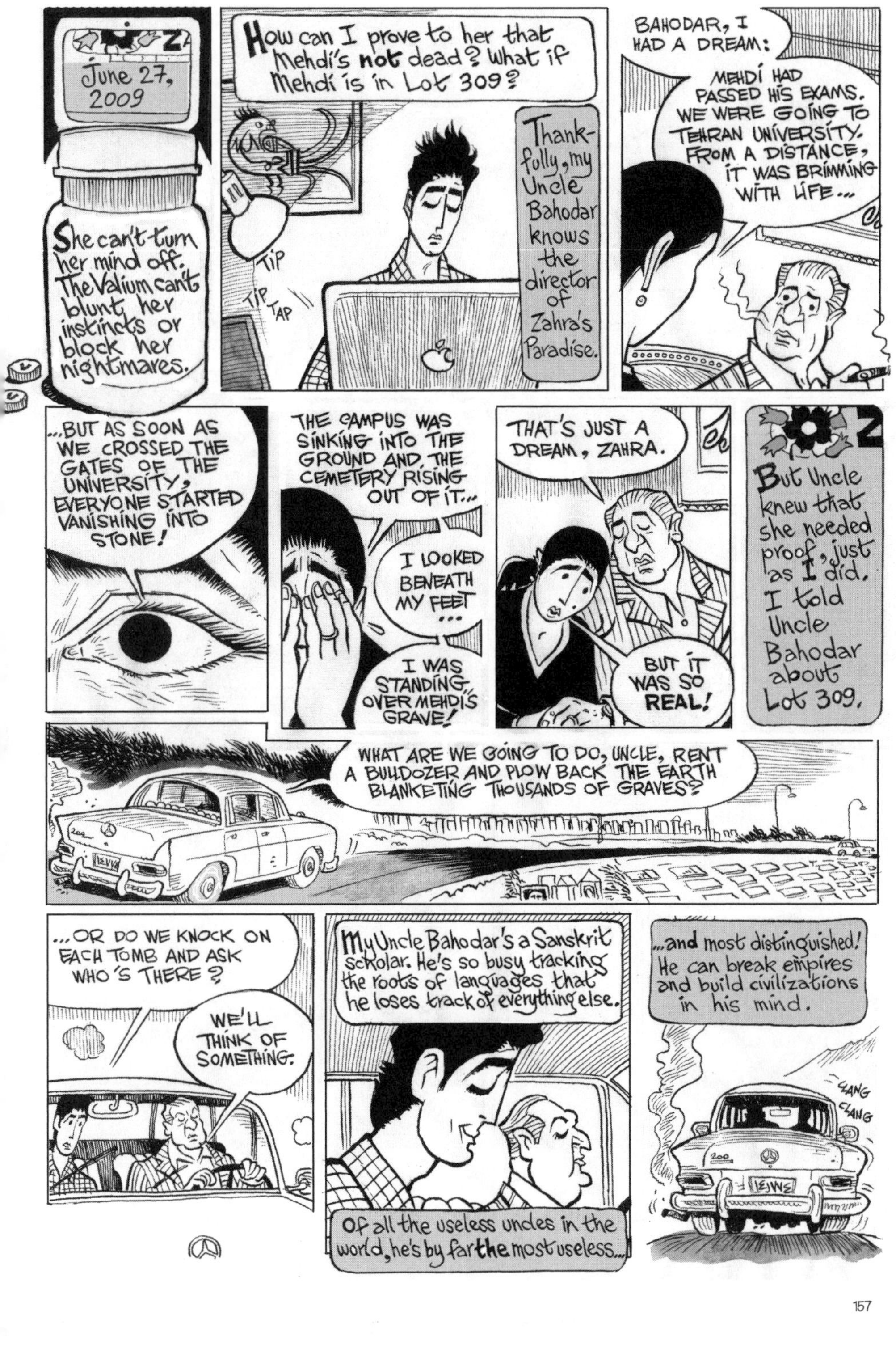
June 27, 2009
She can't turn her mind off. The Valium can't blunt her instincts or block her nightmares.
How can I prove to her that Mehdi's **not** dead? What if Mehdi is in Lot 309?
TIP TIP TAP
Thankfully, my Uncle Bahodar knows the director of Zahra's Paradise.
BAHODAR, I HAD A DREAM:
MEHDI HAD PASSED HIS EXAMS. WE WERE GOING TO TEHRAN UNIVERSITY. FROM A DISTANCE, IT WAS BRIMMING WITH LIFE...
...BUT AS SOON AS WE CROSSED THE GATES OF THE UNIVERSITY, EVERYONE STARTED VANISHING INTO STONE!
THE CAMPUS WAS SINKING INTO THE GROUND AND THE CEMETERY RISING OUT OF IT...
I LOOKED BENEATH MY FEET...
I WAS STANDING OVER MEHDI'S GRAVE!
THAT'S JUST A DREAM, ZAHRA.
BUT IT WAS SO **REAL**!
But Uncle knew that she needed proof, just as I did. I told Uncle Bahodar about Lot 309.
WHAT ARE WE GOING TO DO, UNCLE, RENT A BULLDOZER AND PLOW BACK THE EARTH BLANKETING THOUSANDS OF GRAVES?
...OR DO WE KNOCK ON EACH TOMB AND ASK WHO'S THERE?
WE'LL THINK OF SOMETHING.
My Uncle Bahodar's a Sanskrit scholar. He's so busy tracking the roots of languages that he loses track of everything else.
Of all the useless uncles in the world, he's by far **the** most useless...
...**and** most distinguished! He can break empires and build civilizations in his mind.
CLANG CLANG

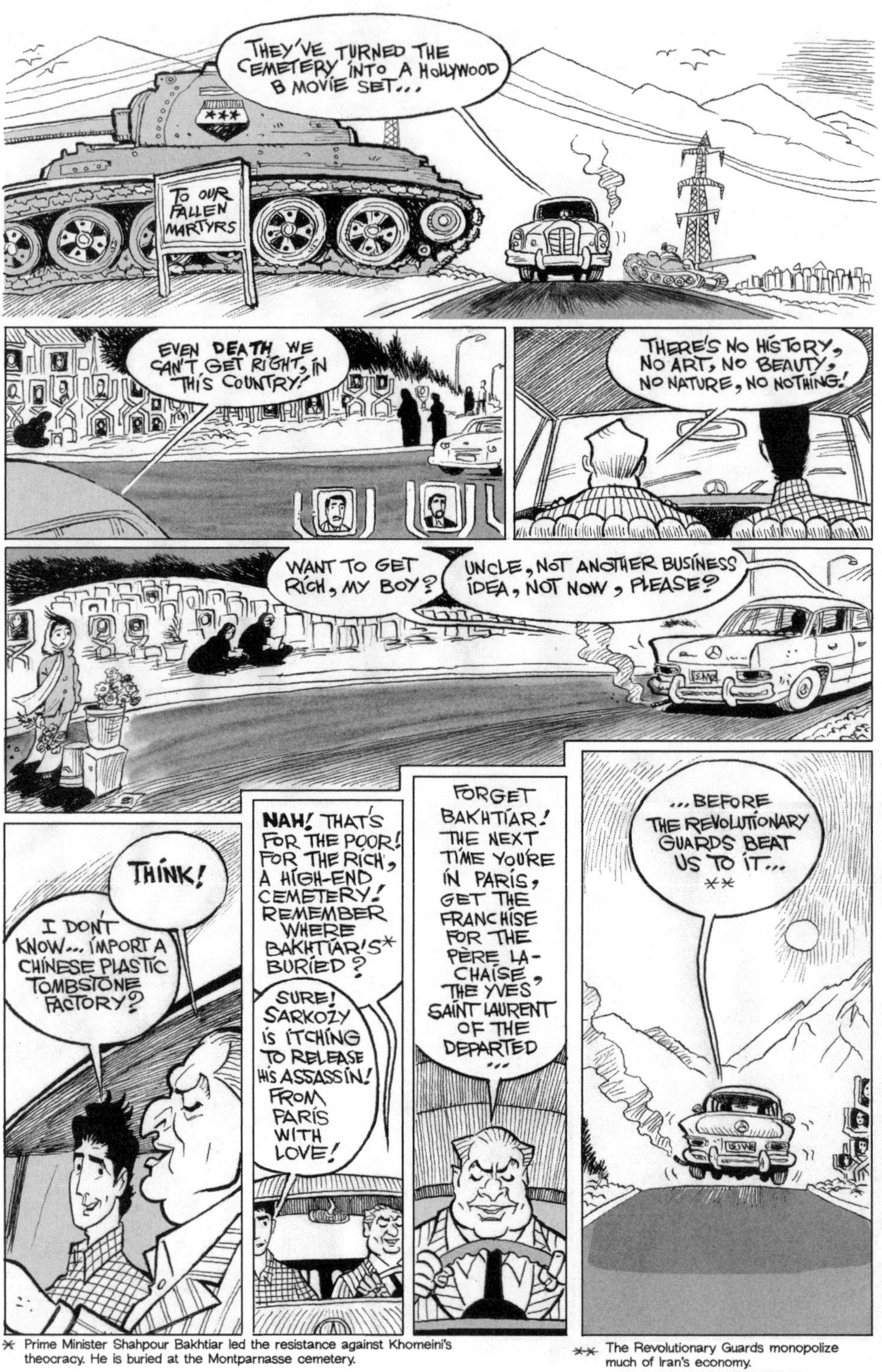
THEY'VE TURNED THE CEMETERY INTO A HOLLYWOOD B MOVIE SET...
TO OUR FALLEN MARTYRS
EVEN DEATH WE CAN'T GET RIGHT, IN THIS COUNTRY!
THERE'S NO HISTORY, NO ART, NO BEAUTY, NO NATURE, NO NOTHING!
WANT TO GET RICH, MY BOY?
UNCLE, NOT ANOTHER BUSINESS IDEA, NOT NOW, PLEASE?
THINK!
I DON'T KNOW... IMPORT A CHINESE PLASTIC TOMBSTONE FACTORY?
NAH! THAT'S FOR THE POOR! FOR THE RICH, A HIGH-END CEMETERY! REMEMBER WHERE BAKHTIAR'S* BURIED?
SURE! SARKOZY IS ITCHING TO RELEASE HIS ASSASSIN! FROM PARIS WITH LOVE!
FORGET BAKHTIAR! THE NEXT TIME YOU'RE IN PARIS, GET THE FRANCHISE FOR THE PÈRE LA-CHAISE, THE YVES SAINT LAURENT OF THE DEPARTED...
...BEFORE THE REVOLUTIONARY GUARDS BEAT US TO IT... **

* Prime Minister Shahpour Bakhtiar led the resistance against Khomeini's theocracy. He is buried at the Montparnasse cemetery.

** The Revolutionary Guards monopolize much of Iran's economy.

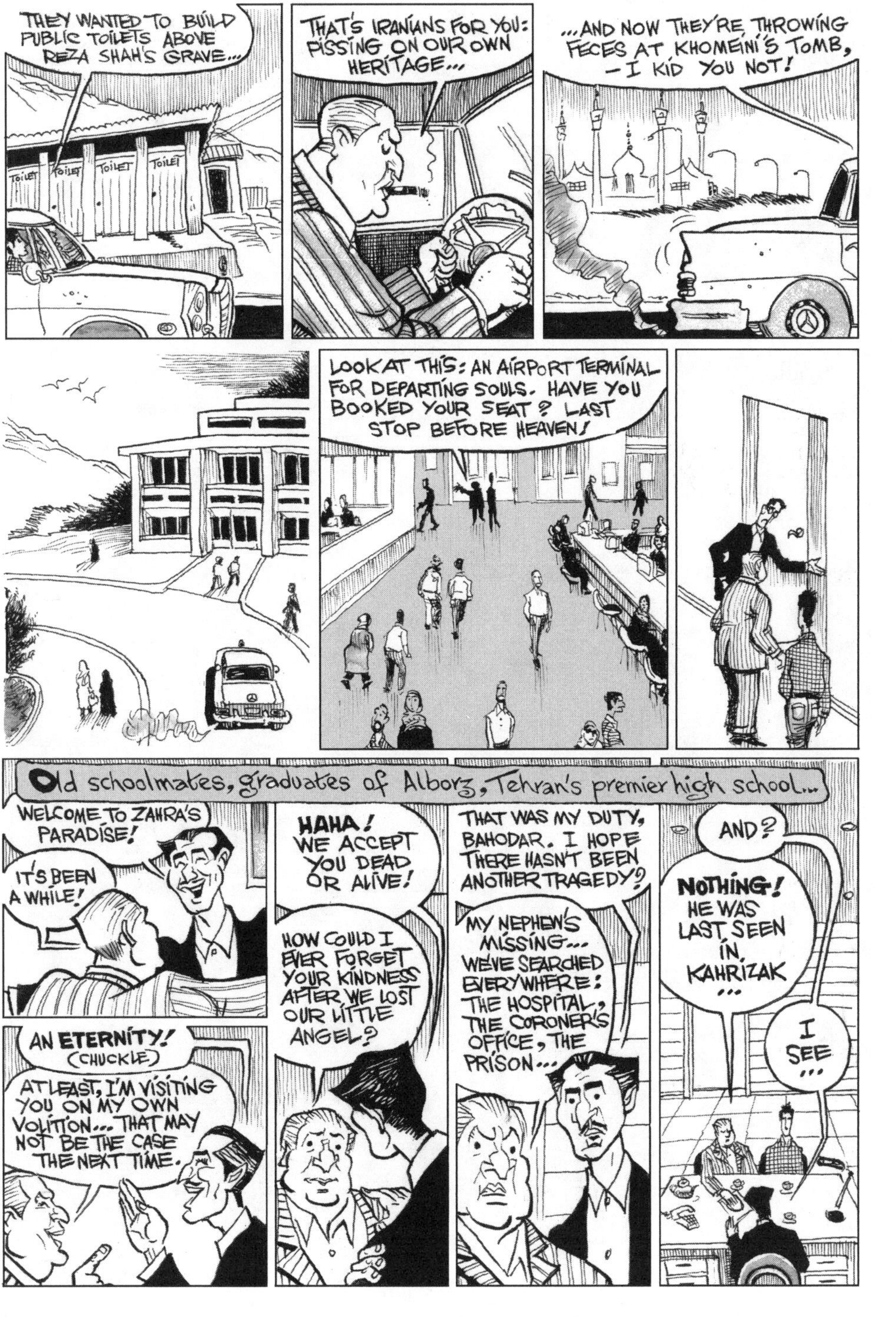

THEY WANTED TO BUILD PUBLIC TOILETS ABOVE REZA SHAH'S GRAVE...
TOILET TOILET TOILET TOILET
THAT'S IRANIANS FOR YOU: PISSING ON OUR OWN HERITAGE...
...AND NOW THEY'RE THROWING FECES AT KHOMEINI'S TOMB, —I KID YOU NOT!
LOOK AT THIS: AN AIRPORT TERMINAL FOR DEPARTING SOULS. HAVE YOU BOOKED YOUR SEAT? LAST STOP BEFORE HEAVEN!
Old schoolmates, graduates of Alborz, Tehran's premier high school...
WELCOME TO ZAHRA'S PARADISE!
IT'S BEEN A WHILE!
AN ETERNITY! (CHUCKLE)
AT LEAST, I'M VISITING YOU ON MY OWN VOLITION... THAT MAY NOT BE THE CASE THE NEXT TIME.
HAHA! WE ACCEPT YOU DEAD OR ALIVE!
HOW COULD I EVER FORGET YOUR KINDNESS AFTER WE LOST OUR LITTLE ANGEL?
THAT WAS MY DUTY, BAHODAR. I HOPE THERE HASN'T BEEN ANOTHER TRAGEDY?
MY NEPHEW'S MISSING... WE'VE SEARCHED EVERYWHERE: THE HOSPITAL, THE CORONER'S OFFICE, THE PRISON...
AND?
NOTHING! HE WAS LAST SEEN IN KAHRIZAK...
I SEE...

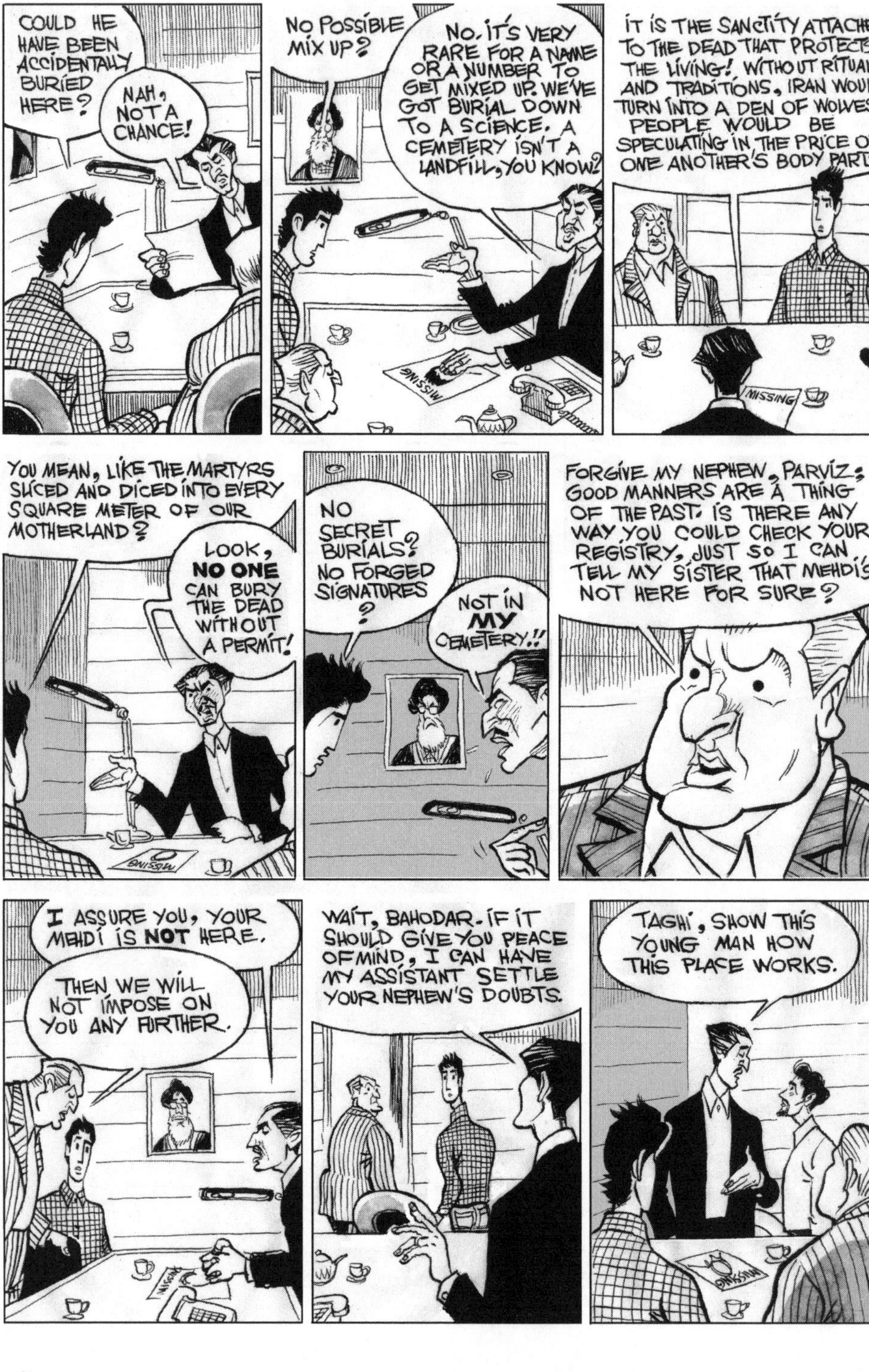
COULD HE HAVE BEEN ACCIDENTALLY BURIED HERE?
NAH, NOT A CHANCE!
NO POSSIBLE MIX UP?
NO. IT'S VERY RARE FOR A NAME OR A NUMBER TO GET MIXED UP. WE'VE GOT BURIAL DOWN TO A SCIENCE. A CEMETERY ISN'T A LANDFILL, YOU KNOW!
MISSING
IT IS THE SANCTITY ATTACHED TO THE DEAD THAT PROTECTS THE LIVING! WITHOUT RITUALS AND TRADITIONS, IRAN WOULD TURN INTO A DEN OF WOLVES! PEOPLE WOULD BE SPECULATING IN THE PRICE OF ONE ANOTHER'S BODY PARTS!
MISSING
YOU MEAN, LIKE THE MARTYRS SLICED AND DICED INTO EVERY SQUARE METER OF OUR MOTHERLAND?
LOOK, NO ONE CAN BURY THE DEAD WITHOUT A PERMIT!
MISSING
NO SECRET BURIALS? NO FORGED SIGNATURES?
NOT IN MY CEMETERY!!
FORGIVE MY NEPHEW, PARVIZ; GOOD MANNERS ARE A THING OF THE PAST. IS THERE ANY WAY YOU COULD CHECK YOUR REGISTRY, JUST SO I CAN TELL MY SISTER THAT MEHDI'S NOT HERE FOR SURE?
I ASSURE YOU, YOUR MEHDI IS NOT HERE.
THEN WE WILL NOT IMPOSE ON YOU ANY FURTHER.
MISSING
WAIT, BAHODAR. IF IT SHOULD GIVE YOU PEACE OF MIND, I CAN HAVE MY ASSISTANT SETTLE YOUR NEPHEW'S DOUBTS.
TAGHI, SHOW THIS YOUNG MAN HOW THIS PLACE WORKS.
MISSING

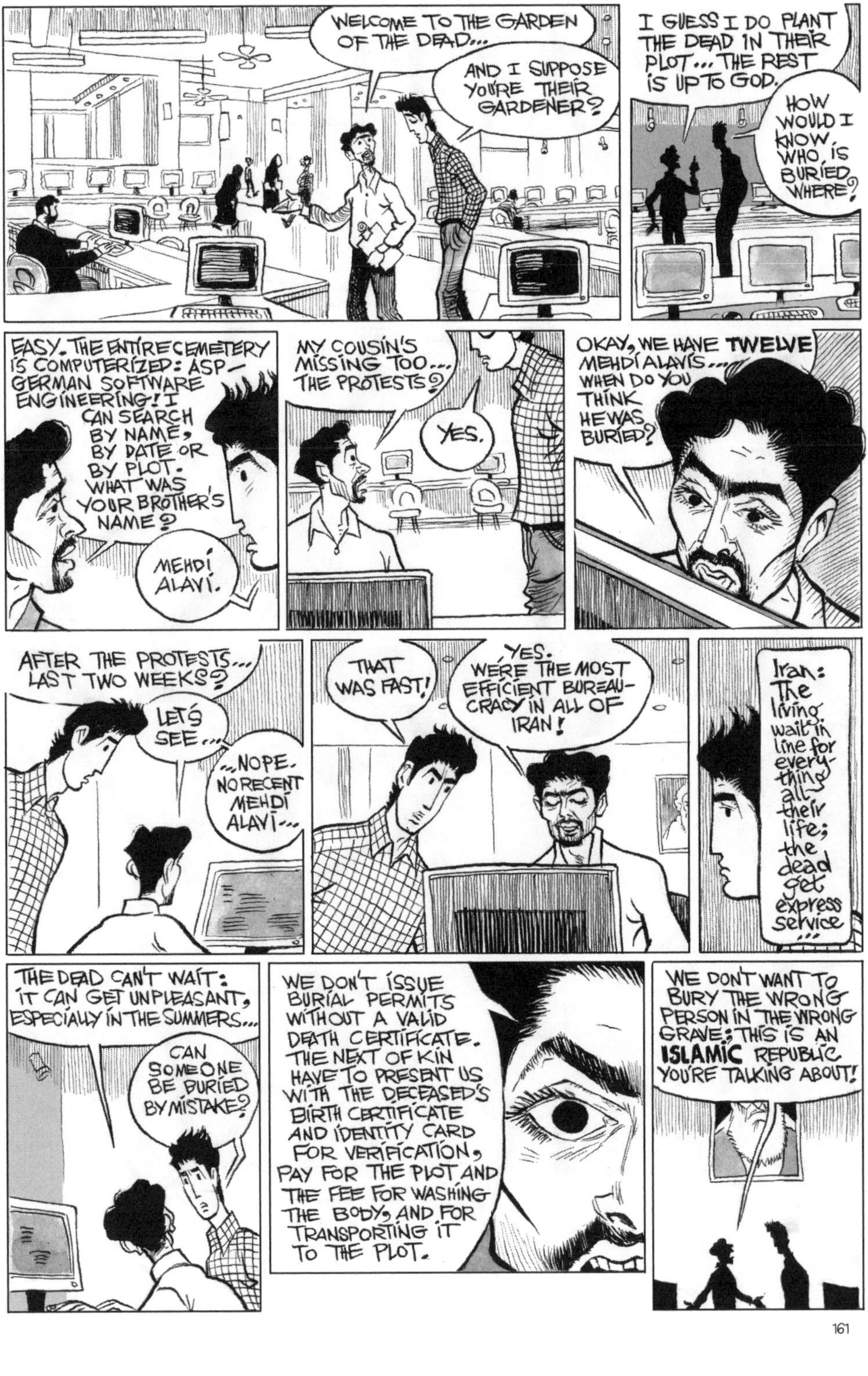
WELCOME TO THE GARDEN OF THE DEAD...
AND I SUPPOSE YOU'RE THEIR GARDENER?
I GUESS I DO PLANT THE DEAD IN THEIR PLOT... THE REST IS UP TO GOD.
HOW WOULD I KNOW, WHO, IS BURIED, WHERE?
EASY. THE ENTIRE CEMETERY IS COMPUTERIZED: ASP—GERMAN SOFTWARE ENGINEERING! I CAN SEARCH BY NAME, BY DATE OR BY PLOT. WHAT WAS YOUR BROTHER'S NAME?
MEHDI ALAVI.
MY COUSIN'S MISSING TOO... THE PROTESTS?
YES.
OKAY, WE HAVE TWELVE MEHDI ALAVIS... WHEN DO YOU THINK HE WAS BURIED?
AFTER THE PROTESTS... LAST TWO WEEKS?
LET'S SEE...
...NOPE. NO RECENT MEHDI ALAVI...
THAT WAS FAST!
...YES. WE'RE THE MOST EFFICIENT BUREAUCRACY IN ALL OF IRAN!
Iran: The living wait in line for everything all their life; the dead get express service...
THE DEAD CAN'T WAIT: IT CAN GET UNPLEASANT, ESPECIALLY IN THE SUMMERS...
CAN SOMEONE BE BURIED BY MISTAKE?
WE DON'T ISSUE BURIAL PERMITS WITHOUT A VALID DEATH CERTIFICATE. THE NEXT OF KIN HAVE TO PRESENT US WITH THE DECEASED'S BIRTH CERTIFICATE AND IDENTITY CARD FOR VERIFICATION, PAY FOR THE PLOT AND THE FEE FOR WASHING THE BODY, AND FOR TRANSPORTING IT TO THE PLOT.
WE DON'T WANT TO BURY THE WRONG PERSON IN THE WRONG GRAVE; THIS IS AN ISLAMIC REPUBLIC YOU'RE TALKING ABOUT!

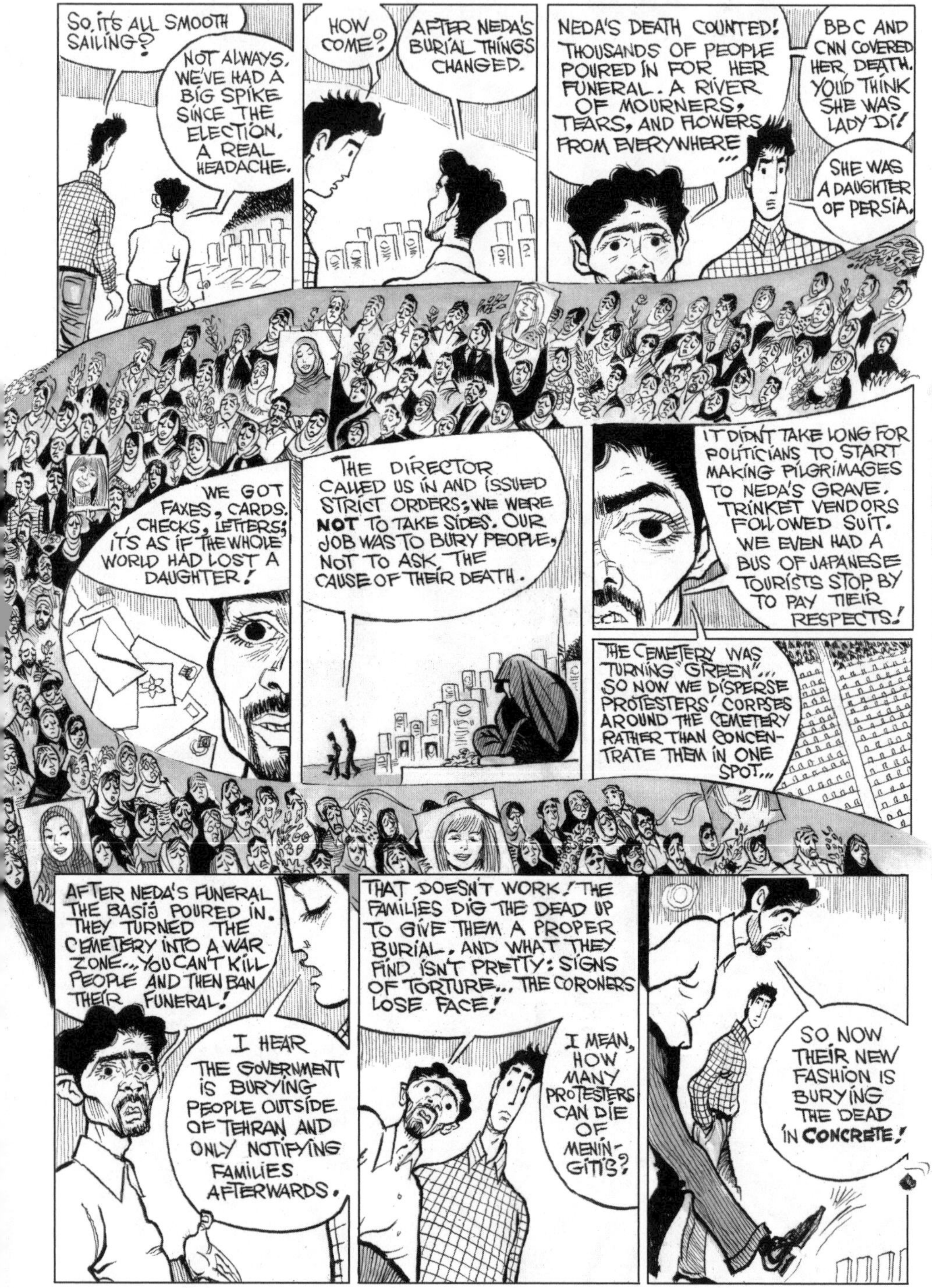

SO, IT'S ALL SMOOTH SAILING?
NOT ALWAYS. WE'VE HAD A BIG SPIKE SINCE THE ELECTION. A REAL HEADACHE.
HOW COME?
AFTER NEDA'S BURIAL THINGS CHANGED.
NEDA'S DEATH COUNTED! THOUSANDS OF PEOPLE POURED IN FOR HER FUNERAL. A RIVER OF MOURNERS, TEARS, AND FLOWERS FROM EVERYWHERE...
BBC AND CNN COVERED HER DEATH. YOU'D THINK SHE WAS LADY DI!
SHE WAS A DAUGHTER OF PERSIA.
NEDA
WE GOT FAXES, CARDS, CHECKS, LETTERS; IT'S AS IF THE WHOLE WORLD HAD LOST A DAUGHTER!
THE DIRECTOR CALLED US IN AND ISSUED STRICT ORDERS; WE WERE **NOT** TO TAKE SIDES. OUR JOB WAS TO BURY PEOPLE, NOT TO ASK THE CAUSE OF THEIR DEATH.
IT DIDN'T TAKE LONG FOR POLITICIANS TO START MAKING PILGRIMAGES TO NEDA'S GRAVE. TRINKET VENDORS FOLLOWED SUIT. WE EVEN HAD A BUS OF JAPANESE TOURISTS STOP BY TO PAY THEIR RESPECTS!
THE CEMETERY WAS TURNING "GREEN"... SO NOW WE DISPERSE PROTESTERS' CORPSES AROUND THE CEMETERY RATHER THAN CONCENTRATE THEM IN ONE SPOT...
AFTER NEDA'S FUNERAL THE BASIJ POURED IN. THEY TURNED THE CEMETERY INTO A WAR ZONE... YOU CAN'T KILL PEOPLE AND THEN BAN THEIR FUNERAL!
I HEAR THE GOVERNMENT IS BURYING PEOPLE OUTSIDE OF TEHRAN AND ONLY NOTIFYING FAMILIES AFTERWARDS.
THAT DOESN'T WORK! THE FAMILIES DIG THE DEAD UP TO GIVE THEM A PROPER BURIAL, AND WHAT THEY FIND ISN'T PRETTY: SIGNS OF TORTURE... THE CORONERS LOSE FACE!
I MEAN, HOW MANY PROTESTERS CAN DIE OF MENINGITIS?
SO NOW THEIR NEW FASHION IS BURYING THE DEAD IN **CONCRETE**!

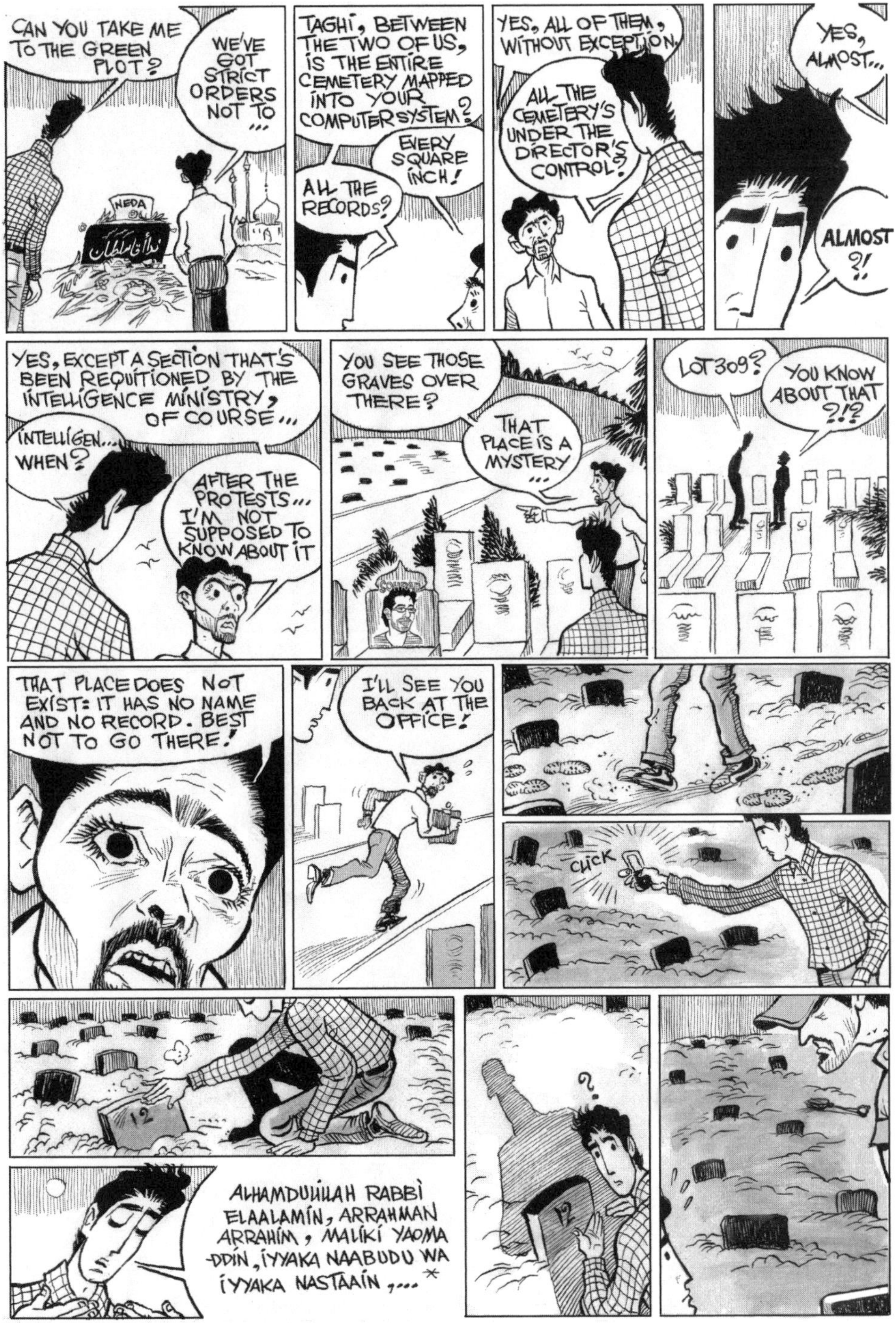
CAN YOU TAKE ME TO THE GREEN PLOT?
WE'VE GOT STRICT ORDERS NOT TO ...
NEDA
TAGHI, BETWEEN THE TWO OF US, IS THE ENTIRE CEMETERY MAPPED INTO YOUR COMPUTER SYSTEM?
EVERY SQUARE INCH!
ALL THE RECORDS?
YES, ALL OF THEM, WITHOUT EXCEPTION.
ALL THE CEMETERY'S UNDER THE DIRECTOR'S CONTROL?
YES, ALMOST...
ALMOST ?!
YES, EXCEPT A SECTION THAT'S BEEN REQUITIONED BY THE INTELLIGENCE MINISTRY, OF COURSE...
INTELLIGEN... WHEN?
AFTER THE PROTESTS... I'M NOT SUPPOSED TO KNOW ABOUT IT
YOU SEE THOSE GRAVES OVER THERE?
THAT PLACE IS A MYSTERY ...
LOT 309?
YOU KNOW ABOUT THAT ?!?
THAT PLACE DOES NOT EXIST: IT HAS NO NAME AND NO RECORD. BEST NOT TO GO THERE!
I'LL SEE YOU BACK AT THE OFFICE!
CLICK
12
?
ALHAMDULILAH RABBI ELAALAMÍN, ARRAHMAN ARRAHÍM, MALÍKI YAOMA -DDÍN, ÍYYAKA NAABUDU WA ÍYYAKA NASTAAÍN ,...*

* The opening verse of the Qur'an, or Fatiha, is used in prayers for the dead.

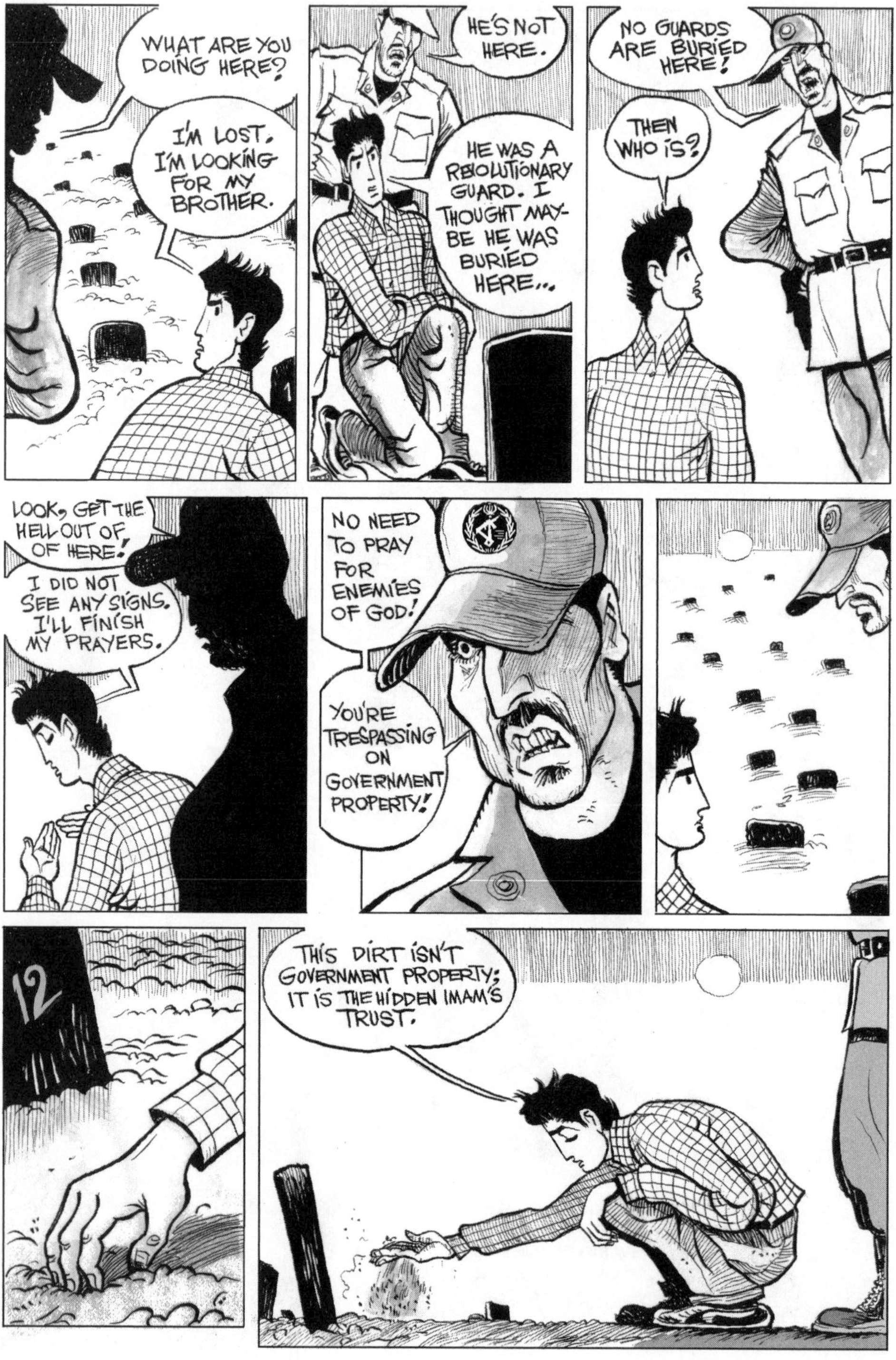
WHAT ARE YOU DOING HERE?
I'M LOST. I'M LOOKING FOR MY BROTHER.
HE'S NOT HERE.
HE WAS A REVOLUTIONARY GUARD. I THOUGHT MAY-BE HE WAS BURIED HERE...
NO GUARDS ARE BURIED HERE!
THEN WHO IS?
LOOK, GET THE HELL OUT OF OF HERE!
I DID NOT SEE ANY SIGNS. I'LL FINISH MY PRAYERS.
NO NEED TO PRAY FOR ENEMIES OF GOD!
YOU'RE TRESPASSING ON GOVERNMENT PROPERTY!
12
THIS DIRT ISN'T GOVERNMENT PROPERTY; IT IS THE HIDDEN IMAM'S TRUST.

THE HACKER

CHAPTER THIRTEEN

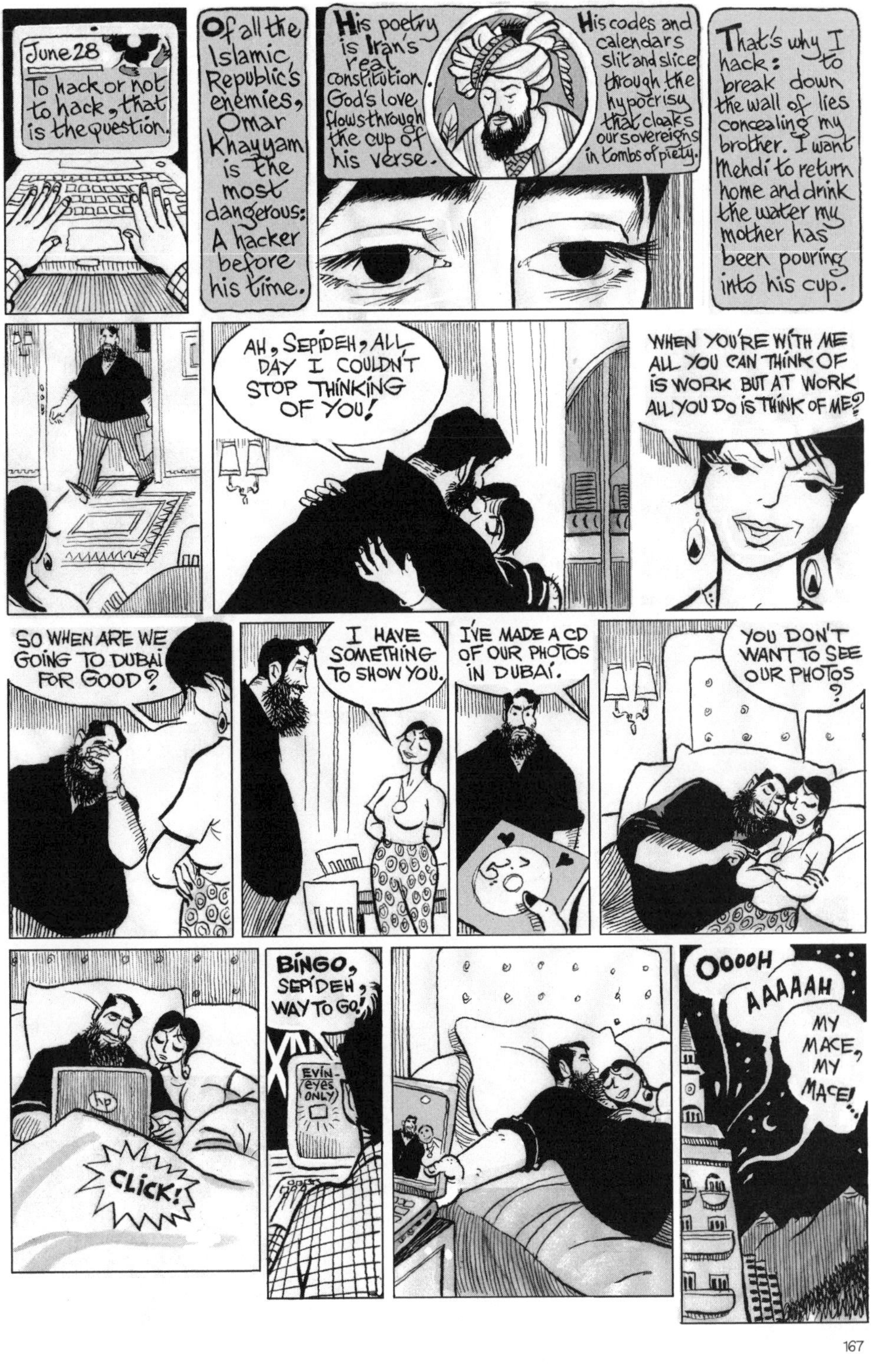
June 28
To hack or not to hack, that is the question.
Of all the Islamic Republic's enemies, Omar Khayyam is the most dangerous: A hacker before his time.
His poetry is Iran's real constitution. God's love flows through the cup of his verse.
His codes and calendars slit and slice through the hypocrisy that cloaks our sovereigns in tombs of piety.
That's why I hack: to break down the wall of lies concealing my brother. I want Mehdi to return home and drink the water my mother has been pouring into his cup.
AH, SEPIDEH, ALL DAY I COULDN'T STOP THINKING OF YOU!
WHEN YOU'RE WITH ME ALL YOU CAN THINK OF IS WORK BUT AT WORK ALL YOU DO IS THINK OF ME?
SO WHEN ARE WE GOING TO DUBAI FOR GOOD?
I HAVE SOMETHING TO SHOW YOU.
I'VE MADE A CD OF OUR PHOTOS IN DUBAI.
دبي
YOU DON'T WANT TO SEE OUR PHOTOS?
hp
CLICK!
BINGO, SEPIDEH, WAY TO GO!
EVIN (eyes ONLY)
OOOOH
AAAAAH
MY MACE, MY MACE!...

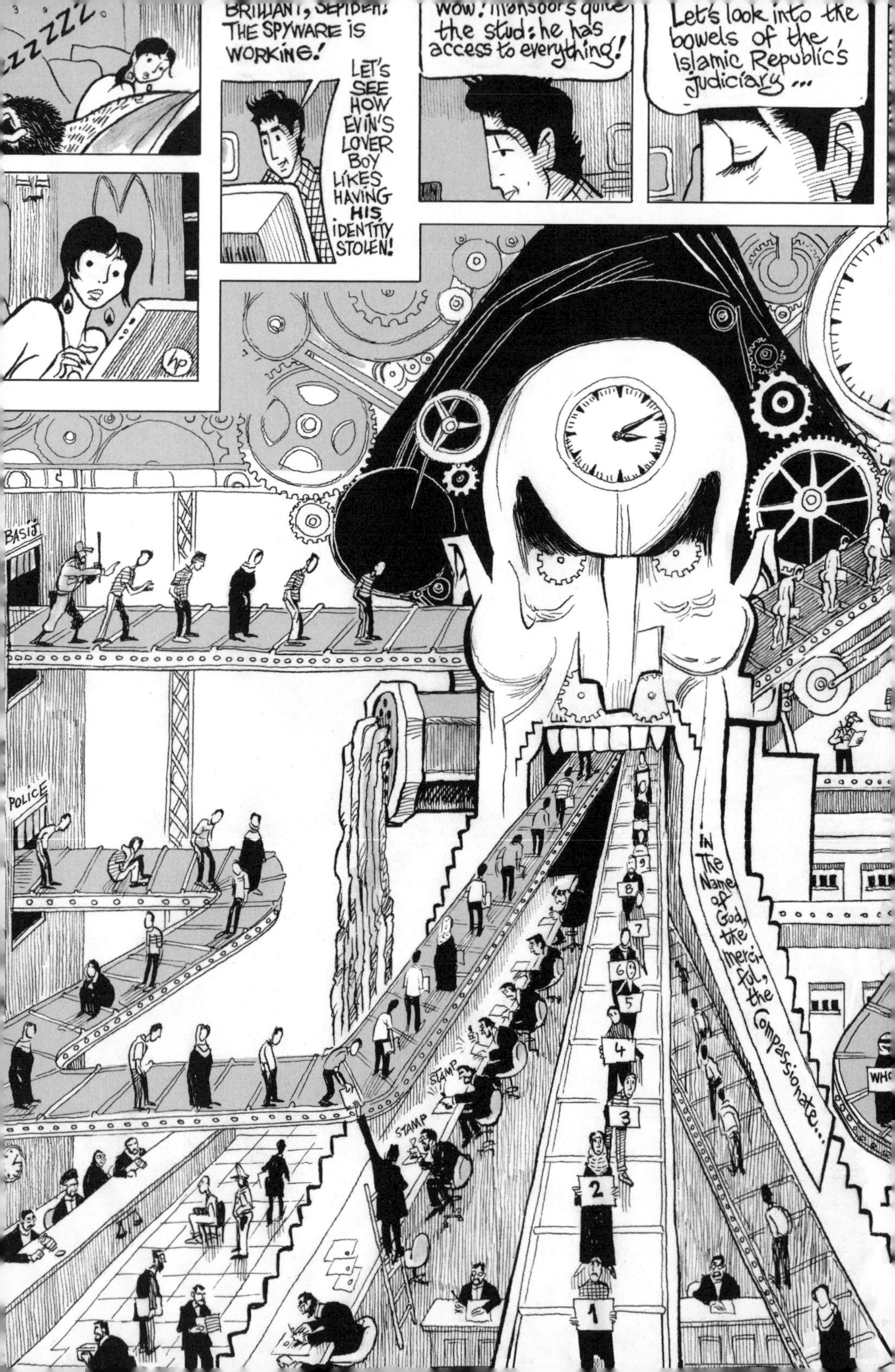
ZZZZZZ
BRILLIANT, SEPIDEH! THE SPYWARE IS WORKING!
LET'S SEE HOW EVIN'S LOVER BOY LIKES HAVING HIS IDENTITY STOLEN!
WOW! MANSOOR'S QUITE THE STUD: HE HAS ACCESS TO EVERYTHING!
Let's look into the bowels of the Islamic Republic's judiciary...
BASIJ
POLICE
IN The Name of God, the merciful, the Compassionate...
STAMP
STAMP
10
9
8
7
6
5
4
3
2
1
WHO

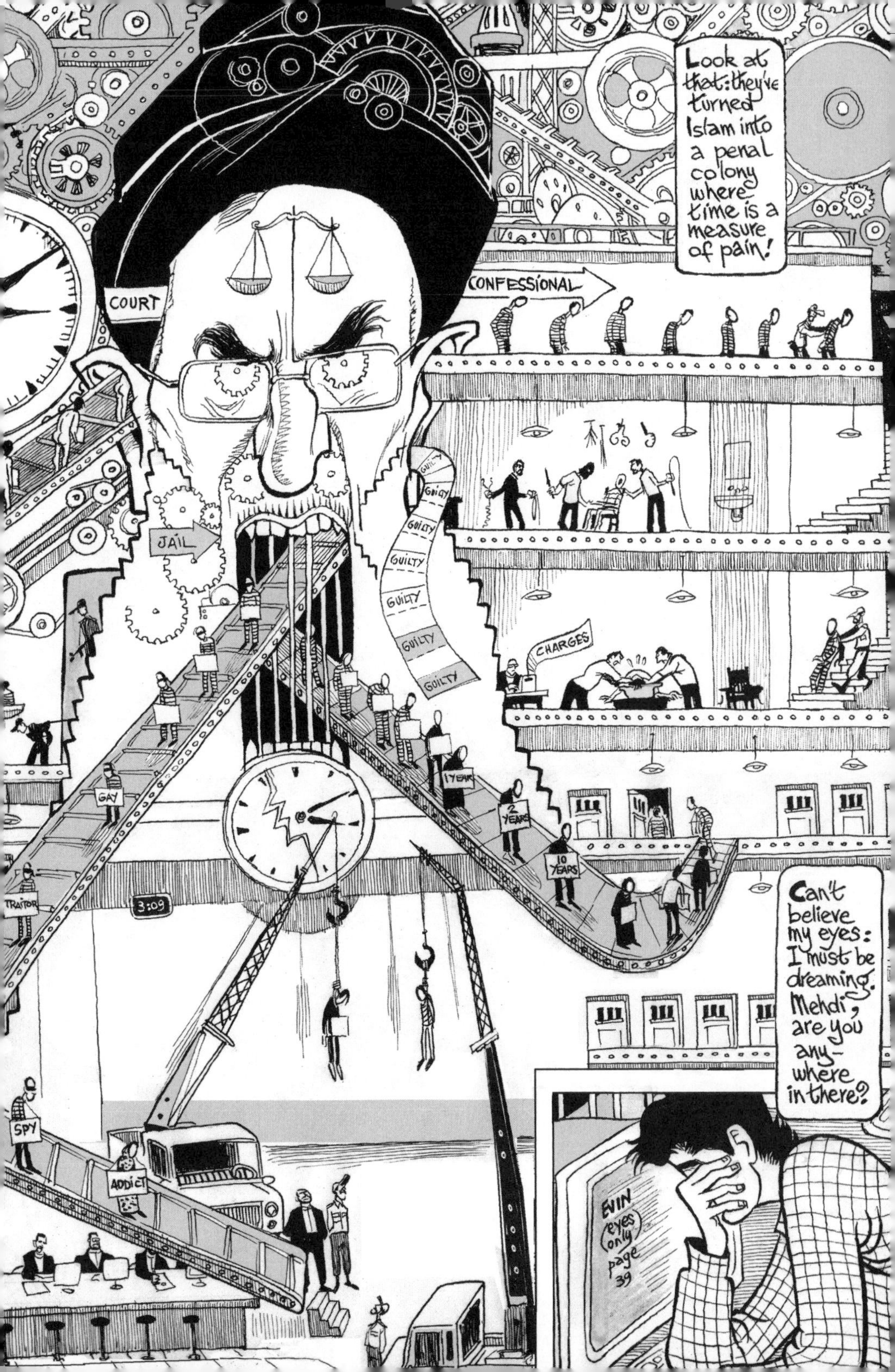
Look at that: they've turned Islam into a penal colony where time is a measure of pain!
COURT
CONFESSIONAL
JAIL
GUILTY
GUILTY
GUILTY
GUILTY
GUILTY
GUILTY
GUILTY
GUILTY
CHARGES
GAY
1 YEAR
2 YEARS
10 YEARS
TRAITOR
3:09
SPY
ADDICT
Can't believe my eyes: I must be dreaming. Mehdi, are you any-where in there?
EVIN (eyes only) page 39

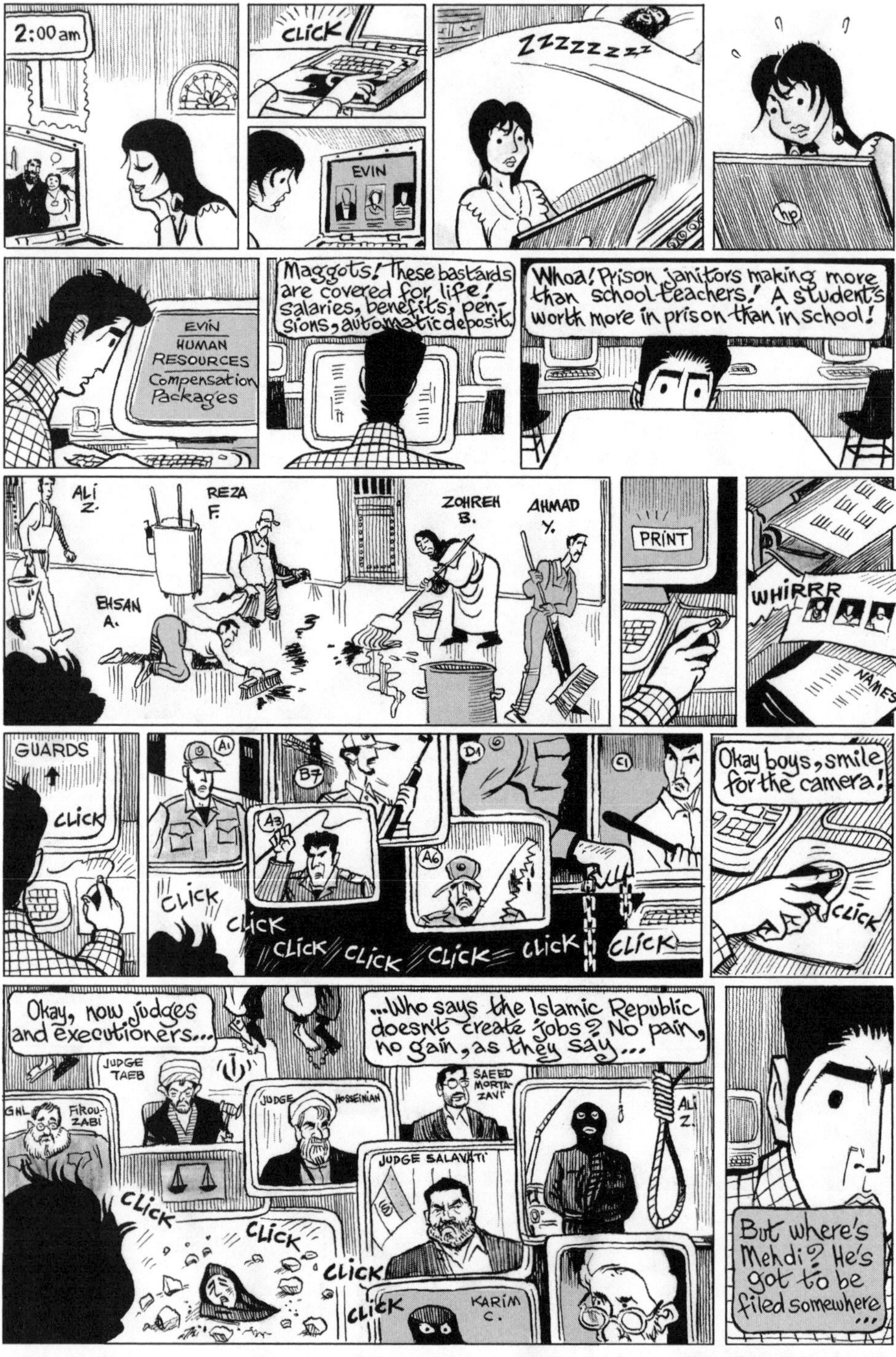
2:00 am
CLICK
EVIN
ZZZZZZZZ
hp
EVIN
HUMAN
RESOURCES
Compensation
Packages
Maggots! These bastards are covered for life! salaries, benefits, pensions, automatic deposit.
Whoa! Prison janitors making more than school teachers! A student's worth more in prison than in school!
ALI Z.
REZA F.
EHSAN A.
ZOHREH B.
AHMAD Y.
PRINT
WHIRRR
NAMES
GUARDS
CLICK
A1
B7
D1
C1
A3
A6
CLICK
CLICK
CLICK
CLICK
CLICK
CLICK
CLICK
Okay boys, smile for the camera!
CLICK
Okay, now judges and executioners...
...Who says the Islamic Republic doesn't create jobs? No pain, no gain, as they say...
JUDGE TAEB
GNL. FIROUZABI
JUDGE HOSSEINIAN
SAEED MORTAZAVI
ALI Z.
JUDGE SALAVATI
KARIM C.
CLICK
CLICK
CLICK
CLICK
But where's Mehdi? He's got to be filed somewhere...

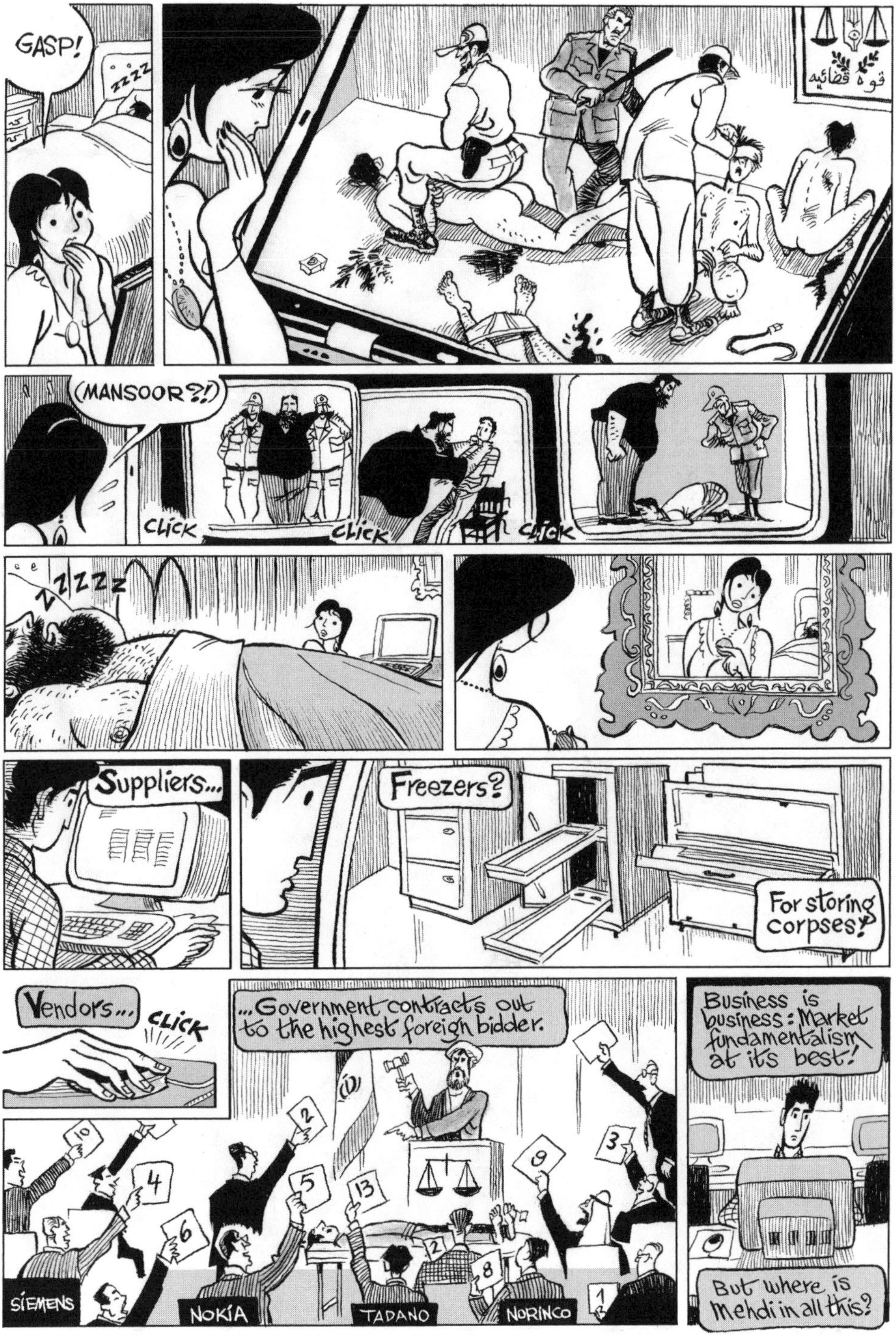
GASP!
ZZZZ
(MANSOOR?!)
CLICK
CLICK
CLICK
ZZZZ
Suppliers...
Freezers?
For storing corpses!
Vendors...
CLICK
...Government contracts out to the highest foreign bidder.
Business is business: Market fundamentalism at it's best!
SIEMENS
NOKIA
TADANO
NORINCO
But where is Mehdi in all this?

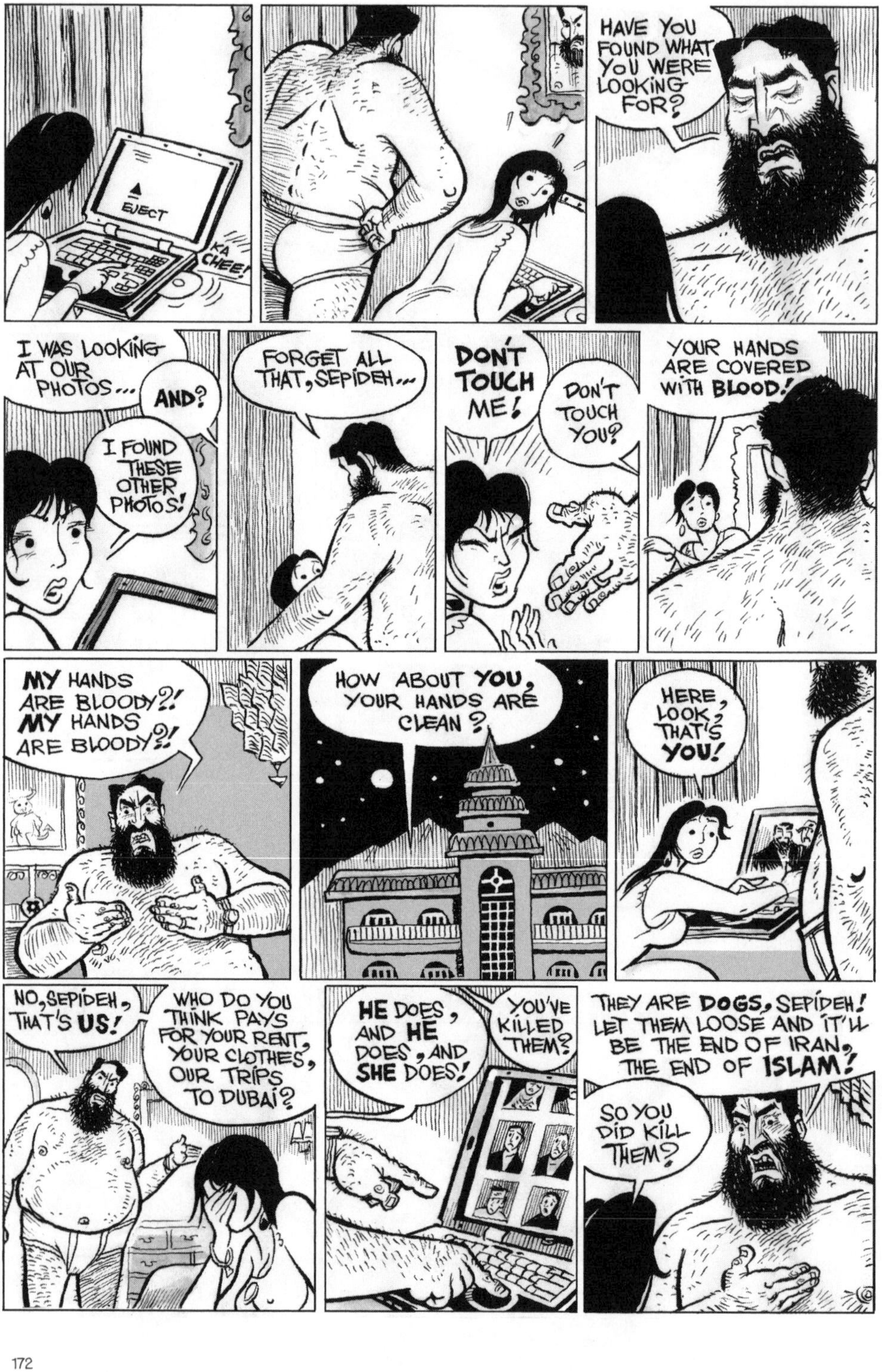
EJECT
KA CHEE!
HAVE YOU FOUND WHAT YOU WERE LOOKING FOR?
I WAS LOOKING AT OUR PHOTOS...
AND?
I FOUND THESE OTHER PHOTOS!
FORGET ALL THAT, SEPIDEH...
DON'T TOUCH ME!
DON'T TOUCH YOU?
YOUR HANDS ARE COVERED WITH BLOOD!
MY HANDS ARE BLOODY?! MY HANDS ARE BLOODY?!
HOW ABOUT YOU, YOUR HANDS ARE CLEAN?
HERE, LOOK, THAT'S YOU!
NO, SEPIDEH, THAT'S US!
WHO DO YOU THINK PAYS FOR YOUR RENT, YOUR CLOTHES, OUR TRIPS TO DUBAI?
HE DOES, AND HE DOES, AND SHE DOES!
YOU'VE KILLED THEM?
THEY ARE DOGS, SEPIDEH! LET THEM LOOSE AND IT'LL BE THE END OF IRAN, THE END OF ISLAM!
SO YOU DID KILL THEM?

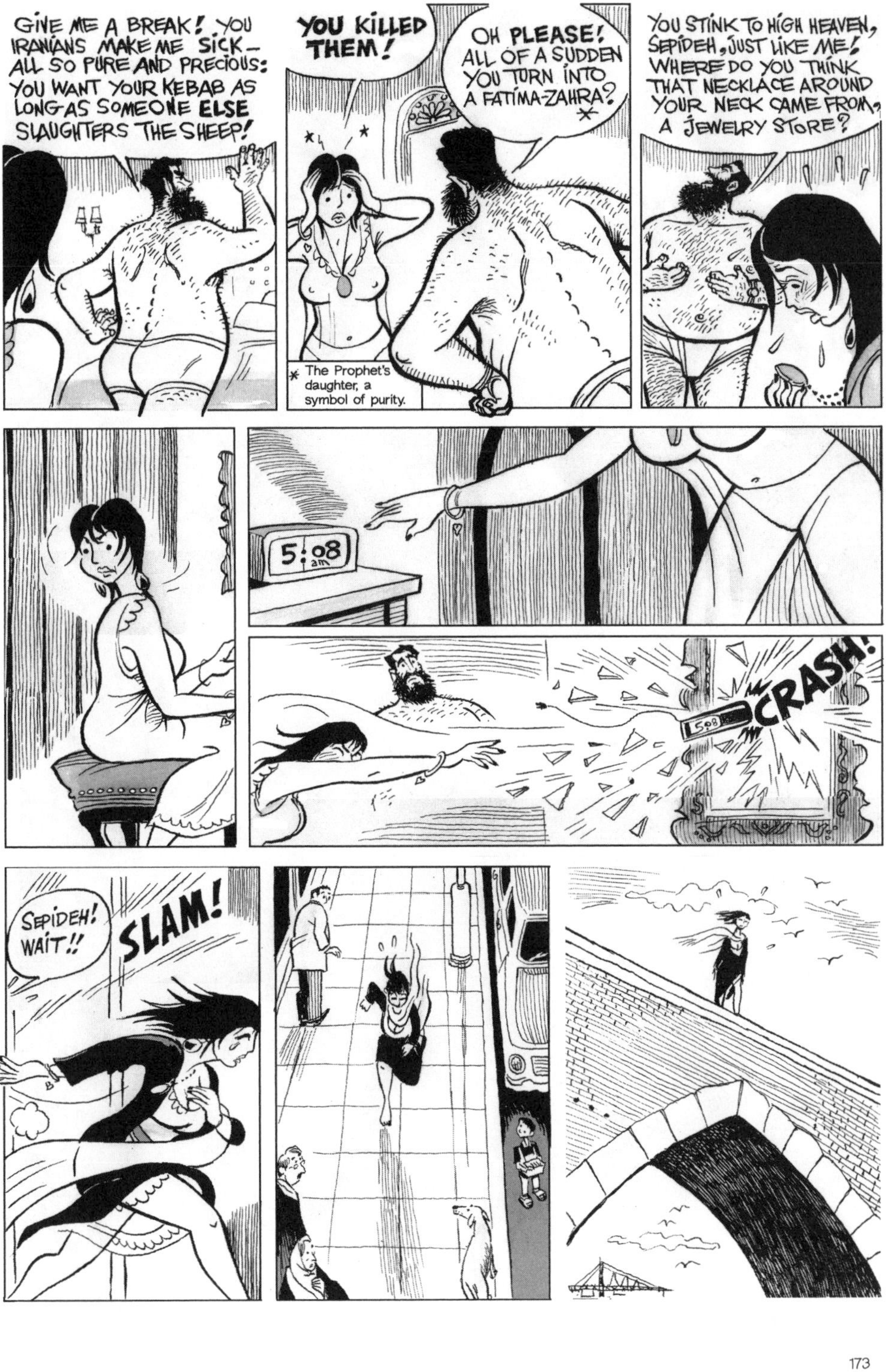
GIVE ME A BREAK! YOU IRANIANS MAKE ME SICK— ALL SO PURE AND PRECIOUS: YOU WANT YOUR KEBAB AS LONG AS SOMEONE ELSE SLAUGHTERS THE SHEEP!
YOU KILLED THEM!
OH PLEASE! ALL OF A SUDDEN YOU TURN INTO A FATIMA-ZAHRA? *
* The Prophet's daughter, a symbol of purity.
YOU STINK TO HIGH HEAVEN, SEPIDEH, JUST LIKE ME! WHERE DO YOU THINK THAT NECKLACE AROUND YOUR NECK CAME FROM, A JEWELRY STORE?
5:08 am
CRASH!
SEPIDEH! WAIT!!
SLAM!

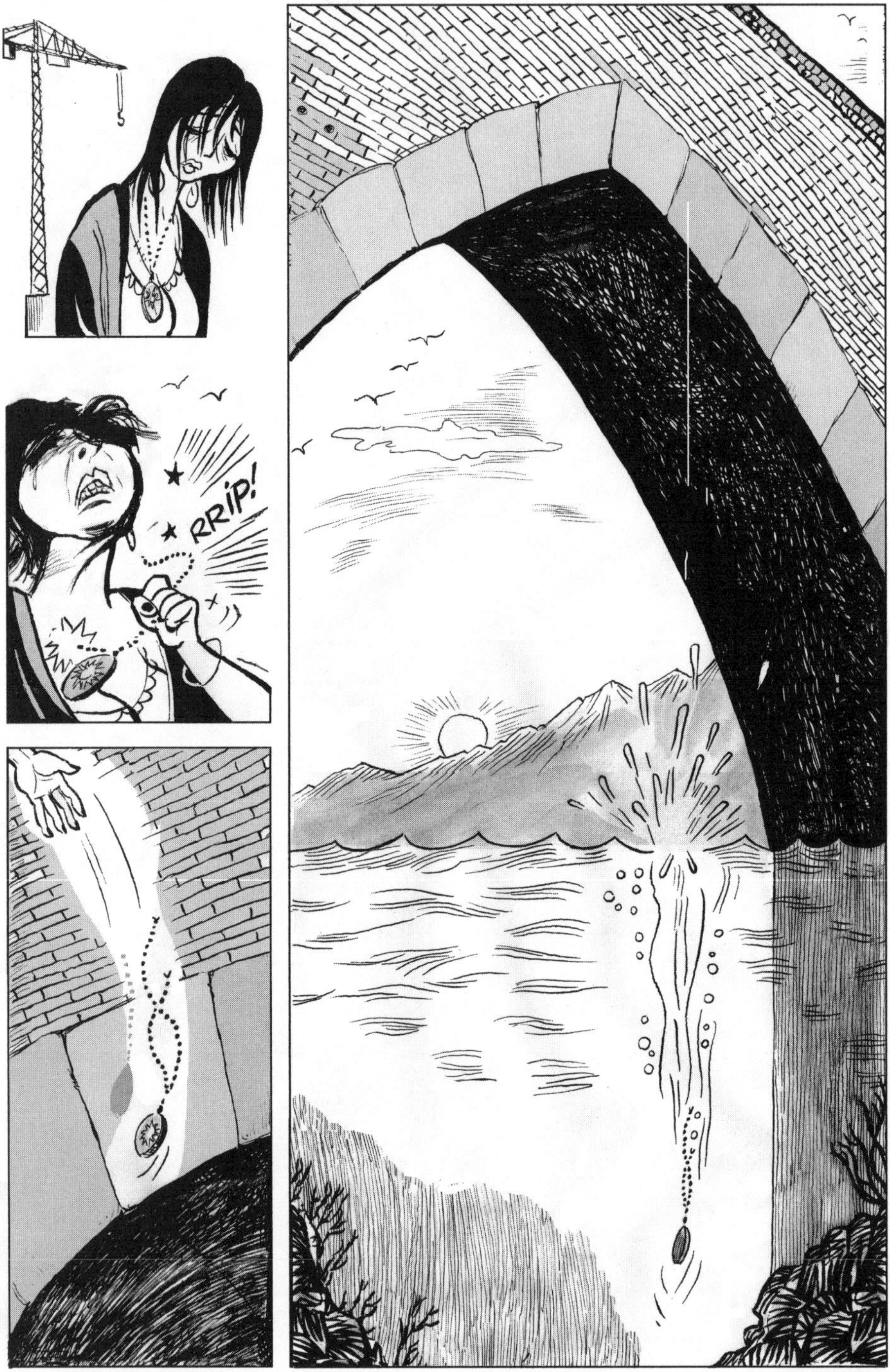
RRIP!

TAKHTI'S REVENGE

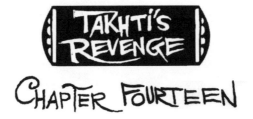

CHAPTER FOURTEEN

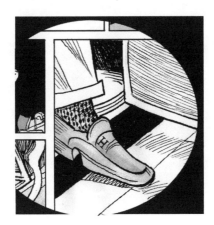

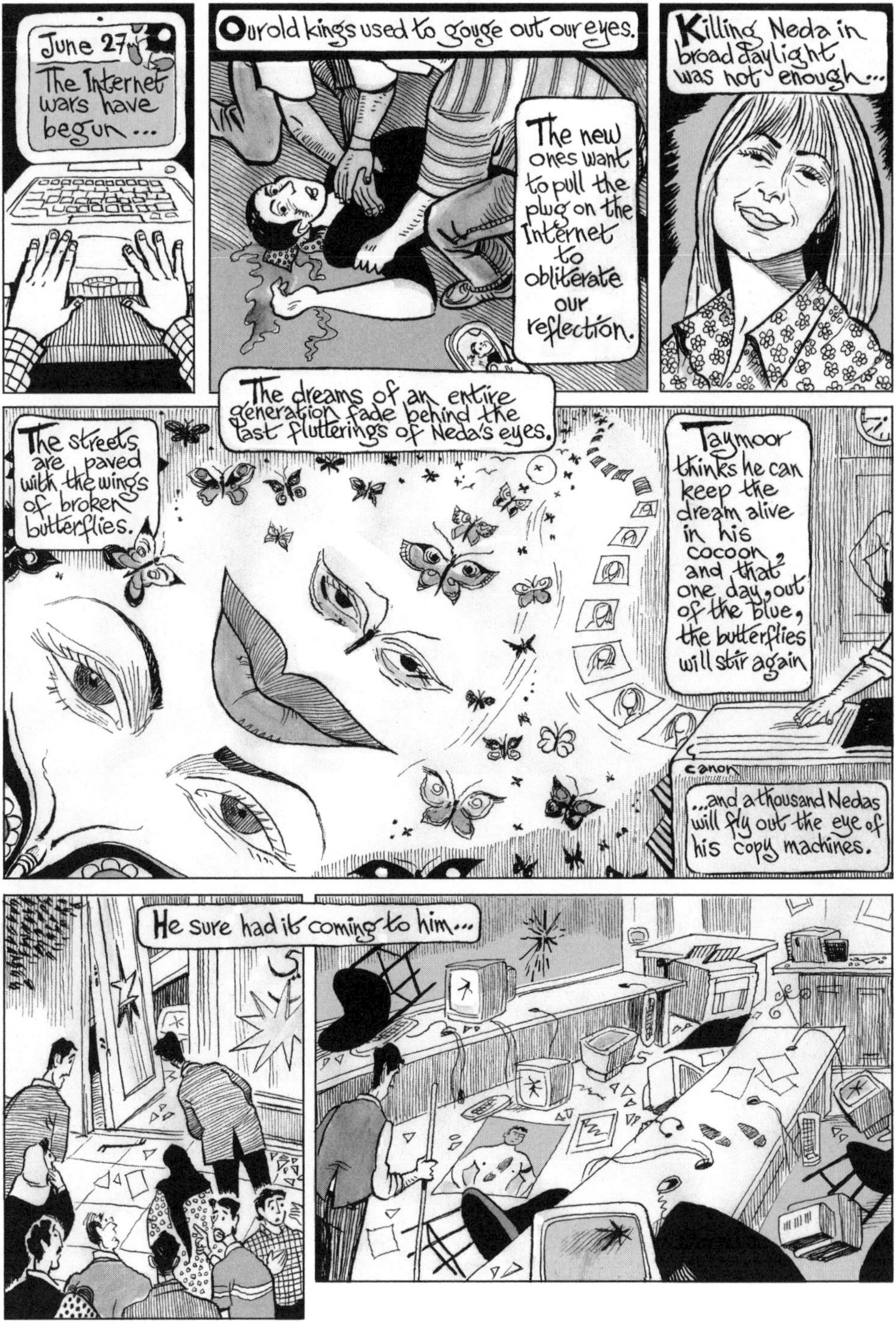
June 27
The Internet wars have begun...
Our old kings used to gouge out our eyes.
The new ones want to pull the plug on the Internet to obliterate our reflection.
Killing Neda in broad daylight was not enough...
The dreams of an entire generation fade behind the last flutterings of Neda's eyes.
The streets are paved with the wings of broken butterflies.
Taymoor thinks he can keep the dream alive in his cocoon, and that one day, out of the blue, the butterflies will stir again
canon
...and a thousand Nedas will fly out the eye of his copy machines.
He sure had it coming to him...

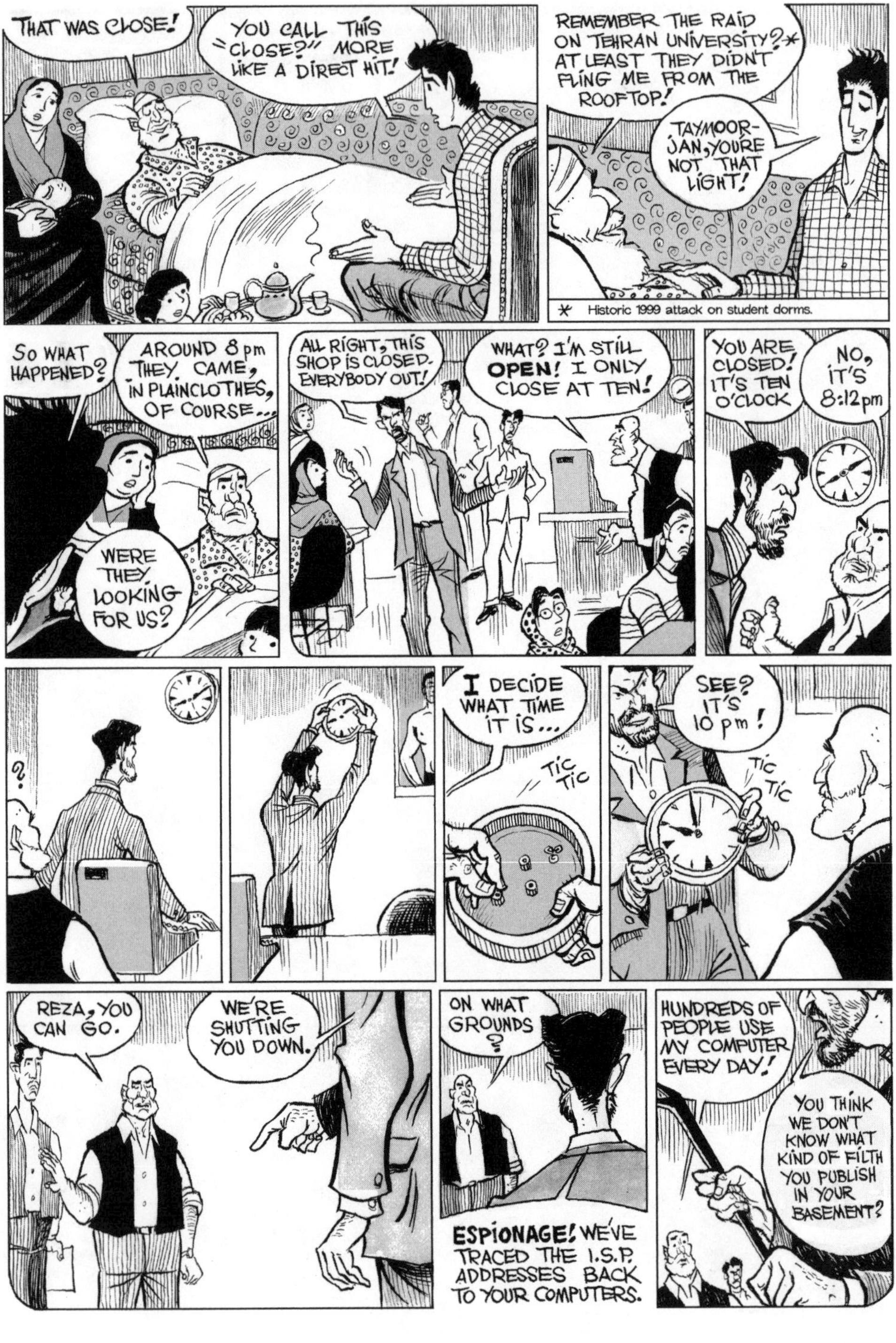
THAT WAS CLOSE!
YOU CALL THIS "CLOSE?" MORE LIKE A DIRECT HIT!
REMEMBER THE RAID ON TEHRAN UNIVERSITY?* AT LEAST THEY DIDN'T FLING ME FROM THE ROOFTOP!
TAYMOOR-JAN, YOU'RE NOT THAT LIGHT!
* Historic 1999 attack on student dorms.
SO WHAT HAPPENED?
AROUND 8 pm THEY CAME, IN PLAINCLOTHES, OF COURSE...
WERE THEY LOOKING FOR US?
ALL RIGHT, THIS SHOP IS CLOSED. EVERYBODY OUT!
WHAT? I'M STILL OPEN! I ONLY CLOSE AT TEN!
YOU ARE CLOSED! IT'S TEN O'CLOCK
NO, IT'S 8:12 pm
?
I DECIDE WHAT TIME IT IS...
TIC TIC
SEE? IT'S 10 pm!
TIC TIC
REZA, YOU CAN GO.
WE'RE SHUTTING YOU DOWN.
ON WHAT GROUNDS?
ESPIONAGE! WE'VE TRACED THE I.S.P. ADDRESSES BACK TO YOUR COMPUTERS.
HUNDREDS OF PEOPLE USE MY COMPUTER EVERY DAY!
YOU THINK WE DON'T KNOW WHAT KIND OF FILTH YOU PUBLISH IN YOUR BASEMENT?

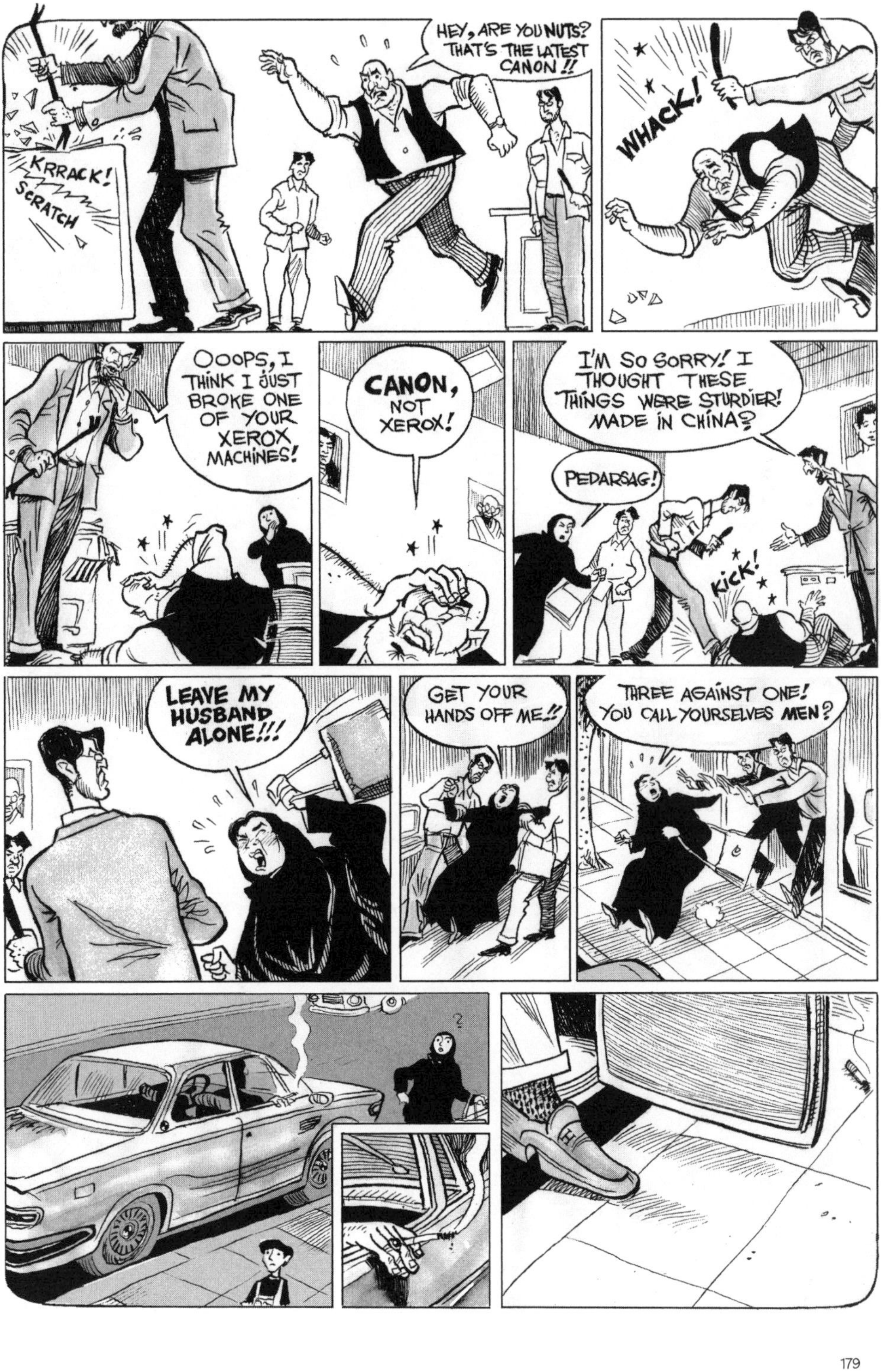

KRRACK!
SCRATCH
HEY, ARE YOU NUTS? THAT'S THE LATEST CANON!!
WHACK!
OOOPS, I THINK I JUST BROKE ONE OF YOUR XEROX MACHINES!
CANON, NOT XEROX!
I'M SO SORRY! I THOUGHT THESE THINGS WERE STURDIER! MADE IN CHINA?
PEDARSAG!
KICK!
LEAVE MY HUSBAND ALONE!!!
GET YOUR HANDS OFF ME!!
THREE AGAINST ONE! YOU CALL YOURSELVES MEN?

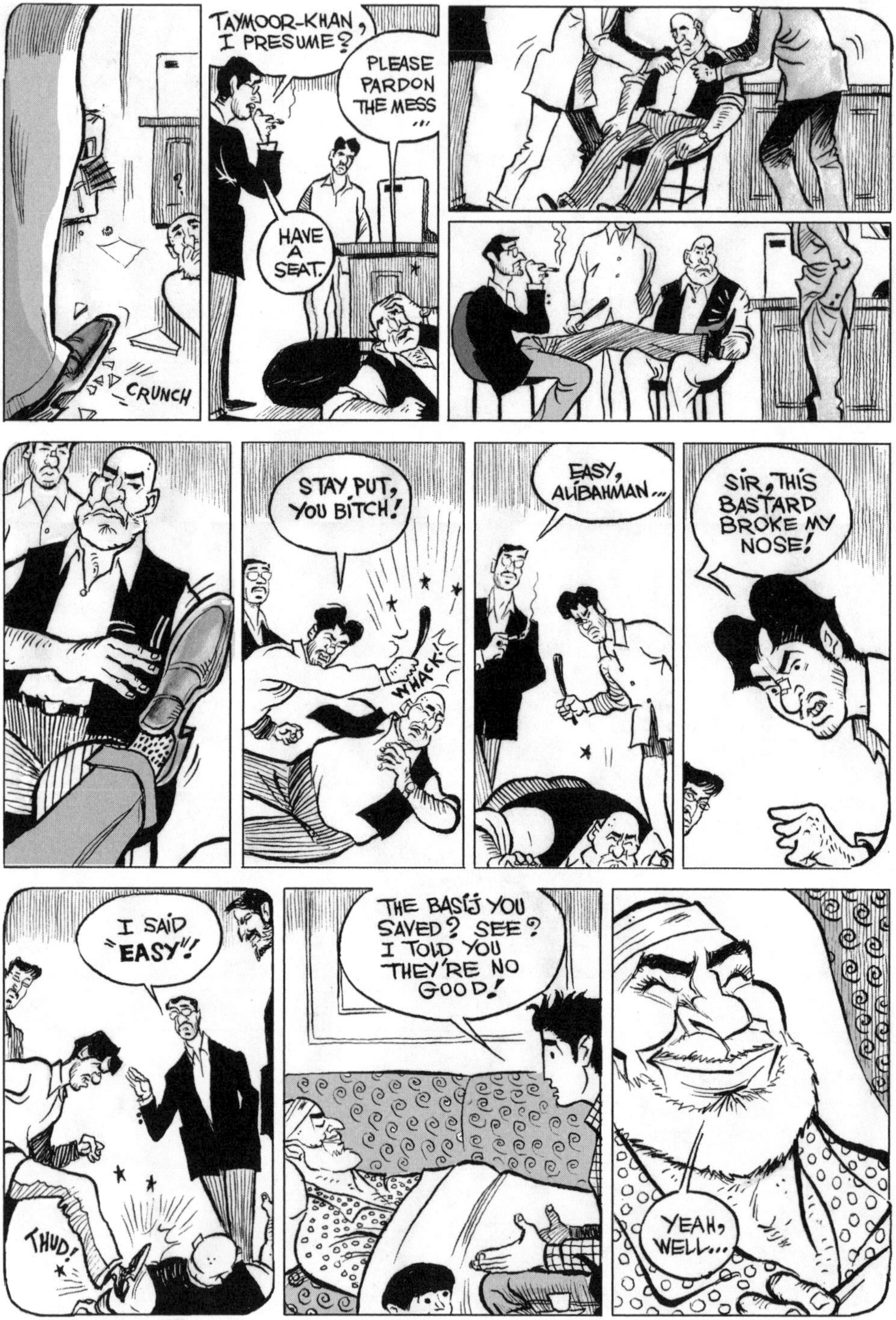
CRUNCH
TAYMOOR-KHAN, I PRESUME?
PLEASE PARDON THE MESS ...
HAVE A SEAT.
STAY PUT, YOU BITCH!
WHACK!
EASY, ALIBAHMAN...
SIR, THIS BASTARD BROKE MY NOSE!
I SAID "EASY"!
THUD!
THE BASIJ YOU SAVED? SEE? I TOLD YOU THEY'RE NO GOOD!
YEAH, WELL...

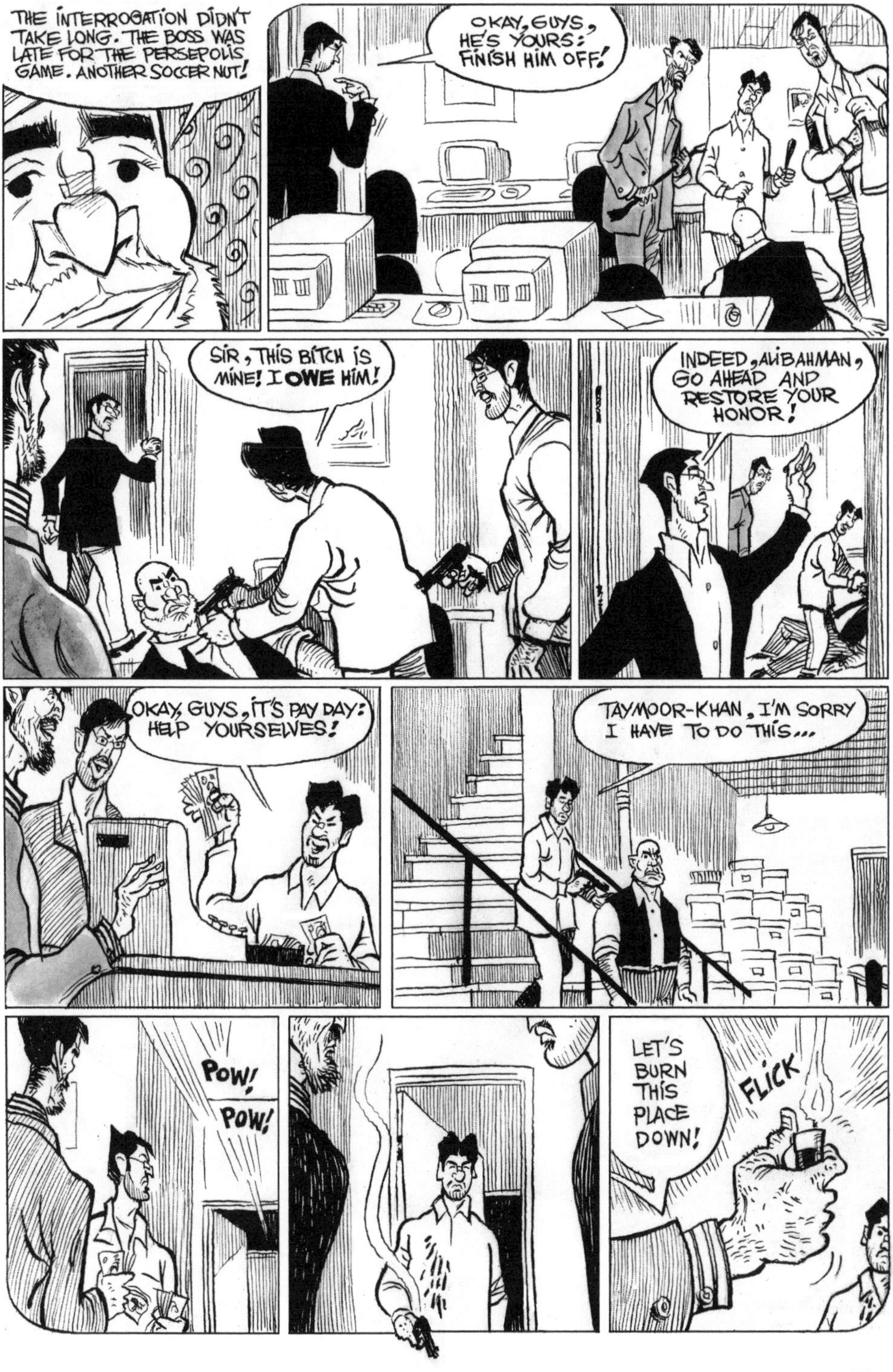
THE INTERROGATION DIDN'T TAKE LONG. THE BOSS WAS LATE FOR THE PERSEPOLIS GAME. ANOTHER SOCCER NUT!
OKAY, GUYS, HE'S YOURS: FINISH HIM OFF!
SIR, THIS BITCH IS MINE! I OWE HIM!
INDEED, ALIBAHMAN, GO AHEAD AND RESTORE YOUR HONOR!
OKAY, GUYS, IT'S PAY DAY: HELP YOURSELVES!
TAYMOOR-KHAN, I'M SORRY I HAVE TO DO THIS...
POW!
POW!
LET'S BURN THIS PLACE DOWN!
FLICK

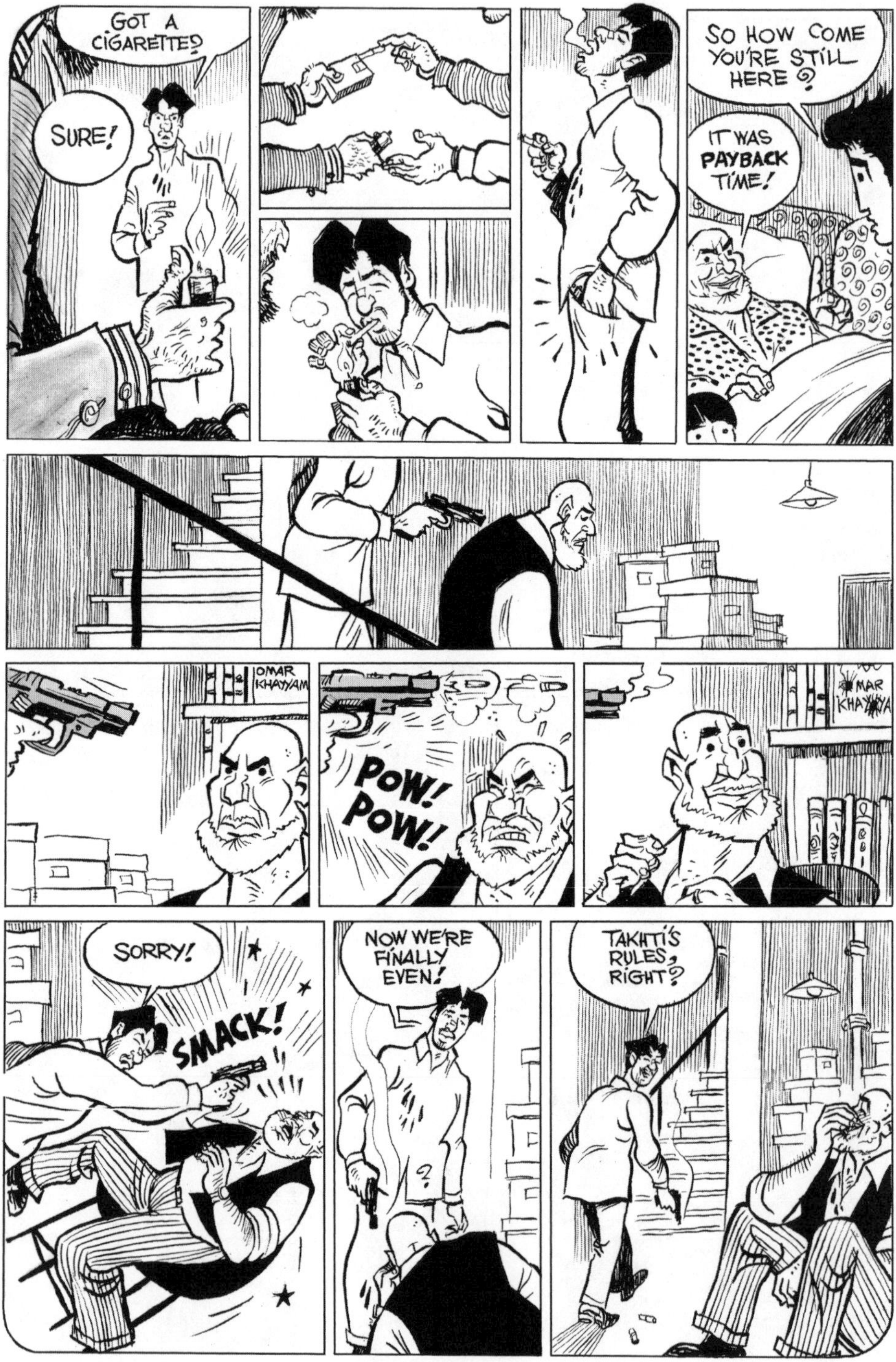
GOT A CIGARETTE?
SURE!
SO HOW COME YOU'RE STILL HERE?
IT WAS **PAYBACK** TIME!
OMAR KHAYYAM
POW! POW!
MAR KHAYYAM
SORRY!
SMACK!
NOW WE'RE FINALLY EVEN!
TAKHTI'S RULES, RIGHT?

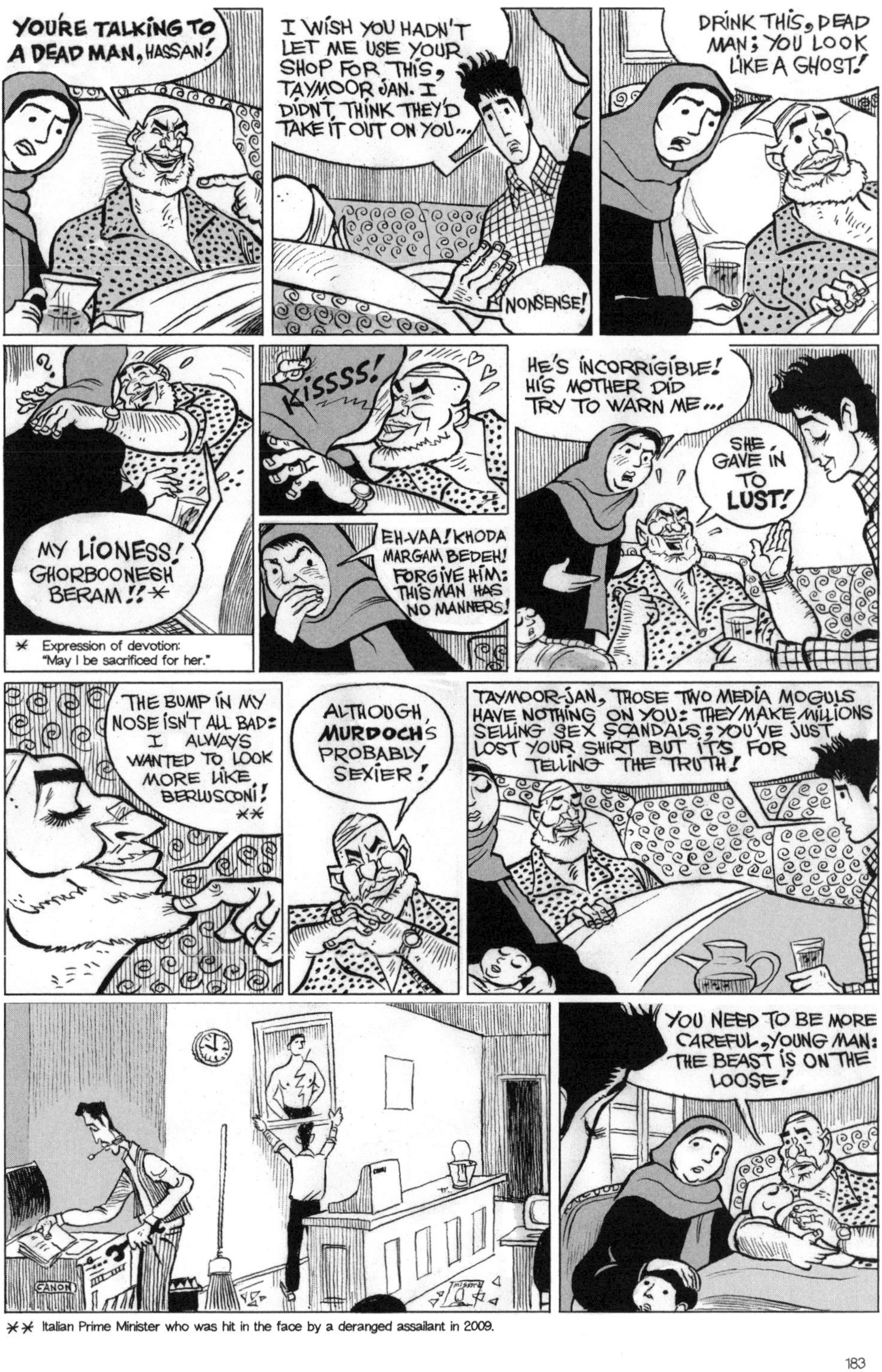
YOU'RE TALKING TO A DEAD MAN, HASSAN!
I WISH YOU HADN'T LET ME USE YOUR SHOP FOR THIS, TAYMOOR JAN. I DIDN'T THINK THEY'D TAKE IT OUT ON YOU...
NONSENSE!
DRINK THIS, DEAD MAN; YOU LOOK LIKE A GHOST!
MY LIONESS! GHORBOONESH BERAM!! *
KISSSS!
EH-VAA! KHODA MARGAM BEDEH! FORGIVE HIM: THIS MAN HAS NO MANNERS!
HE'S INCORRIGIBLE! HIS MOTHER DID TRY TO WARN ME...
SHE GAVE IN TO LUST!
THE BUMP IN MY NOSE ISN'T ALL BAD: I ALWAYS WANTED TO LOOK MORE LIKE BERLUSCONI! **
ALTHOUGH, MURDOCH'S PROBABLY SEXIER!
TAYMOOR-JAN, THOSE TWO MEDIA MOGULS HAVE NOTHING ON YOU: THEY MAKE MILLIONS SELLING SEX SCANDALS; YOU'VE JUST LOST YOUR SHIRT BUT IT'S FOR TELLING THE TRUTH!
CANON
YOU NEED TO BE MORE CAREFUL, YOUNG MAN: THE BEAST IS ON THE LOOSE!

* Expression of devotion: "May I be sacrificed for her."

** Italian Prime Minister who was hit in the face by a deranged assailant in 2009.

THE NECKLACE

CHAPTER FIFTEEN

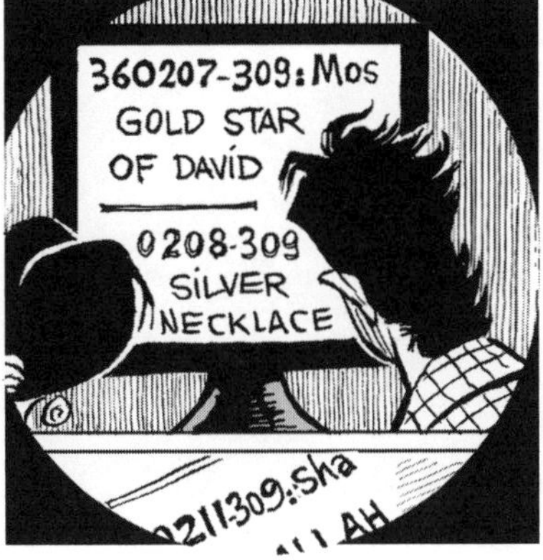
360207-309: Mos
GOLD STAR OF DAVID
0208-309
SILVER NECKLACE

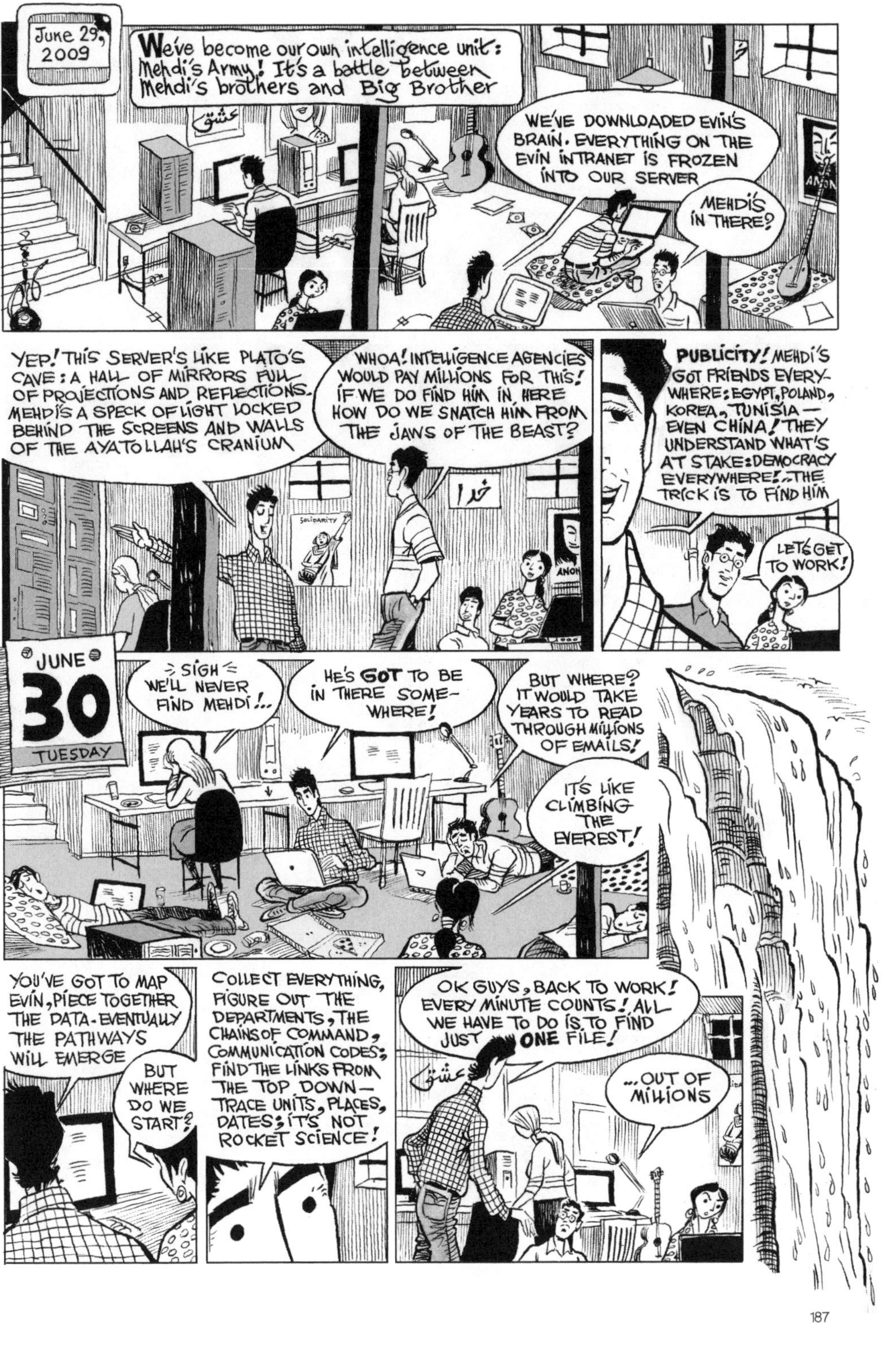
June 29, 2009
We've become our own intelligence unit: Mehdi's Army! It's a battle between Mehdi's brothers and Big Brother
WE'VE DOWNLOADED EVIN'S BRAIN. EVERYTHING ON THE EVIN INTRANET IS FROZEN INTO OUR SERVER
MEHDI'S IN THERE?
YEP! THIS SERVER'S LIKE PLATO'S CAVE: A HALL OF MIRRORS FULL OF PROJECTIONS AND REFLECTIONS. MEHDI'S A SPECK OF LIGHT LOCKED BEHIND THE SCREENS AND WALLS OF THE AYATOLLAH'S CRANIUM
WHOA! INTELLIGENCE AGENCIES WOULD PAY MILLIONS FOR THIS! IF WE DO FIND HIM IN HERE HOW DO WE SNATCH HIM FROM THE JAWS OF THE BEAST?
SOLIDARITY
ANON
PUBLICITY! MEHDI'S GOT FRIENDS EVERYWHERE: EGYPT, POLAND, KOREA, TUNISIA — EVEN CHINA! THEY UNDERSTAND WHAT'S AT STAKE: DEMOCRACY EVERYWHERE!... THE TRICK IS TO FIND HIM
LET'S GET TO WORK!
JUNE 30 TUESDAY
SIGH WE'LL NEVER FIND MEHDI!..
HE'S GOT TO BE IN THERE SOMEWHERE!
BUT WHERE? IT WOULD TAKE YEARS TO READ THROUGH MILLIONS OF EMAILS!
IT'S LIKE CLIMBING THE EVEREST!
YOU'VE GOT TO MAP EVIN, PIECE TOGETHER THE DATA - EVENTUALLY THE PATHWAYS WILL EMERGE
BUT WHERE DO WE START?
COLLECT EVERYTHING, FIGURE OUT THE DEPARTMENTS, THE CHAINS OF COMMAND, COMMUNICATION CODES; FIND THE LINKS FROM THE TOP DOWN — TRACE UNITS, PLACES, DATES; IT'S NOT ROCKET SCIENCE!
OK GUYS, BACK TO WORK! EVERY MINUTE COUNTS! ALL WE HAVE TO DO IS TO FIND JUST ONE FILE!
...OUT OF MILLIONS

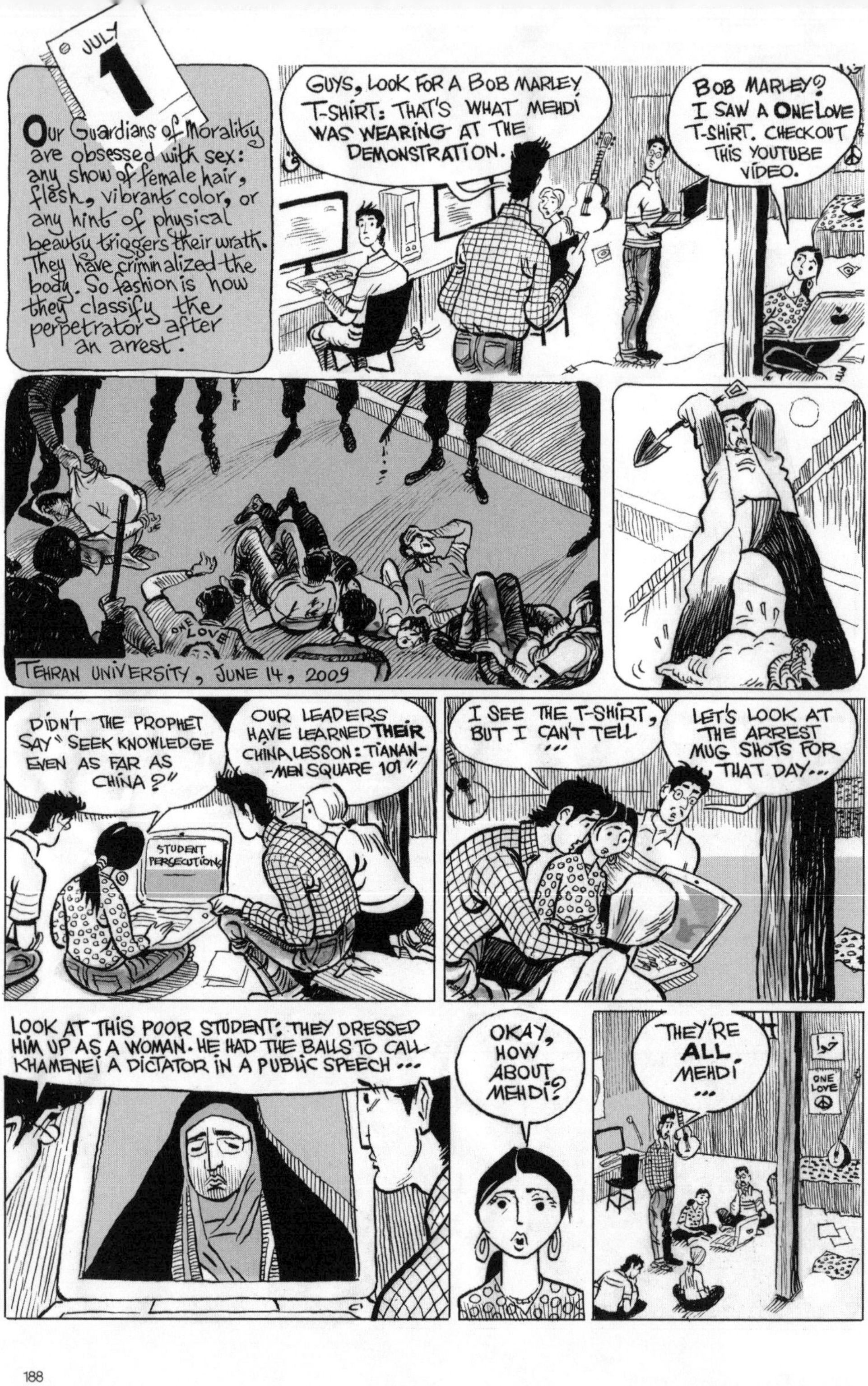
JULY
1
Our Guardians of Morality are obsessed with sex: any show of female hair, flesh, vibrant color, or any hint of physical beauty triggers their wrath. They have criminalized the body. So fashion is how they classify the perpetrator after an arrest.
GUYS, LOOK FOR A BOB MARLEY T-SHIRT: THAT'S WHAT MEHDI WAS WEARING AT THE DEMONSTRATION.
BOB MARLEY? I SAW A ONE LOVE T-SHIRT. CHECKOUT THIS YOUTUBE VIDEO.
ONE LOVE
TEHRAN UNIVERSITY, JUNE 14, 2009
DIDN'T THE PROPHET SAY "SEEK KNOWLEDGE EVEN AS FAR AS CHINA?"
OUR LEADERS HAVE LEARNED THEIR CHINA LESSON: TIANAN-MEN SQUARE 101"
STUDENT PERSECUTIONS
I SEE THE T-SHIRT, BUT I CAN'T TELL ...
LET'S LOOK AT THE ARREST MUG SHOTS FOR THAT DAY...
LOOK AT THIS POOR STUDENT: THEY DRESSED HIM UP AS A WOMAN. HE HAD THE BALLS TO CALL KHAMENEI A DICTATOR IN A PUBLIC SPEECH ...
OKAY, HOW ABOUT MEHDI?
THEY'RE ALL MEHDI ...
خوا
ONE LOVE

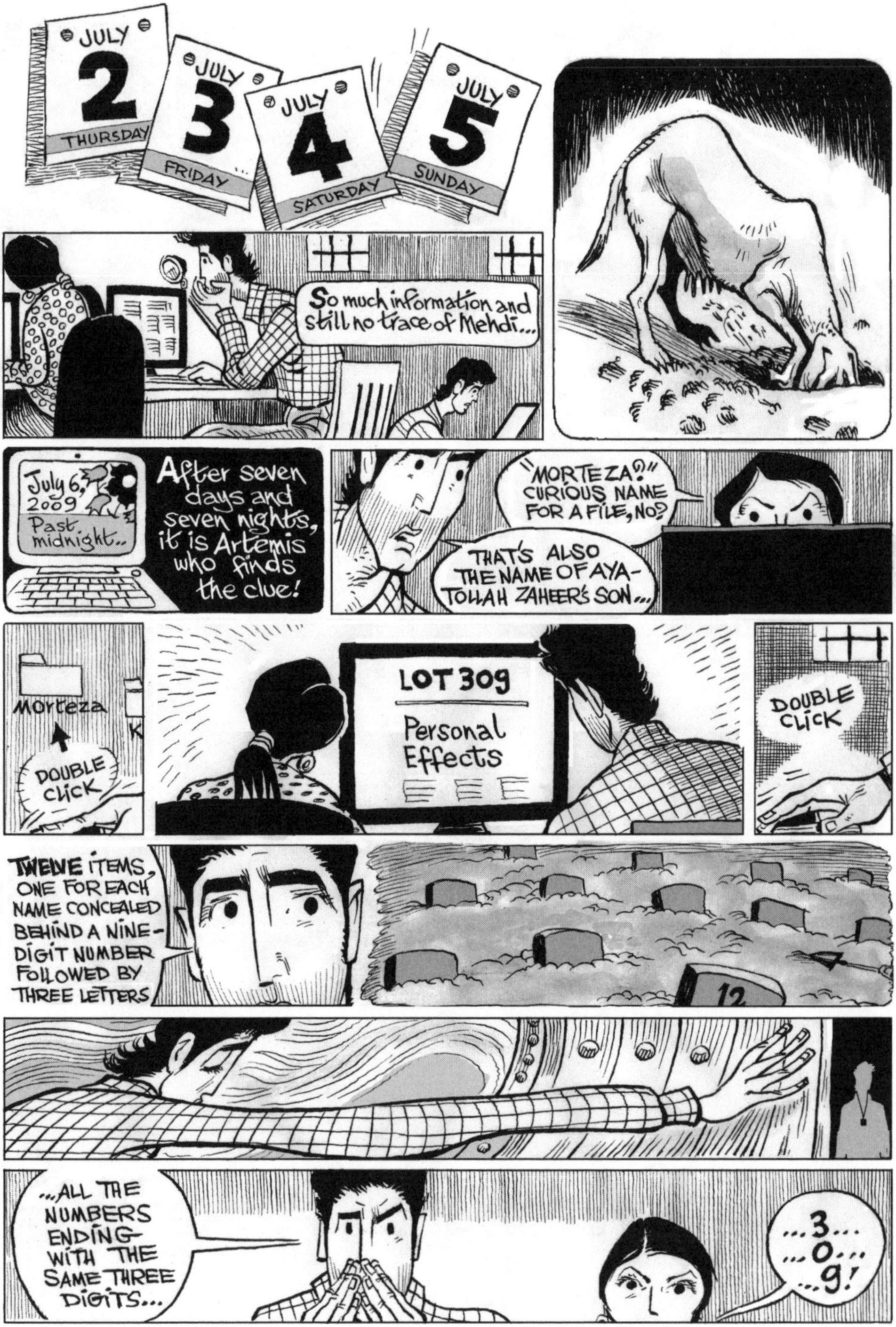

JULY 2 THURSDAY
JULY 3 FRIDAY...
JULY 4 SATURDAY
JULY 5 SUNDAY
So much information and still no trace of Mehdi...
July 6, 2009 Past midnight...
After seven days and seven nights, it is Artemis who finds the clue!
"MORTEZA?" CURIOUS NAME FOR A FILE, NO?
THAT'S ALSO THE NAME OF AYATOLLAH ZAHEER'S SON...
Morteza
DOUBLE CLICK
LOT 309
Personal Effects
DOUBLE CLICK
TWELVE ITEMS, ONE FOR EACH NAME CONCEALED BEHIND A NINE-DIGIT NUMBER FOLLOWED BY THREE LETTERS
12
...ALL THE NUMBERS ENDING WITH THE SAME THREE DIGITS...
...3... ...0... ...9!

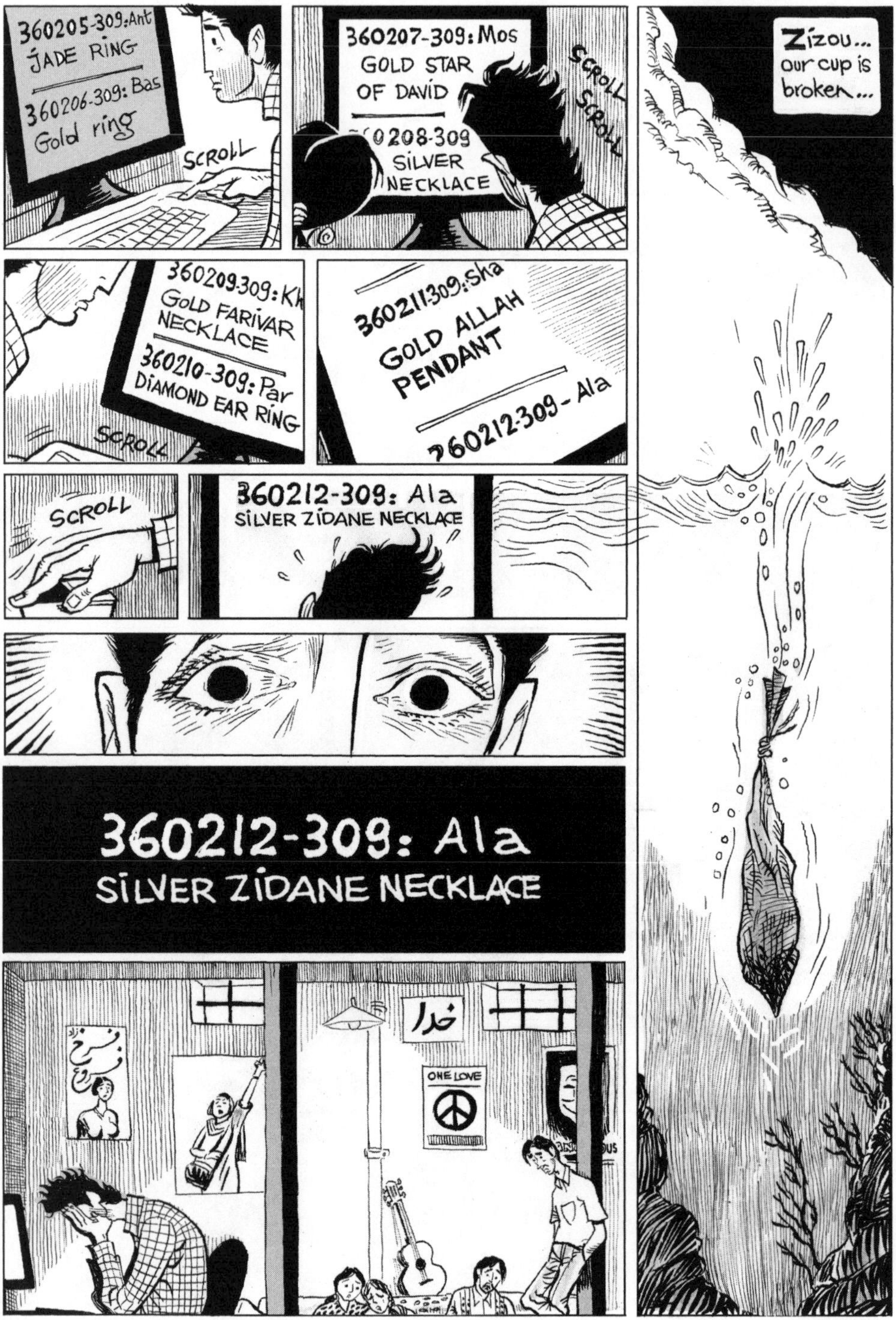

360205-309: Ant
JADE RING
360206-309: Bas
Gold ring
SCROLL
360207-309: Mos
GOLD STAR OF DAVID
SCROLL
SCROLL
SILVER NECKLACE
Zízou... our cup is broken...
360209-309: Kh
GOLD FARIVAR NECKLACE
360210-309: Par
DIAMOND EAR RING
SCROLL
360211-309: Sha
GOLD ALLAH PENDANT
360212-309 - Ala
SCROLL
360212-309: Ala
SILVER ZIDANE NECKLACE
360212-309: Ala
SILVER ZIDANE NECKLACE
خدا
ONE LOVE

THE PRAYER
CHAPTER SIXTEEN

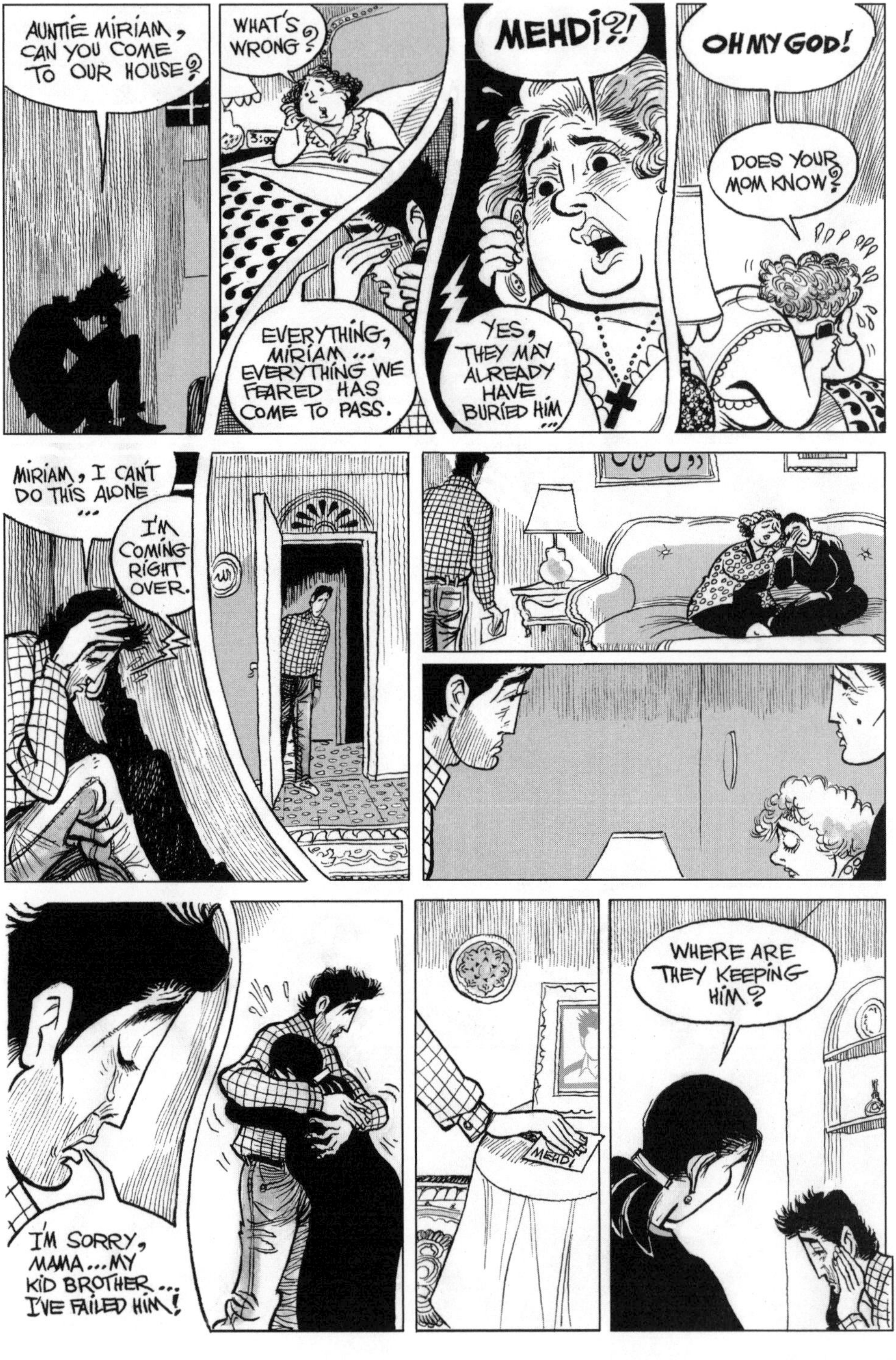

AUNTIE MIRIAM, CAN YOU COME TO OUR HOUSE?
WHAT'S WRONG?
EVERYTHING, MIRIAM... EVERYTHING WE FEARED HAS COME TO PASS.
MEHDI?!
YES, THEY MAY ALREADY HAVE BURIED HIM...
OH MY GOD!
DOES YOUR MOM KNOW?
MIRIAM, I CAN'T DO THIS ALONE...
I'M COMING RIGHT OVER.
I'M SORRY, MAMA... MY KID BROTHER... I'VE FAILED HIM!
MEHDI
WHERE ARE THEY KEEPING HIM?

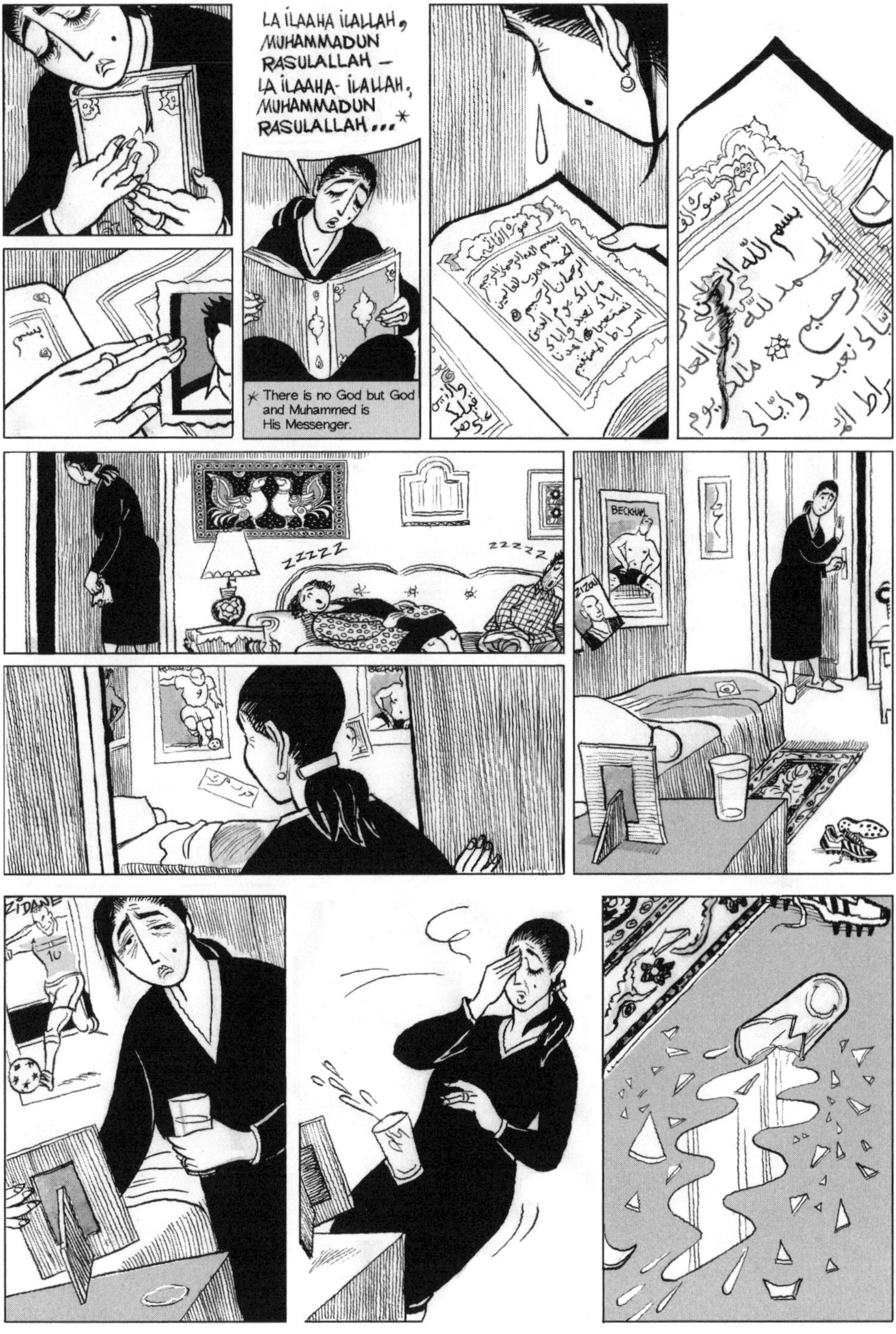
LA ILAAHA ILALLAH, MUHAMMADUN RASULALLAH — LA ILAAHA ILALLAH, MUHAMMADUN RASULALLAH...*
* There is no God but God and Muhammed is His Messenger.
BECKHAM
ZIZOU
ZIDANE

THE
RETRIEVAL
CHAPTER SEVENTEEN

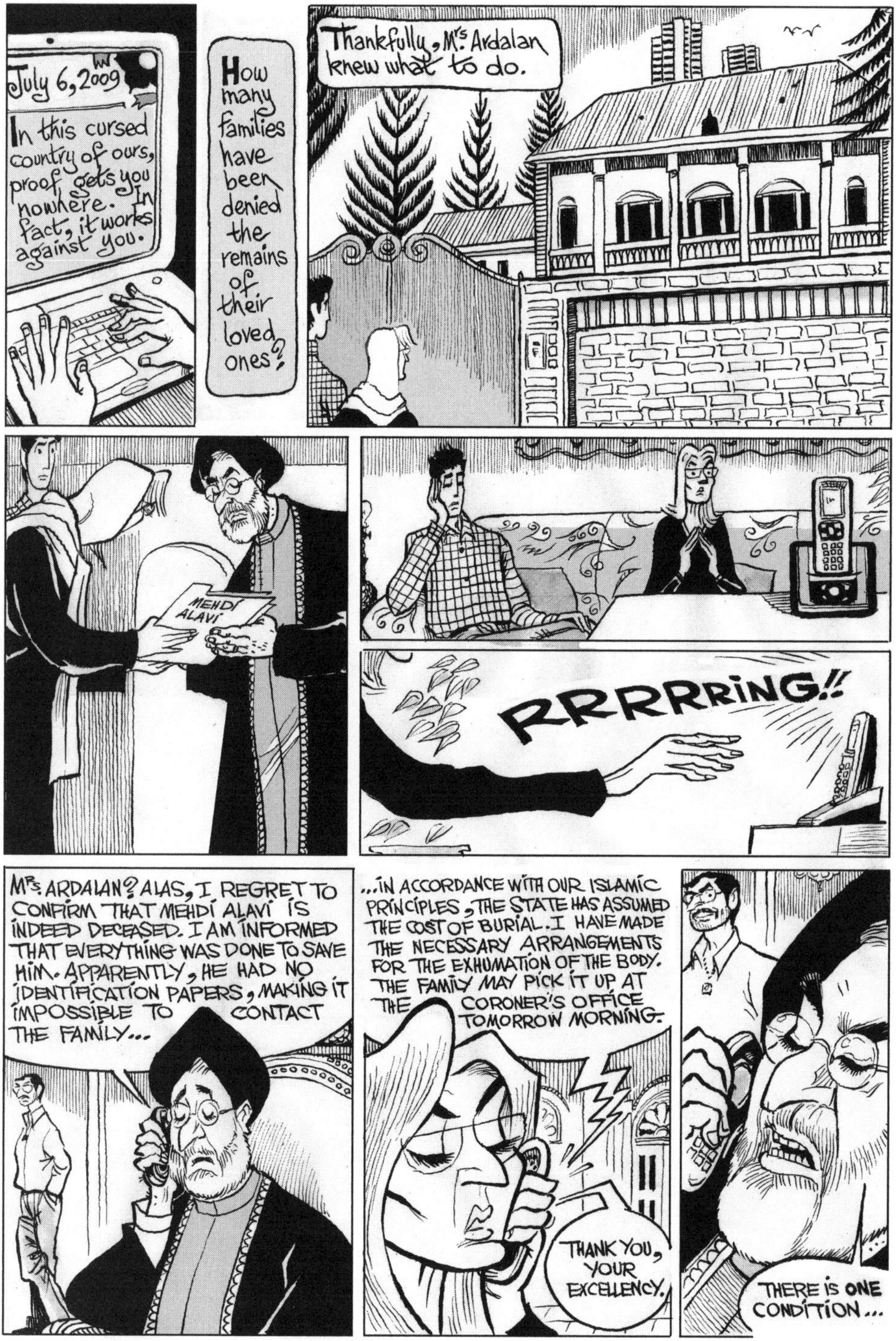
July 6, 2009
In this cursed country of ours, proof gets you nowhere. In fact, it works against you.
How many families have been denied the remains of their loved ones?
Thankfully, Mrs. Ardalan knew what to do.
MEHDI ALAVI
RRRRRING!!
Mrs. ARDALAN? ALAS, I REGRET TO CONFIRM THAT MEHDI ALAVI IS INDEED DECEASED. I AM INFORMED THAT EVERYTHING WAS DONE TO SAVE HIM. APPARENTLY, HE HAD NO IDENTIFICATION PAPERS, MAKING IT IMPOSSIBLE TO CONTACT THE FAMILY...
...IN ACCORDANCE WITH OUR ISLAMIC PRINCIPLES, THE STATE HAS ASSUMED THE COST OF BURIAL. I HAVE MADE THE NECESSARY ARRANGEMENTS FOR THE EXHUMATION OF THE BODY. THE FAMILY MAY PICK IT UP AT THE CORONER'S OFFICE TOMORROW MORNING.
THANK YOU, YOUR EXCELLENCY.
THERE IS ONE CONDITION...

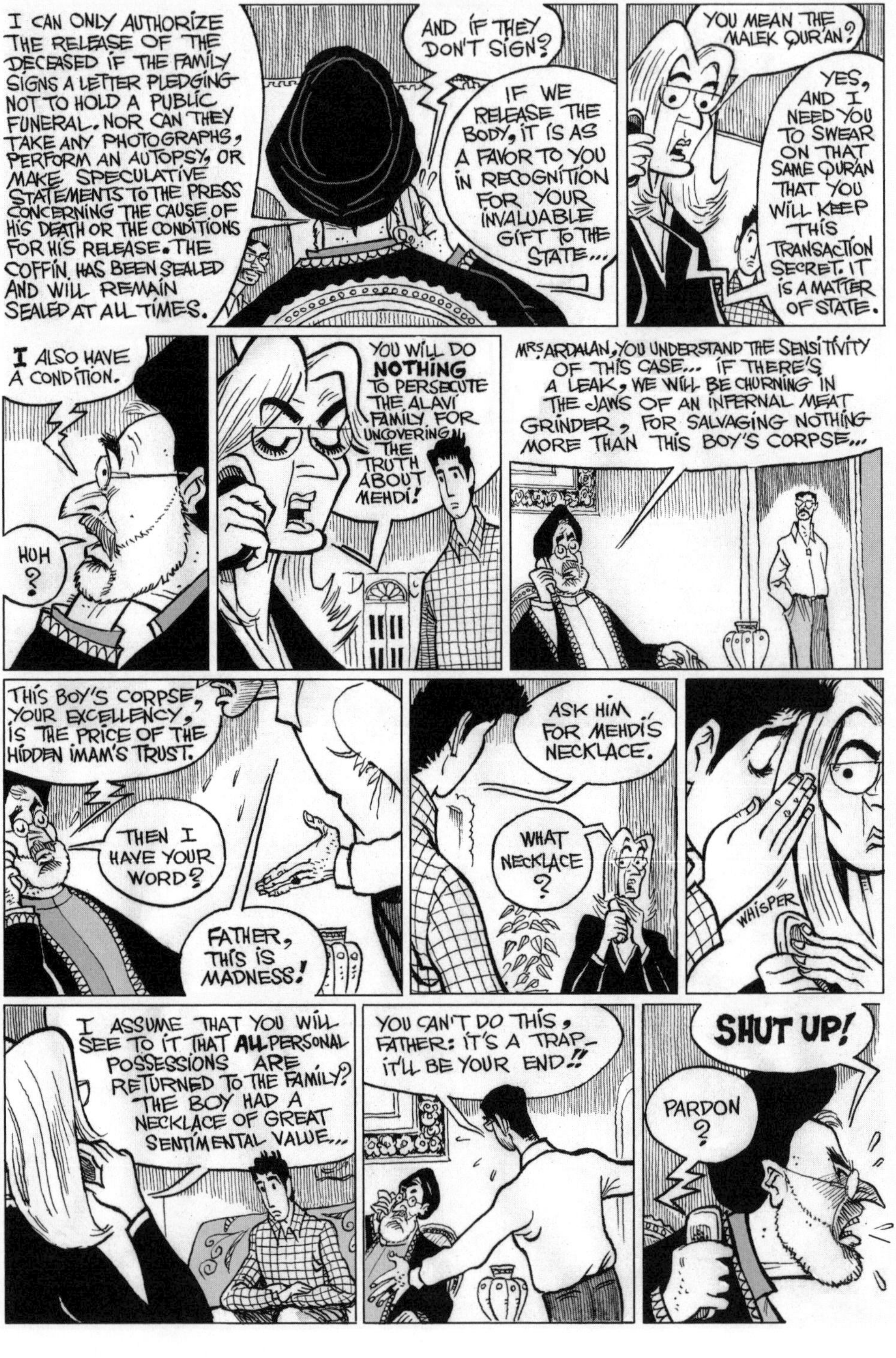
I CAN ONLY AUTHORIZE THE RELEASE OF THE DECEASED IF THE FAMILY SIGNS A LETTER PLEDGING NOT TO HOLD A PUBLIC FUNERAL. NOR CAN THEY TAKE ANY PHOTOGRAPHS, PERFORM AN AUTOPSY, OR MAKE SPECULATIVE STATEMENTS TO THE PRESS CONCERNING THE CAUSE OF HIS DEATH OR THE CONDITIONS FOR HIS RELEASE. THE COFFIN HAS BEEN SEALED AND WILL REMAIN SEALED AT ALL TIMES.
AND IF THEY DON'T SIGN?
IF WE RELEASE THE BODY, IT IS AS A FAVOR TO YOU IN RECOGNITION FOR YOUR INVALUABLE GIFT TO THE STATE...
YOU MEAN THE MALEK QUR'AN?
YES, AND I NEED YOU TO SWEAR ON THAT SAME QUR'AN THAT YOU WILL KEEP THIS TRANSACTION SECRET. IT IS A MATTER OF STATE.
I ALSO HAVE A CONDITION.
HUH?
YOU WILL DO NOTHING TO PERSECUTE THE ALAVI FAMILY FOR UNCOVERING THE TRUTH ABOUT MEHDI!
MRS. ARDALAN, YOU UNDERSTAND THE SENSITIVITY OF THIS CASE... IF THERE'S A LEAK, WE WILL BE CHURNING IN THE JAWS OF AN INFERNAL MEAT GRINDER, FOR SALVAGING NOTHING MORE THAN THIS BOY'S CORPSE...
THIS BOY'S CORPSE, YOUR EXCELLENCY, IS THE PRICE OF THE HIDDEN IMAM'S TRUST.
THEN I HAVE YOUR WORD?
FATHER, THIS IS MADNESS!
ASK HIM FOR MEHDI'S NECKLACE.
WHAT NECKLACE?
WHISPER
I ASSUME THAT YOU WILL SEE TO IT THAT ALL PERSONAL POSSESSIONS ARE RETURNED TO THE FAMILY? THE BOY HAD A NECKLACE OF GREAT SENTIMENTAL VALUE...
YOU CAN'T DO THIS, FATHER: IT'S A TRAP-IT'LL BE YOUR END!!
SHUT UP!
PARDON?

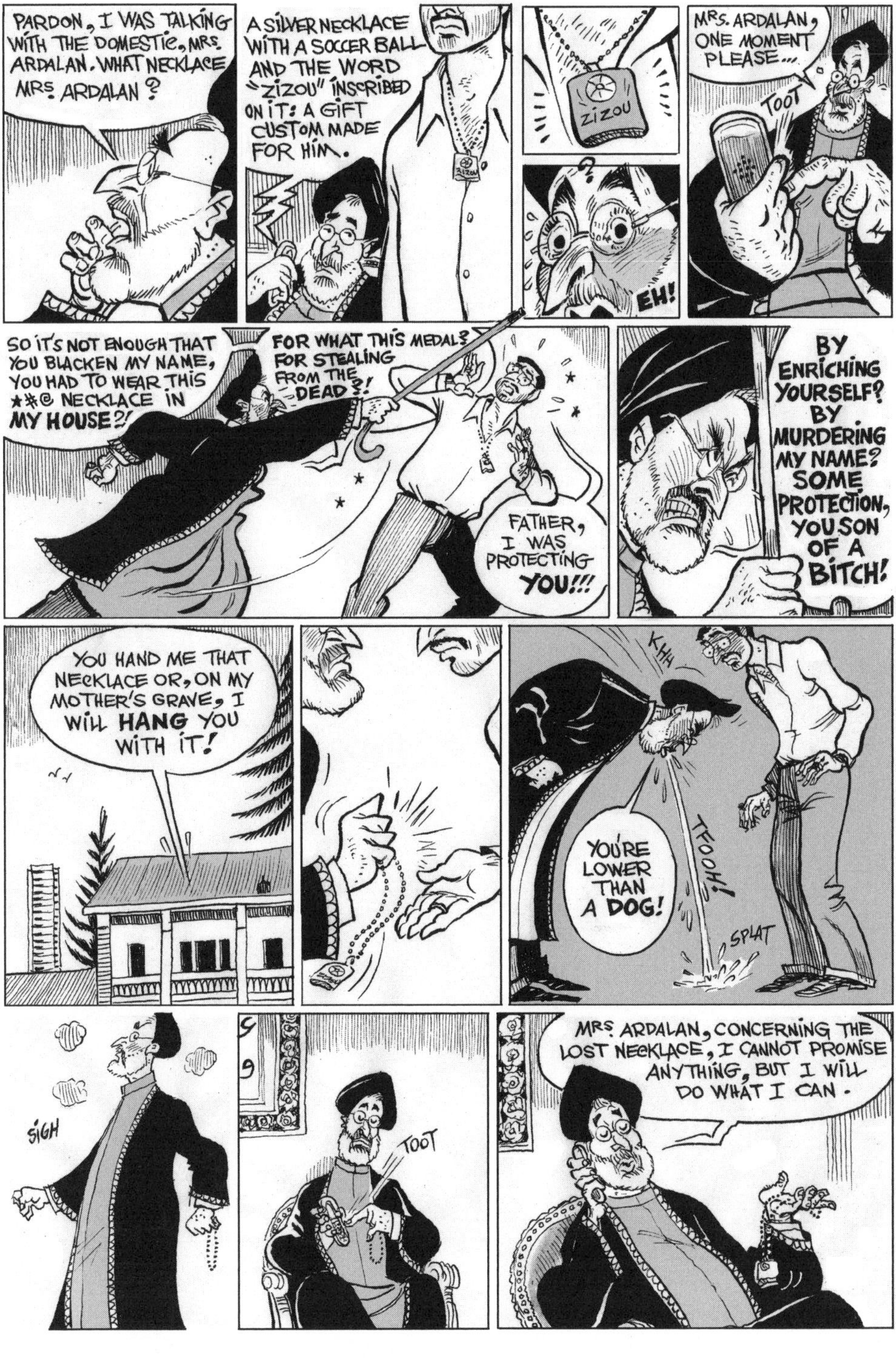
PARDON, I WAS TALKING WITH THE DOMESTIC, MRS. ARDALAN. WHAT NECKLACE MRS. ARDALAN?
A SILVER NECKLACE WITH A SOCCER BALL AND THE WORD "ZIZOU" INSCRIBED ON IT: A GIFT CUSTOM MADE FOR HIM.
ZIZOU
EH!
MRS. ARDALAN, ONE MOMENT PLEASE...
TOOT
SO IT'S NOT ENOUGH THAT YOU BLACKEN MY NAME, YOU HAD TO WEAR THIS *#@ NECKLACE IN MY HOUSE?!
FOR WHAT THIS MEDAL? FOR STEALING FROM THE DEAD?!
FATHER, I WAS PROTECTING YOU!!!
BY ENRICHING YOURSELF? BY MURDERING MY NAME? SOME PROTECTION, YOU SON OF A BITCH!
YOU HAND ME THAT NECKLACE OR, ON MY MOTHER'S GRAVE, I WILL HANG YOU WITH IT!
KHH
YOU'RE LOWER THAN A DOG!
TFOOH!
SPLAT
SIGH
TOOT
MRS. ARDALAN, CONCERNING THE LOST NECKLACE, I CANNOT PROMISE ANYTHING, BUT I WILL DO WHAT I CAN.

THE ANNOUNCEMENT

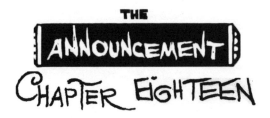

CHAPTER EIGHTEEN

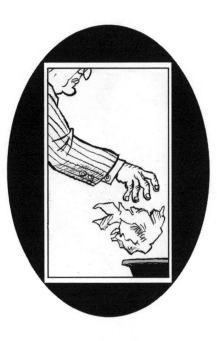

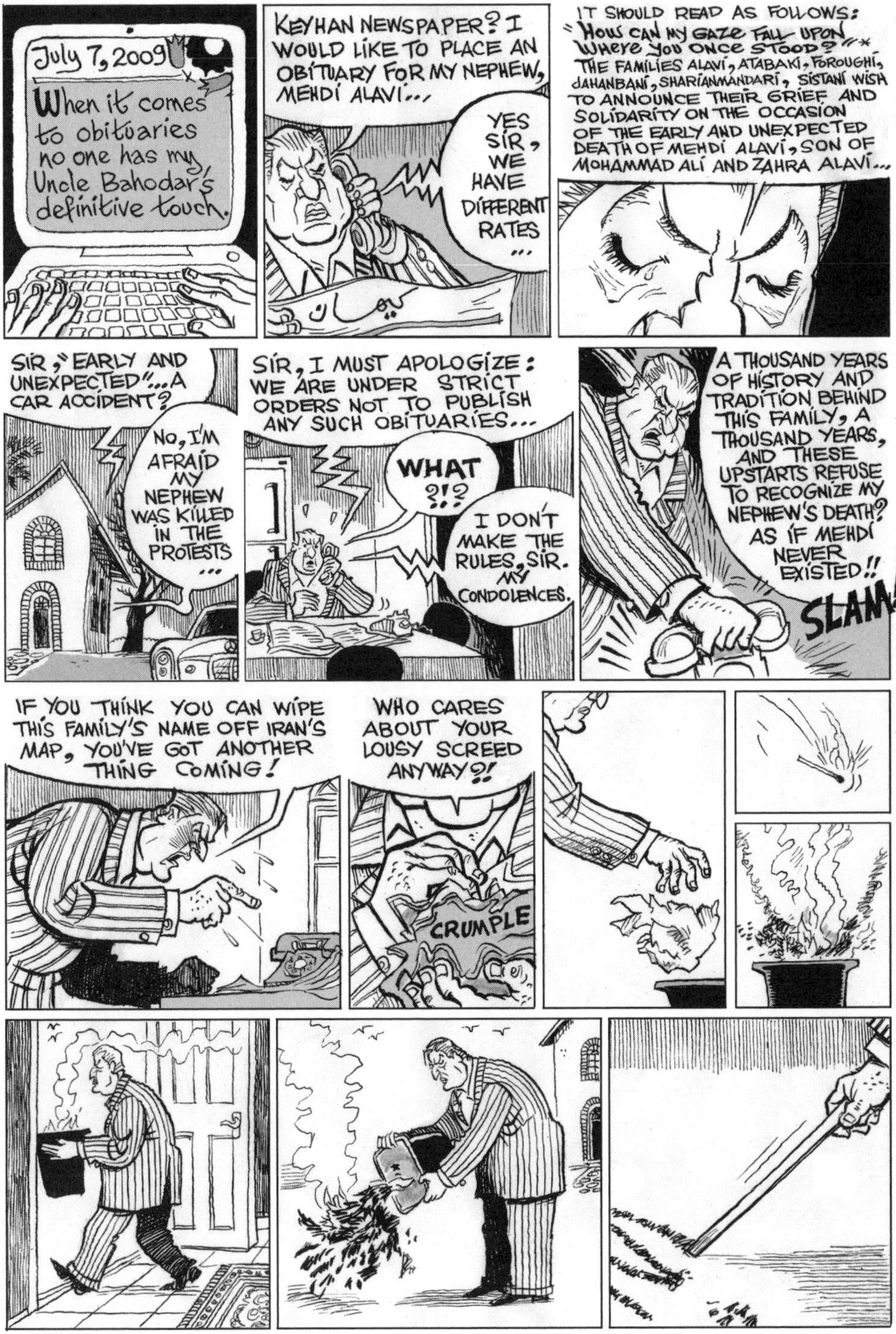
July 7, 2009
When it comes to obituaries no one has my Uncle Bahodar's definitive touch.
KEYHAN NEWSPAPER? I WOULD LIKE TO PLACE AN OBITUARY FOR MY NEPHEW, MEHDI ALAVI...
YES SIR, WE HAVE DIFFERENT RATES...
IT SHOULD READ AS FOLLOWS: "HOW CAN MY GAZE FALL UPON WHERE YOU ONCE STOOD?"* THE FAMILIES ALAVI, ATABAKI, FOROUGHI, JAHANBANI, SHARIANMADARI, SISTANI WISH TO ANNOUNCE THEIR GRIEF AND SOLIDARITY ON THE OCCASION OF THE EARLY AND UNEXPECTED DEATH OF MEHDI ALAVI, SON OF MOHAMMAD ALI AND ZAHRA ALAVI...
SIR, "EARLY AND UNEXPECTED"... A CAR ACCIDENT?
NO, I'M AFRAID MY NEPHEW WAS KILLED IN THE PROTESTS...
SIR, I MUST APOLOGIZE: WE ARE UNDER STRICT ORDERS NOT TO PUBLISH ANY SUCH OBITUARIES...
WHAT ?!?
I DON'T MAKE THE RULES, SIR. MY CONDOLENCES.
A THOUSAND YEARS OF HISTORY AND TRADITION BEHIND THIS FAMILY, A THOUSAND YEARS, AND THESE UPSTARTS REFUSE TO RECOGNIZE MY NEPHEW'S DEATH? AS IF MEHDI NEVER EXISTED!!
SLAM!
IF YOU THINK YOU CAN WIPE THIS FAMILY'S NAME OFF IRAN'S MAP, YOU'VE GOT ANOTHER THING COMING!
WHO CARES ABOUT YOUR LOUSY SCREED ANYWAY?!
CRUMPLE

* Verse by twelfth-century poet Faridudin Attar.

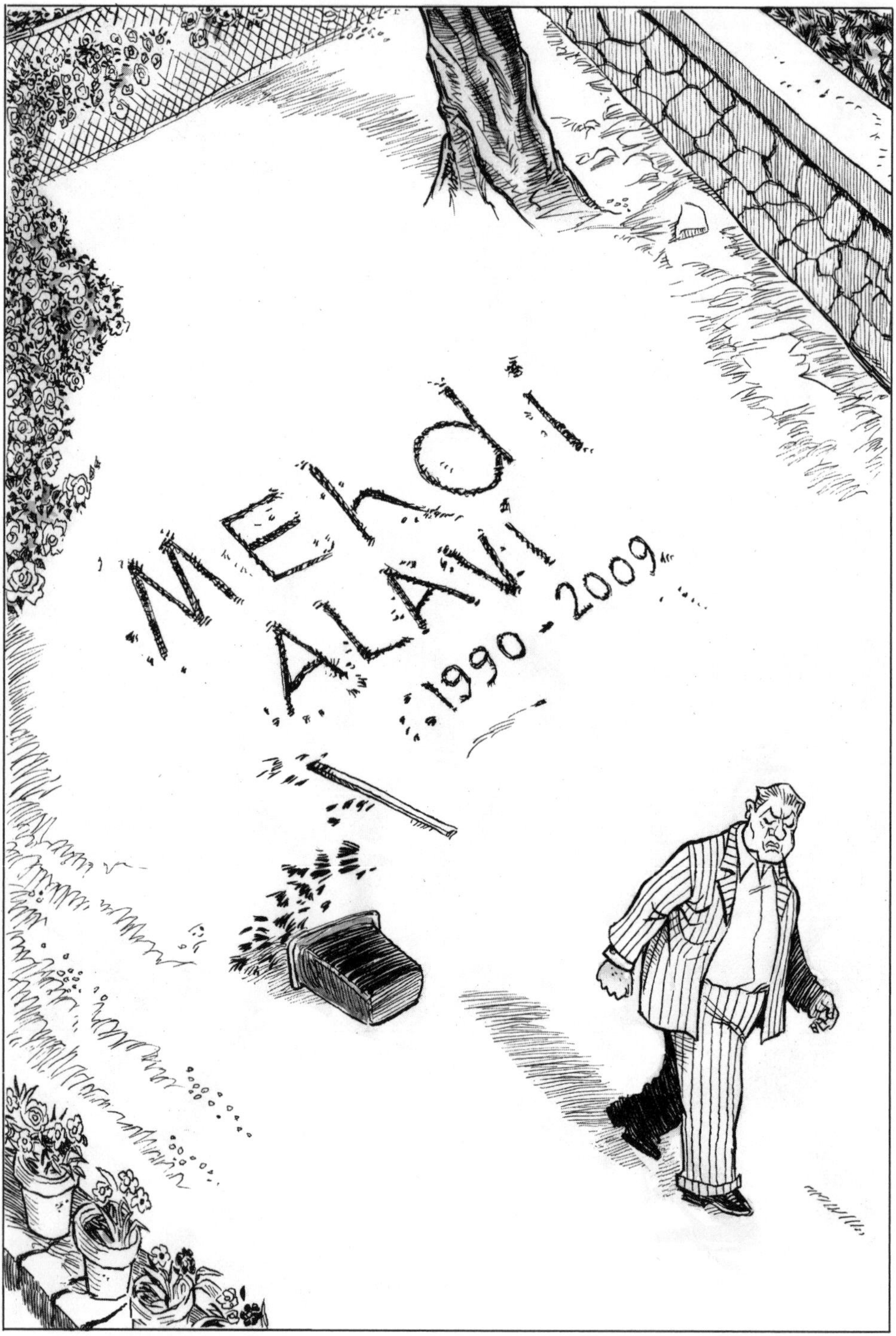
MEHDI
ALAVI
1990 - 2009

THE VISIT
CHAPTER NINETEEN

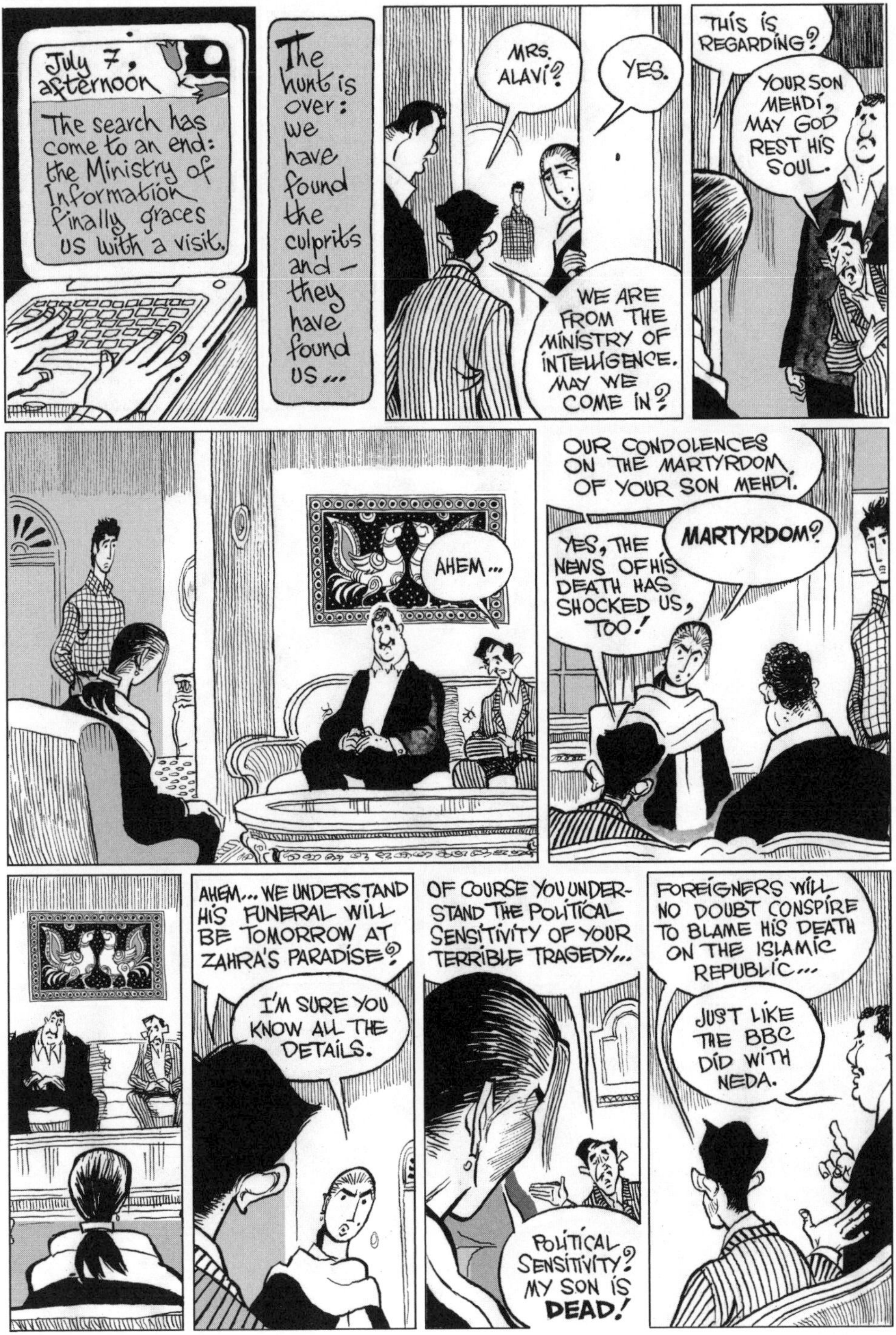
July 7, afternoon
The search has come to an end: the Ministry of Information finally graces us with a visit.
The hunt is over: we have found the culprits and — they have found us...
MRS. ALAVI?
YES.
WE ARE FROM THE MINISTRY OF INTELLIGENCE. MAY WE COME IN?
THIS IS REGARDING?
YOUR SON MEHDI, MAY GOD REST HIS SOUL.
AHEM...
OUR CONDOLENCES ON THE MARTYRDOM OF YOUR SON MEHDI.
MARTYRDOM?
YES, THE NEWS OF HIS DEATH HAS SHOCKED US, TOO!
AHEM... WE UNDERSTAND HIS FUNERAL WILL BE TOMORROW AT ZAHRA'S PARADISE?
I'M SURE YOU KNOW ALL THE DETAILS.
OF COURSE YOU UNDERSTAND THE POLITICAL SENSITIVITY OF YOUR TERRIBLE TRAGEDY...
POLITICAL SENSITIVITY? MY SON IS **DEAD**!
FOREIGNERS WILL NO DOUBT CONSPIRE TO BLAME HIS DEATH ON THE ISLAMIC REPUBLIC...
JUST LIKE THE BBC DID WITH NEDA.

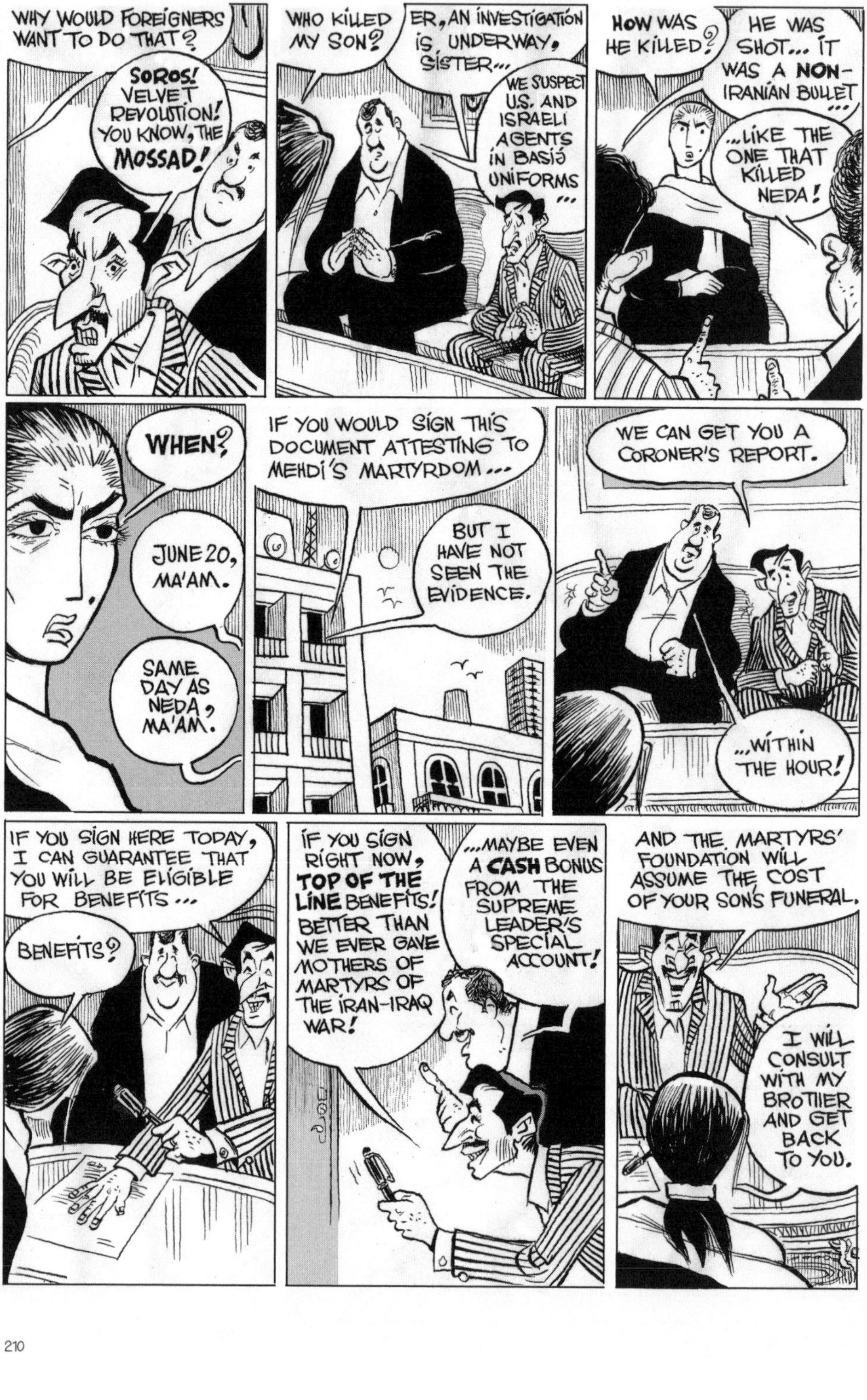
WHY WOULD FOREIGNERS WANT TO DO THAT?
SOROS! VELVET REVOLUTION! YOU KNOW, THE MOSSAD!
WHO KILLED MY SON?
ER, AN INVESTIGATION IS UNDERWAY, SISTER...
WE SUSPECT U.S. AND ISRAELI AGENTS IN BASIJ UNIFORMS...
HOW WAS HE KILLED?
HE WAS SHOT... IT WAS A NON-IRANIAN BULLET...
...LIKE THE ONE THAT KILLED NEDA!
WHEN?
JUNE 20, MA'AM.
SAME DAY AS NEDA, MA'AM.
IF YOU WOULD SIGN THIS DOCUMENT ATTESTING TO MEHDI'S MARTYRDOM...
BUT I HAVE NOT SEEN THE EVIDENCE.
WE CAN GET YOU A CORONER'S REPORT.
...WITHIN THE HOUR!
IF YOU SIGN HERE TODAY, I CAN GUARANTEE THAT YOU WILL BE ELIGIBLE FOR BENEFITS...
BENEFITS?
IF YOU SIGN RIGHT NOW, TOP OF THE LINE BENEFITS! BETTER THAN WE EVER GAVE MOTHERS OF MARTYRS OF THE IRAN-IRAQ WAR!
...MAYBE EVEN A CASH BONUS FROM THE SUPREME LEADER'S SPECIAL ACCOUNT!
AND THE MARTYRS' FOUNDATION WILL ASSUME THE COST OF YOUR SON'S FUNERAL.
I WILL CONSULT WITH MY BROTHER AND GET BACK TO YOU.

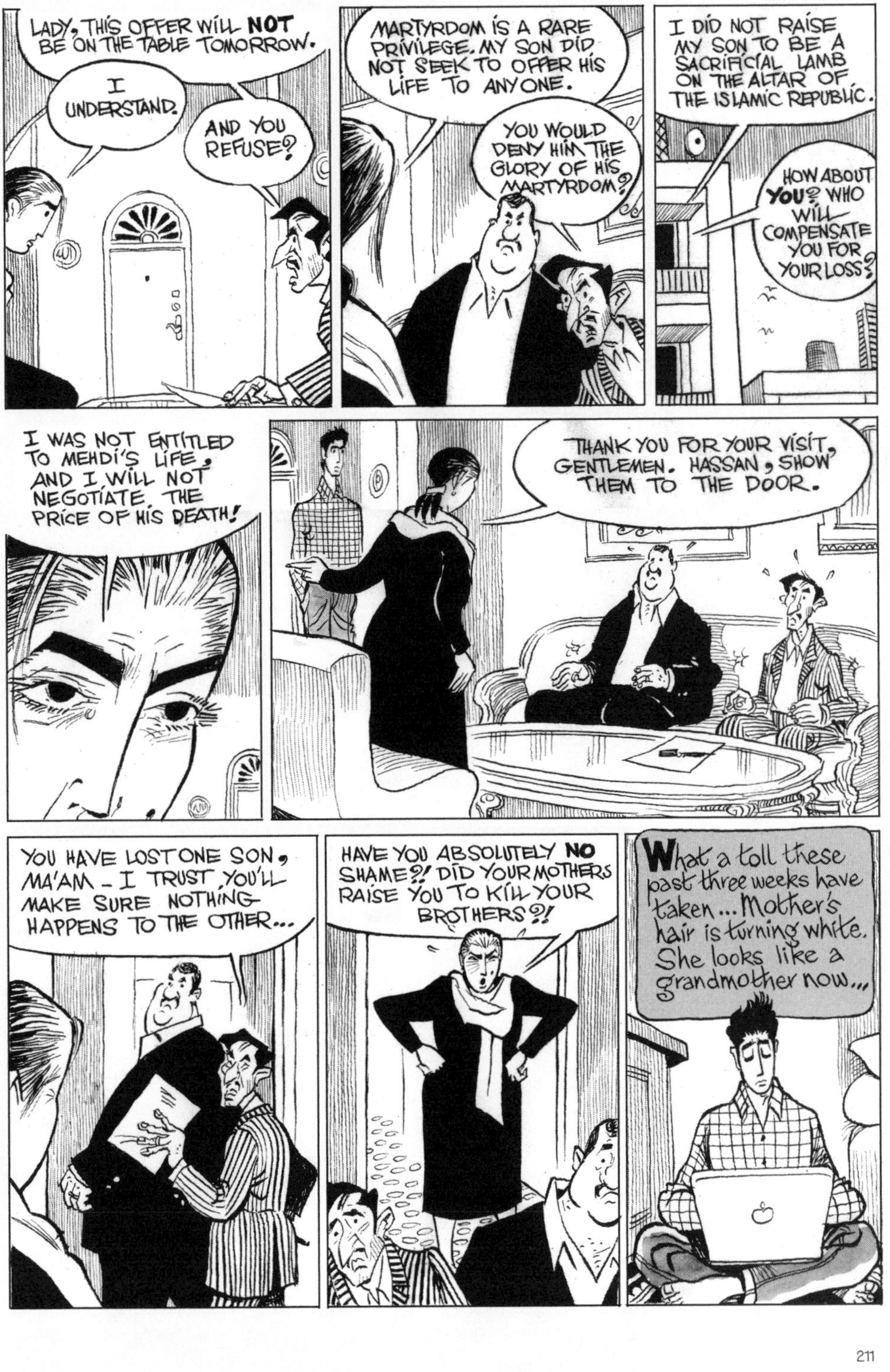
LADY, THIS OFFER WILL NOT BE ON THE TABLE TOMORROW.
I UNDERSTAND.
AND YOU REFUSE?
MARTYRDOM IS A RARE PRIVILEGE. MY SON DID NOT SEEK TO OFFER HIS LIFE TO ANYONE.
YOU WOULD DENY HIM THE GLORY OF HIS MARTYRDOM?
I DID NOT RAISE MY SON TO BE A SACRIFICIAL LAMB ON THE ALTAR OF THE ISLAMIC REPUBLIC.
HOW ABOUT YOU? WHO WILL COMPENSATE YOU FOR YOUR LOSS?
I WAS NOT ENTITLED TO MEHDI'S LIFE, AND I WILL NOT NEGOTIATE THE PRICE OF HIS DEATH!
THANK YOU FOR YOUR VISIT, GENTLEMEN. HASSAN, SHOW THEM TO THE DOOR.
YOU HAVE LOST ONE SON, MA'AM - I TRUST YOU'LL MAKE SURE NOTHING HAPPENS TO THE OTHER...
HAVE YOU ABSOLUTELY NO SHAME?! DID YOUR MOTHERS RAISE YOU TO KILL YOUR BROTHERS?!
What a toll these past three weeks have taken... Mother's hair is turning white. She looks like a grandmother now...

THE FURIE'S

CHAPTER TWENTY

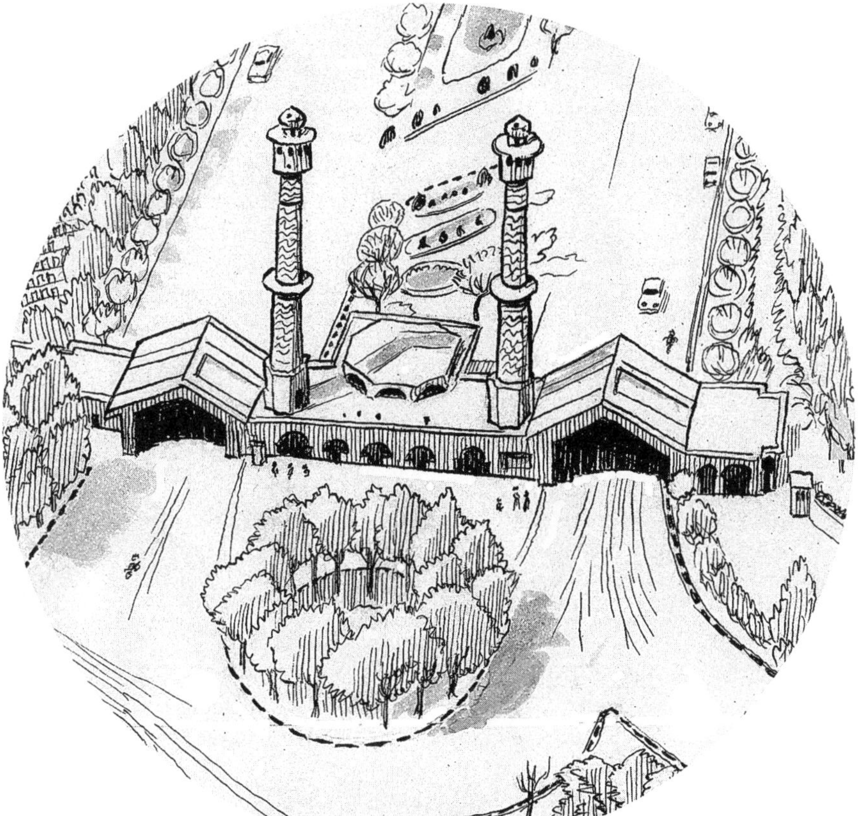

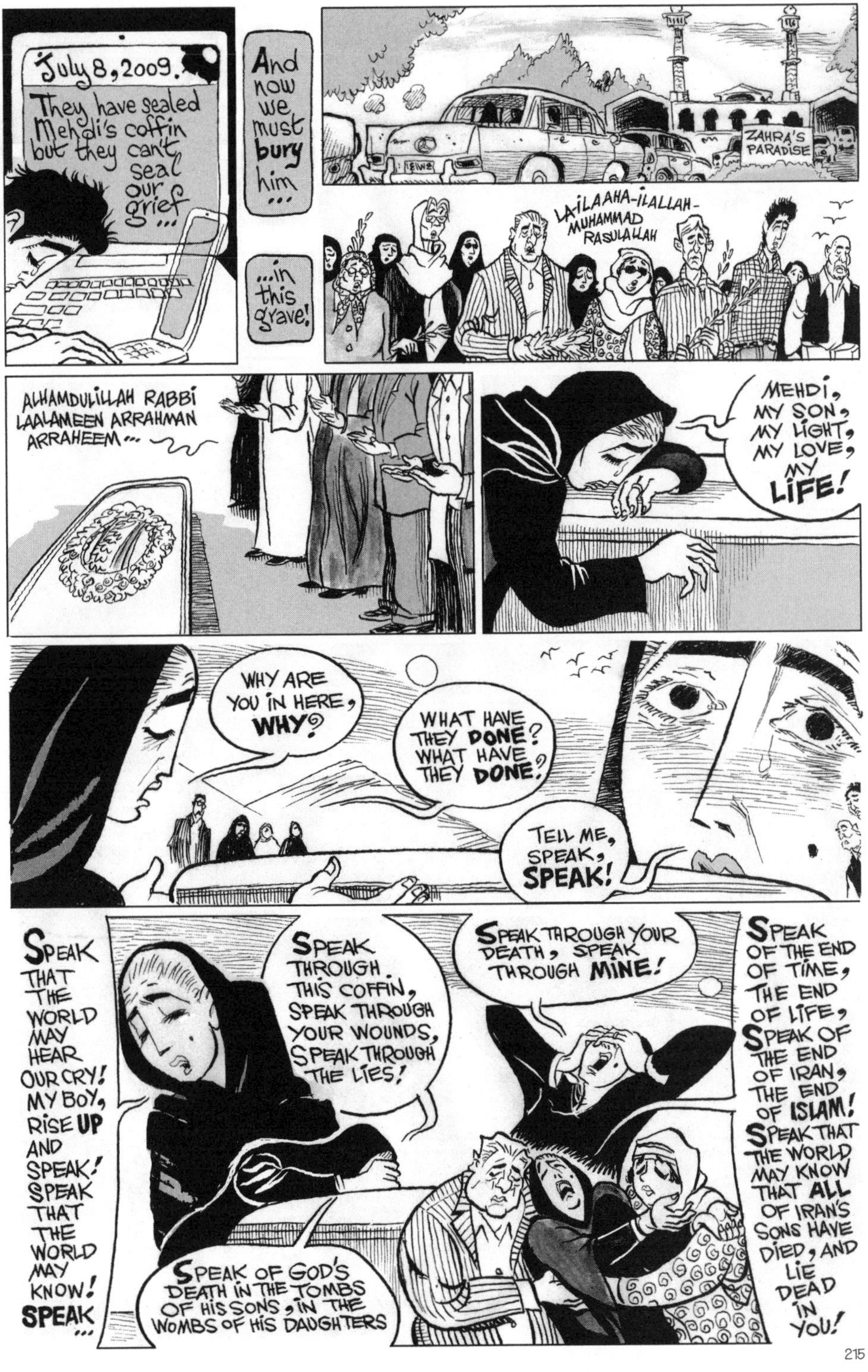
July 8, 2009.
They have sealed Mehdi's coffin but they can't seal our grief...
And now we must bury him...
...in this grave!
ZAHRA'S PARADISE
LA ILAAHA-ILALLAH-MUHAMMAD RASULALLAH
ALHAMDULILLAH RABBI LAALAMEEN ARRAHMAN ARRAHEEM...
MEHDI, MY SON, MY LIGHT, MY LOVE, MY LIFE!
WHY ARE YOU IN HERE, WHY?
WHAT HAVE THEY DONE? WHAT HAVE THEY DONE?
TELL ME, SPEAK, SPEAK!
SPEAK THAT THE WORLD MAY HEAR OUR CRY! MY BOY, RISE UP AND SPEAK! SPEAK THAT THE WORLD MAY KNOW! SPEAK...
SPEAK THROUGH THIS COFFIN, SPEAK THROUGH YOUR WOUNDS, SPEAK THROUGH THE LIES!
SPEAK THROUGH YOUR DEATH, SPEAK THROUGH MINE!
SPEAK OF GOD'S DEATH IN THE TOMBS OF HIS SONS, IN THE WOMBS OF HIS DAUGHTERS
SPEAK OF THE END OF TIME, THE END OF LIFE, SPEAK OF THE END OF IRAN, THE END OF ISLAM! SPEAK THAT THE WORLD MAY KNOW THAT ALL OF IRAN'S SONS HAVE DIED, AND LIE DEAD IN YOU!

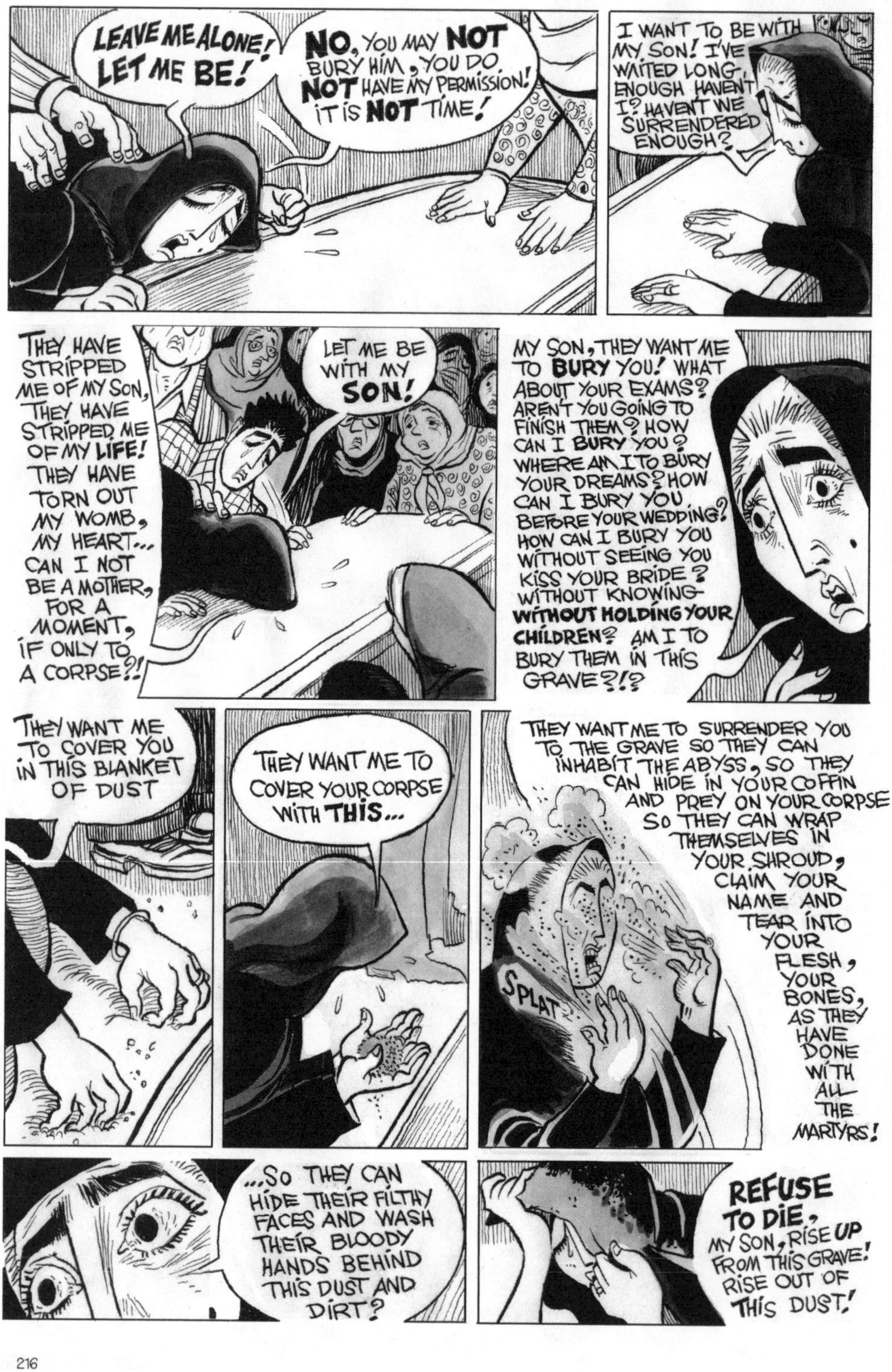
LEAVE ME ALONE! LET ME BE!
NO, YOU MAY NOT BURY HIM, YOU DO NOT HAVE MY PERMISSION! IT IS NOT TIME!
I WANT TO BE WITH MY SON! I'VE WAITED LONG ENOUGH HAVEN'T I? HAVEN'T WE SURRENDERED ENOUGH?
THEY HAVE STRIPPED ME OF MY SON, THEY HAVE STRIPPED ME OF MY LIFE! THEY HAVE TORN OUT MY WOMB, MY HEART... CAN I NOT BE A MOTHER, FOR A MOMENT, IF ONLY TO A CORPSE?!
LET ME BE WITH MY SON!
MY SON, THEY WANT ME TO BURY YOU! WHAT ABOUT YOUR EXAMS? AREN'T YOU GOING TO FINISH THEM? HOW CAN I BURY YOU? WHERE AM I TO BURY YOUR DREAMS? HOW CAN I BURY YOU BEFORE YOUR WEDDING? HOW CAN I BURY YOU WITHOUT SEEING YOU KISS YOUR BRIDE? WITHOUT KNOWING-WITHOUT HOLDING YOUR CHILDREN? AM I TO BURY THEM IN THIS GRAVE?!?
THEY WANT ME TO COVER YOU IN THIS BLANKET OF DUST
THEY WANT ME TO COVER YOUR CORPSE WITH THIS...
THEY WANT ME TO SURRENDER YOU TO THE GRAVE SO THEY CAN INHABIT THE ABYSS, SO THEY CAN HIDE IN YOUR COFFIN AND PREY ON YOUR CORPSE SO THEY CAN WRAP THEMSELVES IN YOUR SHROUD, CLAIM YOUR NAME AND TEAR INTO YOUR FLESH, YOUR BONES, AS THEY HAVE DONE WITH ALL THE MARTYRS!
SPLAT
...SO THEY CAN HIDE THEIR FILTHY FACES AND WASH THEIR BLOODY HANDS BEHIND THIS DUST AND DIRT?
REFUSE TO DIE, MY SON, RISE UP FROM THIS GRAVE! RISE OUT OF THIS DUST!

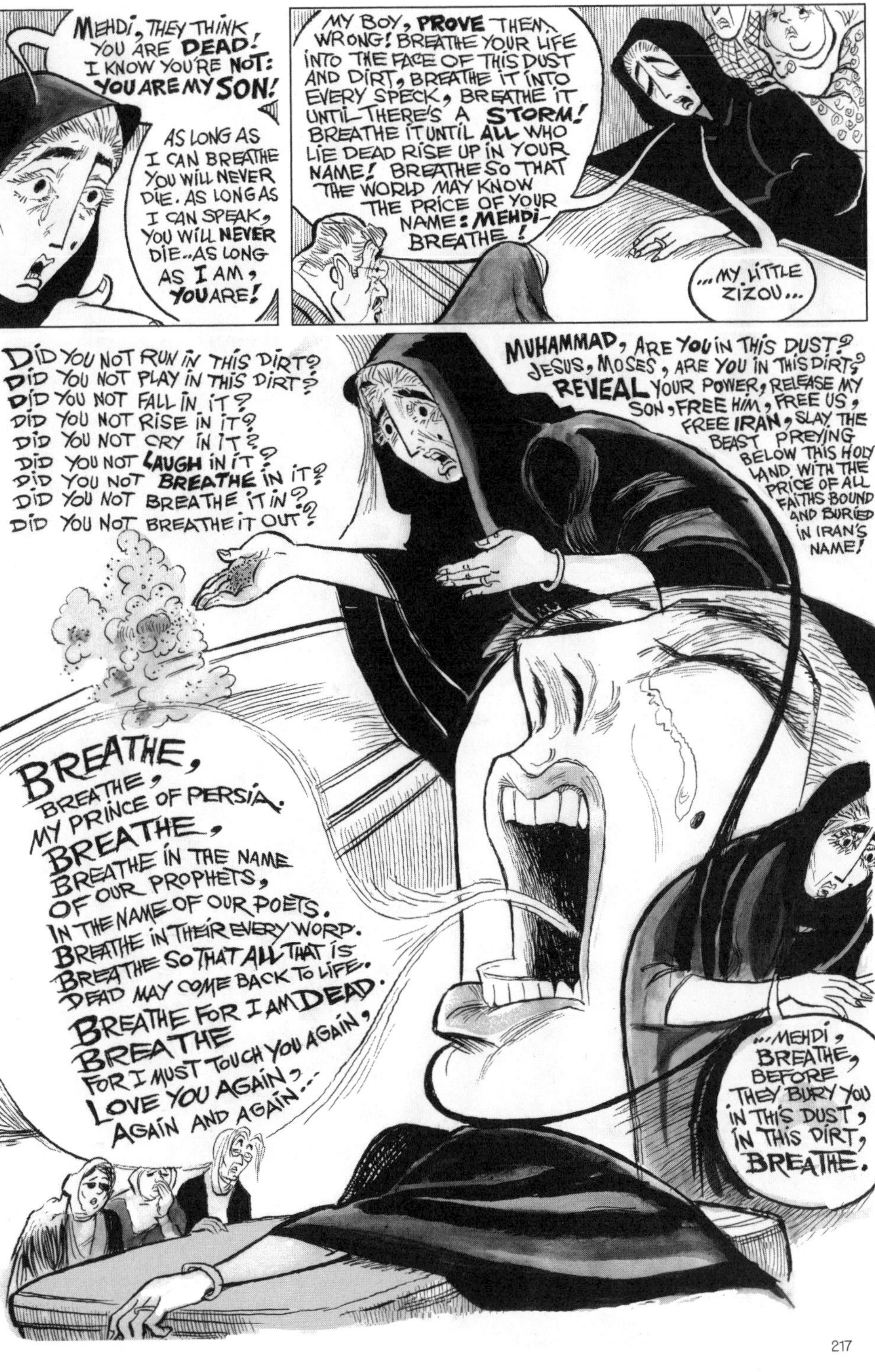
MEHDI, THEY THINK YOU ARE DEAD! I KNOW YOU'RE NOT: YOU ARE MY SON!
AS LONG AS I CAN BREATHE YOU WILL NEVER DIE. AS LONG AS I CAN SPEAK, YOU WILL NEVER DIE.. AS LONG AS I AM, YOU ARE!
MY BOY, PROVE THEM WRONG! BREATHE YOUR LIFE INTO THE FACE OF THIS DUST AND DIRT, BREATHE IT INTO EVERY SPECK, BREATHE IT UNTIL THERE'S A STORM! BREATHE IT UNTIL ALL WHO LIE DEAD RISE UP IN YOUR NAME! BREATHE SO THAT THE WORLD MAY KNOW THE PRICE OF YOUR NAME: MEHDI-BREATHE!
...MY LITTLE ZIZOU...
DID YOU NOT RUN IN THIS DIRT? DID YOU NOT PLAY IN THIS DIRT? DID YOU NOT FALL IN IT? DID YOU NOT RISE IN IT? DID YOU NOT CRY IN IT? DID YOU NOT LAUGH IN IT? DID YOU NOT BREATHE IN IT? DID YOU NOT BREATHE IT IN? DID YOU NOT BREATHE IT OUT?
MUHAMMAD, ARE YOU IN THIS DUST? JESUS, MOSES, ARE YOU IN THIS DIRT? REVEAL YOUR POWER, RELEASE MY SON, FREE HIM, FREE US, FREE IRAN, SLAY THE BEAST PREYING BELOW THIS HOLY LAND, WITH THE PRICE OF ALL FAITHS BOUND AND BURIED IN IRAN'S NAME!
BREATHE, BREATHE, MY PRINCE OF PERSIA. BREATHE, BREATHE IN THE NAME OF OUR PROPHETS, BREATHE IN THE NAME OF OUR POETS. BREATHE IN THEIR EVERY WORD. BREATHE SO THAT ALL THAT IS DEAD MAY COME BACK TO LIFE. BREATHE FOR I AM DEAD. BREATHE FOR I MUST TOUCH YOU AGAIN, LOVE YOU AGAIN, AGAIN AND AGAIN...
...MEHDI, BREATHE, BEFORE THEY BURY YOU IN THIS DUST, IN THIS DIRT, BREATHE.

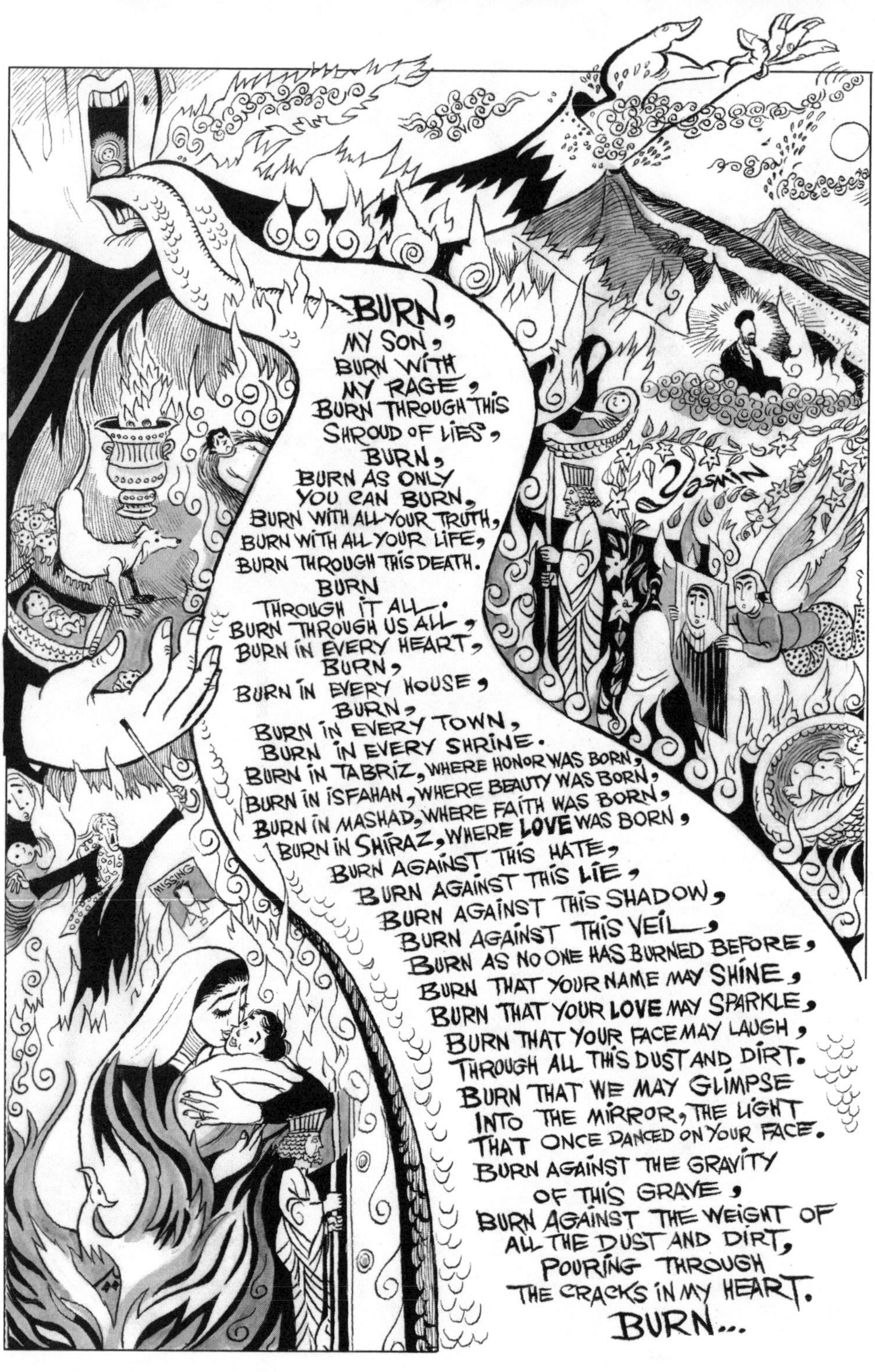

Yasmin
MISSING
BURN,
MY SON,
BURN WITH
MY RAGE,
BURN THROUGH THIS
SHROUD OF LIES,
BURN,
BURN AS ONLY
YOU CAN BURN,
BURN WITH ALL YOUR TRUTH,
BURN WITH ALL YOUR LIFE,
BURN THROUGH THIS DEATH.
BURN
THROUGH IT ALL.
BURN THROUGH US ALL,
BURN IN EVERY HEART,
BURN,
BURN IN EVERY HOUSE,
BURN,
BURN IN EVERY TOWN,
BURN IN EVERY SHRINE.
BURN IN TABRIZ, WHERE HONOR WAS BORN,
BURN IN ISFAHAN, WHERE BEAUTY WAS BORN,
BURN IN MASHAD, WHERE FAITH WAS BORN,
BURN IN SHIRAZ, WHERE LOVE WAS BORN,
BURN AGAINST THIS HATE,
BURN AGAINST THIS LIE,
BURN AGAINST THIS SHADOW,
BURN AGAINST THIS VEIL,
BURN AS NO ONE HAS BURNED BEFORE,
BURN THAT YOUR NAME MAY SHINE,
BURN THAT YOUR LOVE MAY SPARKLE,
BURN THAT YOUR FACE MAY LAUGH,
THROUGH ALL THIS DUST AND DIRT.
BURN THAT WE MAY GLIMPSE
INTO THE MIRROR, THE LIGHT
THAT ONCE DANCED ON YOUR FACE.
BURN AGAINST THE GRAVITY
OF THIS GRAVE,
BURN AGAINST THE WEIGHT OF
ALL THE DUST AND DIRT,
POURING THROUGH
THE CRACKS IN MY HEART.
BURN...

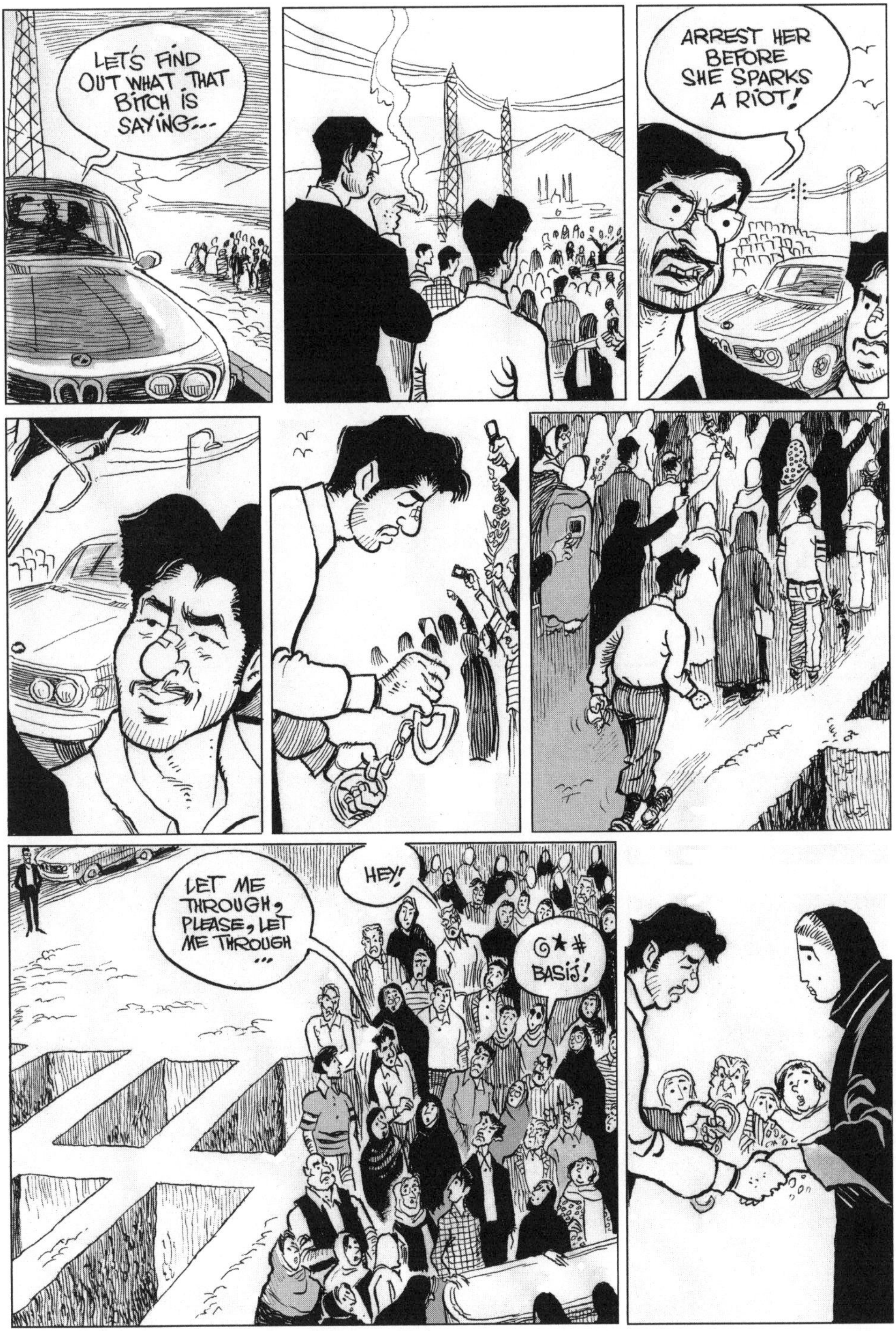
LET'S FIND OUT WHAT THAT BITCH IS SAYING...
ARREST HER BEFORE SHE SPARKS A RIOT!
LET ME THROUGH, PLEASE, LET ME THROUGH...
HEY!
@*# BASIJ!

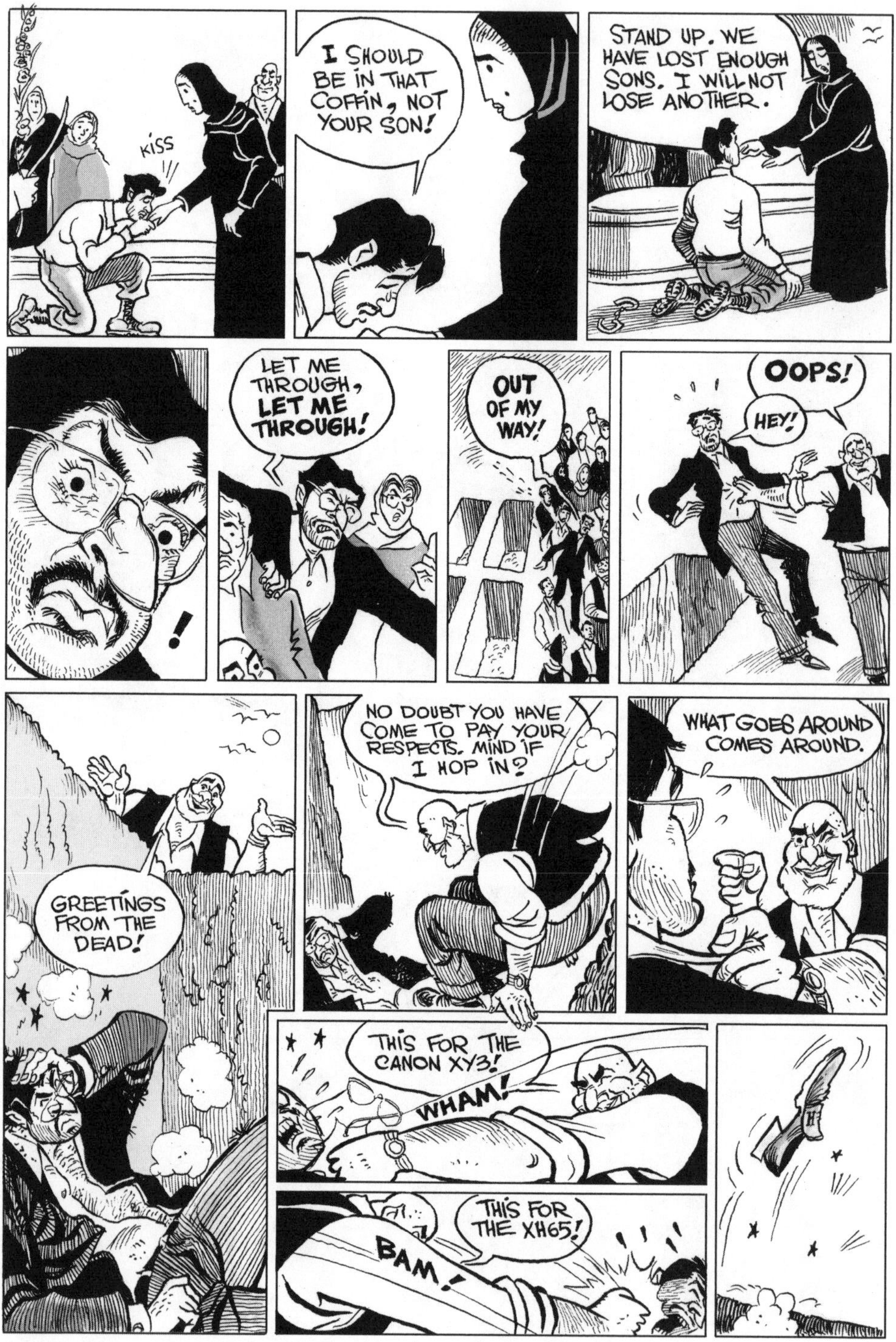
KISS
I SHOULD BE IN THAT COFFIN, NOT YOUR SON!
STAND UP. WE HAVE LOST ENOUGH SONS. I WILL NOT LOSE ANOTHER.
LET ME THROUGH, LET ME THROUGH!
OUT OF MY WAY!
OOPS!
HEY!
GREETINGS FROM THE DEAD!
NO DOUBT YOU HAVE COME TO PAY YOUR RESPECTS. MIND IF I HOP IN?
WHAT GOES AROUND COMES AROUND.
THIS FOR THE CANON XY3!
WHAM!
THIS FOR THE XH65!
BAM!

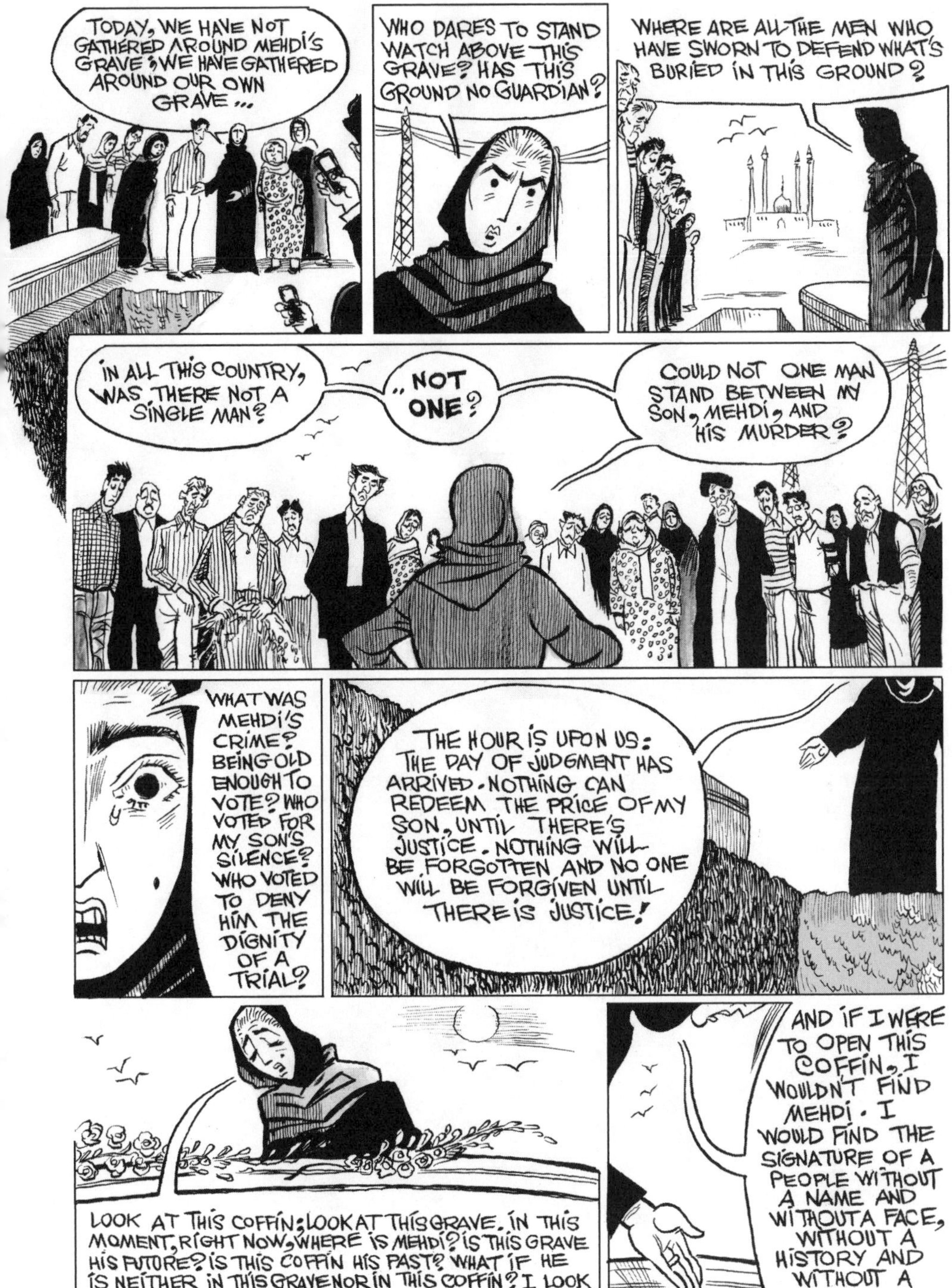
TODAY, WE HAVE NOT GATHERED AROUND MEHDI'S GRAVE; WE HAVE GATHERED AROUND OUR OWN GRAVE...
WHO DARES TO STAND WATCH ABOVE THIS GRAVE? HAS THIS GROUND NO GUARDIAN?
WHERE ARE ALL THE MEN WHO HAVE SWORN TO DEFEND WHAT'S BURIED IN THIS GROUND?
IN ALL THIS COUNTRY, WAS THERE NOT A SINGLE MAN?
...NOT ONE?
COULD NOT ONE MAN STAND BETWEEN MY SON, MEHDI, AND HIS MURDER?
WHAT WAS MEHDI'S CRIME? BEING OLD ENOUGH TO VOTE? WHO VOTED FOR MY SON'S SILENCE? WHO VOTED TO DENY HIM THE DIGNITY OF A TRIAL?
THE HOUR IS UPON US: THE DAY OF JUDGMENT HAS ARRIVED. NOTHING CAN REDEEM THE PRICE OF MY SON, UNTIL THERE'S JUSTICE. NOTHING WILL BE FORGOTTEN AND NO ONE WILL BE FORGIVEN UNTIL THERE IS JUSTICE!
LOOK AT THIS COFFIN; LOOK AT THIS GRAVE. IN THIS MOMENT, RIGHT NOW, WHERE IS MEHDI? IS THIS GRAVE HIS FUTURE? IS THIS COFFIN HIS PAST? WHAT IF HE IS NEITHER IN THIS GRAVE NOR IN THIS COFFIN? I LOOK AT THIS GRAVE AND I DON'T SEE MEHDI...
AND IF I WERE TO OPEN THIS COFFIN, I WOULDN'T FIND MEHDI. I WOULD FIND THE SIGNATURE OF A PEOPLE WITHOUT A NAME AND WITHOUT A FACE, WITHOUT A HISTORY AND WITHOUT A FUTURE!

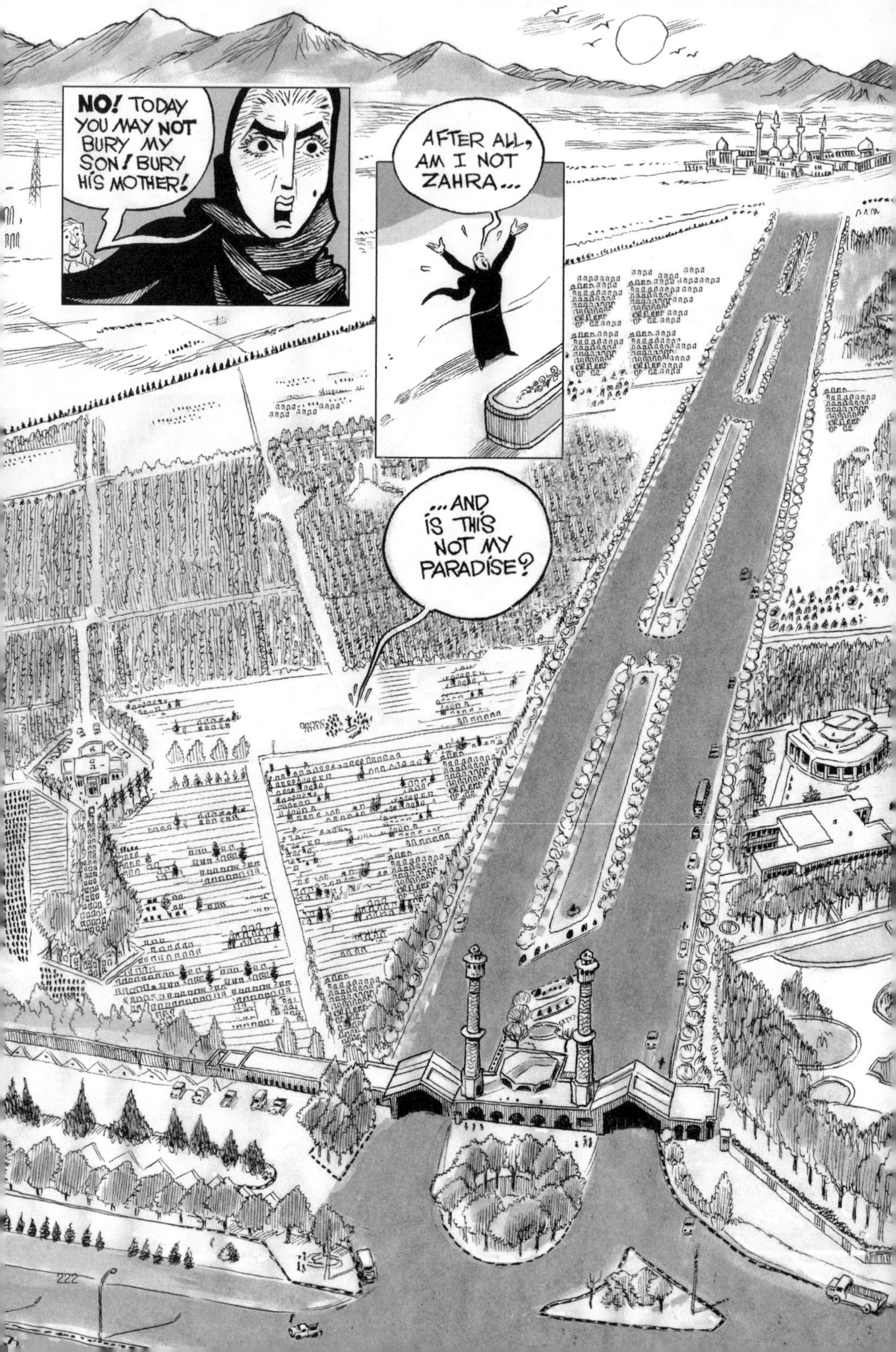
NO! TODAY YOU MAY NOT BURY MY SON! BURY HIS MOTHER!
AFTER ALL, AM I NOT ZAHRA...
...AND IS THIS NOT MY PARADISE?

EPILOGUE

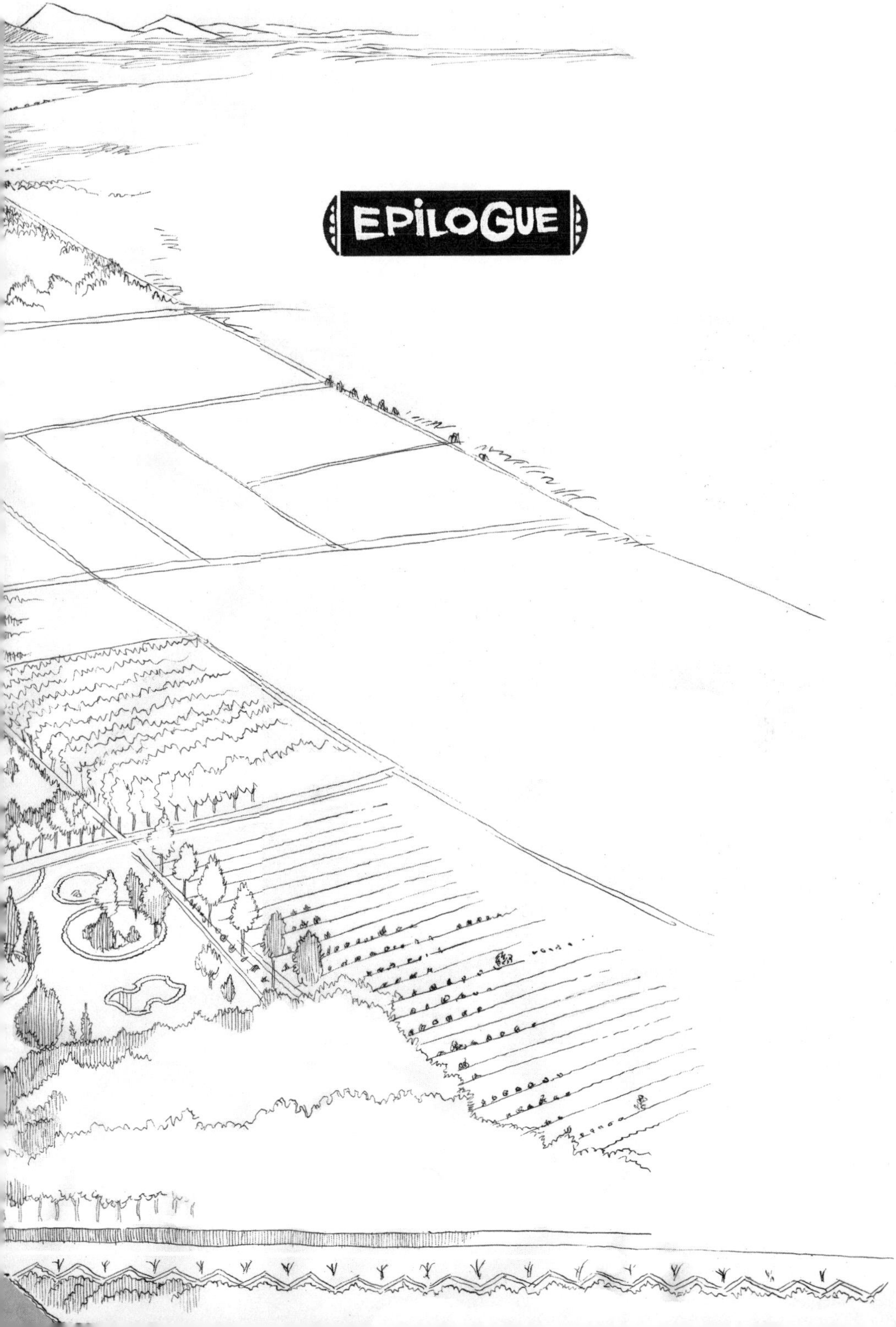

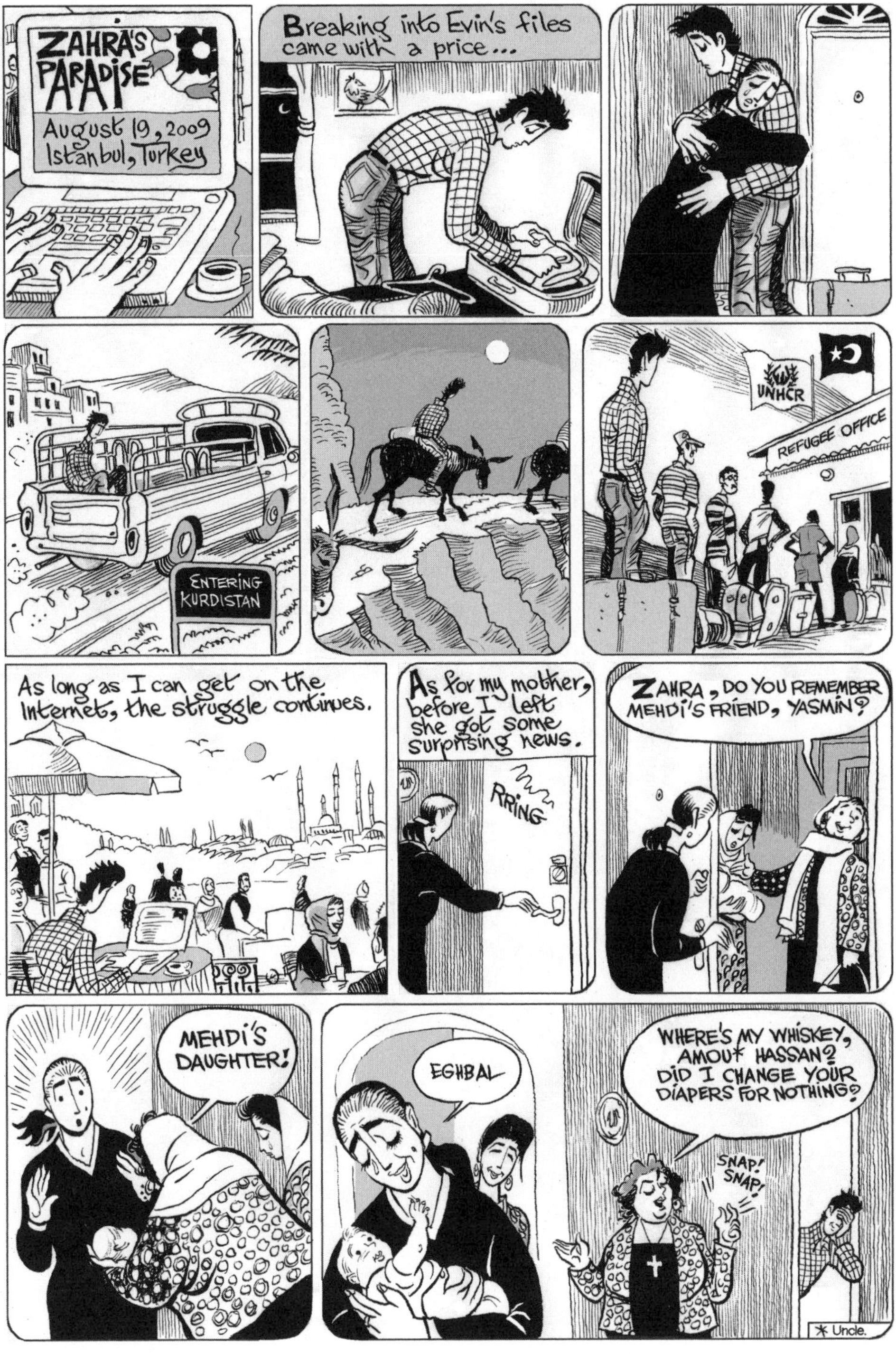
ZAHRA'S PARADISE
August 19, 2009
Istanbul, Turkey
Breaking into Evin's files came with a price...
ENTERING KURDISTAN
UNHCR
REFUGEE OFFICE
As long as I can get on the Internet, the struggle continues.
As for my mother, before I left she got some surprising news.
RRING
ZAHRA, DO YOU REMEMBER MEHDI'S FRIEND, YASMIN?
MEHDI'S DAUGHTER!
EGHBAL
WHERE'S MY WHISKEY, AMOU* HASSAN? DID I CHANGE YOUR DIAPERS FOR NOTHING?
SNAP! SNAP!
* Uncle.

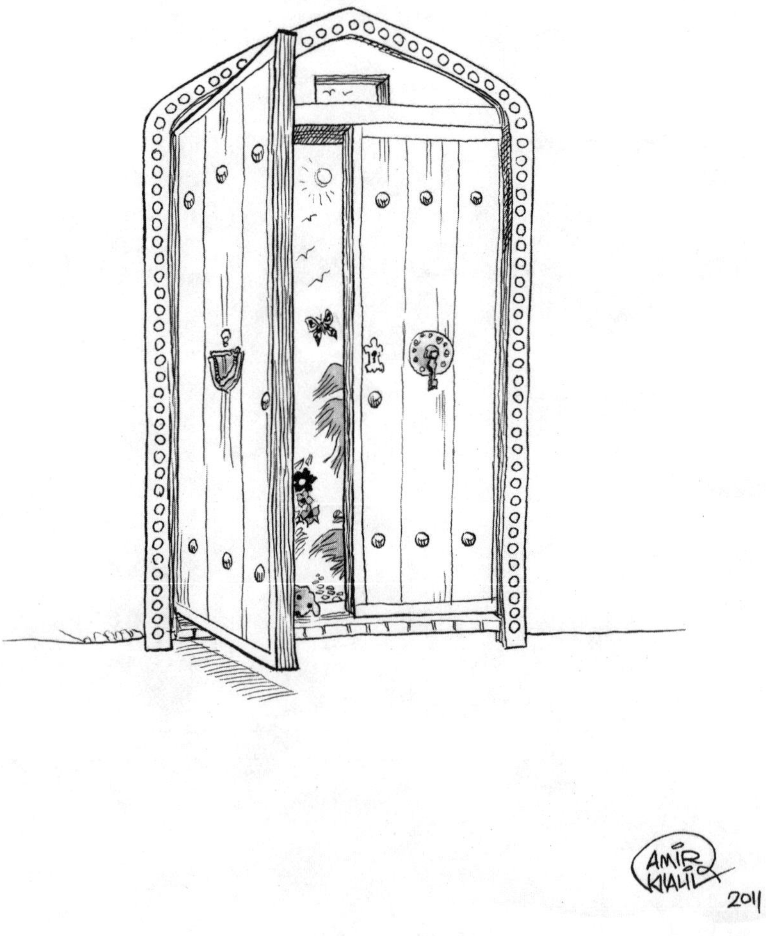
AMIR KHALIL
2011

Glossary

Ab hendooneh—Watermelon juice, the ultimate summer drink in Iran.

Abu Ghraib—Prison in Iraq, notorious as the site of the U.S. torture scandal, photographs of which leaked to the world.

Ahmadinejad, Mahmoud—President of Iran (2005–), and former mayor of Tehran (1999–2005), he is a conservative and populist politician. His re-election in 2009 was disputed by opposition groups and international observers who accused him of tampering with votes.

Alborz—One of Tehran's best high schools.

Al-e Ahmad, Jalal (1923–1969)—Prominent Iranian intellectual who coined the term "Gharbzadegi," or "Westoxification." His writings called for a return to authentic traditions and cultural roots, and resonated with the left and fundamentalists who rejected the Pahlavi state's pro-American policies and Western aspirations.

Allahu Akbar—"God Is Great," one of the religious slogans that animated Iran's revolution of 1979, Allahu Akbar gained renewed currency after Iran's 2009 presidential elections as an expression of popular opposition to the Islamic Republic's reliance on force, fear, and fraud.

Ashura—The tenth day of the month of Muharram in the Shia Islamic calendar, it is the day Muslims commemorate the martyrdom of Imam Hussein, the Prophet's grandson, and his companions, in the Battle of Karbala.

Atash—fire.

Attar, Farid ud-Din—A twelfth-century Persian poet, Attar is one of the great masters of Sufism. His most famous work is *The Conference of the Birds*.

Ayatollah—Literally means "Sign of God," religious title bestowed on the most respected and learned Shi'a clerics by devotees. Since 1979, the Islamic regime has politicized the title, bestowing it on those who support the regime.

Azadi Square—A massive public square in Tehran that served as the rallying point for the 1979 revolution and the 2009 protests.

Baha'I faith—A monotheist religion founded by Bahá'u'lláh in nineteenth-century Iran that emphasizes oneness and the unity of humankind.

Bakhtiar, Shapur—The last prime minister under the monarchy. He was appointed by the Shah in January 1979. A social democrat who rejected religious despotism, Bakhtiar was assassinated in Paris on August 7, 1991, while under the protection of the French government.

Behesht—paradise.

Bismillah ir- Rahman ir- Rahim—"In the Name of God, the Merciful, the Compassionate."

Boz keshi—A precursor of polo, an Afghan sport in which horsemen compete for control over the carcass of a dead goat, a metaphor for the Great Game in which great powers fight for control over the carcass of Middle Eastern and Central Asian nations.

Cossack Brigade—Elite Persian cavalry unit led by Russian officers under the Qajar dynasty. During Iran's constitutional revolution (1906–1911), the Cossacks were used by the central government to attack the Parliament. Reza Shah, the founder of the Pahlavi dynasty, was an officer in the Cossack Brigade and used his military power to centralize the Iranian state.

Council of Guardians—Powerful conservative body whose twelve members act as the final authority on parliamentary legislation and electoral certification. The Council vets candidates, supervises elections, and monitors laws as guardians of Islamic principles.

Deev—demon.

Deev Sepid—White Demon, one of the most ferocious demons defeated by Rostam in Ferdowsi's *Shahnameh*.

Eghbal—(Farsi) chance, good fortune.

Evin—A village on the outskirts of Tehran; also the name of a notorious prison located there in which countless political prisoners have vanished.

Ey Baba—(Farsi) For God's sake, a term of exasperation.

Ferdowsi, Hakim Abul Qasim (940-1020)— One of the giants of Persian literature, Ferdowsi's Book of Kings, the *Shahnameh*, is Iran's national epic. Ferdowsi is credited with guarding the sanctity of Persian culture and civilization in the aftermath of the Arab conquests.

Foozool— (Farsi) An inquisitive person who inquires about people's private affairs. Often used in an affectionate sense.

Gumsho—(Farsi) Get lost.

Hafez, Shamsuddin Mohammad—fourteenth-century poet and mystic. Born in Shiraz, Hafez is one of Iran's greatest lyric poets. His collection of lyric poetry, *The Divan of Hafez*, is a masterpiece of Persian culture and literature, and an integral part of the Iranian world's traditions.

Hoveyda, Amir Abbas (1919–1979)—Prime Minister of Iran from 1965 to 1977. The Islamic regime executed Hoveyda on the charge of "corruption on earth."

Isfahan—major Iranian city, renowned for its stunning Islamic art and architecture.

Istaghfirallah—(Arabic) "May God Forgive Me."

Jahanam—(Farsi and Arabic) Hell.

Jannati, Ahmad—A senior conservative ayatollah. Jannati heads the Guardian Council, a twelve-member body whose responsibilities include the supervision of elections, the vetting of candidates, and insuring compliance of laws passed by the parliament with Islamic principles.

Javanmardi—Persian code of chivalry and fair play embodied by Takhti, as well as other warriors and athletes.

Kahrizak—Detention center outside Tehran.

Karbala—A shrine city in modern-day Iraq. Also the site of an historic battle between the Prophet Muhammad's grandson, Imam Hossein, and the much larger armies of Yazid, the Ummayad Caliph.

Karoubi, Mehdi—Presidential candidate in 2005 and 2009, and former speaker of the Sixth Iranian parliament (2000–2004) Karoubi is one of the leaders of Iran's Green movement.

Kazemi, Zahra (Ziba)—(1949–2003) Canadian-Iranian photojournalist, arrested outside Evin prison for taking pictures of family members of student demonstrators who had gone missing in Evin. Kazemi was beaten, raped, and tortured while under the custody of the Islamic Republic. Her death, and its subsequent cover-up by the Iranian government led to an international outcry against the Islamic regime. She was buried in Shiraz against the wishes of her son, Stephan Kazemi (Hashemi).

Khafehsho—(Farsi) shut up. Alternatively, the more affectionate term, "kewft."

Khanoom—(Farsi) Madame.

Khamenei, Ali—Iran's president 1981 to 1989, he became Iran's supreme leader after Khomeini's designated successor, Ayatollah Montazeri, fell from grace. He was crowned Supreme Leader by the Assembly of Experts, a council of Islamic scholars. As Supreme Leader, he controls the Iranian state through the Guardian Council, judiciary, revolutionary guards, intelligence services, media, and religious foundations. Denounced as a dictator for usurping his office to sanctify the election of Ahmadinejad and for authorizing the use of force against the people.

Khatami, Mohammad—Former president of Iran (1997–2005), a reformist, Khatami is credited with salvaging the Islamic Republic's image at home and abroad by pursuing a reformist and liberal cultural agenda within the framework of the system.

Khavaran—Mass grave where victims of 1988 prison massacre are buried.

Khayyam, Omar (1048–1131)— Mathematician, astronomer, and poet, in his poetry he challenged orthodox codes and conventions premised on piety, morality, fear, and death. He dismisses the speculations of saints and sages stuck between two worlds, and celebrates the presence of love and life as they unfold in the moment.

Khomeini, Ruhollah—A dissident cleric, Ayatollah Khomeini was the founder of the Islamic Republic of Iran. His vision of an Islamic state paved the way for the establishment of a theocracy following the Shah's overthrow in 1979. He assumed the right to rule in the name of the Hidden Imam (the Mahdi, or Messiah, in the Shia tradition) and ordered the execution of thousands of Iranians, including the massacre of political prisoners. Khomeini's decapitation of the Iranian military and support for the hostage crisis radicalized the revolution, and paved the way for a cultural revolution at home and an eight-year war with Saddam Hussein of Iraq.

Hajj Hussein Agha Malek—Founder of the Malek National Library and Museum, which houses a magnificent collection of rare manuscripts and objects.

Imam—Title used for Muslim religious leaders as well as for Friday prayer leaders. In the Shi'a tradition, the Imams are believed to be divinely appointed, sinless and infallible successors of the Prophet Muhammad from the line of Ali. Most Iranians are "Twelver Shia" and believe that at the end of time, the Twelfth Imam (or "Hidden Imam") will appear and fill the world with justice. In 1979, Ayatollah Khomeini assumed the title Imam. He advanced a theory of government called "Velayat-i Faqih," or rule of the jurisprudent, premised on his right to rule Iran as the infallible guardian and trustee of the Hidden Imam.

Laleh Park—A park in Tehran, the gathering ground of grieving mothers.

Larijani, Ali—Speaker of the Iranian parliament, he denied allegations about the rape and abuse of detainees in the aftermath of the 2009 elections.

Larijani, Sadeq—Brother of Ali Larijani and head of the judiciary appointed by Khamenei.

Loobiya polo—A delicious Persian dish made from rice and beans.

Marmoolak—(Farsi) Rascal, scoundrel; literally, a small lizard. It is also the title of a popular film.

Mashad—A shrine city near the Afghan border.

Mast-o-khiyar—A refreshing summer dish, yogurt with cucumbers, raisins, walnuts, mint, and more.

Mohareb—Enemy of God, a legal and religious term the Islamic Republic uses to label dissidents it wishes to intimidate or eliminate.

Montazeri- Najafabadi, Hussein-Ali (1922-2009)—An early advocate of Ayatollah Khomeini's theory of Islamic government, Montazeri turned against Khomeini after the prison massacres of 1988. He lost his position as Khomeini's successor, and became one of the leading critics of the Islamic Republic, which he declared was "neither Islamic nor a Republic."

Mortazavi , Saeed—Former judge and Prosecutor General of Tehran, known as the "Butcher of the Press." He was also blamed by the Iranian parliament for covering up the murder of Zahra Kazemi. Following the Kahrizak prison scandal, he was removed from office, only to be appointed Iran's drug czar. Mortazavi symbolizes the Iranian judiciary's persecution of the press and opponents of the regime.

Mossadegh, Mohammad (1882-1967)—Democratically elected Prime Minister of Iran from 1951 to 1953, Mossadegh sought to nationalize Iran's oil industry by limiting the economic and political influence of Britain, as exercised through the Anglo-Iranian Oil Company. He was overthrown in 1953 in a coup staged by the CIA.

Mottahari, Morteza (1920-1979)—a prominent religious scholar and cleric, Mottahari was one of the intellectual leaders of Iran's Islamic revolution and a critic of materialist schools of Islam. He was assassinated in 1979.

Mousavi, Mir Hossein—Presidential candidate in 2009, and former prime minister (1982-1988), Mir Hossein Mousavi is the leader of Iran's Green movement. Mousavi claimed to have won Iran's presidential elections in 2009.

Muhammad (pbuh)—The founder of the religion of Islam, also referred to as the messenger, lawgiver. The Prophet Muhammad proclaimed the oneness of God and called upon his followers to join his religion by witnessing that "There was no God but God and that Muhammad was the Prophet of God." Muhammad was an orphan who got his start in life as a merchant. After receiving revelation, he became a teacher and a dissident. He was severely persecuted by his elders in Mecca for denouncing the pagan idolatry of his own tribe, the Quraysh. He was forced to flee Mecca to escape assassination, and migrated to the city of Medina (Yathrib), where he founded his community. The Prophet's teachings represented a major reform in the predatory tribal traditions and customs of Arabia. His story is the basis of the Islamic world's calendar, as well as its concepts of history, knowledge, authority, legitimacy, justice, and love. After his death, different companions, relatives, dynasties, schools, and sects have clashed with one another over the question of succession to the mantle of the Prophet. These doctrinal disputes and disagreements have often led to division and war over the nature of law and location of sovereignty. Khomeini's disciples claim to rule Iran—and thus justify the execution of Iranians—in the name of representing the Prophet and guarding the constitution of the Twelfth Imam, based on the consensus of the clergy and the consent of the people.

Neda Agha Soltan (1983-2009)—Young Iranian woman who was shot to death during the 2009 presidential elections and became a symbol of the Iranian government's crackdown on its people.

Pedarsag—(Farsi) Son of a dog (literally, your father is a dog), an insult used both as a term of endearment and as a rude expression (depending on the occasion).

Persepolis—Capital of the Achaemenid Empire and burial ground of Cyrus the Great. Looted and burned by Alexander the Not So Great and his Macedonian barbarians. In an attempt to destroy Iran's pre-Islamic heritage, Ayatollah Khalkhali demolished Reza Shah's mausoleum and famously wanted to bulldoze Persepolis to wipe out the memory of Cyrus the Great.

Qadissiya—Decisive battle against Arab armies of the Caliph Omar in 637 C.E., Qadissiyah led to the collapse of the Sassanian empire and the subsequent conquest and conversion of Iran.

Rafsanjani, Ali Akbar—Former president (1989–1997) and speaker of the parliament (1982–1989), he is a major figure in the Islamic Republic. As head of the Assembly of Experts, Rafsanjani played a crucial role in crowning Ali Khamenei as Khomeini's successor. During the elections, Ahmadinejad attacked Rafsanjani's family for corruption.

Rahbar—Title of the Supreme Leader, Ali Khamenei

Rahnavard, Zahra—One of the leaders of Iran's reform movement, she was the Chancellor of al-Zahra University and an adviser to President Khatami. She is married to Mir Hossein Mousavi.

Reza Shah (1878-1944)—Founder of the Pahlavi dynasty, Reza Shah toppled the Qajar dynasty (1794–1925). Using the military, he centralized the Iranian state by crushing tribal revolts. Reza Shah modeled Iran's development on Ataturk's secular and Western reforms in Turkey. A ferocious nationalist, he was forced to abdicate in favor of his son, Mohammad Reza Pahlavi, by the British in 1941.

Rostam—Legendary hero from Ferdowsi's tenth-century epic, *The Shahnameh*.

Rumi—A Thirteenth-century poet and mystic for whom devotion and love, separation and union with the beloved, is the source of faith, poetry, dance, and movement. A spiritual giant, his open celebration of his boundless love for Shams of Tabriz scandalized the orthodox beliefs and conventions of his time. The inscription on his tomb reads: "When we are dead seek not our tomb in the earth but in the hearts of men."

Saadi—A thirteenth-century Persian mystic poet, Saadi lived during the Mongol invasion of Iran. His "Boostan" ("Orchard") and "Golestan" ("Rose Garden") are among the greatest treasures of Persian literature and culture. His words on the oneness of humanity grace the entrance of the Hall of Nations in New York and are regularly quoted by dignitaries straining to find a polite way to remind Iran's leaders—the rapacious descendants of Mongol invaders—that it is love and compassion, not cruelty and carnage, that defines Iran's heritage and culture. Good luck!

Shah—King, title of Mohammad Reza Shah Pahlavi, the last king of Iran, deposed in 1979.

Shaheed—martyr.

Shariati, Ali (1933-1977)—French-educated utopian philosopher and sociologist who popularized the concept of revolution in Iran by blending Marxism and Shi'ism. Opposed to Western imperialism, Shariati sanctified violence, martyrdom, and sacrifice as a force for purifying society by purging criminal classes and categories. Ayatollah Khomeini borrowed much of Shariati's anti-imperialist and leftist categories in the revolution against the Shah, often referring to the Iranian people as the Oppressed (mostazaf) while demonizing the United States as the Great Satan.

Shariatmadari, Kazem (1905-1986)—A ranking conservative cleric and a strong defender of constitutional democracy, Ayatollah Shariatmadari represented the traditional Shi'a view of separation of mosque and state. He opposed Ayatollah Khomeini's theory of Islamic government on the grounds that the clergy's direct involvement in government would damage religion by contaminating it with politics.

Sepideh—(Farsi) Sepid means *white*. Sepideh is a popular name for girls. Deev-e Sepid, the White Demon, is one of Rostam's great enemies in the *Shahnameh*.

Sohrab—Son of Rostam. In the *Shahnameh*, Sohrab is a mighty warrior who is killed by his father in combat.

Shiraz—Renowned city of love in Fars province, famous for its gardens, wine, poets, and literature.

Supreme Leader—Title of the political and religious leader of the Islamic Republic of Iran, Ali Khamenei.

Tabriz—The city at the heart of Iran's constitutional revolution, renowned for the courage and faith of its inhabitants.

Takhti, Gholamreza (1930-1968)—One of the most popular wrestlers in Iranian history. As a world champion, "Jahan Pahlavan" Takhti embodied ideals of chivalry and sportsmanship. His name is synonymous in Iran with "javanmardi," the innate quality of a man whose character is reflected in his respect for codes of justice and fair play governing his sport.

Taleqani, Mahmood (1911–1979)—An influential cleric, Taleqani was one of the leaders of the 1979 revolution. He was member of the Freedom Movement of Iran.

Taymoor (Tamerlane)—Fourteenth century conqueror and founder of the Timurid dynasty. A legendary military leader, he sacked Baghdad, Damascus and Delhi and many other cities, leaving behind a trail of destruction that connected much of Asia. A genius at propaganda, he struck fear in the heart of his enemies by exaggerating the cruelty and size of his armies. Also a great patron of the arts.

Ya Hazrat-i Abbas—Revered Shi'a figure whose name is often invoked for protection.

Zizou—Nickname of Zinedine Zidane, legendary French football (soccer) player of Algerian descent.

Zulfiqar—The name of Imam Ali's legendary sword, a bit like King Arthur's Excalibur.

What is in a Name?

Mahdi/Mehdi—The rightly guided one. In Shi'a tradition, the Mahdi is the Twelfth Imam, who has been in Occultation since 872, and will return at the end of time to fill the world with justice. Over the years many have claimed the title of the Mahdi to legitimize their claims to political and religious authority. Ayatollah Khomeini advanced a theory of Islamic government asserting that during the Mahdi's absence, clerics had the obligation to govern as the guardians and trustees of the Mahdi's trust. He also assumed the title of Imam.

Paradise—Derived from an old Iranian word, a garden enclosed by a wall.

Yasmin—Jasmine, name of a flower, popular Persian name, also the name given to the Tunisian revolution.

Zahra—(Arabic) Flower. Also name of a revered figure in Islamic history. Fatima Zahra was the Prophet Muhammad's only child from his first wife, Khadijah. She was married to Muhammad's cousin, Ali, and was the mother of Imam's Ali and Hassan. In the Islamic tradition, she is a symbol of purity, dignity, generosity, and grace. Iran's main cemetery, Zahra's Paradise, is named after her. Presumably, burying the dead in the womb of a cemetery—sacred ground named after the Prophet's daughter—would lead to their rebirth in Paradise. Zahra is also the first name of Zahra (Ziba) Kazemi, the Canadian-Iranian photographer killed while in the custody of the Islamic Republic and buried in Shiraz.

Zahra's Paradise—(Behesht-i Zahra) Massive cemetery on the outskirts of Tehran named after the Prophet's daughter.

Afterwords

About Origins

IN THE MUQADDIMAH, THE INTRODUCTION TO HISTORY, one of the classics of history and Islamic civilization, the great Muslim historian Ibn Khaldun bemoaned the fact that most scholars of history did not have a technique for separating truth from falsehood. Being a historian had become "a stupid occupation" as a result. Concerned about the sanctity of his discipline, Ibn Khaldun went further: "Ordinary people with no firm foundation of knowledge considered it a simple matter to study and know history, to delve in it and sponge on it. Strays got into the flock, bits of shells were mixed with the nuts, truth was adulterated with lies."

To qualify as an historian, he thought, a scholar had to be able to sift through historical time to learn the rules of politics and nature of things, as well "as the differences among nations, places, periods with regard to ways of life, character, qualities, customs, sects, schools and everything else." Ibn Khaldun did not stop there, oh no.

The historian had to be "aware of the differing origins and beginnings of different dynasties and religious groups, as well as of the reasons and incentives that brought them into being and the circumstances and history of the persons who supported them. His goals must be to have complete knowledge of the reasons for every happening and to be acquainted with the origins of every event."

In ZAHRA'S PARADISE, we have approached history through the prism of fiction. Neither of us was in a position to document the facts about Iran's presidential elections. Nor did we want to mislead our readers by presenting ZAHRA'S PARADISE as an objective work of history (or journalism) with any definitive claim to the truth or any pretense of neutrality. We have not set out to establish the facts about the nature and extent of fraud in Iran's presidential elections.

What mattered to us when we started this project, and what matters to us now, is witnessing the plight and reversing the tragedy that has befallen the Iranian people. That tragedy is personal. Its details and dimensions are unfathomable. It is also legal, political, religious, and cultural.

It was hard for us, like millions of other people outside Iran, to watch Iranian mothers and fathers grieve over the loss of their sons and daughters in Zahra's Paradise—the actual cemetery—and not feel singed by their grief or touched by their dignity. That is the origin of this work. It is their gift to us. And ours to them.

We have tried to capture and reflect the Iranian's people's dignity, humanity, love, and grief in the mirror of ZAHRA'S PARADISE. And yes, also the violence, cruelty, and ignorance that causes so many to suffer around their absent children, children who lie beaten, betrayed, buried—but not forgotten—in the bottom of a constitution and tradition established in the name of the Hidden Imam.

As the creators of ZAHRA'S PARADISE, we can't pretend there is no connection between fiction and reality. We have had thousands of collaborators, some living, some dead. They too are the authors of this work. Without them, it would not come to life. It would have no origin and no voice, truth be told, no meaning and no purpose. In the end, ZAHRA'S PARADISE does not matter. Their stories do. If we succeed, it is because fiction can open a window into reality when reality is too painful, distant, silent, or hard to reach. What happens through that window is anyone's guess. It is certain that words and images have the power to expose truths that can break through some very thick walls.

Over the past year, hundreds of thousands of Iranians have turned their cell phones into mirrors for witnessing each other's presence. Instead of remaining or accepting absence, they disrupted lies and exploded pretenses. As journalists, they recorded, documented, and established facts. Those facts have split the image of the Iranian people, and much of the Islamic world, from that of their rulers. No one can claim that human dignity and freedom are the exclusive properties of one culture, or that subjugation by tyranny and terror is the fate of other cultures. The Iranian people have paid the ultimate price to capture the cruel and criminal nature of the Islamic Republic, and they have done so on a canvas stained with the flesh and blood of Neda and countless others.

These facts are not established cheaply. They were and are being purchased at grave risk every day. The stories that are constructed out of them—what is remembered and what is forgotten—matter.

Once Ayatollah Khamenei had ruled in favor of Mahmoud Ahmadinejad, the outcome of the presidential race was settled as far as he was concerned. Facts about fraud did not matter. As the point of reference, his authority was self-evident. The Iranian people had no choice but to accept his ruling as Khomeini's heir and Islamic Iran's caliph. Yet the Iranian people did no such thing. They dared to step out of "God's shadow on earth," in much the same way, that they had dared to defy the Shah, and in much the same way, they had dared to launch the Constitutional Revolution of 1906.

The era of Khomeini and Khamenei was over. Tyranny and terror were losing their grip on Iran. And the scarecrows were shivering and trembling. Yet, it's also true that the scarecrows are still with us. They cast their shadow on the living.

Virtually all Iranians who revealed their face during the protests (whether in the real streets, rooftops, universities, and seminaries or in the virtual realm of the Internet, Twitter, YouTube, and newspapers) were exposing themselves to the wrath of an Ayatollah—yet another abusive holy father—whose idea of law and religion is bludgeoning and raping Iran's sons and daughters in the dark corners of his divine shrine: the Kahrizak detention center, Evin prison, and countless other secret prisons. And from there, having his men dispose of the corpses of detainees in the desert or, if they are lucky, in unmarked graves in Zahra's Paradise.

Still, Ibn Khaldun would caution you about reading ZAHRA'S PARADISE as historical truth. After all, Mehdi, the protester who has vanished in the dungeons of the Islamic Republic, is a fictional character. And the dungeons and guards are just drawings flowing out of the tip of an artist's pen. The old master of history would want you to search deeper. He would want you to ask your own questions and check your own facts. He would want you to go back to the origins of the Islamic Republic, read the foundational documents. He would want you to compare sources and cases to see if there is any truth behind Mehdi, or if ZAHRA'S PARADISE is just fiction with no point of reference in history. He would want you to question everything, not for doubt's sake, but for truth's sake.

With a new generation and movement redefining the future of Iran, Islam, and democracy, and the relations within and between civilizations, it's important to search beyond the story of Mehdi to understand what has happened and what is happening to protesters in Iran and why. As the protests sweeping through the Middle East and North Africa make clear, the stakes could not be higher.

ZAHRA'S PARADISE concludes with the Omid memorial, a list of 16,901 names of individuals killed by the Islamic Republic since 1979. Fortunately, we have not had to do this alone. The Omid memorial is a list compiled over the past decade by the Abdurrahman Boroumand Foundation—history as an act of love if there ever was one.

We have benefitted from the extraordinary work and dedication of human rights organizations, lawyers, scholars, journalists, and activists inside and outside Iran. They know who they are and need no acknowledgment. But if these organizations exist at all, it is ultimately because thousands of Iranians have held onto their loved ones and told their stories, insisted in a thousand ways to keep the dead alive, to keep the absent present, as names, as words, as images, as memories, as joy, and as grief until there is justice. As long as there is time. Until the end of time.

The real Mehdis in Iran—Majid Tavakoli, Nasrin Sotoudeh, Ayatollah Seyyed Hossein Borujerdi, Emadeddin Baghi, Mansour Osanloo and thousands of other dissidents and rebels—are paying the price of time in Evin and other prisons right now. We on the outside can bear witness to the worth of their life, and our own.

In *Long Walk to Freedom*, the world's most famous political prisoner, Nelson Mandela, distilled the lesson of his years as a political prisoner on Robben Island. He wrote, "There is nothing more encouraging in prison as learning that people outside are supporting the cause for which you are inside." ZAHRA'S PARADISE is our way of joining our voice to that of the Iranian families whose chants of Allahu Akbar are breaking through the gates of Evin prison.

Ibn Khaldun, that great North African chronicler of civilization would have to admit that in the age of the internet, life, love and light transcend the old boundaries of time, space, language, race and religion. We—all of us, Muslim, Christian, Jew, Buddhist, and atheist—are of one essence, and if we are to ever become human and our world to become whole, it is with and through each other.

After all, the only place where we can truly come to life is in one another's hearts.

The rest is nonsense. The rest is fiction.

For further reading please see: Ibn Khaldun, 'The Muqaddimah, An Introduction to History', transl. Rosenthal, Franz, Bollingen Series XLIII (Princeton University Press: Princeton, 1967)

Iran's 2009 Presidential Elections

IRAN'S 2009 PRESIDENTIAL ELECTIONS TOOK PLACE ON JUNE 12, 2009. The Council of Guardians approved four candidates for this election: the incumbent, Mahmoud Ahmadinejad, former Prime Minister Mir Hussein Mousavi, former Commander of Revolutionary Guards and Secretary of the Expediency Council, Mohsen Rezai, and former Speaker of Majles (Parliament) Mehdi Karoubi. Early polls showed a close race between Ahmadinejad and Mousavi.

The Candidates

The four candidates were approved from an original pool of 476 men and women. Although Iran's constitution allocates significant power to the Council of Guardians "as the supervisory body for all elections in the Islamic Republic," electoral legislation since 1989 has increased the Council's powers to vet and screen candidates in accordance with ideological guidelines adopted by the Council.

Mahmoud Ahmadinejad: A populist politician, Ahmadinejad was the victor in the 2005 elections and a former mayor of Tehran. His victory in 2005 was challenged by Karoubi, who claimed Ahmadinejad's campaign had resorted to fraudulent tactics.

Mir Hussein Mousavi: A reformist candidate and leader of the Green movement, Mousavi was Prime Minister of Iran from 1981 to 1988. Mousavi has shunned any political involvement since his position was eliminated in 1989.

Mohsen Rezai: A conservative candidate, Rezai was best known for his service on the Supreme Leader's Expediency Council and his role as a former Revolutionary Guard Corps Chief Commander.

Mehdi Karoubi: A reformist candidate, Karoubi previously served as the Speaker of the Majlis, Iran's parliament. Karoubi was the only cleric in this election.

The Official Results: The official results, announced early the morning of June 13, 2009, portrayed a clear and decisive victory for Mahmoud Ahmadinejad:

Ahmadinejad: 63 percent

Mousavi: 34 percent

Mohsen Rezai: less than 2 percent

Mehdi Karoubi: less than 2 percent

The Disputes: Following the announcement of the results, both Ahmadinejad and Mousavi each declared he had won the election. International observers stated concern over "irregularities" in the way the election was run, and the Mousavi camp denounced the results as fraudulent. Ahmadinejad depicted the accusation of ballot manipulation as an attempt by foreign media to undermine the Iranian government.

The Guardian Council, a twelve-member body charged with monitoring the elections, promised a recount of disputed votes on June 16. On June 18, the Supreme Leader, Ayatollah Ali Khameini endorsed Ahmadinejad's election as president. He hailed the historic turnout as a victory for the Islamic Republic and added that despite their differences, all the presidential candidates were loyal supporters of the Islamic system. In the crackdowns that followed, thousands were arrested and beaten, and dozens killed. The focus of the protests shifted from demanding a recount, captured in the slogans "Where is my vote?" and "Ahmadinejad's a liar," to chants of "death to the dictator" and "Khamenei's a murderer, his rule is null and void" (Khamenei Qatil-i, Wilayat-ish Batil-i).

The Council of Guardians declared Ahmadinejad the victor after a partial recount. Mahmoud Ahamdinejad was sworn into office on August 5. Russia and China congratulated Ahmadinejad on his victory.

The Protests: Protests began immediately after the election results were announced and continued for several weeks. The demonstrations spread quickly as thousands took to the streets in Tehran, Qom, and other major Iranian cities. Al Jazeera (English) described the protests as the "biggest unrest since the 1979 revolution." During a rally on June 15, as many as 3 million protesters turned out in support of the opposition.

The Toll: According to a report by the International Campaign for Human Rights in Iran, the opposition placed the number of people killed during the protests at 73. On August 11, the Judiciary announced the arrest of around 4,000 citizens since the elections. And Amnesty International reported that in the 50 days after the elections, Iran executed 115 convicted prisoners, an "alarming spike" intended to strike fear in demonstrators. The International Campaign also reported being informed that "as many as 100 cases of rape have been filed with the Speaker of the Parliament, Ali Larijani, but he has dismissed them as false."

The Slogans: On June 14, at a victory rally covered by the *Guardian*'s Robert Tait, Mahmoud Ahmadinejad dismissed the street protests as dust and dirt (*khas o khashak* in Farsi), compared his opponents to hooligans after a lost soccer match, and accused them of "officially recognizing thieves, homosexuals, and scumbags" in exchange for votes. His insults further inflamed the protests, and led to counterslogans, tweets, and poems.

Neda Agha Soltan: Neda Agha Soltan, a young musician and philosophy student, was shot on June 20, shortly after Khamenei's ordered his militia to crack down on protestors. Her death on the pavements of Tehran was captured on video and went viral after appearing on Brazilian author Paulo Coelho's Web site. It became one the most watched clips around the world. Neda's tragedy led to public chants that "Our Neda is not dead, the government is dead," and "Khamenei's a murderer, his rule is nullified."

For more, see: *For Neda*: HBO documentary.

Kahrizak Prison Scandal: Kahrizak prison, located in southern Tehran, became the final destination for a number of protesters following the election. Those who were later released reported beatings and torture while interned at Kahrizak. The government later officially acknowledged that at least three prisoners were beaten to death while at Kahrizak, including Mohsen Ruholamini, son of a high-ranking conservative figure. The cause of their deaths was initially falsified as "meningitis." Ramin Pourandanjani, the Kahrizak doctor whose testimony exposed the cover-up of abuse, was reported to have "committed suicide" shortly thereafter. The Supreme Leader ordered the prison shut down for being "substandard."

The Mass Trials: The government staged mass "show trials" in which leading opposition figures were forced to make televised confessions retracting their claims that the elections were stolen and admitting to plotting a "Velvet Revolution." It was later revealed that many of these admissions of guilt were obtained by torture and threats to the family or property of those detained. Former Vice President and Karoubi adviser Mohammad Ali Abtahi was among the detainees.

The House Arrests: The opposition leaders Mir Hossein Mousavi and Mehdi Karoubi and their wives were reported to have been placed under house arrest. They were also subjected to constant surveillance, harassment, and intimidation, including attacks on their persons, cars, homes, and family members.

Montazeri Funeral: The death of Grand Ayatollah Montazeri, a dissident cleric who had criticized both Ahmadinejad and the Supreme Leader Ali Khamenei on repeated occasions, and characterized the Islamic Republic as "neither Islamic nor a Republic," fueled further opposition protests. Montazeri had challenged the elections results and called for three days of public mourning for the death of Neda Agha Soltan. After his death on December 21, the government's attempts to ban commemorations led to clashes in Isfahan and other major cities.

Ashura Protests: In December 2009, during the religious holiday of Ashura, commemorating the martyrdom of Imam Hossein, the attacks on protestors left eight people dead prompting opposition leader Karoubi to question the legitimacy of an Islamic Republic that engages in bloodshed on a religious holiday.

Mousavi Nephew: Ali-Habibi Mousavi, the opposition leader's nephew, was shot to death at close range on December 26. Hossein Shariatmadari, the editor of Kayhan, was reported to have accused Mr. Mousavi of staging the assassination of his relative to "drum up sympathy for the opposition." His corpse was reportedly removed from the Tehran hospital to deter mourners from using his funeral as an occasion for more protests.

The Arab Spring: The success of protest movements in Tunisia and Egypt at toppling their dictators energized Iran's opposition movement. On February 15, 2010, after a massive opposition rally called to express the Iranian people's solidarity with the people of Tunisia and Egypt, 70 conservative members of Parliament staged a rally in front of Speaker Larijani, calling for the execution of Mousavi and Karoubi. The slogan coined at these protests was "Mubarak, Ben Ali, it's your turn, Seyyed Ali [Khamenei],", "Freedom, freedom, the cry of all Iranians," "Khamenei should know, he'll be toppled soon" (Khamenei bedooneh, bezoodi sarnegooneh).

Green Charter: On June 15, 2010, the first anniversary of the tenth presidential elections, Mir Hussein Mousavi published a charter for the Green movement. In the Charter, he condemned the beating, torture, and murder of prisoners by corrupt seekers of tyranny disguised as saints. He linked Iran's protest movement to the Iranian people's century-long struggle for constitutional and accountable government based on the rule of law.

Allahu Akbar

What do these two little words actually mean in Arabic and Farsi?

IN WESTERN MEDIA, the commonly used literal translation ("God Is great") is, if anything, rather misleading and confusing. It isn't even a correct literal translation.

Word for word, "God Is Greatest," would be much more accurate than "God Is Great," more encompassing and not an expression of automatic—and often inexplicable—delight in the face of tragedy.

In Hollywood movies that stereotype Arabs/Muslims, Allahu Akbar is shorthand for religious fanaticism, intolerance, and hate. Whenever a bomb explodes or a massacre is perpetrated, some deranged Arab- or Muslim-looking character will invariably shout those two words at the top of his lungs.

And yet, those two little words convey so much more, most of the time: humility, sadness, pride, joy, wonder, among other powerful emotions.

The common thread in all the different meanings of Allahu Akbar, depending on context and occasion, is a transcendence of the ordinary. Whenever emotion becomes too much, one will evoke the infinite wisdom of a higher power, remembering, after all, that "God Is Greatest."

Inconsolable after losing a loved one? Never despair: God knows best, and nothing happens without a sound divine reason. Nothing occurs randomly or senselessly. God is there, put your trust in your Creator.

During the 2009 marches in Iran, in addition to the feelings of strength in unity and solidarity, Allahu Akbar also came to convey special irony and sarcasm. Repeated chants of "God is the greatest," theoretically music to the ears of a theocratic regime, came to be understood as a reproach and a taunt by an ostensibly godly, yet illegitimate, regime.

Allahu Akbar!

From Zahra to Yasmin:
Iran and the Arab Spring

THE CHANTS OF "ALLAHU AKBAR," cell phones in the air, victory signs, cool shades and sassy sunglasses, green wristbands—even some of the same exuberant hairstyles that no headscarves could ever hope to attenuate: who could possibly miss the Iranian connection when watching Tunisia's Jasmine Revolution on their TV screens in January 2011?

Had young protestors in the streets of Tunis—and then Cairo—spontaneously, subliminally, adopted Iran's revolutionary chic, broadcast worldwide through cell phone videos, blogs, and tweets—or had they simply reinvented it for themselves, demanding their democratic and human rights as well, often at the peril of their lives, just as their Iranian brothers and sisters had done a year and a half before?

Like a daisy chain, the Zahra-Jasmine contagion has spread as far as China and Madison, Wisconsin.

And it will inevitably return to the perfumed gardens of Iran, where Paradise once was invented.

Of Cranes and the Death Penalty

PEOPLE HAVE BEEN HANGING EACH OTHER FOR CENTURIES. I think of the civil rights movement in the United States, and it is hard not to think of African-Americans being lynched on trees.

A lot goes into a hanging. There's gravity, the ultimate executioner. There's usually a knot of some kind, so a state of suspension. And then there's the neck, the strangling and gagging and all. The executioner fastens a noose around someone's neck, and then kicks the chair or trap door out from under them. Their weight does the rest. All that's required is a fall—enough of a gap between the ground and the person's feet. Relative to other ways of killing people, say the guillotine, hangings are not terribly bloody or messy. Not much scrubbing and washing. And they are fairly expeditious and cheap. Finally, they are pretty hands off.

But whoever has heard of executions by cranes?

That's one of these odd anomalies about the beloved judges guarding our Islamic Republic. As far as I know, there is nothing Islamic about crane killings. It's not in the Shari'a. There are simply no legal schools, religious or otherwise, that endorse crane killing. Iran's supreme leader and other phony legal and religious luminaries running Iran's judiciary would have a tough time sugarcoating their appetite for crane killings by citing traditions of the Prophet and his companions. Like most other things about the Islamic Republic, hanging people off cranes is a modern legal and religious innovation—mechanized murder.

Of course, defenders of hanging by crane would point out that the Islamic Republic deserves credit for being practical. They can attach their cranes to a truck, and so there is plenty of mobility. You can basically perform an execution in any neighborhood. With or without trees. And you can hang the bodies as high as you want, making it much harder for crowds to cut the noose. There's also the entertainment value—a tall crane guarantees a wider audience. And all you've got to do is push a button. And the chances of botching an execution aren't as high as relying on a feeble branch. So, why not rent a fleet of cranes to criss-cross Iran as a kind of travelling judicial circus— hanging judges, mobile executioners, a heavenly noose for purging every earthly sin?

But how did God's word turn into a rope wrapped around the Iranian people's neck? And how did God's hand turn into a crane lifting Iran's children up into the heavens? Do Iran's holy books come with a Sura of the Crane? How did the crane supplant the scales as the symbol of God's justice?

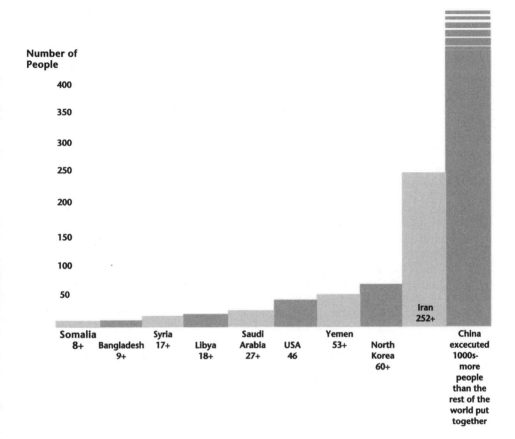

COUNTRIES WITH THE HIGHEST NUMBER OF EXECUTIONS IN 2010

+ Indicates that the figure Amnesty International has calculated is a minimum.

Number of People

400

350

300

250

200

150

100

50

Somalia
8+

Bangladesh
9+

Syria
17+

Libya
18+

Saudi
Arabia
27+

USA
46

Yemen
53+

North
Korea
60+

Iran
252+

China
excecuted
1000s-
more
people
than the
rest of the
world put
together

Source: Amnesty International

Seeing Neda
Of Paulo Coelho and Arash Hejazi

IN ZAHRA'S PARADISE WE TOUCH BRIEFLY ON THE STORY of Neda Agha Soltan. But an account of how Neda's reflection, the last fluttering of her light and life, touched so many hearts, has its own alchemy. And that mystery—seeing Neda—had much to do with Brazil.

The Brazilian Connection: The Alchemy of Neda

Paulo Coelho is a force of nature. The bestselling author of *The Alchemist* is Latin America's answer to the great Persian mystics Hafez, Rumi, Saadi, and Khayyam. Coelho's work, and life, resonates with spiritual connections, coincidences, and convergences. In the aftermath of the protests that shook Iran, Coelho was drawn into a story that even he could not have conjured.

Coelho's editor and publisher in Iran, Dr. Arash Hejazi, was shown in video footage kneeling over Neda, trying to save her life. The Neda video went viral after it appeared on Coelho's Web site. Although Ayatollah Khamenei had ordered the Basij to crack down on protestors, Neda's death was blamed on foreign powers. Dr. Hejazi was accused of conspiring in an international plot to murder Neda. Hejazi managed to escape to Britain, where he wrote his memoir, *The Gaze of the Gazelle*.

Coelho's books were banned in Iran, and his publishing house, Caravan, was shut down. Coelho and the Brazilian government objected to the ban. The Iranian embassy in Brazil denied the charge of censorship. Later, Coelho wrote the foreword to *The Gaze of the Gazelle*. He also published his exchanges with Hejazi in his blog. Their friendship—the fusion of history, literature, technology, commerce, and spirituality—is a reminder of the force that binds Iran to the rest of the world. The East in the West, the West in the East.

Coelho on Iran
(Little did he know. . .)

> Finally I was in Iran, and while I had been looking forward to visiting Iran for some time, I had no idea what to expect. I didn't know what the implications of my visit were going to be, or if Christina and I were in any kind of danger. However, I had made the decision to venture this visit; I already knew that I had thousands of readers there waiting for me and I was ecstatic at the thought of seeing the land of Rumi, Saadi, Hafiz and Omar Khayyam.
>
> —Coelho, Foreword to *The Gaze of the Gazelle*

Coelho on Neda, in The Gaze of the Gazelle

On 20 June 2009, a brief video clip was circulated all over the world. It showed the death of a young, unarmed woman called Neda, who had been shot in the chest while taking part in a protest in Tehran and was bleeding to death on the street. Few images in the contemporary world have had such an instant and powerful impact. This footage was so intense it raised the awareness of the world on what was happening in Iran and forced world leaders to condemn the way the Iranian government was treating its citizens.

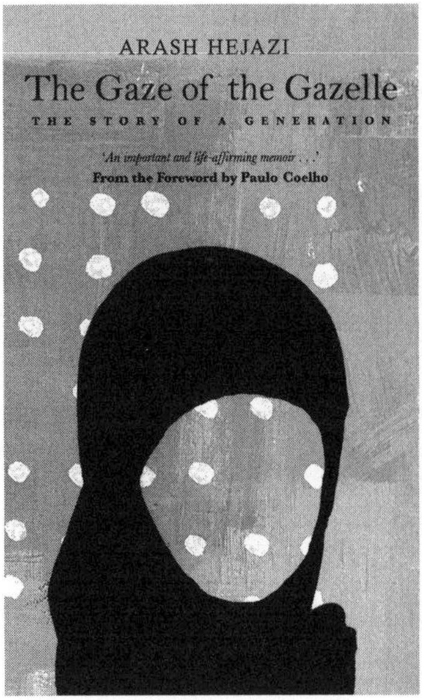
ARASH HEJAZI
The Gaze of the Gazelle
THE STORY OF A GENERATION
'An important and life-affirming memoir . . .'
From the Foreword by Paulo Coelho

For me, however, it was more personal. There was a young man in the video trying to save Neda. He was my friend, Arash.

When I met him for the very first time, I could never have imagined that this slim young man would get caught in the crossroad of history ten years later. Even if I had the power to look into the future and see that this passionate doctor-publisher-author was destined to be present in one of the most important documents of contemporary history, I couldn't have imagined the way he would react to it. I couldn't have imagined that he would have the courage to testify against an unspeakable crime, and be prepared to forsake everything to expose the truth.

Coelho, on Arash, in his memoir

We were in Madrid, in December 2000, when he, with tears in his eyes, told me the legend of Arash the Archer and how he hoped to live up to his name. Arash the Archer was an Iranian mythical hero who, in order to end the war between Iran and its invaders, put his life into his single arrow so that it could fly far enough to land on the original border between the two countries and restore peace. . .

Did Arash live up to his name? I don't know. But he certainly did put his life in his single arrow, the arrow that has unified the aspirations of the Iranians under that image of Neda.

But Arash's story is not summed up in that moment: he has a story of a generation to tell. It came as no surprise when he produced an important and life-affirming memoir. In *The Gaze of the Gazelle,* Arash reveals the true spirit of Iran. He looks unflinchingly into the mirror and reflects on the recent past of his family and of Iran itself. More than many an historical textbook, this memoir illuminates the sense of nationhood and pride that keeps a society together despite the hardships that are thrown at it. A nation that can be stopped by nothing in its pursuit of happiness, and across thousands of years, has learned that there is no tomorrow, there is no yesterday, there's only what you choose to do today, now, this moment.

Arash on why he had to write his memoirs

OK, I was bleeding. I was wounded. The bullet that pierced Neda's chest took her life away, but ripped my life apart. She stared into my eyes and died. She couldn't say anything. But it was as if she was telling me: "Do something!" and I couldn't do anything. . .

. . . I couldn't heal. The memory of those eyes did not leave me. They haunted me, asking me to "do something." I spoke up about her, thinking that she will leave me. I talked to BBC, *The Times* and other media, when I realized that the Iranian government was trying to conceal her death and then blame it on foreign service. But she still didn't leave me. I had to do something else, or else I would have bled to death myself. So I wrote, and when I wrote, I felt better, and the eyes became kinder, and the bleeding stopped whenever I resumed writing. She wanted me to tell her story, the story of the generation, she wanted me to tell how it came to that moment. . . I wrote, because I was in pain, and telling the story eased the pain.

—Arash Hejazi, "Author's Interview with His Shadow"

To learn more about Arash, visit his blog: arashhejazi.com/en/blog/

The Kahrizak Detention Center

About Roya and the Abdorrahman Boroumand Foundation

I DON'T KNOW HOW ROYA DOES IT. For years, Roya, her sister Ladan, and a small band of human rights activists have been telling the story of the Islamic Republic's human rights abuses. Day after day. Victim after victim. Story after story. For years. The count is in the thousands.

Roya deals with hard facts. She does not invent or imagine reality. She documents real stories—the stories of thousands of Zahras and Mehdis. There's very little room for error. The trauma is deep, the wounds severe, the trust fragile. By the time someone comes to the Abdorrahman Boroumand Foundation, they are usually dead, and mostly forgotten. Sometimes, all that is left of them is an initial. Still, they exist. There's a life and story behind the initial. And so Roya has to verify the truth. Did they really exist? What happened to them? Where? When? Why? Sentenced according to which law? By which judge?

For the Islamic Republic's victims, there can be no space. The idea is for them to be locked in their bodies, locked in fear, in silence, in guilt and in time. That is where Roya steps in, a bit like our fictional blogger in Ali's room. And for some reason, the stories gush out.

Take a look inside Roya's world—the mirror of the human rights activist. And you will catch a glimpse of the courage, dignity and resilience of the Iranian people. I have a hunch. It's love that keeps Roya going. And it's love that holds Iranians together. Who can kill love?

To learn more about the Boroumand Foundation's work, please visit

http://www.iranrights.org

From Roya Boroumand:

Kahrizak, depicted as fiction in ZAHRA'S PARADISE, is not the product of the authors' imagination. Initially meant to store goods, Kahrizak was conceived as hell on earth, a place to punish those the Iranian regime categorizes as "hooligans." Protesters who were sent to Kahrizak on a hot day in July 2009 were left completely naked in the courtyard for half an hour and then beaten with batons and hoses. But before this humiliating and painful welcoming ceremony, they were greeted by a prison official. "Kahrizak," he explained to them, "means the end of the world. Here, bestiality [bestial traits] will soon become second nature for you. No one leaves this place alive."

The magnitude of the violence that detainees were subjected to at Kahrizak matches the stupidity of those who believe that extreme physical pain and mental anguish can eradicate ideas they fear or break the will of people who defy them. Individuals who are subjected to such absurd levels of cruelty and injustice may, at times, experience discouragement or struggle with life-long physical and psychological effects of torture. In my experience however, many also become more resilient and determined.

I am the co-founder of the Abdorrahman Boroumand Foundation, a Washington-based organization founded in April 2001 with the aim of promoting human rights and democracy in Iran. Our main project, Omid, is an online memorial and library through which we document all the executions carried out by Iranian authorities, remember victims, protest against the death penalty and torture, and draw attention to the violation of due process of law in Iran. Over the past ten years, we have interviewed or collected testimonies of hundreds of individuals who have lost family members or were in prison and tortured, including some of the refugees who left Iran in the aftermath of the 2009 presidential election.

I met a detainee from Kahrizak last winter in Europe. The ordeal he described continues to haunt me today. Yet, this young man, whom we call Sa'id, had dignity, kindness, and resolve. He decided to tell his story in memory of those cellmates who did not survive their detention. "There were so many of us," he said of the windowless container-type cell he was kept in. "We couldn't sit down. . . Half of us sat and half of us stood. We were not allowed to go to the toilet. Each of us passed out numerous times. It was very hot."

They were kept semi-naked in unsanitary conditions, denied food and water in the extreme heat of Tehran's summer, and constantly humiliated and beaten. They witnessed the suffering of others and the death of one man who was arrested with his son before them. But this was not enough punishment for individuals who had defied the wishes of the Supreme Leader:

"The third or fourth day [July 13th or 14th], around 12 p.m., they took us to the courtyard. They made half of us crawl on our hands and knees around the courtyard while carrying the other prisoners on our backs. We had to carry them in a circle around the courtyard. The ground was so hot, we were burning. After five minutes, I only saw blood on the ground from other people's knees and hands. I carried an old man on my back. We circled the courtyard maybe twenty or twenty five times. If we stopped, they beat us."

The absurd violence and dehumanization aimed at changing or neutralizing individuals whose existence bothers the state is not new in Iran (or elsewhere). The number of people who were subjected to

To read Sa'id's full testimony about Kahrizak, please see "Iran July 2009: A Witness to State Crimes in Kahrizak Detention Center" by visiting www.iranrights.org

this kind of treatment at Kahrizak, or died in detention during the years it operated, remains unknown. Sa'id and his cellmates were lucky as one of the detainees, Mohsen, was the son of an influential member of the Islamic Republic's ruling elite. Their stay in Kahrizak did not last. They were taken to Evin Prison and eventually released. Mohsen and two others died, Kahrizak became a national scandal, and the Spiritual Leader ordered its closure.

So, Kahrizak was closed and we all feel better. But we shouldn't. This development doesn't change the fact that many of us here, and in Iran, had heard about the horrifying and deadly conditions of Kahrizak long before the summer of 2009. Very few of us however, made a serious effort to campaign for its closure. Why? Perhaps because human rights organizations are often under-staffed, under-resourced, and overwhelmed with so many ongoing human rights violations. Perhaps because the victims, those the Iranian authorities call "hooligans," seemed less relevant to our work. Regardless, as long as Iran is plagued with a culture of impunity, there will be other Kahrizak-type prisons. Let us hope that Sa'id's ordeal, and his courage to defy his captors by giving us an account of his detention, will serve as a lesson so that when we hear about the intolerable again, we do what we can to stop it.

On Secret Prisons, excerpts of a letter from Iran's President Ahmadinejad to U.S. President Bush

Mr. President

(. . .) There are prisoners in Guantanamo Bay that have not been tried, have no legal representation, their families cannot see them and are obviously kept in a strange land outside their own country. There is no international monitoring of their conditions and fate. No one knows whether they are prisoners, POWs, accused or criminals.

European investigators have confirmed the existence of secret prisons in Europe too. I could not correlate the abduction of a person, and him or her being kept in secret prisons, with the provisions of any judicial system. For that matter, I fail to understand how such actions correspond to the values outlined in the beginning of this letter, i.e. the teachings of Jesus Christ (Peace Be Upon Him), human rights and liberal values."

(. . .) History tells us that repressive and cruel governments do not survive. God has entrusted the fate of men to them. The Almighty has not left the universe and humanity to their own devices. Many things have happened contrary to the wishes and plans of governments. These tell us that there is a higher power at work and all events are determined by Him.

Source: *Washington Post*, May 9, 2006

In Memoriam

THE OMID MEMORIAL IS A PROJECT of the Abdorrahman Boroumand Foundation for the Promotion of Human Rights and Democracy in Iran (ABF). It lists the names of 16,901 individuals executed, shot in demonstrations, or assassinated since the establishment of the Islamic Republic of Iran. The majority of the names are those of individuals killed between 1979 and 1989. Some names belong to individuals executed in the 1990s, and the years 2005–2009. All that remains of some is the fragment of a first or last name, or even initials, as remembered or reported by fellow prisoners, officials, and other sources. These names are those of people deliberately killed by the Islamic Republic. It is only a glimpse at the tragedy of war, displacement, exodus, and depression that has claimed the lives of hundreds of thousands of Iranians, and shattered the homes, hopes, and dreams of millions.

The names listed in following pages are drawn from several sources:

1. Testimony and interviews with family and friends of victims

2. Documents published by political organizations, the United Nations, and international human rights groups

3. Reports by the Islamic Republic as well as semi-official media in Iran

4. Memoirs and other statements by officials of the Islamic Republic

5. ABF's daily surveys of more than fifty newspapers, Web sites, and blogs.

ABF verifies the names drawn from various sources to the best of its ability and compares them to avoid duplication. This verification is not always easy, as official reports may contain mistakes, people with similar names may be killed in different locations at different times, and members of the same family may have been killed but those reporting their death may not have known their first or last names. Reports are not always systematic and complete, and the Iranian authorities do not allow independent investigations and monitoring of cases where the death penalty is enforced. Until and unless an official body is mandated to investigate executions with free access to official documents and witnesses, the list will remain a work in progress; a first step in finding out the truth about the number of executions in Iran and the identity of the victims.

For more information, please visit **www.iranrights.org/english/memorial.php**

Omid

THE MEN AND WOMEN NAMED ON THESE NEXT PAGES
are now all citizens of a silent city named Omid
("hope" in Persian). There, victims of persecution
have found a common life whose substance is
memory.

Omid's citizens were of varying social origins,
nationalities, and religions; they held diverse,
and often opposing, opinions and ideologies.
Despite the differences in their personality, spirit
and moral fiber, they are all united in Omid by
their natural rights and their humanity. What
makes them fellow citizens is the fact that one
day each of them was unfairly and arbitrarily
deprived of his or her life. At that moment, while
the world watched the unspeakable happen, an
individual destiny was shattered, a family was
destroyed, and an indescribable suffering was
inflicted.

If you wander around this city, you will
realize that, through their common ordeal, the
citizens of Omid have created another Iran, an
imaginary Iran: a democratic polity, pluralistic
and diverse, where citizens posthumously enjoy
their human rights.

Visit Omid, meet its citizens, and, by doing so,
bring them back in memory. Let them challenge
our conscience so that in the future we will pre-
vent this kind of tragedy from happening again.

('Abbasi) Mojtaba * (Bagheri) Hossein * (brother of Amu Oghlu) Ahmad * (Esfandiari) Aliakbar * (Gorzedin) Farhad * (Nayebi) Ardalan * (Rajabi) * (Ramezani) Jamshid (Ramezan) * (Samadi) Kiarash * (Samim) Roshan * (Tarjomeh) Hosei
* ? Hasan * ? Iran * _Amir Kiya' Baqa Shidrukh * A Sohrab Mohammad * A A. * A B. * A H. * A Vahid *A. Abdollah * A. Ali * A. Mahmud * A. Mohammad * A. Mohammad Sa'id * A. Sohrabmohammad * A. Mehdi * A. Ali * A. M. * A. Mehr
* A. Eydi * A. Ebrahim * A. Saeid * A. Abbas * A. Morteza * A. N. * A. AliReza * A. GholamReza * A. Gholamhazrat * A. Shahmir * A. H. * A. Javad * A. Mahmud * A. Mohsen * A. Firuz * A. Hamid * A. V. * A. Abdollah * A. Allahgholi * A. *
* A. Ahmad * A. Mohammad * A. Hamid * A. Kian * A. Hossein * A. Abdolmajid * A. A. * A. Mohammad Saeid * A. Majid * A. Aziz * A. Hushang * A. Naser * A. Omid * A. Reza * A. Mohammad * A. GholamReza * A. Hamid * A. Hadi * A
Mehdi * A. Ghodrat * A. Mohammad * A. Reza * A. Ramezan'ali * A. Kh. * A. A. * A. Nader * A. Pejman * A. Hassan * A. Asghar * A. Nosratollah * A. M. * A. A. * A. M. * A. M. * A. M. * A. Hassan * A. A. * A. Esmail * A. Ahmad * A. J. * A. Mohammad
* A. Hamid * A. Reza * A. Omid * A. A. * A. Abdi * A. Z. * A. Karim * A. Bahador * A. Mohammad Sadeq * A. Rahim * A. Omid * A. Abdollah * A. Torab * A. A. * A. Sa'id * A. Reza * A. A. * A. Shahram * A. A. * A. M. * A. Mohammad * A
Dariush * A. Asqar * A. Hossein * A. Gh. * A. A. * A. Manuchehr * A. A. * A. Masud * A. J. * A. Nurbakhsh * A. Khodabakhsh * A. A. * A. Abdolkhalegh * A. (Biglari) Mohammad * A. (Ebrahimi) Faraz * A. (R.) Mojtaba * Aali Hossein * Aalipu
N'emat * Ab Hamid * Abad Musa * Abad Khiz (Abad Kheir) Ardeshir * Abadegan (Amadegan) Sadeq * Abadi Soleiman * Abadian Ali * Abadian Fatemeh * Abadian Taregh * Abadian Amira'ali * Abadian Amira'ali * Abadi Karam * Abaqun
Mas'ud * Abar Ramezan Ali * Abareqi * Abarqu'i Khalil * Abashian Baqer * Abayi Zahra * Abbas Zadeh Safieh * Abbas Zadeh Dehqani Ruhanguiz * Abbasalipoor * Abbashi Abdol-Reza * Abbasi * Abbasi * Abbasi Abbas * Abbasi Ahmad * Abbasi abdolreza
far * Abbasi Ebrahim * Abbasian Behrouz * Abbasian Bijan * Abbasian Hasan * Abbasian Baratollah * Abbasian Mohammad * Abbaspur Hossein * Abbaspur Seyed Ali * Abbaspur Hossein * Abbaspur Atashgah Yadollah * Abbasi Zade
Bahih * Abbass Zadeh Majid * Abbass Zadeh Seromi Majid * Abbassi Abdolmajid * Abbassi Alireza * Abbassi Gholamreza * Abbassi Hossein (Bahman) * Abbassi M.Javad * Abbassi M.Reza * Abbassi Magh
soud * Abbassi Mahmoud * Abbassi Mehrdad * Abbassi Sirous * Abbassi Shiraz Mansour * Abbassian Hosseini Maryam * Abbas-Zadeh Bahram * Abdali Tahmaseb * Abdanabi Akhtarjan * Abdani Behzad * Abdeli Haj Reza * Abdi * Abdi Aza
* Abdi Bakhtiar * Abdi Esfandiar * Abdi Hosein * Abdi Mohammad Esma'il * Abdi Qanbar * Abdi Shahla * Abdi Jamshid * Abdi Vahid * Abdi Gholam'ali * Abdi Hossein * Abdi Amir * Abdi Pirbazari Foruzan * Abdinejad Mohammad * Abdiza
deh Reza * Abdobakry Mohammad * Abdol Rahim Kashi Mariam * Abdolahzadeh Mohsen * Abdolali * Abdolali Pour Fatemeh * Abdolaziz Khalil * Abdolghani Mohammad * Abdolhossein * Abdolhosseini Gholamhossein * Abdol-Hosse
ini Akbar * Abdol-Hosseini Morteza * Abdolhossein (Ruzbehani) Mohsen * Abdoli Abdolhamid * Abdoli Abdolhamid (Sirus) * Abdoli Fatemeh * Abdoli Fattah * Abdoli Hassan * Abdoli Kazem * Abdoli Mina * Abdoli Kazem * Abdoli Ka
mali Majid * Abdolizadeh Ruhollah * Abdollah Mohammadi Sufi * Abdollah Zadeh Abdollah * Abdollahi Abolfazl * Abdollahi Abolhassan * Abdollahi Behzad * Abdollahi Fatemeh * Abdollahi Hossein * Abdollahi Javad * Abdollahi Khorshi
* Abdollahi Mirfattah * Abdollahi Mohammad * Abdollahi Moharram Ali * Abdollahi Molud * Abdollahi Nazir * Abdollahi Rahman * Abdollahi Shahnaz * Abdollahi Aliahmad * Abdollahi Nazir * Abdollahi Hossein
Abdollahi Karam * Abdollahi Qasem * Abdollahi Davud * Abdollahmohammadi Soofi * Abdollahzadeh Seif Ali * Abdollahzadeh Nader * Abdolmarzuqi * Abdolvahab Hossein * Abed Esmail * Abed Ebrahimi Ahmad * Abedi * Abedi Al
Reza * Abedi Bahram * Abedi Ebrahim * Abedi Hasan * Abedi Kazem * Abedi Mostafa * Abedi Seyyed Abbas * Abedi Seyyed Kazem * Abedi Alireza * Abedi Rahman * Abedi Mohammad * Abedi Zadeh Se-Sari Khalil * Abedian Fatemeh
Abedini Abbas * Abedini Esmaiel * Abedini Hosein * Abedini Mariam * Abedini Monireh * Abedini Parvin * Abedni Qasem * Abedini Abkenari Mostafa * Abedini Marghzari Qasem * Abedisir Gholam Reza * Abedpur Hossein * Aberi Behza
* Aberumand Azar Fereidun * Abestan Ali * Abhesht Yadollah * Abkari Behzad * Abkhun Yusef * Abnar ghanbar'ali * Abnus Hamid * Aboarda Davud * Aboarda Hasan * Abolahrar Shirazi Leyla * Abolbaei Behrooz * Abolfathi Soraya
Abolhassani Fatemeh * Abolhassani Khalil * Abolhassani Majid * Abolhassian Hassan * Abolqasem Hasan * Abolqasem Ahmad * Abolqasemi Esmail * Abolqasemi Gholamhossein * Abolvardi Asghar * Abootora
Asghar * Abootorab Saeid * Abrahami Jasem * Abrandi * Abrari Esma'il * Abrari Mehran * Abresani Hushang * Abrisham Baf Asghar (Fathollah) * Abrishamchi Mehdi * Abroshan Haj Sharif * Abrumand Kheshtmajid Hassan * Abrush Qarna
Haji Sharif * Absari Doustali * Abtahi Naser * Abu Ali Qasem * Abu 'Ali Shamshiri Fereydun * Abu Talebi Zonuz Behruz * Abu Talebi Zonuz Firuz * Abu Talebian Majid * Abu-Massih Riyad * Abusa'idi Mas'ud * Abuyi Radkashki Fereshteh
Abuyi Radkashti Mehdi * Abyaneh Afghani Asghar * Abyari Abbas * Abyat Bani * Abyat Karim * Abzam Mohammad * Achazgehi Abdolhabib * Achek Zehi Gol Mohammad * Achkarhi Ne'matollah * Adab - Avaz Hosein
Adab-Avaz Esmat * Adab-Avaz Fatemeh * Adab-Avaz Hossein * Adam Raufi Mohammad * Adam Ra'ufi Abdolaziz * Adeli Abolqasem * Adeli Jamshid * Adeli Reza * Adelshahri Saeid * Adelshahri Sani Hashem * Adelzadeh Ali * Ade
zadeh Ali * Adhami Abolfazl * Adhami Mohammad * Adib Amir * Adib Kamal * Adib Tofiq * Adibi Ahmad * Adibi Mahmud * Adibi Sirus (Gholam Reza) * Adibpur Manuchehr * Adigzal Ebrahim * Adineh Pur Qorban * Adi-Shirinpur Ali
Adlu Leila * Adnan Khalaf 'Adel * Adrian Ahmad * A'ein Parast Mir Majid * Aeineh Youssef * Afandi Hossein * Afaq Mehrangiz * Afghani Aliakbar * Afghan Behruz * Afghan Rasul * Afghan Behruz * Afghani Sattar * Afghani
Ruhollah * Afghani * Afghani Hassan * Afjeh hezari Mohammad Kazem * Afkhami Abbas * Afkhami Mansureh * Aflatuni Hashem * Afnan Bahram * Afra'i Abolqasem * Afrajudi Raheleh * Afrashteh Mohsen * Afrashteh Ya'qub * Afrasiab
Asad * Afrasiabi Bizhan * Afrasiabi Fatemeh * Afrasiabi Fatemeh * Afrasiabi Habib * Afravi Naji * Afravi Ali * Afrazeh Abbas * Afrazeh Ahmad * Afrazi Shah Mohammad * Afri Nejad Zahra * Afrousheh Abbas * Afruzeh Seyyed Ahmad
Afsahi Behzad * Afsaneh Mohammad 'Ali * Afsar Majid * Afsar Zadeh A'tefeh * Afsar Zadeh Esfehani A'tefeh * Afsardehi Mojtaba * Afsardir Mojtaba * Afsar Abdollah * Afsari Abdollah * Afsari Ali * Afsari Hamid * Afsari Mohammad * Afsari
* Afshar * Afshar * Afshar Ahmad * Afshar Akbar * Afshar Farokh * Afshar Fatemeh * Afshar Fazollah * Afshar Jahanbakhsh * Afshar Ma'sumeh * Afshar Mahmud * Afshar Mariam * Afshar Nadereh * Afshar Nahid * Afshar Pari * Afsha
Parviz * Afshar Qodrat * Afshar Reza * Afshar Shahpur * Afshar Tayefeh * Afshar Bakshlu Mohsen * Afshar Shandi Rasul * Afshari Abdonnabi * Afshari Ali * Afshari Ezat * Afshari Mahin * Afshari Manoochehr * Afshari Mitra * Afshari Abbas
Afshari Nasab Farrokh * Afshari Nasab Mahmud * Afshari Niku Hassan * Afsharlu Ahmad * Afsharlu Behnaz * Afsharzadeh Abdollah * Afshin Iradj * Afshin Sa'id * Afshin Ghobad * Afshoon Alireza * Afshoon Zinolabedin * Aftut Bijan * Afvia
Sharifeh * Afzali Bahram * Afzali Esma'il * Afzali M.Reza * Afzali Mohammad Reza * Afzallipoor Ali * Afzalnia Afsaneh * Afzal-Nia Azizeh * Afzaly Mansour * Agah Ali * Agahi Abdolhossein * Agahi Abdolhossein * Agahi Abdolhossein * Agahi Hossein Reza * Agha
beighi Ali * Aghabeighi Dianat * Aghabeigi Ali * Aghabeigi Dianat * Aghabozorgi Hossein * Aghabozorgi Majid * Aghaei Hamid * Aghaei Majid * Aghai Ahad * Aghai' Samir * Aghajani Gholamhossein * Aghajari Abbas * Aghajari Mohammad
* Aghakhani Saied * Aghanejad Yuness * Aghapoor Rahim * Aghapour Jafar * Aghasizadeh Mohsen * Aghbashlu Akbar * Aghdaghi Mojtaba * Aghdashi Mahmud * Aghedu Safar'ali * Agheli Rahim * Aghili Hamid * Aghlorian Farhad
Aghsami Ghasem * Ahadi * Ahadi Jalal * Ahadi Seyyed Hasan * Ahanchi * Ahang Sa'id * Ahangar Behruz * Ahangar Javad * Ahangar Ghorbani Alireza * Ahangaran Roqiyeh * Ahangari Alireza * Ahangari (Ahangaran) Davud * Ahangaria
Behruz * Ahangarian Behrus * Ahani Khanjan * Ahashti (Ahu Dashti) Fazlollah * Ahi Ali * Ahi Gholamreza * Ahiyari Ozra * Ahkami Jamshid * Ahmad Ali * Ahmad Faz'l * Ahmad Naser * Ahmad Doost Zahra * Ahmad Dust Ali * Ahmad Du
Zahra * Ahmad Goltapeh Jahangir * Ahmad Goltapeh Jahangir (Jahan) * Ahmad Karami Haj Qolam * Ahmad Khani Hasan * Ahmad Khatiri Nader * Ahmad Pour Mohammad * Ahmad Pur Abbas * Ahmad Pur Mohammad Ali * Ahmad Pu
Shahin * Ahmad Raji Hasan * Ahmad Rasti Ekhlasi Ahmad * Ahmad Simab Hasan * Ahmad Zadeh Ali * Ahmad Zadeh Keramat * Ahmad Zadeh Mahmud * Ahmad Zadeh Siavosh * Ahma
Zadeh (Mojaver Mahalehi) Seyed Taqi * Ahmadi-Nawara Ali * Ahmadi * Ahmadi * Ahmadi Abdollah * Ahmadi Abolfazael * Ahmadi Abubakr * Ahmadi Ahmad * Ahmadi Ahmad * Ahmadi Ali * Ahmadi Ali
Ali * Ahmadi Ali Asghar * Ahmadi Ali Qoli * Ahmadi Aliyar * Ahmadi Aref * Ahmadi Ayub * Ahmadi Azar * Ahmadi Batul * Ahmadi Changiz * Ahmadi Ebrahim * Ahmadi Esma'il * Ahmadi Esmaiel * Ahmadi Esmail
Ahmadi Esmat * Ahmadi Farahnaz * Ahmadi Fariba * Ahmadi Farid * Ahmadi Firuz * Ahmadi Gholamreza * Ahmadi Habib * Ahmadi Hasan * Ahmadi Homeyra * Ahmadi Hosein * Ahmadi Hosein * Ahmadi
Hossein * Ahmadi Houshang * Ahmadi Hushang * Ahmadi Jabar * Ahmadi Jan Ali * Ahmadi Karim * Ahmadi Khosro * Ahmadi M.Reza * Ahmadi Mansour * Ahmadi Manuchehr * Ahmadi Mariam * Ahmadi Mas'ud * Ahmadi Mehdi * Ahmadi
Mohammad * Ahmadi Mohammad Ali * Ahmadi Mohammad Hadi * Ahmadi Moharram Ali * Ahmadi Monireh * Ahmadi Morad Ali * Ahmadi Morteza * Ahmadi Mozaffar * Ahmadi Nader * Ahmadi Nasser * Ahmadi Noruz Ali * Ahmadi
Omar * Ahmadi Qodrat * Ahmadi Qodratollah * Ahmadi Ra'uf * Ahmadi Sattar * Ahmadi Setareh * Ahmadi Seyyed Ebrahim * Ahmadi Seyyed Hasan * Ahmadi Shamseddin * Ahmadi Shiraza * Ahmadi Shokrollah * Ahmadi Gholam'ali
Ahmadi Ali * Ahmadi Hossein * Ahmadi Darvish'ali Khan * Ahmadi Esmail * Ahmadi Hasan * Ahmadi Abdollah * Ahmadi Alipasha * Ahmadi Haj * Ahmadi Rahi * Ahmadi Kazem * Ahmadi Nejat
Ahmadi Naser * Ahmadi Mohammadmehdi * Ahmadi (Mansuri) Kiumars * Ahmadi (Qayem Nezhad) Setareh * Ahmadi Aloonabadi Ashraf-ol Sadat * Ahmadi Atuie Abbas * Ahmadi Danesh Ashtiani Morteza * Ahmadi Nia Mohammad Kazem
* Ahmadi Nureh Mashallah * Ahmadi Qotbi Nassir * Ahmadi Sarkhooni Ali * Ahmadi Siahpush Hamid Reza * Ahmadi Zadeh * Ahmadi Zade Tarakomi Asl Ashraf (Nasrin) * Ahmadi Zadeh Tarakomi Asl Zahra * Ahmadian Bijan * Ahmadian
Bizhan * Ahmadian Faramarz * Ahmadian Mahmoud * Ahmadian-Moqaddas Ahmad * Ahmadinaghi Ebrahim * Ahmadi-Nawara Mezgin * Ahmadinejad Sa'id * Ahmadinezhad Esmail * Ahmadinia Gholam
Hossein * Ahmadi-vand Maqsoud * Ahmadizadeh Jaber * Ahmadizadeh Tarako Ashraf Amir * Ahmadlu Sa'id * Ahmadnejad Fatemeh * Ahmadnejad Sureh Qasem * Ahmadnia Ramazan * Ahmadpur Abdolkhaleq * Ahmadpur
pur Abdollah * Ahmadzadeh Ashtiani Morteza * Ahmadshahi Raj * Ahmadvand Morteza * Ahmadvand Yusef * Ahmadvand Hadi * Ahmadvand Hassan * Ahmadvand Mehdi * Ahmady Khosrow * Ahmady Mansour * Ahmady
* Ahmadzadeh Bidokhti Zahra * Ahmadzadeh Zabihollah * Ahmadzadeh Javad * Ahmad-zadeh M.Reza * Ahmadzadeh Rezwan * Ahmadzadeh- Tarakomi Asl Ashraf * Ahmadzadeh-Tarakomi Asl Zahra * Ahmardi-far Akbar * Ahrabi Gholam Hos
sein * Ahrari Dhiya'u'llah * Ahrari Leyla * Ahsan Khosro * Aimyari Abdolmajid * A'ineh Varzan Hossein * A'ineh Varzani Ali * A'ineh Varzani Mohammad * Ai'ni Feizollah * Ajam Ali * Ajam Hasan * Ajami Gholam Hossein * Ajam
Saleh * Ajami Gholamhossein * Ajdani Aqdas * Ajdari Moqadam Hushang * Ajeli Fariba * Aji Habibollah * Ajili Reza * Ajini Sohan * Ajirabi Abdolkarim * Ajoodani Isma'il * Ajorlu Mohammad Reza * Ajorpi Gholam Reza * AjparAbi Abulkarim
* Ajrlu Mahdi * Akasheh Zahra * Akbar Abdollah * Akbarfard Ahmad Ali * Akbari Abbas * Akbari Alireza * Akbari Fatemeh * Akbari Feyzollah * Akbari Naser * Akbari Reza * Akbari Mohammad * Akbari Yusef * Akbari Ak
sein * Akbari Ibrahim * Akbari Leyla * Akbari Mahmood * Akbari Mansur * Akbari Maqdam * Akbari Minu * Akbari Mohtaram * Akbari Mohammad * Akbari Nasrin * Akbari Akbar * Akbari Mohammad * Akbari Yusef * Akbari Ak
Seyyed Mohammad * Akbari Mohammad'ali * Akbar Habib * Akbari Ahangari Vahid * Akbari Diba Abdorreza * Akbari Diba Farhad * Akbari Diba Abdolreza * Akbari Diba Farhad * Akbari Kordestani Kasra * Akbari Monfared Abdollah
Akbari Monfared Roqiyeh * Akbari Namdar Gholamreza * Akbari Shandi Ali Reza * Akbari Tehrani Shamsi * Akbarian Abdolsaheb * Akbarian Hamid * Akbarian Motlagh AliReza * Akbaridust Rahim Ali * Akbari-Moqa
ddam Giti * Akbarisefat Ebrahim * Akbarkhah Roqieh * Akbarkhah Roghieh * Akbar-Mofarah Roqiyeh * Akbarnezhad Hurieh * Akbarpur Javad * Akbarpur Sarvestani Rostam * Akbar-Shahi Mariam * Akbarzadeh
Davud * Akbarzadeh Mohammad'ali * Akbarzadeh Shokuhi Siavash * Akbarzadeh Yusefi Mohammed Hossein * Akbarzad-Yousefi Nasser * Akharfateh Hassan * Akhavan Jalal * Akhavan Shrafieh Fereidun * Akhavan
hasherni Mohammad * Akhavanahashemi Mohammad * Akhgar Javad * Akhlaghi Asghar * Akhlaghi Seyed Mohammad * Akhlaghi Alimohammadi Akhmadreza * Akhlaghi Reza * Akhlaqi Abdorrahman * Akhlaqi Gholam Reza * Akhlaqi Mohammad
Nastaran * Akhlaqi Rahman * Akhlaqi Taqi * Akhlaqi Vahid * Akhoo'i Javad * Akhrot Abdolgafur * Akhtar Ardishir * Akhtar-Khavari Nuru'llah * Akhtarnasimi Gholamhosein Ali (Behroz) * Akhundi Mohammad Esmail
Akhundi Mahtab Amir Ahmad * Akhyari Bahman * Akbari Reza * Alami * Akram Mohammad Karim * Akrami Naser * Akrami Shahbazi * Akrami Farhad * Akrami Farshad * Akrami Mohammad * Akrami Mohammad
Reza * A'l - Aqa' Alireza * A'l - Aqa' Hamid * Al Asieh Gholamreza * Al Davudi Sadr-ol-Sadat * Al e Bu Ali Fazel * Al e Naser Faraj * A'l Es'haq Es'haq * Al Hashemi Narges * Al Nabi Taqi * A'l Taher Marziyeh * Al Taher Raziye
* A'l Taher Marziyeh * Ala'eddini Masoud * Ala'i Gholamreza * A'laei Bakhshayesh * A'laei Huriyeh * A'laei Masoud * Alafchin Soraya * Alaghmand Mohammad'ali * A'la'i Mahmud * Ala'i Khastu Masud * Ala'inejad Asghar * Ala'i-ni Huriel
* Alam Ahmad * A'lam Jamshid * Alam Huli Shirin * A'lam Mehrjerdi Nader * Alam Rajabi Ozra * Alamdaran Akbar * Alami Mahmud * Alami Mahmud * Alami Jalal * A'lami Naser * Alamzadeh Harjandi Batoul * Alamzadeh Harjandi Sedighe
* Alaqmand Manijeh * Alaqmand Zahra * Alave Babolhakim Seyyed Ali * Alavi Mehdi * Alavi Mehrdad * Alavi Seyed Reza * Alavi Shushtari Mehdi * Alavi Tafreshi Nushin * Alavian Sharifeh * Alaviyan Buzurg * Alayeri
Kazem * 'Alayi Gholamhossein * A'layi Abdol Kazem * Alborz Manijeh * Albu'ali Adnan * Albughabish Majid * Aldaghi (Aldaqi) Jamaloddin * Aldaghi (Aldaqi) Javad * Ale-Kan'an Sasan * Ale-Kasir Abdorreza * Ale-Kena'n Sasa
* Ale'ali Adel * Alekan'an Yadollah * Alemi Esma'il * Alemi Mohammad-Reza * Alemi Reza * Alemitabar Abdollah * Ale-s'haq Mehdi * Al-E-Taha * Alghusi Majid * Alghusi Majid * Alguea de Rodriguez Silvana * Ali Halabi Abdallah * Al-Hashim Yolla * Ali Jome'khan * Ali Taghavi * Ali Changiz * Ali (Mohammadsaleh) Kak Jalil (Moradi) * Ali Abdollah Seyyed Abdollah * Ali Akbarian Kahani Majid * Ali Beik (Beik Ali) Ali * Ali Dusti Mc
hamad Reza * Ali Miri Abbas * Ali Mohammad Mehdi * Ali Mohammadi Hossein * Ali Mohammadi Tabrizi Ramazan Ali * Ali Yazdan Panahi Ali'Akbar * Ali zehi Jonmohammad * Ali zehi Shirahmad * Alia
Aliaqa * Alibakhshi Manuchehr * Alibakhtari Masud * Alidadi Karim * Alidoost Ghanbar * Alidoost Reza * Alidoost Mohammad Qoli * Alidusti Qohfarrokhi Ali * Aligorji Malekeh * Ali-Haderi Ali Ahmad * Ali Hosseiny Fahimeh * Alijani Asghar
* Alijani Hossein * Alijani Khodadad * Alijoni Solat * Alijouzadeh * Alikhademi Farideh * Alikhah Ali * Alikhani Hajeh * Alikhani Majid * Alikhani Mohammad Aman * Alikouzohdi-Danz Hedayatollah * Aliku Asghar * Alimohamadi Mas'ume
* Alimohamadi Mansureh * Alimohammadi Hasan * Alimohammadi Musa * Alimoradi Ali Akbar * Alimoradi Behruz * Alimoradi Alireza * Alimoradi Aziz * Alimorad Zadeh Haj * Alimzehi Amanat * Alinaghipur Mostafa * Alinejad Davud
Alinia Sediq * Alipanah Sedigheh * Alipour Hamid * Alipour Hassan * Alipour Hossein * Alipur Guldanih * Alipur Hassan * Alipur Mehr * Alipur Qasem * Alipur Zahra * Alipur Zahra * Alipur Hossein * Aliq
Aliasghar * Alipur Hamid * Alipur Ali * Alipur 'Abdolhamid * Alipur Abdolmajid * Alipur (Soleimani) Qasem * Alipur Kermani Habibollah * Aliqoli Haj Reza * Aliqoli Shapur * Aliqolipoor Naser * Alirahi Mohammad * Alirezaii Farideh
Alirezania Mohammad Reza * Alirezania Mohammad Taqi * Alishahi Gita * Alishahnejad Hamid Reza * Alitab' Yusef * AliTab'e Yussef * Aliverdi Tahereh * Aliyannejad Mehri * Alizad Rafi' Ja'far Mohammad * Alizade Hassan * Alizade
Alizadeh Ja'far Sadeq * Alizadeh Kabus * Alizadeh Mahmud * Alizadeh Maqsud * Alizadeh Mehdi * Alizadeh Mehdi (Bijan) * Alizadeh Mohammad Ali * Alizadeh Reza Karam * Alizadeh Sha'ban Ali * Alizadeh Reza * Alizade
Shiragha * Alizadeh Hashem * Alizadeh Karim Hossein * Alizadeh Khosrow * Alizadeh Farzad * Alizadeh Safarqolikomodi Jamal * Alizadeh Zahed-sefat Qassem * Alizadehkurani Kobra * Alizaghi Zia * Alizehi Abdol
lah * Alizehi Abdolzaher * Alizehi Abdorra'uf * Alizehi Gol Mohammad * Alizehi Havalikhan * Alizehi Iran * Alizehi Mohammad Vali * Alizehi Shirahmad * Alizehi Sattar * Alizehi Nasir * Alizehi Nurmohammad * Alizehi Sharif
'Alizehi Mostafa * Alkuzei' Mohammadsarvar * Allah Verdi Sakineh * Allahdadi Ghader * Allahverdi Ma'edin * Allahyari Mehrab * Allahyari Sarbaz * Allahyari Sara'i * Allame Arqoy Homayoun * Allameh Ha'eri Fazilat * Alma
* Almasi Akbar * Almasi Ali Reza * Almasi Hamzeh * Almasi Mohammad * Almasi Siarnak * Almasi Moqadam Saleh * Almasian Naser * Almasian Parviz * Almasizadeh Mari'am * Almasizadeh Reza * Alsadat Jozi Giti * Alshafie Mostafa
* Aluki Qassem * Alvand Masoud * Alvandi Ramazan * Alvandi Shirin * Alvandpur Parvaneh * Alvani * Alvani Yusef * Alyani Reza * Alyani Yusef * Amadadian Zahra * Aman Dori Jafar * Amanat Abbas * Amanat Reza * Amani Ya'qub * Amani
* Amani Jamshid * Amani Hadi * Amani Mohammad * Amani Rabi' * Ameli Fariba * Amel-Tehrani Abdollah * Ameri * Ameri Tusi Reza * Ameriani Tusi Sadeq (Jamal) * Ameri Ozra * Ameri Hadi * Ames Robert C. * Amin Mahammad * Amin Masoud
Amin Reza * Amin Mohammadreza * Amin Amin Mehdi * Aminchordeh Mohammad * Amini Ayyoub * Amini Behruz * Amini Hadi * Amini Hossein * Amini Ma'sumeh * Amini Masud * Amini Mohammad
madreza * Amini Mostafa * Amini Nasru'llah * Amini Osman * Amini Rahmatollah * Amini Reza * Amini Reza * Amini Rahmatollah * Amini Habib * Amini Mohammadtaghi * Amini Payam * Amini Majid * Amini Naqi * Amini
Amini Afshar Byok * Amini Afshar Iraj * Amini Aftar Parviz * Amini Khah Mashallah * Amini Khah Seyyed Mehdi * Amini Najafi Dariush * Aminian Afsaneh * Aminian Alireza * Aminian Jamshid * Aminian Mansur * Aminian Masoud * Amir
ian Zahra * Aminifar Baratali * Amininia Jamshid * Aminipour Jamshid * Aminisangar Ahmad * Aminolro'ayaee Mohammad * Aminottolleh Seyyed Shams * Aminzadeh Rasul * Aminzadeh Mahmud * Amir Akram Isma'il * Amir
Ataollah * Amir Bahrami Mohammad * Amir Hossein Saber * Amir Hosseini Saber * Amir Shahkarami Shamsoddin * Amirfathi Hojjatollah * Amirhosseini Fahimeh * Amirhosseini Mir Hadi * Amirhosseini Amir Hamid
* Amiri Hossein * Amiri Houshang * Amiri Jahanbakhsh * Amiri Mehrdad * Amiri Ali * Amiri Mojtaba * Amiri Morteza * Amiri Mostafa * Amiri Naser * Amiri Parvin * Amiri Rakhboda * Amiri Soheylah * Amiri Ya'qub * Amiri
Zabihollah * Amiri Mostafa * Amiri Ali * Amiri Mojtaba * Amiri Ahmad * Amiri Jahanbakhsh * Amiri Alam * Amiri Shadollah * Amiri Mojtaba * Amiri (Amini) Mohsen * Amiri Kiomars * Amirjahed Danablu Jebra'il * Amirmorad Rasul
Amirnejad Naser * Amirpour Esfandiyar * Amirpur Hushang * Amirshahi Javad * Amirshekari Ali * Amirshekari Sa'id * Amirvaziri Mohammad * Amjadi Hassan * Amjadi Mahmud * Amjadi Torshizi Hadi * Amlashi Reza * Amlashi
Mohammadsafar * Amlashi Khahar * Ammari Mehdi * Amoli Ahmad * Amouzgar Ali * Amouzgar Alireza * Amouzgar Mehri * Amuzgar Navid * Amri Farideh * Amshasband Mehdi * Amtar Sarvar * Amusheikhi Dolar'i * Gholam Hossein
Amuzegar Abbas * Amuzegar Mohammad Naser (Mohammad Reza) * Amuzeidy Zahra * Amuzgar Reza * Ana'i Ali Asghar * Ana'i Asghar * Anab Hashem * Anabarnia Hashem * Anboozadeh
Anbuzadeh Shahlah * Ancheshki Azar * Anchezadeh Gholamreza * Andakhideh Hossein * Andisheh Gilan * Anethi Aliasghar * Anghouti Khedmat-Ali * Anghuti Khedmat'ali * Anoshyirvani Bahrami Hashem * Anoshyirvani
Kazem * Ansari Fariba * Ansari Faryba * Ansari Jaber * Ansari Majid * Ansari Mani'a * Ansari Mas'ud * Ansari Say'ed * Ansari Tayyeb * Ansari Zadeh Asadollah * Ansaripoor Poorandokht * Ansaripoor Mehdi * Ansarizadeh Saeid * Ansi Se
diqeh * Antunez Jorge * Anushiravani Nasrollah * Anushirvan Ebrahimi * Anvar Ardalan * Anvar Abbas * Anvar Meskin Karim * Anvari Mehdi * Anvari Morteza * Anzidani Amir * Aq Atabay Fereydun * Aq Banu Dr.
Aqa Baba'i Karim * Aqa Maleki Sa'id * Aqa Maleki Sa'id (Amaneh) * Aqa Marandi Asadollah * Aqa Mohammadi Aqdas * Aqa Mohammadi Bahram * Aqa Mohammadi Bahram * Aqa Mohammadi Ramezan Ali * Aqa Salehi Adel * Aqa'i Sichani Hamid * Aqa'al-ge
Bahram * Aqaali-Sichani Nasrin * Aqa'ali-Sichani Nasrin * Aqababa Amir Hushang * Aqababa'i Abbas * Aqababayi Abbas * Aqabeigi Karim * Aqa-davudi Mohammad Ali * Aqagolian Jamileh * Aqahaseni Mohammad * Aqahasani
Aqa'i Amrollah * Aqa'i Keramat * Aqa'i Naqi * Aqa'i Forushani Taqi * Aqa'i (Agha_) Faramarz * Aqa'i Forushani Hosein (Alireza) * Aqajani Naser * Aqajani Esmail * Aqajani Gholam Hossein * Aqajani Naser * Aqajan
Aqajan-Pur Zahra * Aqaji Sakineh * Aqaji Tahereh * Aqakhan Moqadam Tahereh * Aqakhani Javad * Aqakhanian Razmik * Aqamiri (Amiri) Mojtaba (Hamid) * Aqa-Nejad Mohammadi Aqdas * Aqa-Nejad Mohammadi
Aqanur Shahnaz * Aqapur Ali * Aqapur Ezat * Aqapur Bonab Rahim * Aqaqorehsvii Ali * Aqa-Soltan Neda * Aqaqoreyshi Ali * Aqasi Zahra * Aqayan (Yadegar) Karim * Aqayani Reza * Aqayem Gholam Hossein * Aqazadeh
deh Soraya * Aqazadeh Qahremani Ramin * Aqbashlu Babak * Aqcheman Esma'il * Aqda'i Talha * Aqdam Shahpur * Aqel Hossein * Aqeli Alireza * Aqeli Nabzali * Aqelli Majid * Aqili Hossein * Aqili Yadollah * Aqilu
Mahalli * Aqvami Mehdi * Aqvamipanah Mohammad Hossein * Aqyapur Abdul * Aqyapur Ezat * Arab Alahyar * Arab Ali * Arab Ali Reza * Arab Ali Reza * Arab Fatemeh * Arab Hossein * Arab Hossein *
Kazem * Arab Abdolhagh * Arab Mohammadhossein * Arab Abdolsattar * Arab Latif * Arab Zarif * Arab Masud * Arab Mohajed Ali * Arab Taheri Asghar * Arab Tehrani Ghassem * Arab Teymuri Safar'ali * Arab Vaziri Alireza